I0793971

YOUR STUDY OF

THE BOOK OF MORMON

• MADE EASIER •

FOR TEENS

PART ONE: 1

1 NEPHI THROUGH WORDS OF MORMON

BOOKS BY DAVID J. RIDGES

THE GOSPEL STUDIES SERIES

- *Isaiah Made Easier, Second Edition*
- *The New Testament Made Easier, Part 1, Second Edition*
- *The New Testament Made Easier, Part 2, Second Edition*
- *Your Study of The Book of Mormon Made Easier, Part 1*
- *Your Study of The Book of Mormon Made Easier, Part 2*
- *Your Study of The Book of Mormon Made Easier, Part 3*
- *Your Study of The Doctrine and Covenants Made Easier, Part 1*
- *Your Study of The Doctrine and Covenants Made Easier, Part 2*
- *Your Study of The Doctrine and Covenants Made Easier, Part 3*
- *The Old Testament Made Easier, Part 1*
- *The Old Testament Made Easier—Selections from the O.T., Part 2*
- *The Old Testament Made Easier—Selections from the O.T., Part 3*
- *Your Study of the Pearl of Great Price Made Easier*
- *Your Study of Jeremiah Made Easier*
- *Your Study of The Book of Revelation Made Easier, Second Edition*
- *Gospel Studies Series Deluxe Sets*

ADDITIONAL TITLES BY DAVID J. RIDGES

- *Our Savior, Jesus Christ: His Life and Mission to Cleanse and Heal*
- *Mormon Beliefs and Doctrines Made Easier*
- *The Proclamation on the Family: The Word of the Lord on More Than 30 Current Issues*
- *100 Signs of the Times Leading Up to the Second Coming of Christ*
- *Doctrinal Details of the Plan of Salvation: From Premortality to Exaltation*
- *To This End Was I Born: Walking with the Savior in His Final Week*
- *Temples: Sacred Symbolism, Eternal Blessings*
- *Priesthood Power Unlocked*
- *Using the Signs of the Times to Strengthen Your Testimony*
- *The Red Porsche*
- *The Righteous Role of a Father*
- *A Mother's Perfect Hope*
- *Seasons of a Mother's Love*
- *Born to the Virgin Mary*
- *Gospel Questions, Gospel Answers*

YOUR STUDY OF

THE BOOK OF MORMON

• MADE EASIER •

FOR TEENS

PART ONE: 1

1 NEPHI THROUGH WORDS OF MORMON

DAVID J. RIDGES

CFI

An imprint of Cedar Fort, Inc.
Springville, Utah

ISBN 13: 978-1-4621-3683-4 (Volume 1)
ISBN 13: 978-1-4621-3579-0 (Set)

Published by CFI, an imprint of Cedar Fort, Inc.
2373 W. 700 S., Springville, UT 84663
Distributed by Cedar Fort, Inc., www.cedarfort.com

LIBRARY OF CONGRESS CATALOGING-IN-PUBLICATION DATA

Names: Ridges, David J., author.
Title: The Book of Mormon made easier for teens / David J. Ridges.
Description: Springville, Utah : CFI, an imprint of Cedar Fort, Inc., [2019] | Includes bibliographical references.
Identifiers: LCCN 2019018562 (print) | LCCN 2019020853 (ebook) | ISBN 9781462135790 (perfect bound : alk. paper)
Subjects: LCSH: Book of Mormon--Commentaries. | Mormon youth--Religious life.
Classification: LCC BX8627 .R533 2019 (print) | LCC BX8627 (ebook) | DDC 289.3/22--dc23
LC record available at https://lccn.loc.gov/2019018562
LC ebook record available at https://lccn.loc.gov/2019020853

Cover design by Shawnda T. Craig

Edited by Nicole Terry

Printed in the United States of America

10 9 8 7 6 5 4 3 2 1

Printed on acid-free paper

CONTENTS

THE JST REFERENCES IN STUDY GUIDES BY DAVID J. RIDGES

Note that some of the JST (The Joseph Smith Translation of the Bible) references I use in my study guides are not found in our LDS Bible in the footnotes or in the Joseph Smith Translation section in the reference section in the back. The reason for this, as explained to me while writing curriculum materials for the Church, is simply that there is not enough room to include all of the JST additions and changes to the King James Version of the Bible (the one we use in the English speaking part of the Church). As you can imagine, as was likewise explained to me, there were difficult decisions that had to be made by the Scriptures Committee of the Church as to which JST contributions were included and which were not.

The Joseph Smith Translation of the Bible in its entirety can generally be found in or ordered through LDS bookstores. It was originally published under the auspices of the Reorganized Church of Jesus Christ of Latter Day Saints in Independence, Missouri. The version of the JST I prefer to use is a parallel column version, Joseph Smith's "New Translation" of the Bible, published by Herald Publishing House, Independence, Missouri, in 1970. This parallel column version compares the King James Bible with the JST side by side and includes only the verses that have changes, additions, or deletions made by the Prophet Joseph Smith.

By the way, some members of the Church have wondered if we can trust the JST since it was published by a breakaway faction from our Church. They worry that some changes from Joseph Smith's original manuscript might have been made to support doctrinal differences between us and the RLDS Church. This is not the case. Many years ago, Robert J. Matthews of the Brigham Young University Religion Department was given permission by leaders of the RLDS Church to come to their Independence, Missouri, headquarters and personally compare the original JST document word for word with their publication of the JST. Brother Matthews was thus able to verify that they had been meticulously true to the Prophet's original work.

INTRODUCTION

Welcome to the Book of Mormon Made Easier for Teens (and adults who would like a bit more help studying the Book of Mormon). These three study guide volumes combined contain every verse in the Book of Mormon. So, as you read and study, you will be reading the entire Book of Mormon word for word.

This study guide series was written for you. It is designed to help you learn to see applications in your own life from what you are reading and learning in the Book of Mormon. That way, it will be more interesting for you to read and study.

One of the things that typically stands in the way of understanding the scriptures is the vocabulary and overall language used in the scriptures. And so, I am going to help you learn "Scriptureze," or, in other words, the language of the scriptures, as we go along. In effect, you will learn a new language. Especially at first, I will define many words as we come to them. As you get to the point that you no longer need some of the words defined, you can ignore my definitions, realizing that you are actually making good progress in learning the language of the scriptures.

The Prophet Joseph Smith taught that we can get closer to God by living according to the teachings of the Book of Mormon than through any other book. The exact quote is, "I told the brethren that the Book of Mormon was the most correct of any book on earth, and the keystone of our religion, and a man would get nearer to God by abiding by its precepts, than by any other book." (See Book of Mormon, Introduction, paragraph 6.) So, there is probably nothing more valuable that you can do than to read and study the Book of Mormon.

The difference between this version and the regular Book of Mormon Made Easier study guides published several years ago is that these three volumes have many more definitions of scriptural terms that can be difficult for younger readers and also for many adults. They also contain a number of additional explanations of the teachings and principles taught in the Book of Mormon, and some longer and more technical notes and commentary have not been included.

You will see as we go along that I have used bold for many words and phrases. You can use this as a guide to mark your own scriptures with colored pencils, or highlight them if you are using digital scriptures. Also, you will see that by marking certain key words and phrases in a verse, you can, in effect, make brief notes as to what the verse is about. Later, as you re-read and study your Book of Mormon, you can glance at a verse and quickly see what it is about because of what you have marked in it.

Most important of all, the Book of Mormon is true. It is the word of God. And it is a sure way to bring the Spirit into your heart and mind whenever you choose to read and study it.

—David J. Ridges

THE FIRST BOOK OF NEPHI

1 NEPHI 1

As you first meet Nephi, when he introduces himself here in chapter one, you might be like many readers who tend to think of him as probably in his teens as he is writing this. He probably was in his teens as these events took place—in other words, when his father, Lehi, took his family and fled from Jerusalem, about 600 years before the birth of Christ. But Nephi is probably actually in his fifties as he is writing this now. If you were to check his writings in 2 Nephi 5:28–33, you would find that it has already been thirty years since they landed in America. Also, since it was eight years from the time the family left Jerusalem before they even got on their ship to sail to America (2 Nephi 17:4), Nephi has to be somewhere in his fifties at the time he is writing what we see here in chapter one.

The point is, Nephi is a mature adult at the time he is writing this to us, and he is looking back at what took place many years ago, in his young life, as he shares with us his thoughts. He is picking out things he feels would be important to teach us from his own life's experiences. For example, look at verse one, next, and see if you can pick out important messages he wants you to learn from what he is writing.

Also, just a reminder that Jerusalem, at the time in history referred to here, is a very wicked city located in the country of Israel at the eastern end of the Mediterranean Sea, north of Egypt, in the tops of the mountains.

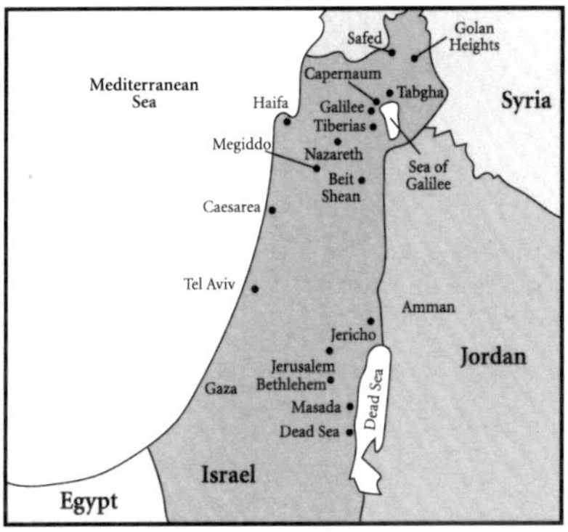

Let's join Nephi now as he introduces himself to us.

1 **I, NEPHI, having been born of goodly parents** [*"goodly" is an Old Testament word meaning praiseworthy, noble, or morally good, according to* Strong's Exhaustive Concordance of the Bible], therefore **I was taught** somewhat **in all the learning of my father**; and **having seen many afflictions** [*troubles*] in the course of my days [*during my life so far*], **nevertheless, having been highly**

favored [*greatly blessed*] **of the Lord** in all my days; yea, having had a great knowledge of the goodness and the mysteries [*basic doctrines of the gospel*] of God, therefore I make a record of my proceedings in my days.

What did you pick out? Did you see that he appreciates and respects his parents? Did you notice that, even though he had had "many afflictions," he chooses now to emphasize that he had been "highly favored of the Lord in all my days"? In other words, he is an optimist. He chooses to emphasize the positives in his life. This is a major message for us from his writings.

For perspective, we might just take a quick look at a few of the "many afflictions" in Nephi's life up to this point. He was nearly murdered four times by his own brothers (1 Nephi 7:16, 1 Nephi 16:37, 1 Nephi 17:45, 2 Nephi 5:4). Laban tried to kill him and his brothers (1 Nephi 3:25). They spent eight difficult years in the wilderness. He had much opposition in building the ship (1 Nephi 17), plus being tied up on the ship (1 Nephi 18). And after they arrived in America, his brothers again tried to kill him (2 Nephi 5:2–4).

By the way, don't forget that the Holy Ghost is THE teacher for us as we study and apply the Book of Mormon to our lives. He will prompt and teach you constantly as you study this sacred volume of scripture. And remember, experience has shown that it really helps to start each session of your study of the Book of Mormon with a prayer, asking Heavenly Father for help in understanding and applying the Book of Mormon to your personal life. You may also wish to end your study session with a prayer, expressing gratitude for what you have learned and the feelings you have had.

Next, Nephi tells us what language he uses as he engraves his history on the metal plates and also bears testimony to us of the truthfulness of what he writes. One of the wonderful and important things here is that the Holy Ghost can also bear testimony to us of the truthfulness of Nephi's testimony. This witness can come to us in many ways, including as feelings in our hearts, impressions and emphases in our minds, peace, clarity of thinking—for example, a simple clear impression that Nephi is right!

2 Yea, **I make a record** [*a written history*] **in the language of my father**, which consists of the learning of the Jews and the language of the Egyptians.

3 And **I know that the record which I make is true**; and I make it with mine own hand;

and I make it according to my knowledge.

Next, Nephi will mention Zedekiah, king of Judah, which includes the area around Jerusalem in southern Israel. This is about 600 BC, meaning that it is about 600 years before the birth of Christ. King Zedekiah is a wicked, twenty-one-year-old king (see 2 Kings 24:18–19). He will reign for eleven years, during which time, among other evil deeds, he will imprison the prophet Jeremiah in a miserable dungeon with deep mud (see Jeremiah, chapters 38–39). Finally, after Lehi and his family have been run out of Jerusalem by angry mobs, King Zedekiah will be captured by King Nebuchadnezzar's forces, from Babylon, about 587 BC. Zedekiah's sons (except for Mulek) will be killed before his eyes, and he will be blinded and carried as a prisoner to Babylon (basically where Iran and Iraq are today). (See 2 Kings 25.) Somehow, Mulek will end up in America, and we will meet his descendants in Omni 1:14–15, Mosiah 25:1, and elsewhere in the Book of Mormon.

Next, we see that the Lord is warning the wicked inhabitants of Jerusalem and the surrounding area that they will be destroyed unless they repent.

4 For it came to pass [*Now this is what happened*] in the commencement [*the beginning*] of the first year of the reign [*rule*] of Zedekiah, king of Judah, (my father, Lehi, having dwelt [*lived*] at Jerusalem in all his days); and in that same year **there came many prophets** [*including Jeremiah, Nahum, Habakkuk, and Zephaniah*], **prophesying** [*teaching about the future*] **unto the people that they must repent**, or the great city Jerusalem must be [*would be*] destroyed.

5 Wherefore [*therefore*] it came to pass that **my father, Lehi**, as he went forth **prayed** unto the Lord, yea, even with all his heart, in behalf of [*for*] his people.

In verses 6–16, next, you will see that Nephi's father, Lehi, was indeed a great prophet. We will underline and **bold** words and phrases in these verses to show you this.

6 And it came to pass as he prayed unto the Lord, **there came a pillar of fire and dwelt upon a rock before** [*in front of*] **him; and he saw and heard much**; and because of the things which he saw and heard he did quake and tremble exceedingly [*a whole lot*].

7 And it came to pass that he returned to his own house at Jerusalem; and he cast himself [*lay down*] upon his bed, being

overcome with the Spirit and the things which he had seen.

Next, in verse 8, we run into an interesting phrase which causes some readers to ask, "Why doesn't it come right out and say that Lehi saw God, rather than saying that he thought he saw God?" The answer is simple. In order to avoid even the slightest chance of using the name of God inappropriately (like people nowadays constantly using "god" as a swear word and so forth), ancient prophets sometimes used the "polite indirect" reference rather than using "God" outright. Lehi did see God the Father, but in writing about it, Nephi uses the indirect "thought he saw God." We see other examples of this indirect mode in the scriptures. For instance, in Abraham 3:24, Abraham refers to the premortal Christ as one "that was like unto God." In Daniel 3:25, Christ is referred to as "like the Son of God." In Revelation 1:13, Jesus is referred to as "one like unto the Son of man."

8 And being thus overcome with the Spirit, he was **carried away in a vision, even that he saw the heavens open, and he thought he saw God** [*he saw Heavenly Father, compare with Revelation 4:2*] **sitting upon his throne, surrounded with numberless concourses of angels** [*more angels than you could possibly count*] **in the attitude of singing and praising their God**.

9 And it came to pass that **he** [*Lehi*] **saw One** [*Christ*] **descending** [*coming down*] **out of the midst of heaven, and he beheld that his luster** [*brightness*] **was above that of the sun at noon-day**.

Next, Lehi will see in vision the future Twelve Apostles following Christ.

10 And **he also saw twelve others following him** [*the Savior*], and their brightness did exceed that of the stars in the firmament [*the sky*].

11 And they came down and went forth upon the face of the earth; and **the first** [*Christ, see verse 9*] **came and stood before my father, and gave unto him a book, and bade him that he should read** [*told him to read the book*].

12 And it came to pass that as he read, **he was filled with the Spirit of the Lord**.

13 And he read, saying: Wo, wo, [*bad things are coming*] unto Jerusalem, for I have seen thine abominations [*terrible wickedness*]! Yea, and **many things did my father read concerning Jerusalem—that it should be destroyed, and the inhabitants thereof; many should perish** [*die*] **by the sword,**

and many should be carried away captive into Babylon [*a powerful enemy nation with headquarters about 500 miles east of Jerusalem*].

14 And it came to pass that when **my father had read and seen many great and marvelous things**, he did exclaim many things unto the Lord; such as: Great and marvelous are thy works, O Lord God Almighty! Thy throne is high in the heavens, and thy power, and goodness, and mercy are over all the inhabitants of the earth; and, because thou art merciful, thou wilt not suffer [*allow*] those who come unto thee [*the righteous*] that they shall perish!

15 And after this manner was the language of my father in the praising of his God [*these are the kinds of words my father used to praise God*]; for his soul did rejoice, and his whole heart was filled, because of the things which he had seen, yea, which the Lord had shown unto him.

16 And now I, Nephi, do not make a full account [*a complete record*] of the things which my father hath written, for **he hath written many things which he saw in visions and in dreams; and he also hath written many things which he prophesied** and spake unto his children, of which I shall not make a full account.

17 But **I shall make an account of** [*tell about*] **my proceedings** in my days [*make a history of my life*]. Behold, I make an abridgment [*a shortened version*] of the record of my father, upon plates which I have made with mine own hands [*this brief summary of his father's writings goes through 1 Nephi chapter 8*]; wherefore, after I have abridged the record of my father then will I make an account of mine own life.

Next, Nephi tells us that, after his father was given the tremendous revelations mentioned in the previous verses, he started preaching to the Jews and warning them what would happen if they did not repent. Pay attention to how the inhabitants of Jerusalem reacted to his message from the Lord to them.

18 Therefore, I would that ye should know [*I want you to know*], that after the Lord had shown so many marvelous things unto my father, **Lehi**, yea, concerning the destruction of Jerusalem, behold he **went forth among the people, and began to prophesy** and to declare unto them concerning the things which he had both seen and heard.

19 And it came to pass that **the Jews did mock** [*make fun of, laugh at*] **him** because of the things which he testified of them; for he truly testified of their wickedness and their abominations [*extra bad wickedness*]; and he testified that the things which he saw and heard, and also the things which he read in the book [*mentioned in verse 11*], manifested [*showed*] plainly of **the coming of a Messiah** [*meaning "a deliverer," one who would set them free, in other words, Christ*] and also the redemption of the world [*the saving of the world by Christ through His Atonement*].

20 And **when the Jews heard these things they were angry with him**; yea, even as with the prophets of old [*in the past*], whom they had cast out, and stoned [*threw rocks at them until they died*], and slain [*killed*]; and **they also sought his life**, that they might take it away [*tried to kill Lehi*]. But behold, I, Nephi, will show unto you that the tender mercies of the Lord are over all those whom he hath chosen, because of their faith, to make them mighty even unto the power of deliverance [*Nephi will show us that the Lord will show great and tender mercy to all who have faith in Him and will give them power to be saved*].

1 NEPHI 2

In this chapter, Lehi is warned by the Lord to take his family and flee into the wilderness—in other words, to quickly get away from his enemies in the Jerusalem area and go into the barren desert areas southeast of the Holy Land. Lehi is a wealthy man, and this will involve leaving his wealth and worldly possessions behind. You will see that two of Nephi's older brothers, Laman and Lemuel, are unhappy about leaving their comfortable lifestyle in the Jerusalem area and will complain a lot. Some readers are inclined to ask why Lehi didn't just leave Laman and Lemuel home, rather than being subjected to the problems they continued to cause. While Lehi and his wife, Sariah, are best qualified to respond to this question, perhaps we may venture a few responses. First of all, faithful parents continue to hope that wayward children will repent, and they often do. Another facet of the answer may be that in each family, it is not just the wayward or rebellious members who need to learn lessons, but the faithful members also have the need to grow in patience, wisdom, forgiving, striving to bring them back, etc., and to learn countless other attributes that Heavenly Father wants us to gain.

1 FOR behold, it came to pass that [*Now this is what happened*] **the Lord spake** [*spoke*] **unto my father**, yea, even in a dream, and said unto him: Blessed art thou Lehi, because of the things which

thou hast done; and because thou hast been faithful and declared unto this people [*told these people*] the things which I commanded thee, behold, they seek to take away thy life [*and, as you can see, they now want to kill you*].

2 And it came to pass that **the Lord commanded my father**, even in a dream, **that he should take his family and depart into the wilderness** [*the desert-like area southeast of Jerusalem*].

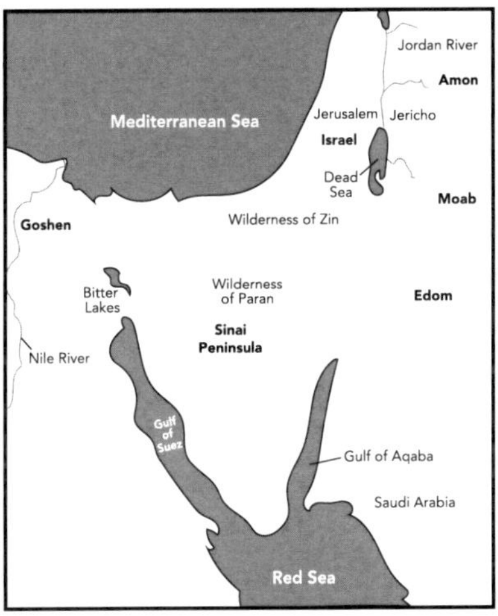

3 And it came to pass that **he was obedient** unto the word of the Lord, wherefore [*and so*] he did as the Lord commanded him.

Next, in verse 4, watch what Lehi has to leave behind as he obeys the Lord's command to get out of Jerusalem quickly. What does that tell you about him?

4 And it came to pass that he departed into the wilderness. And **he left his house**, and the land of his inheritance [*the land and property he had received from his father*], and **his gold**, and his **silver**, and his **precious things**, and took nothing with him, save it were his family, and provisions [*food and supplies*], and tents, and departed into the wilderness.

Did you notice how many times "and" is used in verse four, above? It is used ten times. Your school teacher would probably not give you a passing grade on a homework paper you wrote if you used "and" so many times, rather than mostly commas. The use of "and" like this in the Book of Mormon is strong evidence that it is translated from an ancient Near Eastern (Jerusalem area) language in which they used "and" instead of commas (think the gold plates that Joseph Smith received from Moroni).

5 And **he came** down by the borders **near the shore of the Red Sea** [*180–200 miles or 290–320 kilometers from Jerusalem*]; and he traveled in the wilderness in the borders which are nearer the Red Sea; and he did travel in the wilderness with **his family**, which consisted of my mother, **Sariah**, and my elder [*older*] brothers, who were **Laman**, **Lemuel**, and **Sam**.

We know that Nephi's parents are still young enough to have more children because they will have two more sons (Jacob and Joseph) plus daughters during the time they travel in the wilderness. See 2 Nephi 5:6.

6 And it came to pass that when **he** had **traveled three days** in the wilderness, he pitched his tent in a valley by the side of a river of water.

7 And it came to pass that **he built an altar** of stones, and made an offering unto the Lord, **and gave thanks unto the Lord** our God.

The building of an altar and giving an offering to the Lord in verse 7, above, is a reminder that Lehi and his family worshipped God according to Old Testament laws and ceremonies given to the people by the prophet Moses (see, for example, Exodus 20:24–26). The Book of Mormon people will continue to keep the Old Testament law of Moses until the Savior appears as recorded in 3 Nephi and gives them the higher laws of the New Testament.

8 And it came to pass that he called the name of the river, Laman, [*this was quite an honor given to Laman*] and it emptied into the Red Sea; and the valley was in the borders near the mouth thereof.

9 And when my father saw that the waters of the river emptied into the fountain of the Red Sea [*probably one of the source rivers of the Red Sea*], **he spake** [*spoke*] **unto Laman**, saying: O that thou mightest be like unto this river, continually running into the fountain of all righteousness [*always living righteously*]!

10 And **he also spake unto Lemuel**: O that thou mightest be like unto this valley, firm and steadfast, and immovable in keeping the commandments of the Lord!

We can sense from Lehi's wishes expressed to Laman and Lemuel in verses 9 and 10, above, that he is worried about them and wants them to know their potential for good and faithfulness to God.

Next, Nephi will confirm that his father is worried about Laman and Lemuel.

11 Now this he spake [*said*] **because of the stiffneckedness** [*lack of humility and unwillingness to obey*] **of Laman and Lemuel**; for behold **they did murmur** [*complain*] **in many things against their father**, because he was a visionary man [*had visions and revelations from God*], and had led them out of the land of Jerusalem, to leave the land of their inheritance, and their gold, and their silver, and their precious things, to perish [*die*] in the wilderness. And this they said he had done because of the foolish imaginations of his heart [*they didn't believe he had actually seen visions and had revelations from God*].

12 And thus Laman and Lemuel, being the eldest, did murmur [*gripe, complain*] against their father. And **they did murmur because they knew not the dealings of that God who had created them**.

The last sentence of verse 12, above, leads us to believe that Laman and Lemuel either did not want religion to get in the way of their lives much, if at all, or had already rebelled against religion at this point in their lives.

In fact, the first part of verse 13, next, says clearly that they did not believe the prophets.

13 **Neither did they believe that Jerusalem**, that great city, **could be destroyed** according to the words of the prophets. And **they were like unto the Jews who were at Jerusalem**, who sought to take away the life of my father.

The last half of verse 13, above, leaves no doubt that Laman and Lemuel were already wicked and rebellious in their hearts. It says that they were just like the wicked Jews in Jerusalem. The prophet Jeramiah tells us that the Jews at that time were deeply involved in all kinds of wickedness, including sexual immorality (Jeremiah 5:7–8, 6:15, 9:2–3). This makes it easy for us to believe that Laman and Lemuel had several wicked friends back in Jerusalem and that they were mad about having to leave them and follow their father on what they considered to be a crazy and uncomfortable trip into the dangerous wilderness.

Next, Father Lehi is filled with the Spirit of the Lord and speaks so strongly that Laman and Lemuel are completely stopped in their complaining, and, in fact, they feel the Spirit so strongly that they shake with fear and don't dare say anything against their father.

14 And it came to pass that **my father did speak unto them** in the valley of Lemuel, **with power, being filled with the Spirit**, until their frames [*bodies*] did shake

before him. And he did confound them [*they were terrified*], that they durst not utter [*didn't dare speak*] against him; wherefore [*therefore*], they did as he commanded them.

One of the important lessons we learn from verse 14, above, is that the Lord loves everyone, even those who are wicked and rebellious, and gives them miraculous evidence that He exists so that they have a chance to repent.

15 And **my father dwelt in a tent**.

It may be that Nephi adds what is in verse 15, above, just to remind us that Lehi gave up wealth and comfortable living conditions back in the Jerusalem area in order to be obedient to the Lord's commandment to flee into the wilderness. It's a good reminder for us to give up our comforts and worldly things when necessary to follow what the Lord asks, such as going on missions, going to church on Sunday, paying tithing, participating in service projects, saying our prayers, ministering, and so forth.

16 And it came to pass that I, **Nephi**, being exceedingly [*very*] young, nevertheless **being large in stature** [*was already very big*], and also having great desires to know of the mysteries [*the basics of the gospel*] of **God**, wherefore, I did cry [*pray*] unto the Lord; and behold he **did visit me, and did soften my heart** that **I did believe all the words which had been spoken by my father**; wherefore, **I did not rebel** against him like unto my brothers.

There is an important lesson to learn from Nephi in verse 16, above. Some people ask whether it is wrong to doubt or wonder about matters related to the gospel. Given the fact that individual agency is a gift from God, the answer has to be "No." But it is wrong and foolish to rebel. It is what we do about doubts when they arise in our hearts that makes or breaks us. When doubts about their father and his visions, etc., arose in Laman and Laman's minds, they chose to murmur and rebel. A careful reading of verse 16 may indicate that Nephi also had doubts in his heart, because he tells us that the Lord "did soften my heart that I did believe all the words which had been spoken by my father; wherefore, I did not rebel . . ." Nephi's approach was different from that of his two older brothers. He had an honest heart, a great desire to know the basic truths and doctrines of the gospel, and a desire to know the truthfulness of what his father taught. He humbly prayed to the Lord until he received the sweet, reassuring answer about the truthfulness of his father's revelations. Thus, he had full ownership of faithfully following his prophet father.

17 And I spake unto **Sam**, making known unto him the things which the Lord had manifested unto me by his Holy Spirit. And it came to pass that he **believed in my words**.

Sam is one of my favorite people in the Book of Mormon. I have tender feelings for him and hope to meet him some day. Though older than Nephi, he faithfully follows him and assists him. He reminds me of Hyrum Smith, Joseph Smith's older brother. Though they were older brothers, both Sam and Hyrum seemed to have the gift of believing the words of others (a gift of the Spirit spoken of in D&C 46:14). They both followed and faithfully supported their younger prophet brothers throughout the rest of their lives.

18 But, behold, **Laman and Lemuel would not hearken** [*listen*] **unto my words**; and being grieved [*worried*] because of the hardness of their hearts [*their rebellion*] **I cried** [*prayed*] **unto the Lord for them**.

19 And it came to pass that **the Lord spake unto me**, saying: Blessed art thou, Nephi, because of thy faith, for thou hast sought me diligently [*made great effort to find Me*], with lowliness of heart [*with humility*].

20 And **inasmuch as** [*as long as*] **ye shall keep my commandments, ye shall prosper** [*do very well, be greatly blessed*], and shall be led to a land of promise; yea, even a land which I have prepared for you; yea, a land which is choice above all other lands [*America*].

21 **And inasmuch as** [*if*] **thy brethren shall rebel** against thee, **they shall be cut off** from the presence of the Lord [*they will not get into heaven nor will they get His help now during their lives*].

There is quite an important lesson here for us. It may be that Nephi did not get the answer he wanted. He had obviously been praying for the salvation of Laman and Lemuel. Instead of being reassured that they would be saved, he is reminded that they have agency and their judgment on Judgment Day will depend on how they use it. However, in the next verse, he is reassured that if he, himself, continues to keep the commandments, he will be saved. Thus, we are reminded that we need to do all we can to save others, including praying continually for them. But we cannot force anyone to be saved in heaven against his or her agency.

22 **And inasmuch as** [*if*] **thou** [*you*] **shalt keep my commandments, thou shalt be made a ruler and a teacher over thy**

brethren [*this prophecy will be fulfilled as the Book of Mormon continues*].

23 For behold, in that day that they shall rebel against me, **I will curse them** even with a sore [*severe, heavy*] curse [*instead of blessings from Me, they will have much misery and trouble in their lives*], and **they shall have no power over thy seed** [*Nephi's posterity, children, grandchildren, etc.*] **except** [*unless*] **they shall rebel against me also**.

24 And **if** it so be that **they** [*Nephi's posterity*] **rebel** against me, they [*Laman and Lemuel's posterity*] shall be a scourge [*trouble*] unto thy seed, to stir them up in the ways of remembrance [*to encourage them to live the gospel and repent as needed*].

1 NEPHI 3

In this chapter, Lehi's sons will be commanded to go back to Jerusalem to get the brass plates of Laban. These plates contained the scriptures written upon thin metal plates made of brass (much more durable than parchment or scrolls). The writings included the first part of our Bible—the Old Testament up to the writings of the prophet Jeremiah—plus a record of Lehi's own genealogy, meaning his ancestors. Laban is a powerful and influential man in Jerusalem who is the keeper of these plates. He is most likely Lehi's relative and the one in the family who keeps the family's genealogical records. The journey back through the dangerous wilderness to Jerusalem will be around 200 miles (or 320 kilometers) one way.

Remember, as Nephi comes back into camp, he has been in a very sacred, spiritual environment, having just finished speaking with the premortal Jesus Christ (Jehovah, the God of the Old Testament, at that time, who was still a spirit). He will be very well prepared for the commandment his father gives even though his older brothers are already complaining about it.

1 AND it came to pass that I, Nephi, returned from speaking with the Lord, to the tent of **my father**.

2 And it came to pass that he **spake** [*spoke*] unto me, saying: Behold I have dreamed a dream, in the which the Lord hath commanded me that **thou** [*you*] **and thy** [*your*] **brethren** [*brothers*] **shall return to Jerusalem**.

3 For behold, Laban hath the record [*history*] of the Jews and also a genealogy [*record*] of my forefathers [*ancestors*], and they are engraven [*written with an engraving tool*] upon plates of brass.

4 Wherefore, **the Lord hath commanded me that thou** [*you*] **and thy** [*your*] **brothers should**

go unto the house of Laban, and **seek** [*ask for*] **the records, and bring them down hither** [*here*] into the wilderness.

> Next, we see an important lesson for all of us. When the Lord's prophets ask us to do something, they are not the ones asking us to do it. It is the Lord asking us.

5 And now, behold **thy brothers murmur**, saying it is a hard thing which I have required of them; but behold **I have not required it of them, but it is a commandment of the Lord**.

6 Therefore go, my son, and thou shalt be favored of [*blessed by*] the Lord, **because thou hast not murmured** [*complained*].

> Verse 7, next, is one of the best-known verses in the Book of Mormon. In fact, many missionaries have it printed on their sacrament meeting program when they give their talk prior to leaving on their missions. I was one of them.

7 And it came to pass that **I, Nephi, said unto my father: I will go and do the things which the Lord hath** [*has*] **commanded, for I know that the Lord giveth no commandments unto the children of men** [*people*], **save** [*unless*] **he shall prepare a way for them that they may accomplish** [*do*] **the thing which he commandeth them**.

8 And it came to pass that **when my father had heard these words he was exceedingly** [*very*] **glad**, for he knew that I had been blessed of the Lord.

9 And I, Nephi, and my brethren took our journey in the wilderness, with our tents, to go up to the land of Jerusalem.

> An issue that students sometimes bring up as they study this chapter is the question, "Since the Lord knew that they would need the brass plates, why didn't He tell Lehi before they left the Jerusalem area, instead of having the boys go back 180–200 miles (over 300 kilometers), one way, through a very dangerous wilderness infested with robbers, murderers, and wild beasts?" One possible answer lies in the fact that mortal life is not just an existence for us. It is for our learning and development. In other words, it is a curriculum designed by God for us to help us learn to become like Him. Nephi and his brothers each had many opportunities for increased faith and testimony during the hardships on this trip. Some of them grew spiritually, and some did not.

10 And it came to pass that when we had gone up to the land of Jerusalem, I and my brethren

did consult one with another [*we discussed how to go about getting the brass plates*].

11 And **we cast lots** [*like drawing straws to see who gets the short straw, or rolling dice, and so forth*]—**who of us should go in unto the house of Laban**. And it came to pass that the lot fell upon Laman; and **Laman went in unto the house of Laban**, and he talked with him as he sat in his house.

> Next, Laman asks for the brass plates and is no doubt shocked and scared by the false things Laban accuses him of and the threat he makes.

12 And he desired of Laban the records which were engraven upon **the plates of brass**, which **contained the genealogy of my father**.

13 And behold, it came to pass that **Laban was angry**, and thrust him out from his presence [*chased him out of his house*]; and he would not that he should have the records [*didn't want him to have the brass plates*]. Wherefore, he said unto him: Behold thou art a robber, and I will slay [*kill*] thee.

> In addition to being shocked and scared, having to run for his life to get away, another thing that likely entered Laman's mind here is that Lehi and Nephi had both assured them that this was a mission from the Lord. So, why wasn't it being successful? Why wasn't the Lord helping and protecting them? Why, instead of succeeding in the Lord's work, was he now in danger of losing his life? We will talk about this in a minute.

14 But **Laman fled** out of his presence, and told the things which Laban had done, unto us. And **we began to be exceedingly sorrowful** [*very sad and worried*], and my brethren were about to return unto my father in the wilderness.

> First, based on the middle of verse 14, above, you can see that all, including Nephi, were very disappointed and worried by what had just happened. But watch now as Nephi calms down and begins exercising faith and fulfilling the the prophecy about him given by the Lord in 1 Nephi 2:22 (that he would be a leader over his brothers). He now very firmly tells them that they are not going back to their father until they have the brass plates. We also wonder if this and other situations where he would have to be exceptionally strong and capable physically might be why he told us, back in 1 Nephi 2:16, that he was extra big for his age.

15 But behold I said unto them that: **As the Lord liveth, and as we live**, we will not go down unto our father in the wilderness until

we have accomplished [*done*] the thing which the Lord hath commanded us.

The phrase "As the Lord liveth, and as we live," in verse 15 above, is the strongest way of saying something among the people of Nephi's time. So, you can see that he is telling his older brothers that they will absolutely not go back without getting the plates and taking them back to their father.

Next, he is a bit gentler as he encourages them to do what the Lord asked them to do. He proposes another plan to get the plates.

16 Wherefore [*now*], **let us be faithful in keeping the commandments of the Lord**; therefore let us go down to the land of our father's inheritance [*let's go down to where we lived before father took us into the wilderness*], for behold he left gold and silver, and all manner of riches. And all this he hath done because of the commandments of the Lord.

Next, in verses 17–20, Nephi explains to his worried brothers why their father took them away from the Jerusalem area so quickly and what would have happened if they had not obeyed the Lord's commandment to leave. In a very real way, he is bearing his testimony to them that he knows his father is a true prophet.

17 For **he knew that Jerusalem must be** [*would be*] **destroyed**, **because of the wickedness** of the people.

18 For behold, **they have rejected** [*refused to follow*] the words of **the prophets**. Wherefore [*therefore*], if my father should dwell [*were to live*] in the land after he hath been commanded to flee [*leave quickly*] out of the land, behold, he would also perish [*die*]. Wherefore, it must needs be that he flee out of the land. [*Therefore, it was absolutely necessary for him to leave Jerusalem quickly with us like he did.*]

19 And behold, it is wisdom in God that [*God knows why*] **we should obtain these records** [*the brass plates*], that we may preserve unto our children the language of our fathers [*in other words, having the written language of the brass plates will help keep our language from changing*];

20 And **also that we may preserve** unto them **the words** which have been spoken by the mouth **of all the holy prophets**, which have been delivered unto them by the Spirit and power of God, since the world began, even down unto this present time. [*In other words, we need the scriptures so that we can teach our families the word of God.*]

21 And it came to pass that after this manner of language did I persuade my brethren, [*these are the kinds of words I used to show my brothers why we had to get the brass plates*] that they might be faithful in keeping the commandments of God.

22 And it came to pass that we went down to the land of our inheritance [*down to where we used to live*], and **we did gather together our gold, and our silver, and our precious things**.

23 And after we had gathered these things together, **we went up again unto the house of Laban**.

> Watch now as Laban's greed and true dishonest character come out as Lehi's sons bring all the family's great wealth to him in exchange for the brass plates.

24 And it came to pass that we went in unto Laban, and **desired** him **that he would give unto us the records** which were engraven upon the plates of brass, **for which we would give unto him our gold, and our silver, and all our precious things**.

25 And it came to pass that when **Laban** saw our property, and that it was exceedingly great, he **did lust after it** [*his greedy inner self showed strongly and he wanted it, no matter what*], insomuch that **he thrust us out** [*drove us out*], **and sent his servants to slay us**, that he might obtain our property.

> As you can see, Lehi and Sariah's sons now have to run for their lives. Imagine the terror that filled their souls. Things were not at all working out like they expected!

26 And it came to pass that **we did flee** before the servants of Laban, **and** we were obliged to **leave behind our property** [*we had to leave all our wealth*], and it fell into the hands of Laban.

> So now Laban has all their money and precious things plus his servants are chasing them to kill them. No doubt, this is not what they thought a mission from the Lord was supposed to be like! However, they were young and were able to outrun Laban's servants and so they escaped. But Laman and Lemuel were sure mad!

27 And it came to pass that we fled [*ran*] into the wilderness, and the servants of Laban did not overtake us, and **we hid ourselves in the cavity of a rock** [*in a cave*].

28 And it came to pass that **Laman was angry with me, and** also with **my father**; and **also was Lemuel**, for he hearkened unto the words of Laman. Wherefore Laman and Lemuel did speak many hard words unto us, their

younger brothers, and **they did smite** [*hit*] **us** even **with a rod**.

To be angry with Nephi and Sam and their father is one thing, but to start beating their younger brothers with a rod is quite another. Watch now as an angel interrupts Laman and Lemuel in their wickedness. (By the way, how would you like to be this angel? It could be a rather exciting assignment for you on that particular day!) Pay close attention to how the angel handles the situation and what he prophesies about their next attempt to get the brass plates of Laban.

29 And it came to pass as they smote [*hit*] us with a rod, behold, **an angel of the Lord came and stood before them**, and he spake unto them, saying: Why do ye smite [*hit*] your younger brother with a rod? Know ye not that the Lord hath chosen him to be a ruler over you, and this because of your iniquities [*rebellion, sins, and wickedness*]? Behold ye shall **go up to Jerusalem again, and the Lord will deliver Laban into your hands**.

30 And after the angel had spoken unto us, he departed.

31 And after the angel had departed, **Laman and Lemuel again began to murmur** [*complain*], saying: How is it possible that the Lord will deliver Laban into our hands? Behold, he is a mighty man, and he can command fifty, yea, even he can slay fifty; then why not us?

Did you notice that wickedness does not promote clear thinking? Laman and Lemuel have just seen an angel with their own eyes, and heard his voice scolding them, yet they immediately start complaining again after he leaves. Plus, they have no faith that heaven can protect them from Laban and his soldiers, even though the angel said they would get the plates next time they try. Can you see that intentional wickedness does not leave much room for faith?

1 NEPHI 4

Remember that it was the Lord, Himself, who commanded Lehi to have the brothers return to Jerusalem and get the brass plates. So far, it has been a severe test of faith for them to carry out this mission call from the Lord. Attitude is a major part of having faith, and so far, Laman and Lemuel seem to be failing the test while Nephi and Sam are passing it.

Next, Nephi does his best to encourage his brothers to keep the commandments and to convince them to make another attempt at getting the plates, including reminding them that the Lord is far mightier than Laban and his fifty servants and would be even if Laban had tens of thousands of soldiers. Nephi will even use the Old Testament account of Moses's parting of the waters of the Red Sea so the children of Israel could escape the armies of Pharaoh to remind them of how powerful God is. Remember that the Israelites walked through the parted waters on dry ground while the pursuing soldiers of Egypt were drowned when the waters collapsed down upon them.

1 AND it came to pass that **I spake unto my brethren**, saying: **Let us go up again unto Jerusalem, and let us be faithful in keeping the commandments of the Lord**; for behold he is mightier than all the earth, then why not mightier than Laban and his fifty, yea, or even than his tens of thousands?

2 Therefore let us go up; **let us be strong like unto Moses**; for he truly spake unto the waters of the Red Sea and they divided hither and thither [*the waters parted this way and that*], and our fathers [*ancestors*] came through, out of captivity, on dry ground, and the armies of Pharaoh did follow and were drowned in the waters of the Red Sea.

3 Now behold ye know that this is true; and **ye also know that an angel hath spoken unto you; wherefore can ye doubt** [*so, how can you keep doubting*]? Let us go up; the Lord is able to deliver us, even as our fathers [*our ancestors, the children of Israel*], and to destroy Laban, even as the Egyptians.

4 Now when I had spoken these words, **they were yet wroth** [*angry*], and did still continue to murmur; nevertheless they did follow me up until we came without [*outside of*] the walls of Jerusalem.

5 And it was by night; and I caused that they should hide themselves without the walls. And after they had hid themselves, **I, Nephi, crept into the city and went forth towards the house of Laban**.

Next, as you will see, Nephi is about to meet a very severe test of his faith. He will pass the test, but not before he has been through a real struggle. There is a lesson in this for each of us. Sometimes, as we try to faithfully live the gospel, and to carry out our callings and responsibilities at home and in the Church, we run into problems that we most certainly did not expect. Watch now, as Nephi passes this most difficult test. He will be led by the Spirit, not having any idea where he should go or what to do.

6 And **I was led by the Spirit, not knowing beforehand the things which I should do**.

7 Nevertheless I went forth, and as I came near unto the house

of Laban **I beheld** [*saw*] **a man**, and he had fallen to the earth before me [*in front of me*], for he was **drunken** with wine.

8 And when I came to him I found that **it was Laban**.

9 And **I beheld** [*saw*] **his sword, and I drew it** forth [*pulled it out*] from the sheath thereof; and the hilt [*handle*] thereof was of pure gold, and the workmanship thereof was exceedingly fine [*it was very well made*], and I saw that the blade thereof was of the most precious steel.

Just a thought: We know that Nephi was still a young man when he found Laban completely drunk, lying on the ground. We can't help but note his admiring, detailed description of Laban's fine sword in verse 9, above. It is what we would expect from a typical young man.

Next, we see and feel the struggle in Nephi's mind and heart as he seeks to sort out the teachings of his youth about not killing people, his commitment to follow God, and the commandment from the Spirit to kill Laban. It can remind us that it is not always easy to follow the promptings of the Spirit. Watch, now, as the Spirit and Nephi have a back and forth conversation to help him carry out the will of the Lord here. It is very likely that you will have such conversations on various matters with your conscience at times during your life.

10 And it came to pass that **I was constrained** [*prompted*] **by the Spirit that I should kill Laban**; but I said in my heart: Never at any time have I shed the blood of man. And **I shrunk and would that I might not slay him** [*I hesitated and didn't want to kill him*].

11 And **the Spirit said unto me again**: Behold [*see*] the Lord hath delivered him into thy hands. Yea, and I also knew that he had sought [*tried*] to take away mine own life; yea, and he would not hearken unto [*obey*] the commandments of the Lord; and he also had taken away [*he had stolen*] our property.

12 And it came to pass that **the Spirit said unto me again: Slay him**, for the Lord hath delivered him into thy hands;

13 Behold the Lord slayeth the wicked to bring forth his righteous purposes. **It is better that one man should perish than that a nation should dwindle** [*gradually get worse*] **and perish in unbelief** [*be destroyed because of not believing in God*].

Remember that Nephi has his agency, just as you and I have our agency. God will never violate our agency. Can you see the Spirit here working to convince Nephi to exercise his agency to do whatever is necessary to get the brass plates? Watch this process in the next fews verses as the Spirit guides Nephi's thinking as to why it is so important that he get the brass plates.

14 And now, when I, Nephi, had heard these words, **I remembered the words of the Lord which he spake unto me** in the wilderness, saying that: **Inasmuch as thy seed** [*descendants, posterity, children, grandchildren, etc.*] **shall keep my commandments, they shall prosper** [*do well, thrive*] in the land of promise.

15 Yea, and I also thought that **they could not keep the commandments** of the Lord according to the law of Moses, **save they should have the law** [*unless they have the scripture—in other words, the brass plates—so they can read and study the commandments and words of the Lord*].

16 And I also knew that **the law** [*the law of Moses*] **was engraven upon the plates of brass**.

17 And again, **I knew that the Lord had delivered Laban into my hands** for this cause—that I might obtain the records according to his commandments.

18 Therefore **I did obey** the voice of the Spirit, and took Laban by the hair of the head, and I smote [*cut*] off his head with his own sword.

19 And after I had smitten off his head with his own sword, **I took the garments** [*clothes*] **of Laban and put them upon mine own body**; yea, even every whit [*every bit*]; and I did gird on his armor about my loins [*he strapped Laban's armor on, including his sword—see verse 21*].

20 And after I had done this, **I went forth unto the treasury of Laban**. And as I went forth towards the treasury of Laban, behold, **I saw the servant of Laban** who had the keys of the treasury. And **I commanded him** in the voice of Laban [*made his voice sound like Laban's*], that he should **go with me into the treasury**.

21 And **he supposed me to be his master**, Laban, for he beheld the garments and also the sword girded about my loins [*he thought I was Laban because he saw that I was wearing Laban's clothes and had his armor and sword on me*].

Next, Nephi chats with Laban's servant as if he were Laban, talking about the time he had spent that night among the religious leaders of the Jews. No doubt the

Spirit helped him with the details of this conversation.

22 And he spake [*spoke*] unto me concerning the elders of the Jews [*the Jewish religious leaders*], he knowing that his master, Laban, had been out by night among them.

23 And **I spake unto him as if it had been Laban**.

24 And I also spake unto him **that I should carry** the engravings, which were upon **the plates of brass, to my elder brethren**, who were without the walls [*outside the city walls*].

25 And I also bade him [*requested*] that he should **follow me**.

26 And he, supposing that I spake of the brethren of the church [*the religious leaders of the Jews*], and that I was truly that Laban whom I had slain [*killed*], wherefore [*therefore*] **he did follow me**.

27 And he spake unto me many times concerning the elders of the Jews, as I went forth unto my brethren, who were without the walls [*outside the walls of Jerusalem*].

Remember that Laman, Lemuel, and Sam have been hiding all this time in a cave somewhere outside of the city walls of Jerusalem. You can imagine their fright as they see Laban (it's actually Nephi in Laban's clothes and armor) and his servant coming right toward them.

28 And it came to pass that **when Laman saw me he was exceedingly frightened**, and **also Lemuel and Sam**. And they fled [*ran*] from before my presence; for they supposed it was Laban, and that he had slain me and had sought to take away their lives also.

29 And it came to pass that **I called after them**, and they did hear me [*heard and recognized my voice*]; wherefore **they did cease to flee** from my presence.

The brothers can now relax, because they now know that it is Nephi. But what about Laban's servant?

30 And it came to pass that **when the servant of Laban beheld** [*saw*] **my brethren** [*brothers*] he began to tremble, and was about to flee from before me and return to the city of Jerusalem.

Next, we see that Nephi is indeed a pretty big and strong fellow!

31 And now **I, Nephi, being a man large in stature, and also having received much strength of the Lord**, therefore I **did seize** upon [*I grabbed*] **the servant of**

Laban, and held him, that he should not flee.

Watch next as Nephi firmly holds Laban's servant and makes a very strong promise to him, referred to as an "oath." According to Jewish culture at that time, if you made an oath or promise saying "as the Lord lives" or "as I live," the person to whom you were giving your word could completely rely on it.

32 And it came to pass that **I spake with him**, that **if he would hearken unto** [*listen to and obey*] **my words**, as the Lord liveth, and as I live, even so that if he would hearken unto our words, **we would spare his life** [*we would not kill him*].

33 And **I spake unto him**, even **with an oath**, that he need not fear; **that he should be a free man** like unto us **if he would go down in the wilderness with us**.

34 And **I also spake unto him, saying**: Surely the Lord hath commanded us to do this thing; and shall we not be diligent in keeping the commandments of the Lord? Therefore, if thou wilt go down into the wilderness to my father thou shalt have place with us.

Watch Zoram's reaction now. You can almost see the fear and trembling leave him as Nephi gives him his word and explains what this is all about and invites Zoram to give them his word to stay with them and become one of them. He did, and the problem was solved.

35 And it came to pass that **Zoram did take courage at the words which I spake**. Now Zoram was the name of the servant; and he promised that he would go down into the wilderness unto our father. Yea, and **he also made an oath unto us that he would tarry** [*stay*] **with us** from that time forth.

Next, Nephi explains why they wanted Zoram to stay with them and the family.

36 Now we were desirous that he should tarry with [*stay with*] us for this cause, **that the Jews might not know concerning our flight** [*rapid journey*] **into the wilderness**, lest they should pursue us and destroy us.

37 And it came to pass that **when Zoram had made an oath unto us, our fears did cease concerning him**.

38 And it came to pass that **we took the plates of brass and the servant of Laban** [*Zoram*], and departed into the wilderness, and journeyed **unto the tent of our father**.

1 NEPHI 5

Imagine the joy and relief of Lehi and Sariah as the sons returned safely to camp, along with Zoram! It could easily have been a month or more that Laman, Lemuel, Sam, and Nephi had been gone. They had no way of letting their parents know whether they were safe or not or even still alive. No cell phones, no internet, no nothing! As you read verses 1–6, you will see that Father Lehi knew that they were on a mission from the Lord and that they would return safely. But Mother Sariah did not know that yet and was terribly afraid that their sons were dead and that they, too, would die in this awful wilderness.

As you read further, you will see that this great lady and mother will have her testimony greatly strengthened by the successful return of their sons and will never complain or falter again.

1 AND it came to pass [*and so it happened*] that after we had come down into the wilderness unto **our father**, behold, he **was filled with joy, and also my mother, Sariah**, was exceedingly [*very*] glad, for she truly had mourned because of us [*had been very worried and sad, thinking we had died*].

2 For **she had supposed that we had perished** [*died*] in the wilderness; and **she also had complained against my father**, telling him that he was a visionary man [*telling him he had just imagined having visions*]; saying: Behold thou hast [*you have*] led us forth from the land of our inheritance [*you have led us away from our home*], and my sons are no more, and we perish in the wilderness.

3 And after this manner [*using this kind*] of language had my mother complained against my father.

Watch next as Lehi bears testimony to his wife, Sariah, that he really did see these things in a vision and that their sons will return safely.

4 And it had come to pass that **my father spake unto her, saying**: I know that I am a visionary man; for if I had not seen the things of God in a vision I should not have [*would not have*] known the goodness of God, but had tarried [*would have stayed*] at Jerusalem, and had perished with my brethren.

5 But behold, **I have obtained a land of promise** [*literally, the Americas; symbolically, heaven*], in the which things I do rejoice; yea, and I know that the Lord will deliver my sons out of the hands of Laban, and bring them down again unto us in the wilderness.

6 And **after this manner of language did my father**, Lehi, [*this is the kind of things my father said to*]

comfort my mother, Sariah, concerning us, while we journeyed in the wilderness up to the land of Jerusalem, to obtain the record of the Jews [*the brass plates*].

7 And **when we had returned to the tent of my father, behold their joy was full, and my mother was comforted**.

Watch now as Sariah bears her testimony. Imagine Lehi's joy and comfort as he listens to it, knowing that his wife now knows that he really is a prophet!

8 And she spake [*spoke*], saying: **Now I know of a surety** [*for sure*] that the Lord hath commanded my husband to flee into the wilderness; yea, and **I also know of a surety** that the Lord hath protected my sons, and delivered them out of the hands of Laban, and given them power whereby they could accomplish the thing which the Lord hath commanded them. And after this manner of language did she speak [*these are the kinds of things she said*].

9 And it came to pass that **they did rejoice exceedingly**, and did offer sacrifice and burnt offerings unto the Lord; and **they gave thanks unto the God of Israel**.

Verse 9, above, reminds us that they were still living the law of Moses, including animal sacrifices, symbolic of the future Atonement of Christ. In this sense, we are still in Old Testament times at this point in the Book of Mormon and will be until the visit of the resurrected Savior in Third Nephi.

10 And after they had given thanks unto the God of Israel, **my father, Lehi, took the records which were engraven upon the plates of brass, and he did search them** from the beginning.

Nephi will now give us a detailed description of the contents of the brass plates of Laban according to what his father found in them. You will see that the brass plates were basically their scriptures.

11 And he beheld [*saw*] that they did contain **the five books of Moses** [*Genesis, Exodus, Leviticus, Numbers, and Deuteronomy, as found in the Old Testament in the Bible*], which gave an account of the creation of the world, and also of Adam and Eve, who were our first parents [*our first ancestors*];

12 And also **a record of the Jews** from the beginning, even down to the commencement [*beginning*] of the reign [*rule*] of Zedekiah, king of Judah [*the king in Jerusalem and the surrounding area when Lehi and his family left*];

13 And also **the prophecies of the holy prophets**, [*including Isaiah*] from the beginning, even down to the commencement of the reign of Zedekiah; and also many prophecies which have been spoken by the mouth of Jeremiah.

14 And it came to pass that **my father, Lehi, also found upon the plates of brass a genealogy of his fathers** [*ancestors*]; wherefore [*therefore*] he knew that he was a descendant of Joseph; yea, even that Joseph who was the son of Jacob, who was sold into Egypt, and who was preserved by the hand of the Lord, that he might preserve his father, Jacob, and all his household from perishing with famine.

15 And they [*his ancestors, the children of Israel*] were also led out of captivity and out of the land of Egypt, by that same God who had preserved them.

In verse 16, next, we learn that Lehi and Laban were relatives, though whether close relatives or distant relatives, we don't know.

16 And thus my father, **Lehi, did discover the genealogy of his fathers**. And Laban also was a descendant of Joseph, wherefore [*this is why*] he and his fathers [*ancestors*] had kept the records.

17 And now when **my father** saw all these things, he **was filled with the Spirit**, and began to prophesy concerning his seed [*descendants, posterity*]—

In verses 18 and 19, next, there is a pretty amazing prophecy about the plates of brass, including that they would never be destroyed or even worn by time. With that in mind, it appears that we can plan on seeing them some day, whether in this life or the next.

18 That these **plates of brass should go** forth **unto all nations**, kindreds [*families, tribes*], tongues [*languages*], and people who were of his seed.

19 Wherefore, he said that these **plates of brass should never perish** [*be destroyed*]; neither should they be dimmed any more by time. And he prophesied many things concerning his seed [*descendants*].

Verse 20, next, contains a goal that all of us would do well to work toward, namely to be able someday to look back and honestly say that we have kept the commandments of the Lord.

20 And it came to pass that **thus far I and my father had kept the commandments wherewith the Lord had commanded us**.

21 And **we had obtained the records** [*brass plates*] which the

Lord had commanded us, **and searched** [*studied*] **them** and found that **they were desirable; yea, even of great worth unto us**, insomuch that we could preserve the commandments of the Lord unto our children.

> Did you notice, in verse 21, above, that one of the big purposes of studying the scriptures ourselves is so that we can teach the gospel to our own families and children?

22 Wherefore, it was wisdom in the Lord that **we should** [*that's why the Lord wanted us to*] **carry them with us**, as we journeyed in the wilderness **towards the land of promise**.

1 NEPHI 6

Next, Nephi refers to the special record that the Lord commanded him to write thirty years after they left Jerusalem. See 2 Nephi 5:28–33. We usually refer to this record as the small plates of Nephi. It's the one we are reading and have been reading all along so far. He carefully limits what things he engraves on these small plates to more spiritual matters, lessons, and messages, with just enough history to provide background and setting for what he wants to teach us, as well as his own people. Another set of plates had been kept over the years and are commonly referred to as the large plates of Nephi. See "A Brief Explanation about the Book of Mormon" at the beginning of the regular Book of Mormon for more about the various sets of plates referred to in it. At this point in history, it is about 600–592 BC.

1 AND now **I, Nephi, do not give the genealogy of my fathers in this part of my record**; neither at any time shall I give it after upon these plates [*the small plates*] which I am writing; for it is given in the record which has been kept by my father [*the large plates*]; wherefore [*this is why*], I do not write it in this work.

2 For it sufficeth me [*it is enough for me*] to say that **we are descendants of Joseph** [*the son of Jacob who was sold by his brothers into Egyptian slavery in the Old Testament*].

3 And it mattereth not to me that I am particular to give a full account of all the things of my father, for they cannot be written upon these plates [*the small plates*], for **I desire the room that I may write of the things of God**.

4 For **the fulness of mine intent** [*my whole purpose*] is that I may **persuade men** [*strongly influence people*] **to come unto** the **God** of Abraham, and the God of Isaac, and the God of Jacob [*in other words, Jehovah, who was the premortal Jesus Christ*], and be saved.

Remember that Jesus Christ works under the direction of Heavenly Father to try to finally bring us back to the Father. Christ, as a spirit (before He was born to Mary), was the God of the Old Testament.

5 Wherefore, **the things which are pleasing unto the world** [*to worldly people*] **I do not write**, but the things which are pleasing unto God and unto those who are not of the world [*those who are trying to be righteous, spiritual*].

6 Wherefore, I shall give commandment unto my seed, that they shall not occupy these plates [*small plates*] with things which are not of worth unto the children of men [*all people*].

1 NEPHI 7

In this chapter, you will see the Lord command Father Lehi to take care of a really big problem. Lehi and Sariah have four sons, and the family will now continue traveling in the wilderness and eventually end up in the Americas. But where will the sons get wives when they want to marry and start their own families?

The answer is for the sons to go back to Jerusalem again and ask a man named Ishmael to bring his family and join them on their journey through the wilderness. As you can imagine, this is a huge thing to ask, but the Lord will help, and Ishmael and his family will agree to come.

By the way, you will notice that this time Laman and Lemuel do not complain at all.

You will also see the hand of the Lord in providing a family, in advance, with just the right number of unmarried daughters. We note that there are five who need wives—namely, Laman, Lemuel, Sam, Nephi, and Zoram. Ishmael's family has five unmarried daughters plus two married sons and their families. Also, we are given to understand that Ishmael's two sons had married into Lehi's family. Apostle Erastus Snow said that Joseph Smith said that this was the case. From this we would gather that Lehi and Sariah had two older daughters, and that they had married Ishmael's sons and already had families of their own. Here is the quote from Elder Erastus Snow:

"The Prophet Joseph informed us that the record of Lehi, was contained on the 116 pages that were first translated and subsequently stolen, and of which an abridgement is given us in the first Book of Nephi, which is the record of Nephi individually, he himself being of the lineage of Manasseh; but that Ishmael was of the lineage of Ephraim, and that his sons married into Lehi's family, and Lehi's sons married Ishmael's daughters." (*Journal of Discourses*, 26 vols. [London: Latter-day Saints' Book Depot, 1854–1886], 23: 185–186.)

About 600–592 BC.

1 AND now I would that ye might know [*I want you to know*], that after my father, Lehi, had made an end of prophesying concerning his seed [*his children, their children, their children, and so forth; in other words, his descendants, posterity*], it came to pass that **the Lord spake unto him** again, saying that it was not meet for him [*not good for him*], Lehi, that he should take his family into the wilderness alone; but that **his sons should take daughters to wife**, that they might raise up seed unto the Lord [*so that they could raise righteous families*] in the land of promise [*in America*].

2 And it came to pass that the Lord commanded him that I, Nephi, and my brethren [*brothers*], should again return unto the land of Jerusalem, and **bring** down **Ishmael and his family into the wilderness**.

3 And it came to pass that I, Nephi, did again, with my brethren, go forth into the wilderness to go up to Jerusalem.

In verses 4–5, next, you will see that the Lord helped the brothers convince Ishmael and his family to return with them.

4 And it came to pass that **we went up unto the house of Ishmael**, and we did gain favor in the sight of Ishmael [*Ishmael welcomed us*], insomuch that [*so that*] we did speak unto him the words of the Lord.

5 And it came to pass that **the Lord did soften the heart of Ishmael** [*inspired Ishmael to believe them*], and also his household, insomuch that [*so that*] **they took their journey with** us down into the wilderness to the tent of our father.

Next, you will see Laman and Lemuel and some of the others start causing serious trouble. It is sad that they don't seem to be able to be good for very long. It makes you wonder why some people seem to be able to be good consistently while others are on again, off again righteous. It may be that some people are very serious about wanting to follow the Lord, whereas others don't want to make that serious of a commitment to be righteous. We know that it has to do with how we use our agency.

6 And it came to pass that as we journeyed in the wilderness, behold **Laman** and **Lemuel**, and **two of the daughters of Ishmael**, and **the two sons of Ishmael and their families, did rebel against us**; yea, against me, Nephi, and Sam, and their father, Ishmael, and his wife, and his three other daughters.

7 And it came to pass in the which rebellion [*in the rebellion I just mentioned*], **they were desirous to** [*they wanted to*] **return unto the land of Jerusalem**.

8 And now I, Nephi, being grieved for [*being saddened by*] the hardness of their hearts [*their unrighteousness,*], therefore **I spake unto** them, saying, yea, even unto **Laman** and unto **Lemuel**: Behold ye are mine elder brethren [*older brothers*], and **how is it that ye are so hard in your hearts, and so blind in your minds** [*so spiritually blind*], that ye have need that I, your younger brother, should speak unto you, yea, and set an example for you?

9 How is it that **ye have not hearkened unto** [*listened to and obeyed*] **the word of the Lord**?

10 How is it that ye have forgotten that **ye have seen an angel of the Lord**?

11 Yea, and **how is it that ye have forgotten** what great things the Lord hath done for us, in delivering us out of the hands of Laban, and also that we should obtain the record [*the brass plates*]?

Watch as Nephi, after firmly scolding his brothers and the others and calling them to repentance, now changes his tone of voice and kindly and more gently invites them to exercise faith in the Lord.

12 Yea, and **how is it that ye have forgotten** that the Lord is able to do all things according to his will, for the children of men [*for people*], if it so be that they exercise faith in him? Wherefore, let us be faithful to him.

13 And **if it so be that we are faithful to him, we shall obtain the land of promise**; and ye shall know at some future period that the word of the Lord shall be fulfilled concerning the destruction of Jerusalem; for all things which the Lord hath spoken concerning the destruction of Jerusalem must be fulfilled.

Next, Nephi explains to his brothers why Jerusalem was going to be destroyed.

14 For behold, **the Spirit of the Lord ceaseth** [*stops*] **soon to strive** [*work*] **with them**; for behold, they have rejected the prophets, and Jeremiah [*the prophet*] have they cast into prison. And they have sought [*tried*] to take away the life of my father, insomuch that they have driven him out of the land.

Next, Nephi basically tells Laman and Lemuel and the others who are rebelling that if they want to go back to Jerusalem, go, but if they do, they will die with the inhabitants of that city. Watch how they react!

15 Now behold, I say unto you that **if ye** will **return unto Jerusalem ye shall also perish** [*die*] with them. And now, if ye have choice, go up to the land, and remember the words which I speak unto you, that if ye go ye will also perish; for thus the Spirit of the Lord constraineth me that I should speak.

16 And it came to pass that when I, Nephi, had spoken these words unto my brethren, **they were angry with me**. And it came to pass that **they did lay their hands upon me** [*they grabbed me*], for behold, they were exceedingly wroth [*very angry*], and **they did bind me with cords** [*tied me up with ropes*], for **they sought to take away my life**, that they might leave me in the wilderness to be devoured [*eaten*] by wild beasts.

Verses 17 and 18, next, are favorites of many Book of Mormon readers. Watch how Nephi exercises faith (which he can do because of his personal righteousness). Also, imagine the looks on the faces of these rebellious ones as these next events take place.

17 But it came to pass that **I prayed unto the Lord**, saying: O Lord, **according to my faith which is in thee, wilt thou deliver me from the hands of my brethren**; yea, even give me strength that I may burst these bands [*break these ropes*] with which I am bound [*tied*].

18 And it came to pass that when I had said these words, behold, **the bands were loosed** from off my hands and feet [*the ropes broke*], and I stood before my brethren, and I spake unto them again.

Can you imagine how far gone spiritually you would have to be to do what the brothers did next, after seeing the ropes break because of Nephi's faith and prayer? This is very sad.

19 And it came to pass that **they were angry with me again**, and sought to lay hands upon me; **but** behold, **one of the daughters of Ishmael**, yea, and **also her mother, and one of the sons of Ishmael, did plead with my brethren**, insomuch that they did soften their hearts; and they did cease striving to take away my life.

In verse 19, above, and 20, next, we see what can happen when we speak up to defend the right. (Also, some of us hope that the daughter of Ishmael, in verse 19, who pled for Nephi's life, is the one who will later marry Nephi.)

20 And it came to pass that **they were sorrowful**, because of their

wickedness, insomuch that they did bow down before me, **and did plead with me that I would forgive them** of the thing that they had done against me.

Rather than holding a grudge and making his wicked brothers sweat for a while after they asked his forgiveness, Nephi sets a high standard for us in verse 21, as far as forgiving people who are mean to us is concerned.

21 And it came to pass that **I did frankly** [*simply, without holding anything back*] **forgive them** all that they had done, and I did exhort [*urge, counsel*] them that they would pray unto the Lord their God for forgiveness. And it came to pass that they did so. And after they had done praying unto the Lord we did again travel on our journey towards the tent of our father.

Nephi's example of frankly forgiving his brothers, in verse 21, above, is one of the greatest examples anywhere in the scriptures for showing us how to handle it when others ask us for forgiveness. Not only does it help free them from the burden of guilt but it frees us from the greater burden and damage that comes from holding grudges.

22 And it came to pass that **we did come down unto the tent of our father**. And after I and my brethren and all the house of Ishmael had come down unto the tent of my father, they did give thanks unto the Lord their God; and **they did offer sacrifice and burnt offerings unto him** [*a reminder that they are living according to the Old Testament law of Moses, which will be replaced by the gospel we live that was given by the Savior during His mortal mission*].

1 NEPHI 8

This chapter is one of the best-known chapters of the Book of Mormon. It is the account of Lehi's vision of the tree of life. You may have heard about it already. In the vision, Lehi is shown a tree in a wide field that has delicious fruit on it. The fruit is so white that it is impossible to describe it. There is a river that runs along near the tree and a rod of iron along a path leading along the river. Many of you sang about this "iron rod" in Primary. After Lehi eats some of the fruit, he calls to his family to come and eat some of the fruit also. Sariah, Sam, and Nephi come and partake of the fruit, but Laman and Lemuel refuse to come and partake.

You will see many more details and much symbolism in this dream or vision as you read along now in this chapter. There are many lessons to be learned from it, some of which we will point out. About 600–592 BC.

1 AND it came to pass that we had gathered together all manner

[*all kinds*] of seeds of every kind, both of grain of every kind, and also of the seeds of fruit of every kind.

2 And it came to pass that while **my father** tarried [*waited*] in the wilderness he **spake** unto us, **saying**: Behold, **I have dreamed a dream**; or, in other words, **I have seen a vision**.

> Here, the terms "dream" and "vision" seem to mean the same thing. There may be a message in this for us. Sometimes we can't tell the difference between whether or not we are dreaming something, under the direction and inspiration of the Holy Ghost, or actually seeing real people and objects in a vision. It is probably best not to spend too much time trying to tell the difference, rather, just pay attention to the message the Lord is giving us.
>
> Next, Lehi informs his family that in the vision he saw things about Nephi and Sam that made him happy and things about Laman and Lemuel that caused him to worry.

3 And behold, because of the thing which I have seen, **I have reason to rejoice** in the Lord **because of Nephi and** also of **Sam**; for I have reason to suppose that they, and also many of their seed [*posterity*], will be saved.

4 But behold, **Laman and Lemuel, I fear exceedingly because of you**; for behold, methought [*it seemed like*] **I saw** in my dream, **a dark and dreary wilderness**.

5 And it came to pass that **I saw a man, and he was dressed in a white robe**; and he came and stood before me.

6 And it came to pass that **he** spake [*spoke*] unto me, and **bade** [*asked*] **me follow him**.

7 And it came to pass that as I followed him I beheld myself that I was in a dark and dreary waste.

8 And **after** I had traveled for the space of **many hours** in darkness, **I began to pray** unto the Lord that he would have mercy on me, according to the multitude of his tender mercies.

9 And it came to pass after I had prayed unto the Lord **I beheld** [*saw*] **a large and spacious** [*wide, roomy*] **field**.

10 And it came to pass that **I beheld a tree**, whose **fruit was desirable to make one happy**.

11 And it came to pass that **I did** go forth and **partake** [*ate*] **of the fruit** thereof [*of the tree*]; and I beheld that [*found that*] **it was**

most sweet, above all that I ever before tasted. Yea, and I beheld [*saw*] that **the fruit** thereof **was white**, to exceed all the whiteness that I had ever seen.

12 And **as I partook of the fruit thereof it filled my soul with exceedingly great joy**; wherefore, I began to be **desirous that my family should partake of it also**; for I knew that it was desirable above all other fruit.

13 And as I cast my eyes round about [*as I looked around*], that perhaps I might discover my family also, **I beheld a river of water**; and it ran along, and it was **near the tree** of which I was partaking the fruit.

14 And I looked to behold from whence it came [*to see where it came from*]; and I saw the head thereof a little way off; and at the head thereof **I beheld your mother Sariah, and Sam, and Nephi**; and they stood as if they knew not whither [*where*] they should go.

15 And it came to pass that **I beckoned** [*waved*] **unto them**; and I also **did say** unto them with a loud voice that they should **come unto me, and partake of the fruit**, which was desirable above all other fruit.

16 And it came to pass that **they did come** unto me **and partake** of the fruit also.

17 And it came to pass that **I was desirous that Laman and Lemuel should come and partake of the fruit also**; wherefore, I cast mine eyes [*I looked*] towards the head of the river, that perhaps I might see them.

18 And it came to pass that **I saw them, but they would not come** unto me and partake of the fruit.

It is important here to be aware that one of the Ten Commandments is to "Honor thy Father and thy Mother" (Exodus 20:12). Among the Jews in Jerusalem, where Laman and Lemuel had grown up, it was a very strong rule to honor your parents. So you can see here that Laman and Lemuel are getting way off in their behavior and are violating a very strong teaching as they rebel against their father. It gives us another strong reason to really worry about them.

In verses 19–35, you will see many more details of Lehi's dream.

19 And I beheld [*saw*] **a rod of iron** [*symbolic of the word of God—see 1 Nephi 11:25*], and it extended along [*ran along*] the bank of the river, and led to the tree by which I stood.

20 And I also beheld **a strait and narrow path**, which came along by the rod of iron, even to the tree by which I stood; and it also led by the head of the fountain, unto **a large and spacious field**, as if it had been a world.

Let's study a bit of vocabulary in verse 20, above. The phrase "strait and narrow path" is an interesting one. Look carefully at the spelling of "strait." It is not "straight," which basically means in a straight line. "Strait" means "narrow" or "restricted." So, in effect, we have the phrase "narrow and narrow path." It has been suggested that the phrase can mean "narrow and narrowing" path, meaning that the more righteous you become, the more you limit your behavior and activities to more carefully live the gospel. In other words, you make your own path through life narrower and narrower in order not to risk getting caught up in sin. Perhaps the phrase itself contains an important lesson for us. It is that, as we listen to and obey the promptings of the Holy Ghost, the "covenant path" we are on gets narrower and narrower, by our own choice, thus leading us to exaltation.

In fact, I had an interesting experience with this concept. A friend of mine had gotten way off the gospel path for a time in his life. Through repentance and much effort, he regained his membership in the Church and was doing very well. However, one day he came to see me in my stake president's office. He expressed serious concern about his chances for gaining celestial exaltation. Whereas he had been very confident about his chances for several months now, he was now having serious doubts about himself. His concern boiled down to this: He was now noticing flaws and imperfections in his daily living which he had not even noticed before this time in his life. I guess I startled him when I said, "Rejoice!" Startled, he looked straight at me and said, "President, did you even hear what I just said?" I assured him that I had been listening carefully.

As we chatted, I explained that the fact that he was now noticing things previously unnoticed by him in his life was evidence that he was now much closer to the Spirit than before. He was drawing closer and closer to God and the "light" was shining much brighter on his gospel path so that he was now noticing and worrying about smaller sins in his life. It was a sign that he was doing much better! When he realized this, he paused, then smiled, breathed a big sigh of relief, and left the office very happy. He continued to progress and serve very effectively in the Church and community. Such is the power of travel along the "narrow and narrowing" path.

Next, you will see four different groups or categories of people in Lehi's dream. The first three will have many similarities to begin with, but only one will successfully make it to salvation in heaven. The fourth group will not even get onto the path. See if you can decide which group you want to be in.

Group One (verses 21–23)

21 And I saw **numberless** [*impossible to count*] **concourses** [*crowds, throngs*] **of people**, many of whom were **pressing forward**, that they might **obtain the path** which led unto the tree by which I stood.

22 And it came to pass that **they did come forth, and commence** [*start*] **in the path which led to the tree.**

So far, those in group one want to come unto Christ. They have successfully begun to "press forward" in their lives toward that goal. In fact, according to verse 22, above, they have actually stepped onto the "strait and narrow path" which leads to eternal life. From 2 Nephi 31:17–18, we understand this to mean that they had been baptized into the Church. Next, sadly, these people, who had such good intentions to begin with, will be led astray and off the path.

23 And it came to pass that there arose a **mist of darkness** [*symbolic of the "temptations of the devil" according to 1 Nephi 12:17*] yea, even an exceedingly [*very*] great mist of darkness, insomuch [*so*] that **they** who had commenced in the path **did lose their way**, that they **wandered off and were lost.**

Can you see that, according to the last line of verse 23, above, when people leave the Church or quit going to church, they tend to lose direction in their lives and tend to simply wander around as far as morals and standards and direction in life are concerned? This is a major warning to all of us from this part of Lehi's dream.

Group Two (verses 24–28)

24 And it came to pass that I beheld others **pressing forward**, and they came forth and **caught hold of the end of the rod of iron**; and **they did press forward through the mist of darkness, clinging to the rod of iron**, even until they did come forth and partake of the fruit of the tree.

As you can see in verse 24, above, those in this group start out like the ones in group one, "pressing forward" and getting baptized, but they make it farther along the path. These make it through the "mist of darkness" (Satan's temptations) by holding on to the iron rod. Do you remember what the iron rod symbolizes? It is the "word of God" (see 1 Nephi 11:25). How do we obtain God's word? From reading and studying the scriptures, listening to the words of our living prophets, attending church, and so forth. In fact, the people in this group actually make it to the tree and partake of the fruit. In other words, among other things, they actually have testimonies of the gospel.

We are shown a sad but important fact in the next verses, namely that Satan doesn't quit working on people who have reached "the tree" and partaken of its "fruit," which could include joining the Church and having testimonies. He seems to have some especially powerful weapons designed to take them out and destroy them. One of these is peer pressure.

25 And **after they had partaken of the fruit of the tree they did cast their eyes about** [*look around*] **as if they were ashamed**.

26 And I also cast my eyes round about [*Lehi looked to see where they were looking*], and beheld, on the other side of the **river of water** [*filthiness; see 1 Nephi 15:26-27*], **a great and spacious** [*lots of room*] **building**; and it stood as it were **in the air**, high above the earth.

Two things. First, did you notice that the righteous were separated from the proud, worldly occupants of the "great and spacious building" by the river? And, according to what Nephi was shown later, in 1 Nephi 15:26–27, the river represented filthiness, sin. In other words, sin separates the righteous from the wicked. Second, the huge building with lots of people in it had no foundation! It is not safe to be in! It will fall, guaranteed! (See 1 Nephi 11:36.)

Next, Lehi describes the people he saw in the "great and spacious building."

27 And it was **filled with people**, both old and young, both male and female; and **their manner of dress was exceedingly fine** [*they were very well dressed*]; and they were in the attitude of **mocking** and **pointing their fingers towards those who had come at and were partaking of the fruit** [*they were making fun of the members of the Church who were eating the fruit of the tree, symbolic of peer pressure*].

28 And after they had tasted of the fruit they were ashamed [*embarrassed, ashamed at being members of the Church*], because of those that were scoffing at them [*making fun of them*]; and **they fell away into forbidden paths and were lost**.

Did you notice that those in group one "wandered away," but those in group two "fell away?" Perhaps one lesson we could learn from this is that the more knowledge and testimony you have, the farther and faster you fall if you choose to break your commitments and covenants in the gospel.

29 And now **I, Nephi, do not speak all the words of my father.**

Group three (verse 30 & the last part of verse 33)

Those in this third group are also "pressing forward" like those in groups one and two. These "caught hold of the end of the rod of iron" as did those in group two. So, what are the differences between those in the third group which Lehi saw and those in groups one and two? If we learn our lesson here, we will have some keys to successfully returning home to our Father in Heaven by not falling off the covenant path. Notice that the members in this group do not "wander off" nor do they "fall away." They remain faithful. They are successful. They obtain the prize of eternal life.

30 But, to be short in writing [*to be brief*], behold, he saw other multitudes pressing forward; and they came and caught hold of the end of the rod of iron; and **they did press their way forward, continually** [*not just when they felt like being faithful*] **holding fast to the rod of iron**, until they came forth and **fell down** [*they remained humble*] and **partook of the fruit of the tree.** [*And, according to the last lines of verse 33, they continued partaking of the fruit, with Lehi and those of his family who remained faithful, plus, they "heeded . . . not" those who "did point the finger of scorn" at the righteous. In other words, they did not yield to peer pressure to become involved in wickedness.*]

Group Four (verses 31–33)

Whereas the people in groups one through three appear to be members of the Church, those in group four do not. They doin't even get on the "strait and narrow path." They do not seem to have definite direction, nor do they "press forward." Rather, they "feel" their way through life (verse 31) and "wander" (verse 32).

31 And he also saw other multitudes **feeling their way** towards that great and spacious building.

32 And it came to pass that many were **drowned in the depths of the fountain** [*were overcome by filthiness, sin*]; and many were lost from his view, **wandering** in strange roads [*well-used roads which led away from God*].

33 And great [*large*] was the multitude [*crowd*] that did enter into that strange building [*the great and spacious*

building, verses 26–27]. And after they did enter into that building they did point the finger of scorn at me and those that were partaking of the fruit also; but **we heeded them not** [*we didn't pay any attention to them*]. [*This is a great "short sermon" on how to deal with negative peer pressure.*]

34 These are the words of my father: For as many as heeded them [*those who let the mocking from the "great and spacious building" drive them out of the Church*], had fallen away.

Next, Nephi mentions again that Laman and Lemuel refused to partake of the fruit of the tree in Lehi's dream. This confirms that he is very worried about them.

35 And **Laman and Lemuel partook not of the fruit**, said my father.

36 And it came to pass after my father had spoken all the words of his dream or vision, which were many, he said unto us, because of these things which he saw in a vision, he exceedingly feared for [*was very worried about*] Laman and Lemuel; yea, he feared lest they should be cast off from the presence of the Lord [*would not make it back into the presence of the Lord*].

37 And **he did exhort them** [*counseled and encouraged them*] then with all the feeling of a tender parent, that they would hearken to [*listen to and obey*] his words, that perhaps the Lord would be merciful to them, and not cast them off; yea, my father did preach unto them.

38 And after he had preached unto them, and also prophesied unto them of many things, he bade [*asked*] them to keep the commandments of the Lord; and he did cease [*stopped*] speaking unto them.

1 NEPHI 9

In this chapter, Nephi repeatedly mentions two sets of plates or sets of thin metal plates upon which the history of his people is being kept. As mentioned in the introductory pages of your Book of Mormon, these are the small plates of Nephi and the large plates of Nephi. The small plates contained more of the spiritual matters and gospel teachings and less of the day-to-day history of the people. The large plates contained more of the history and everyday life of his people. In 1 Nephi 1:17, Nephi told us that he would first "make an abridgment (a summary) of the record of my father" upon the small plates, and then he would tell us of his own life. As of the end of 1 Nephi chapter 8, he has now finished his basic summary or abridgment of his father's record. Chapter 9 is a transition between Nephi's abridgment of his father's record and the beginning of his account of his own life and doings which he engraved also on the small plates. We have been reading from Joseph Smith's translation of the small plates ever since chapter 1. About 600–592 BC.

1 AND all these things did my father see, and hear, and speak, as he dwelt in a tent, in the valley of Lemuel, and also a great many more things, which cannot be written upon **these plates** [*the small plates*].

Did you notice in verse 1, above, that Nephi again mentions that his father was living in a tent? He mentioned that before, in 1 Nephi 2:15, for example. It is possible that Nephi is reminding us again that his father left great wealth (1 Nephi 2:4) and, no doubt, a very comfortable home and living conditions near Jerusalem, to follow the Lord's commandment to depart into the wilderness. It appears that he is teaching us the importance of following God's commandments even if it means leaving our comfort zone.

As stated above, Nephi mentions the small set of plates and the large set of plates a number of times in this brief chapter. We will use **bold** and notes in brackets to help you tell which reference is to which set of plates.

2 And now, as I have spoken concerning **these plates** [*the small plates*, behold they are not **the plates** [*the large plates*] upon which I make a full account of the history of my people; for **the plates** [*the large plates*] upon which I make a full account of my people I have given the name of Nephi; wherefore, they are called the **plates of Nephi** [*the large plates*], after mine own name; and **these plates** [*the small plates*] also are called the plates of Nephi.

3 Nevertheless, I have received a commandment of the Lord that I should make **these plates** [*the small plates*], for the special purpose that there should be an account engraven of the ministry of my people.

4 Upon **the other plates** [*the large plates*] should be engraven an account of the reign of the kings, and the wars and contentions of my people; wherefore **these plates** [*the small plates*] are for the more part of the ministry; and **the other plates** [*the large plates*] are for the more part of the reign of the kings and the wars and contentions of my people.

5 Wherefore, the Lord hath commanded me to make **these plates** [*the small plates*] for a wise purpose in him, which purpose I know not [*in other words, Nephi didn't know why the Lord commanded him to make the small plates*].

Nephi is a great and inspired teacher. He knows that people, including you and me, in our day will be reading and studying his words, so he quickly gives us three brief but very important lessons about the Lord in the last verse of this chapter.

6 But the Lord knoweth all things from the beginning; wherefore, he prepareth a way to accomplish all his works among the children of men [*all people*]; for behold, he hath all power unto the fulfilling of all his words. And thus it is. Amen.

One more thing before we leave this chapter. In verse 5, above, Nephi tells us he does not know why the Lord commanded him to make the small plates and keep a separate history of his people on them. He is a wonderful example of simple, pure faith and obedience to the commandments of God. See verse 6. Can you imagine how much extra work it would take to keep this commandment? He would have to find gold ore, melt the rocks down to get the metal out, carefully pound the metal into thin enough sheets so that he could write on them with an engraving tool, and then painstakingly engrave this separate record. This would be very time consuming! But he did it.

We now know one of the major reasons why this separate set of plates was needed. The Lord knows the future. He knew that a man by the name of Martin Harris would serve as a scribe for Joseph Smith, in other words, that Martin would write down the words on paper as Joseph translated from the gold plates. He also knew that Martin would take 116 pages of the completed translation and lose them (see Doctrine and Covenants, sections 3 and 10, including the headings for each section). When Joseph Smith was once again permitted to work on translating the Book of Mormon plates, he was told not to go back and retranslate the portion of the gold plates he had translated while Martin Harris served as his scribe (see D&C 10:30). The lost 116 manuscript pages were the written translation from the large plates of Nephi (see D&C 10:38, including footnote 38a).

Rather than retranslating from the large plates of Nephi (part of the stack of plates Joseph had been given by Moroni on the Hill Cumorah), Joseph was instructed to use the small plates of Nephi, which were also in the stack in the gold plates, and to translate from them to cover the same period of time dealt with in the lost 116 pages. See D&C 10:39–41.

1 NEPHI 10

As Nephi now proceeds to engrave an account of his own life and ministry on the small plates, he will first summarize many things his father prophesied as context and background for his own writings.

This chapter is packed full of important prophesies (things that will take place in the future) and doctrines (facts about the gospel and the Father's plan of salvation for us). You will probably recognize many of them. Remember, Lehi lived about 600 years before Christ was born. His prophesies (predictions about the future) included the destruction of Jerusalem that will take place within a few years of their leaving Jerusalem and that many of the Jews will be taken away as captives to Babylon, an enemy nation about a thousand miles to the east. He will prophesy of the coming of Christ to live on earth (in about 600 years), about John the Baptist, and about the death and resurrection of Christ. He will prophesy about the scattering and gathering of Israel (the descendants of the twelve tribes of Israel—your patriarchal blessing will tell you your lineage, in other words, which of these tribes your blessings come through) and will compare Israel to an olive tree. About 600–592 BC.

1 AND **now I, Nephi, proceed to give an account** [*history*] upon these plates [*the small plates*] **of my proceedings** [*doings*], **and my reign** [*my time as ruler and leader over my people*] **and ministry**; wherefore, to proceed with mine account, **I must speak somewhat of the things of my father, and also of my brethren**.

2 For behold, it came to pass after **my father** had made an end of speaking the words of his dream [*the dream of the tree of life, etc., given in chapter 8*], and also of exhorting them to all diligence [*strongly counseling them to be faithful to God*], he **spake unto them concerning the Jews** [*the inhabitants of Jerusalem and the surrounding area*]—

3 That after **they should be destroyed**, even that great city Jerusalem, and **many be carried away captive into Babylon**, according to the own due time of the Lord [*when the Lord decided that the time was right*], **they should return again**, yea, even be brought back out of captivity; and after they should be brought back out of captivity they should **possess again the land of their inheritance** [*Jerusalem and the surrounding area*].

Watch for several different names for Christ in the next verses.

4 Yea, even six hundred years from the time that my father left Jerusalem, a prophet [*Jesus Christ*] would the Lord God raise up among the Jews—even a **Messiah** [*another name for Christ*], or, in other words, a **Savior of the world**.

5 And he also spake concerning the prophets, how great a number

[*how many of them*] had testified [*taught and borne testimony*] of these things, concerning this **Messiah**, of whom he had spoken, or this **Redeemer of the world**.

6 Wherefore, all mankind were in a lost and in a fallen state, and ever would be save they should rely on this **Redeemer** [*everyone would be lost and nobody would be saved unless they depended on Jesus and lived His gospel*].

7 And he [*Lehi, Nephi's father*] spake [*spoke*] also concerning a prophet [*John the Baptist*] who should come before the **Messiah**, to prepare the way of the Lord—

8 Yea, even he should go forth and cry [*speak loudly*] in the wilderness: Prepare ye the way of the Lord, and make his paths straight; for there standeth one [*Jesus*] among you whom ye know not; and he is mightier than I [*John the Baptist*], whose shoe's latchet I am not worthy to unloose [*I'm not even worthy to unstrap His sandals*]. And much spake my father concerning this thing.

9 And my father said he should [*would*] baptize in Bethabara, beyond Jordan [*a location on the east side of the Jordan River*]; and he also said he should baptize with water; even that he should baptize the **Messiah** with water.

Did you notice how Nephi, who is our teacher here, emphasized that John the Baptist would baptize with water, in other words, by immersion (putting the person being baptized clear under the water) like we do. This is important because some churches just sprinkle a little water on the person and call it baptism. Some churches don't even think water is needed for baptism because they think baptism is just symbolic.

10 And after he had baptized the **Messiah** with water, he should [*would*] behold and bear record [*bear testimony*] that he had baptized the **Lamb of God**, who should [*would*] take away the sins of the world.

11 And it came to pass after my father had spoken these words he spake unto my brethren concerning the gospel [*God's true teachings*] which should be preached among the Jews, and also concerning the dwindling of the Jews in unbelief [*about the fact that the Jews would gradually quit believing in God and would quit keeping God's commandments*]. And after they had slain [*killed*] the **Messiah**, who should [*would*] come, and after he had been slain he should rise from the dead [*be resurrected*], and should make himself manifest, by the Holy Ghost, unto the Gentiles [*people who are not Jews*].

Next, Nephi teaches us about the scattering of Israel, in other words, the scattering of the descendants of the children of Israel throughout the world and the future gathering of Israel. Our prophets today are constantly reminding us that we live in the time when Israel is being gathered again. We are much involved in it. It is a sign that the Second Coming of Christ is getting quite close.

12 Yea, even **my father spake**
much **concerning the Gentiles,**
and also concerning the house
of Israel [*God's covenant people, Jacob's*
descendants, the descendants of the twelve
tribes of Israel], that they should be
compared like unto an olive-
tree, whose **branches** should be
broken off and should be **scat-**
tered upon all the face of the
earth.

13 Wherefore, he said it must
needs be [*it is necessary*] that **we**
should be led with one accord
into the land of promise [*America*],
unto the **fulfilling** of [*in order to ful-*
fill] **the word of the Lord, that we**
should be scattered upon all the
face of the earth.

14 And **after the house of Israel**
[*the twelve tribes of Israel*] **should be**
scattered they should be gath-
ered together again; or, in fine
[*in summary*], **after the Gentiles**
had received the fulness of the
Gospel [*after the Restoration of the true*
gospel through the Prophet Joseph Smith],
the natural branches of the olive-
tree, or **the remnants** [*the remain-*
ing members] **of the house of Israel,**
should be grafted in [*joined in*], or
come to the knowledge of the
true Messiah, their Lord and
their Redeemer.

15 And **after this manner of lan-**
guage did my father prophesy
and speak unto my brethren, and
also many more things which I
do not write in this book [*the small*
plates]; for I have written as many
of them as were expedient for me
[*as I considered necessary*] in mine other
book [*the large plates*].

16 And all these things, of which
I have spoken, were done as my
father dwelt in a tent, in the valley
of Lemuel.

Next, Nephi will tell us that after hearing Lehi tell about his vision of the tree of life and all the details that went along with it, he, Nephi, had a strong desire to see, hear, and know the same things himself, by the power of the Holy Ghost. Among other things, he will teach us how to we can have the help of the Holy Ghost ourselves.

17 And it came to pass **after I,**
Nephi, having **heard all the**
words of my father, concern-
ing the things which he saw in a

vision, and also the things which he spake by the power of the Holy Ghost, which power he received by faith on the Son of God—and the Son of God was the Messiah who should come—**I, Nephi, was desirous also that I might see, and hear, and know of these things**, by the power of the **Holy Ghost**, which **is the gift of God unto all those who diligently seek him** [*work hard to*], as well in times of old [*in Old Testament times*] as in the time that he should manifest himself unto the children of men [*as well as during Christ's mission here on earth*].

18 For **he is the same yesterday, to-day, and forever** [*the plan of salvation and the requirements for exaltation have always been the same and always will be*]; and **the way is prepared** for all men from the foundation of the world [*everyone can make it back to God*], **if it so be that they repent and come unto him**.

19 For **he that diligently seeketh shall find**; and the mysteries of God [*the basic teachings of the gospel*] shall be unfolded [*revealed*] unto them, by the power of the Holy Ghost, as well in these times as in times of old [*the same today as in olden times*], and as well in times of old as in times to come [*the future*]; wherefore [*so, as you can see*], **the course of the Lord is one eternal round** [*the requirements for returning back home to God are always the same*].

Next, Nephi gives us a quick lesson about accountability and Judgment Day.

20 Therefore **remember**, O man, **for all thy doings** [*for everything you do*] **thou shalt be brought into judgment**.

21 Wherefore, **if ye have sought to do wickedly** in the days of your probation [*during your mortal life*], **then ye are found unclean before** the judgment-seat of **God**; and **no unclean thing can dwell** [*live*] **with God**; wherefore, ye must be cast off forever [*you will not be able to return to heaven*].

22 And the Holy Ghost giveth authority that I should speak these things, and deny them not.

1 NEPHI 11

In chapter 10, verse 17, Nephi told us that he desired to "see, and hear, and know" the things which his father saw in his vision of the tree of life, recorded in 1 Nephi, chapter 8. His desire will now be granted by the Lord. 1 Nephi, chapters 11 through 14 will tell us what he saw. He will give us many details and additional explanations about what his father saw.

Nephi gives us three keys to receiving revelation in verse 1. About 600–592 BC.

1 FOR it came to pass after I had **desired** to know the things that my father had seen, and **believing** that the Lord was able to make them known unto me, as I sat **pondering** in mine heart **I was caught away in the Spirit of the Lord**, yea, into an exceedingly high mountain, which I never had before seen, and upon which I never had before set my foot.

As pointed out with **bold**, you saw the three keys to receiving revelation Nephi mentioned: (1) desiring to know, (2) believing, and (3) pondering, in other words, making quiet time to give the Holy Ghost a chance to put revelation and inspiration into your mind.

Many of us who desire revelation and help from the Lord do pretty well at doing the first two things Nephi mentioned. But when it comes to "pondering," it seems that we don't do well at taking the time or making the time to do so. In our fast-paced lives, many of us are out of the habit of providing peaceful, non-pressured time for the Holy Ghost to get a word in edgewise into our minds. Thus, we miss out on much personal inspiration which we would otherwise receive.

Also, did you notice the phrase "exceedingly high mountain" in verse one? This is symbolic, among other things, of perspective, in other words, seeing how things fit in with other things. It is symbolic of seeing things as God sees them. If we are willing, the Lord gives us, through His Spirit, what we can call "high mountain experiences." During such times, the Lord takes our minds up "high," where we can see things from a much broader perspective.

For example, if you just go to church because it is a commandment, you probably don't get all the blessings and benefits from it. But, if you take time to ponder, in other words, think about it during some quiet time, the Holy Ghost can take your mind up much higher where you can look down, so to speak, and see other aspects of your life and see how church attendance strengthens you against temptations from the devil when you are with friends, at school, at work, watching TV, on dates, approached by drug dealers, and a whole bunch of other possible situations in your life. Such a "high mountain" experience could help you pay much better attention to the talks in sacrament meeting and to the discussions in your classes because you now see the great benefit to you in attending church.

As we continue reading, Nephi will experience revelation and perspectives while he is on this "exceedingly high mountain" that will prepare and qualify him to be a tremendous prophet and leader of his people.

It is interesting to see how "interactive" this vision is for Nephi. An active conversation with questions and answers takes place between him and the "Spirit" as we will see, starting in verse 2, next.

2 And the Spirit said unto me: Behold, **what desirest thou** [*what do you want*]?

3 And I said: **I desire to behold** [*see*] **the things which my father saw**.

4 And the Spirit said unto me: **Believest thou** [*do you believe*] that thy father saw the tree of which he hath spoken?

5 And I said: **Yea** [*yes*], thou knowest that I believe all the words of my father.

6 And when I had spoken these words, the Spirit cried [*spoke*] with a loud voice, saying: Hosanna to the Lord [*praise the Lord*], the most high God; for he is God over all the earth, yea, even above all. And blessed art thou, Nephi, **because thou believest in the Son of the most high God** [*Jesus Christ*]; wherefore [*so*], **thou shalt behold** [*you will see*] the things which thou hast desired.

Next, the Spirit prepares Nephi by telling him what he will see first in the vision—namely, the tree of life and the Savior coming down from heaven.

7 And behold this thing shall be given unto thee for a sign, that **after thou hast beheld the tree** [*after you have seen the tree of life*] which bore the fruit which thy father tasted, **thou shalt also behold** [*see*] **a man descending** [*coming down*] **out of heaven**, and him shall ye witness [*you will see Him*]; and after ye have witnessed him ye shall bear record [*bear testimony, stand as a witness*] that **it is the Son of God** [*Jesus*].

Nephi will now see the things that the Spirit told him he would see, in verse 7, above.

8 And it came to pass that **the Spirit said** unto me: **Look!** And **I looked and beheld** [*saw*] **a tree**; and it was **like unto the tree which my father had seen**; and the beauty thereof [*of the tree*] was far beyond, yea, exceeding of [*much more than*] all beauty; and the whiteness thereof did exceed the whiteness of the driven snow.

9 And it came to pass after I had seen the tree, **I said unto the Spirit**: I behold **thou hast** [*I see that you have*] **shown unto me the tree which is precious above all**.

In verse 22, we are told that the tree represents "the love of God." No wonder Nephi said it is the most "precious" thing of all, in other words, the most valuable thing of all, in verse 9, above.

Once again, the Spirit asks Nephi a question (as mentioned previously, this vision is very "interactive," in other words, Nephi and the Spirit of the Lord are talking back and forth with each other as Nephi is shown many things in vision.)

10 And he said unto me: **What desirest thou?**

11 And I said unto him: **To know the interpretation thereof** [*to know what it means*]—for **I spake unto him as a man speaketh; for I beheld that he was in the form of a man**; yet nevertheless, I knew that it was the Spirit of the Lord; and he spake unto me as a man speaketh with another.

Over the years, many members of the Church have asked who the "Spirit of the Lord" is in verse 11, above. Some say that it is the premortal Christ, while others believe him to be the Holy Ghost. We don't know for sure, but we do find out from this verse that spirits have bodies that basically look like we do.

Throughout the rest of this chapter, Nephi is basically shown many things in the future. He is shown what is recorded in the first four books of the New Testament—namely, Matthew, Mark, Luke, and John—starting with the Virgin Mary and the birth of Christ and ending with the Crucifixion of the Savior and persecution of the Apostles.

12 And it came to pass that he said unto me: **Look!** And I looked as if to look upon him, and I saw him not; for he had gone from before my presence [*He had disappeared*].

13 And it came to pass that I looked and beheld the great city of **Jerusalem**, and also other cities. And I beheld the city of Nazareth; and in the city of **Nazareth** I beheld **a virgin** [*Mary, the mother of Jesus*], and she was exceedingly fair [*very beautiful*] and white.

As you will see, another guide now comes and takes over in showing the vision to Nephi.

14 And it came to pass that I saw the heavens open; and **an angel came down** and stood before me; and he said unto me: Nephi, **what beholdest thou** [*what do you see*]?

15 And I said unto him: **A virgin** [*Mary*], **most beautiful and fair above all other virgins**.

Next, the angel asks Nephi yet another question.

16 And he said unto me: **Knowest thou the condescension of God?** [*Meaning God, the Father.*]

Nephi doesn't know the answer, and says so.

17 And I said unto him: I know that he loveth his children; nevertheless, **I do not know the meaning of all things**.

The phrase "condescension of God" will be used twice in this chapter, once in verse 16, referring to Heavenly Father, and again in verse 26, referring to Jesus. The word "condescend," here in the Book of Mormon, means to come down to our level and help and bless us, even though they are both so much more intelligent and powerful than we are. In verse 16, above, it refers to Heavenly Father and means, among other things, that He was willing to be the father of Jesus who was born to Mary. In verse 26, it will refer to Jesus, the Son of God, and it will mean that even though He was already a God, He was willing to come to earth and go through the trials of mortal life, the Crucifixion, and the Atonement in order to provide salvation for us.

18 And he said unto me: Behold [*look*], **the virgin whom thou seest is the mother of the Son of God**, after the manner of the flesh [*in mortality*]. [*The angel is explaining the vision and here tells Nephi that he is seeing Mary, the mortal mother of Christ.*]

19 And it came to pass that I beheld [*I saw*] that **she was carried away in the Spirit**; and after she had been carried away in the Spirit for the space of a time [*for some time*] the angel spake unto me, saying: Look!

20 And **I looked and beheld** [*saw*] **the virgin** [*Mary*] **again, bearing a child** [*carrying baby Jesus*] **in her arms.**

In verse 21, next, you will see two of the many names the scriptures (the Bible, Book of Mormon, Doctrine and Covenants, and Pearl of Great Price) use for Jesus Christ. Then, the angel asks Nephi another question.

21 And the angel said unto me: Behold the **Lamb of God**, yea, even **the Son of the Eternal Father**! **Knowest thou the meaning of the tree which thy father saw?**

22 And I answered him, saying: Yea (yes), **it is the love of God**, which sheddeth itself abroad in the hearts of the children of men [*people*]; wherefore [*and so*], it is the most desirable above all things.

23 And he [*the angel who is Nephi's guide for this part of the vision*] spake unto

me, saying: **Yea, and the most joyous to the soul.**

Next, Nephi will be shown the Savior's mortal ministry, plus, he will be shown the interpretation of many things which his father, Lehi, saw when he was shown this vision in 1 Nephi, chapter 8.

24 And after he had said these words, he said unto me: Look! And I looked, and **I beheld the Son of God going forth among the children of men** [*I saw Jesus among the people while He was on earth*]; and I saw many fall down [*bow down*] at his feet and worship him.

25 And it came to pass that I beheld that **the rod of iron**, which my father had seen, **was the word of God**, which **led to the fountain of living waters**, **or** to **the tree of life**; which **waters are a representation of** [*symbolic of*] **the love of God**; and I also beheld that [*I also saw that*] **the tree of life was a representation of the love of God**.

26 And the angel said unto me again: **Look** and behold **the condescension of God**! [*Look and see the willingness of God the Son, in other words, Christ, to become mortal and redeem us; see note after verse 17, above.*]

Next, Nephi is shown the Savior and John the Baptist.

27 And I looked and beheld [*saw*] **the Redeemer of the world** [*Christ*], of whom my father had spoken; and I also beheld **the prophet** [*John the Baptist*] who should [*who would*] prepare the way before him [*Jesus*]. And the **Lamb of God** [*Jesus*] went forth [*went out*] and **was baptized** of [*by*] him [*John the Baptist*]; and after he was baptized, **I beheld** the heavens open, and **the Holy Ghost come down** out of heaven and abide [*rest*] upon him [*Jesus*] in the form of a dove.

The "form of a dove" here is symbolism. The Prophet Joseph Smith explained that the Holy Ghost does not turn Himself into a dove. Rather, the sign of the dove indicated that the Holy Ghost was present. (You can read more about this in *Teachings of the Prophet Joseph Smith*, by Joseph Fielding Smith, Salt Lake City, Deseret Book Co., 1977], 275–6.)

28 And I beheld that he [*the Savior*] went forth ministering unto the people, in power and great glory; and the multitudes [*crowds*] were gathered together to hear him; and **I beheld that they cast him out from among them** [*Nephi saw that the people rejected Christ*].

29 And I also beheld **twelve others** [*the Savior's Twelve Apostles*] following him. And it came to pass that they were carried away in the

Spirit from before my face, and I saw them not.

30 And it came to pass that the angel spake unto me again, saying: **Look!** And I looked, and I beheld the heavens open again, and I saw **angels descending** [*coming down*] upon the children of men [*the people*]; and they did minister unto them.

From verse 30, above, we learn that angels are very much involved in what goes on here on earth.

Next, in verse 31, Nephi is shown the healing of the sick that the Savior would do about 600 years in the future during His mission on earth, as recorded in the New Testament.

31 And he spake unto me again, saying: **Look!** And I looked, and I beheld **the Lamb of God** [*Jesus*] **going forth among the children of men**. And I beheld multitudes [*large numbers*] of people who were sick, and who were afflicted [*troubled*] with all manner of [*all kinds of*] diseases, and with devils and unclean spirits [*evil spirits*]; and the angel spake and showed all these things unto me. And **they were healed by the power of the Lamb of God**; and the **devils and the unclean spirits were cast out**.

The physical healings shown to Nephi in verse 31, above, are also symbolic of the power of the Savior to heal our spiritual wounds and sicknesses. He can heal "all manner of [spiritual] diseases," including the results of our sins and foolishness. Every time we read of the physical healings performed by the Savior, we would do well to remember that the most important healing of all is the healing of the person who is weighed down by the results of sin, or who feels inadequate in a church calling, or who mourns, etc.

Next, Nephi will see the Crucifixion of the Savior in the vision.

32 And it came to pass that the angel spake unto me again, saying: **Look!** And I looked and beheld **the Lamb of God**, that he was taken by the people; yea, **the Son of the everlasting God** was judged of [*by*] the world [*wicked people*]; and I saw and bear record.

33 And **I, Nephi, saw that he was lifted up upon the cross** [*crucified*] **and slain** [*killed*] **for the sins of the world**.

Next, Nephi will be shown what we know as the rest of the New Testament, beginning with Acts.

34 And after he was slain **I saw the multitudes of the earth**, that they were **gathered together**

to fight against the apostles of the Lamb [*Christ's Apostles, who led the Church after He went to heaven*]; for thus were the twelve called by the angel of the Lord.

Next, Nephi sees that the wicked people who fought against the Savior's Apostles after His Crucifixion and Resurrection were the type of people who were in the large and spacious building Lehi saw in 1 Nephi 8:26.

35 And **the multitude of the earth was gathered together**; and I beheld that **they were in a large and spacious building**, like unto the building which my father saw. And the angel of the Lord spake unto me again, saying: Behold **the world and the wisdom thereof**; yea, behold **the house of Israel hath gathered together to fight against the twelve apostles of the Lamb**.

Remember that one of the things Nephi wanted was to know the interpretation, or what things meant, in Lehi's vision (see 1 Nephi 11:11). In verse 35, above, and verse 36, next, his request was granted as the angel explained that the large and spacious building symbolized the wicked people of the world and their false wisdom or wicked ways of thinking along with their pride.

36 And it came to pass that I saw and bear record, that **the great and spacious building was the pride of the world**; and it fell, and the fall thereof was exceedingly [*very*] great. And the angel of the Lord spake unto me again, saying: **Thus shall be the destruction of all nations, kindreds, tongues, and people** [*in other words, everybody*], **that shall fight against the twelve apostles of the Lamb** [*Christ*].

1 NEPHI 12

Nephi's vision of what his father saw continues in this chapter and will continue to the end of chapter 14. In this chapter he will basically see the whole Book of Mormon.

1 AND it came to pass that the angel said unto me: **Look**, and **behold thy seed**, and **also the seed of thy brethren** [*look at your descendants as well as the descendants of the others in Lehi's group*]. And **I looked and beheld the land of promise** [*America*]; and I beheld **multitudes of people**, yea, even as it were in number as many as the sand of the sea. [*The Nephites and Lamanites multiplied and became very large numbers of people in the Americas.*]

Verse 2, next, would especially represent the books of Alma and Helaman in the Book of Mormon, where we read accounts of many wars and terrible slaughter and destruction.

2 And it came to pass that I beheld multitudes gathered together to battle, one against the other; and **I beheld wars, and rumors of wars, and great slaughters with the sword among my people**.

3 And it came to pass that **I beheld many generations** [*many people and their children, grandchildren, great grandchildren, etc.*] **pass away**, after the manner of wars and contentions in the land; and I beheld many cities, yea, even that I did not number [*count*] them.

Just a quick comment here. Occasionally, you may run into theories that the Book of Mormon peoples represent relatively small numbers of people in scattered villages and small cities. Verses 1–3, above, do not appear to support such theories.

Next, in verses 4–10, Nephi will be shown the events of Third Nephi. In verse 4, he is shown the destruction which took place among the Book of Mormon people at the time of the Savior's Crucifixion. In verse 4, he is especially seeing 3 Nephi, chapter 8, in vision.

4 And it came to pass that **I saw a mist of darkness** [*it was completely dark in America for three days after Christ was crucified; see 3 Nephi 8:19–23*] on the face of the land of promise; and I saw **lightnings, and I heard thunderings, and earthquakes, and all manner of tumultuous** [*all kinds of loud*] **noises; and I saw the earth and the rocks, that they rent** [*were torn apart*]; and I saw mountains tumbling into pieces; and I saw the plains [*flat parts*] of the earth, that they were broken up; and I saw many cities that they were sunk; and I saw many that they were burned with fire; and I saw many that did tumble to the earth, because of the quaking thereof [*of the earth*].

5 And it came to pass after I saw these things, **I saw the vapor of darkness, that it passed from off the face of the earth** [*after three days of total darkness it got light again*]; and behold, **I saw multitudes** [*who were not wicked enough to be destroyed*] **who had not fallen** [*died*] because of the great and terrible judgments [*punishments*] of the Lord.

Next in the vision, Nephi sees the Savior's appearance to the people in Third Nephi. Imagine how everything that he is seeing in this marvelous vision prepares and qualifies him for the responsibilities he will yet have in the future as a prophet.

6 And **I saw the heavens open, and the Lamb of God** [*Jesus*]

descending [*coming down*] **out of heaven; and he came down and showed himself unto them.**

7 **And I also saw and bear record** [*give you my testimony that I know it is true*] that **the Holy Ghost fell upon** [*came upon*] **twelve others** [*the Nephite Twelve Apostles*]; and they were ordained of God, and chosen.

Some members wonder whether or not to refer to the Nephite Twelve as "Apostles." We usually refer to them as the "Twelve Nephite Disciples" as in verse 8, below. But it is also proper to refer to them as "Apostles," since the Prophet Joseph Smith did, as recorded in *History of the Church,* 4:538.

8 And the angel spake unto me, saying: Behold [*see*] **the Twelve Disciples of the Lamb**, who are chosen to minister unto thy seed [*to lead and serve your descendants*].

Next, we are taught some things about the Final Judgment. We discover from what Nephi was shown here that the Twelve Apostles organized by Jesus during His earthly ministry will judge the twelve tribes of Israel. They will also judge the Twelve Nephite Disciples, who, in turn, will judge Nephi's descendants. This is rather interesting, because it seems to tell us that our judgment will involve those who have been our leaders, such as bishops, stake presidents, Apostles, and prophets, throughout our lives. While we do not have much detail as to how this all works out, we do know that Jesus will be our final judge, and that He will have the final say as to our eternal placement in the three degrees of glory after the Judgment Day; see John 5:22.

Next, the angel asks Nephi another question.

9 And he said unto me: Thou rememberest **the Twelve Apostles of the Lamb?** [*In Jerusalem.*] Behold they are they who **shall judge the twelve tribes of Israel;** wherefore [*therefore*], **the twelve ministers of thy seed** [*the Twelve Nephite Disciples; see 3 Nephi 12:1, 19:4*] **shall be judged of** [*by*] **them**; for ye are of the house of Israel.

10 **And these twelve ministers** [*the Nephite Twelve*] whom thou beholdest **shall judge thy seed** [*your descendants*]. And, behold, they [*the Nephite Twelve Apostles*] are righteous forever; for because of their faith in the Lamb of God [*because they have faith in Christ and so they live the gospel*] **their garments** [*symbolic of their lives*] **are made white in his blood** [*they will be forgiven of their sins because of Christ's Atonement, so they will receive exaltation in the highest degree of glory in the celestial kingdom*].

Next, in verses 11–12, Nephi is shown what we read about in Fourth Nephi, where there will be about two hundred years of peace after the Savior departs, then the people will fall away from the Church; in other words, they will go into what we call "apostasy."

11 And the angel said unto me: **Look!** And I looked, and beheld **three generations** [*about three hundred years*] pass away in righteousness; and their garments were white even like unto the Lamb of God. [*In other words, they were worthy of exaltation with Christ.*] And the angel said unto me: **These are made white in the blood of the Lamb, because of their faith in him.**

The symbolism in the phrase "made white in the blood of the Lamb" (verse 11, above) is beautiful and very significant. There is much of color symbolism in the scriptures. The color white symbolizes or means purity, cleansed from sin, worthiness to live in the presence of God forever, and usually means exaltation. Thus, being made white "in the blood of the Lamb" means to have been cleansed and redeemed from sin through the Atonement of Christ and made clean and worthy to live with God forever.

Just one more little bit about the color white. Once you understand what this color symbolizes in the scriptures, it becomes a way of saying things with fewer words. For example, in place of a longer explanation that certain people have attained celestial glory, which is the highest of the three degrees of glory we could be given on Judgment Day, the scriptures could simply say, "They are dressed in white." An example of this is found in the Bible in Revelation 7:9. The people dressed in white robes here have made it to the celestial kingdom or heaven.

A brief list of some colors and associated symbolism often used in scripture follows:

Color Symbolism Often Used in the Scriptures

white: purity; righteousness; exaltation (Example: 1 Ne. 12:10; Rev. 3:4–5)

black: evil; famine; darkness (Example: Rev. 6:5–6)

red: sins; bloodshed (Example: Rev. 6:4; D&C 133:51)

blue: heaven; godliness; remembering and keeping God's commandments (Example: Num. 15:37–40)

green: life; nature (Example: Rev. 8:7)

amber: sun; light; divine glory (Example: D&C 110:2, Rev. 1:15, Ezek. 1:4, 27; 8:2)

scarlet: royalty (Example: Dan. 5:29; Matt. 27:28–29)

silver: worth, but less than gold (Example: Ridges, *Isaiah Made Easier,* Isa. 48:10 notes)

gold: the best; exaltation (Example: Rev. 4:4)

12 And **I, Nephi, also saw many of the fourth generation** who passed away in righteousness [*who lived righteous lives*].

Next, Nephi will see the terrible destruction of his descendants and the descendants of his brothers as described in Mormon in the Book of Mormon. He will also be given more interpretations of what his father saw.

13 And it came to pass that I saw the multitudes of the earth gathered together.

14 And the angel said unto me: **Behold thy seed,** and **also the seed of thy brethren.** [*In other words, the Nephites and the Lamanites as they gather for the final great battles described in Mormon.*]

15 And it came to pass that I looked and beheld **the people of my seed** [*the Nephites*] **gathered together in multitudes against the seed of my brethren** [*the Lamanites*]; and they were gathered together **to battle.**

16 And the angel spake unto me, saying: Behold **the fountain of filthy water** which thy father saw; yea, even **the river of which he spake**; and **the depths thereof are the depths of hell.**

17 And **the mists of darkness are the temptations of the devil**, which blindeth the eyes, and hardeneth the hearts of the children of men [*make people not want to be righteous*], and leadeth them away into broad roads, that they perish and are lost.

Nephi, no doubt, wants us to learn many lessons from what he wrote for us in verse 17, above. Among these things would be that Satan attempts to "blind our eyes" so that we can't see danger, or so that we can't see nor understand spiritual truths and how they can fit into our lives. He takes away wisdom and respect for those who have true wisdom. His success in such "blinding" is very evident in much of what you see around you in your every day life.

Another warning for us from Nephi, in verse 17, is that the devil works and trys to harden our hearts. One definition of "hardened hearts" is lack of feeling, lack of concern about sin, lack of concern for the rights and needs of others.

Yet another warning in this verse is that Satan attempts to lead people into "broad roads." This is an interesting term. When we are on the "strait and narrow path" (1 Nephi 8:20), we have many commandments and we like them. We are blessed "with commandments not a few" (D&C 59:4), and with rules and guidelines from the Lord through the prophets. The cry of the wicked and the quest of the foolish is to do away with restrictions and rules. Thus, they plunge rapidly or wobble slowly down the "broad roads" which finally lead to captivity, remorse, and loss of freedom. On the other hand, those who voluntarily and diligently travel up the "strait and narrow" path gain more and more freedom until they are among the freest people in the universe—namely, the gods—after they have received exaltation.

18 And **the large and spacious building,** which thy father saw, **is vain imaginations and** the **pride** of the children of men [*of people*]. And a **great and a terrible gulf** divideth them; yea, even the word of the **justice** of the Eternal God, and the Messiah who is the Lamb of God, of whom the Holy Ghost beareth record, from the beginning of the world until this time, and from this time henceforth and forever.

The "great and terrible gulf" in verse 18, above, is a reminder that mercy cannot rob justice (see Alma 42:25). Those who do not take advantage of opportunities to repent when mercy could have been extended to them, and thus arrive at the final judgment bar of God "filthy still" (2 Nephi 9:16), will be subject to the law of justice. They will not be worthy to live in the presence of God, and will thus be out of His presence forever (see D&C 29:29, D&C 76:112).

19 And while the angel spake these words, I beheld and saw that the seed [*descendants*] of my brethren did contend [*fight*] against my seed, according to the word of the angel; and because of the **pride** of my seed, and the **temptations of the devil**, I beheld that the seed of my brethren did overpower the people of my seed [*the Lamanites destroyed the Nephite civilization; see Mormon, chapters 6 and 8*].

20 And it came to pass that **I** beheld, and **saw the people of the seed of my brethren** [*the descendants of Laman and Lemuel*] that **they had overcome my seed**; and they went forth in multitudes upon the face of the land.

21 And I saw them gathered together in multitudes; and I saw wars and rumors of wars among them; and in wars and rumors of wars I saw many generations [*hundreds of years*] pass away.

Nephi has now seen the end of the Book of Mormon and beyond in this portion of his vision.

22 And the angel said unto me: Behold these shall dwindle [*gradually fall away from the gospel*] in unbelief.

23 And it came to pass that I beheld, **after they had dwindled in unbelief they became** a **dark,** and **loathsome** [*disgusting*], and a **filthy** people, **full of idleness** [*laziness*] **and all manner of abominations** [*wickedness*].

The final result of pride and intentional wickedness, described in verse 23, above, applies to any people, at any time, anywhere, regardless of race, gender, privilege, or position in life.

1 NEPHI 13

As Nephi's vision continues, he will be shown the formation of a "great and abominable church" and what we usually refer to as the Dark Ages along with some incredible details concerning Christopher Columbus, the pilgrims, the destructions among the Lamanites in the Americas, the thirteen American colonies, the Revolutionary War, and God's help for the new colonies as they fought for independence against Great Britain. In addition, he will be shown that the Bible would be brought by them and that many "plain and precious things" had been taken out of it. He will also be shown the establishment of the United States, the coming forth of the Book of Mormon, the joining together of the Bible and the Book of Mormon, and then a very brief view of the last days.

1 AND it came to pass that the angel spake unto me, saying: **Look!** And I looked and beheld [*saw*] **many nations and kingdoms** [*the nations of Europe*].

2 And **the angel said** unto me: **What beholdest thou** [*what do you see*]? And **I said**: I behold many nations and kingdoms.

3 And **he said** unto me: **These are the nations and kingdoms of the Gentiles** [*people who do not come from the Jerusalem area, meaning mainly people who are not Jews*].

4 And it came to pass that **I saw** among the nations of the Gentiles **the formation of a great church**.

Here, we will be taught about the "great and abominable church." It is Satan's "church" or what we often call "the church of the devil." It includes all of the devil's efforts to teach or promote falsehood or evil, including gangs, lying, stealing, nations or groups or individuals who seek the downfall of democracy, Christianity, or anything that is good and honorable.

5 And **the angel said** unto me: **Behold** [*look and see*] **the formation of a church which is most abominable above all other churches**, which slayeth [*kills*] the saints of

God [*righteous people who are trying to live the gospel and keep God's commandments*], yea, and tortureth them and bindeth them down, and yoketh them with a yoke of iron [*tries to make life miserable for them*], and bringeth them down into captivity.

6 And it came to pass that I beheld this great and abominable church; and **I saw the devil that he was the founder of it** [*he created it*].

We discover in verses 5 and 6, above, that the devil is the "founder" of the "great and abominable church." This teaches us that the great and abominable church is the kingdom of the devil, no matter which organization he may be hiding behind. We are taught this in 1 Nephi 14:10, where we are told that there are basically just two churches, one is the "church of the Lamb" and the other is the "church of the devil."

The word "church" in the phrase "church of the devil" can confuse people a bit. It sometimes makes them think it is referring to a religious organization only. It can be helpful to substitute the word "kingdom" for "church" and thus have the phrase "kingdom of the devil" meaning any groups, individuals, or organizations which fight against that which is right. The phrase "kingdom of the devil" is used in 1 Nephi 22:22.

Next, in verses 7 through 9, we run into what could be termed "Satan's big three tools" for taking people away from God. They are materialism (focusing your life on money and stuff), sexual immorality (sexual sins), and pride. These three major categories of temptation and sin seem to have been terribly effective in leading people astray throughout history, and are still being used effectively by the devil today.

Materialism and Sexual Immorality

7 And I also saw **gold**, and **silver**, and **silks**, and **scarlets**, and **fine-twined linen**, and **all manner of** [*all kinds of*] **precious** [*expensive*] **clothing**; and I saw **many harlots** [*people who get others involved in sexual sin*].

8 And the angel spake unto me, saying: Behold [*look at*] the **gold**, and the **silver**, and the **silks**, and the **scarlets**, and the **fine-twined linen**, and the **precious clothing**, and the **harlots**, are the desires of this great and abominable church.

Pride

9 And also **for the praise of the world** [*to become popular among the wicked*] do they destroy the saints of God, and bring them down into captivity.

10 And it came to pass that **I looked and beheld many waters** [*oceans*]; and they divided the Gentiles [*especially those in Britain and Europe*] from the seed of my brethren [*from the Lamanites in the Americas*].

11 And it came to pass that **the angel said** unto me: Behold **the wrath of God is upon the seed of thy brethren** [*the anger and punishment from the Lord is upon the Lamanites*].

> Next, Nephi will be shown Christopher Columbus in this vision.

12 And **I looked and beheld a man** [*Christopher Columbus*] **among the Gentiles** [*in Europe*], who was separated from the seed of my brethren [*the Lamanites in America*] by the many waters [*oceans*]; and I beheld **the Spirit of God**, that it came down and **wrought upon** [*inspired and worked upon*] **the man**; and he went forth upon the many waters, even unto the seed of my brethren, who were in the promised land [*Columbus sailed across the ocean to America*].

> Next, Nephi sees the pilgrims fleeing oppression in Europe and coming to America.

13 And it came to pass that **I beheld the Spirit of God,** that it **wrought upon other Gentiles** [*the Spirit of the Lord inspired the pilgrims*]; and they went forth out of captivity [*from oppression in Europe*], upon the many waters.

14 And it came to pass that **I beheld many multitudes** [*large numbers*] **of the Gentiles upon the land of promise** [*early colonists, settlers in America*]; and **I beheld the wrath** [*anger*] **of God, that it was upon the seed of my brethren** [*the Lamanites in the Americas*]; and they were scattered before the Gentiles and were smitten [*suffered a lot*].

> In verse 14, above, Nephi sees destruction and death among the Lamanites in America as foreign explorers and colonists come to the Americas and begin to spread out among the Indians.

15 And **I beheld the Spirit of the Lord, that it was upon the Gentiles** [*the colonists in America*], and they did prosper and obtain the land for their inheritance [*they did well and settled in permanently*]; and **I beheld that they were white, and exceedingly fair and beautiful**, like unto my people [*the Nephites*] before they were slain.

16 And it came to pass that I, Nephi, beheld that **the Gentiles** [*who became the thirteen colonies and eventually became the United States*] who had gone forth out of captivity **did humble themselves before the**

Lord; and the power of the Lord was with them.

Next, the prophet Nephi sees the Revolutionary War in his vision. He sees the hand of God helping the small, poorly equipped and undertrained army of the colonists under the leadership of George Washington. He is shown their triumph over vastly better trained and equipped armies of the British.

17 And I beheld that **their mother Gentiles** [*Great Britain, England*] **were gathered** together upon the waters, and upon the land also [*Great Britain sent navies and armies*], **to battle against them** [*the colonists in North America*].

18 And I beheld that **the power of God was with them**, and also that the wrath of God was upon all those that were gathered together against them to battle.

There are many accounts of the power of God exercised in behalf of George Washington and his soldiers. Time and time again, his ragged and struggling fighters were saved against all odds. In a fascinating article in the October 1987 *Ensign* entitled "Delivered by the Power of God," Jonathan A. Dibble gives examples of this power. One excerpt from this article follows:

"The British soon withdrew from Boston and sailed toward New York. Washington, anticipating this move, marched on New York. There, several events led to another miraculous rescue of the American soldiers. Washington split his command and landed most of his troops on Long Island's Brooklyn Heights. He had only ten thousand troops to guard a fifteen-mile front, while General Howe embarked approximately fifteen thousand British and Hessian soldiers at Gravesend Bay, Long Island. He left four thousand soldiers behind on Staten Island as reinforcements. . . . The British, by sailing up the East River, could land troops behind Washington and surround his army. The prospect for the Americans was serious. If Washington were to lose ten thousand men at the outset of the war, the Declaration of Independence would most likely not gain the public support to fuel the fires of freedom.

"However, once again the elements intervened. On 26 August 1776, Howe's reinforcements (the British) were delayed by a strong northeast wind and an ebbing tide that 'compelled the fleet to drop down the bay and come to anchor.' At nine o'clock the next morning, the Americans could hear the British cannons in the American rear. In a brilliant night march, the British General Henry Clinton had slipped by the east side of the Americans and had captured eight hundred prisoners, including Generals John Sullivan and William Stirling.

"At this point, Washington, instead of retreating across the East River, reinforced the American positions on Brooklyn Heights and waited for Howe's assault. Seeing the entrenched American troops, British General Howe decided to delay his attack until the fleet had entered the East River. But the British ships were held back again by another strong northeast wind. Then torrents of rain fell, further hindering the fleet in the East River and subduing the efforts of the British troops on land. Howe began to raise siege works along Washington's lines when, according to historian Henry B. Carrington, 'The rain (became) so incessant, and accompanied by a wind so violent, that the British troops kept within their tents, and their works made slow progress.'

"Finally, on the night of 29 August 1776, Washington, recognizing the opportunity to make a tactical retreat, ordered his troops across the East River. The first unit embarked at ten o'clock. But at midnight, the wind changed. Just as the British advance had earlier been halted by the elements, this time the Americans' retreat was threatened with disaster. Sloops and other sailing craft could not sail, and there were too few rowboats to complete the evacuation in one night. According to Carrington, 'the wind and tide were so violent that even the seamen soldiers of Massachusetts could not spread a close reefed sail upon a single vessel; and the larger vessels, upon which so much depended, would have been swept to the ocean if once entrusted to the current.' "Washington was urged to abandon the evacuation; but then, miraculously, the wind abruptly shifted, allowing the Americans to cross the river in the predawn hours. Nine thousand men were moved in that retreat, and historian Bart McDowell records that after dawn, as the last of the army sailed away, one young captain noted that the boats moved under 'the friendly cover of a thick fog,' which 'increased the danger of panic, but also prevented discovery.' Historian Christopher Ward points out that 'freakish Nature (had) again favored the Americans.' Washington 'had snatched a beaten army from the very jaws of a victorious force, and practically under the nose of the greatest armada ever seen in American waters'" (Dibble, "'Delivered by the Power of God': The American Revolution and Nephi's Prophecy," pp. 45–52).

19 And I, Nephi, beheld that **the Gentiles** that had gone out of captivity [*the American colonists*] **were delivered by the power of God out of the hands of all other nations.**

20 And it came to pass that I, Nephi, beheld that **they did prosper in the land**; and I beheld **a book** [*the Bible*], and it **was carried forth among them**. [*The Christian immigrants brought the Bible with them from their home countries.*]

The angel asks Nephi yet another question.

21 And the angel said unto me: **Knowest thou the meaning of the book?** [*Do you know what book you are seeing now in the vision?*]

22 And I said unto him: **I know not**.

23 And he said: Behold it [*the Bible*] proceedeth out of the mouth of a Jew [*the Bible comes to us from the Jews*]. And I, Nephi, beheld it [*saw the Bible*]; and he said unto me: **The book** that thou beholdest [*which you are seeing*] **is a record** [*history*] **of the Jews**, which **contains** the **covenants** [*promises we make with God to get the blessings He promises us*] of the Lord, which he hath made unto the house of Israel; and it also containeth many of the **prophecies** of the holy prophets; and it is a record like unto the engravings which are upon the plates of brass, save there are not so many; nevertheless, they contain the covenants of the Lord, which he hath made unto the house of Israel; wherefore, they are of great worth unto the Gentiles.

We learn from verse 23, above, that the brass plates contained more Old Testament writings than our current Bible has. Next, Nephi will be shown that much was taken out of the Bible before we got it.

24 And the angel of the Lord said unto me: Thou hast beheld [*you have seen*] that **the book** [*the Bible*] **proceeded forth from the mouth of a Jew;** and **when it proceeded forth** from the mouth of a Jew **it contained the fulness of the** [*the complete*] **gospel of the Lord**, of whom the twelve apostles bear record; and they bear record according to the truth which is in the Lamb of God.

In other words, the original sermons and teachings from which the Bible was eventually put together, contained the full gospel of Jesus Christ.

25 Wherefore [*and so you can see that*], **these things** [*the original writings and teachings of the Bible*] **go forth from the Jews in purity** unto the Gentiles, according to the truth which is in God.

26 And **after they go forth** by the hand of the twelve apostles of the Lamb [*Christ*], from the Jews unto the Gentiles [*non-Jews*], thou seest

the formation of that great and abominable church [*the church of the devil; see 1 Nephi 14:10*], which is most abominable [*which causes the most damage to God's work*] above all other churches; for behold, **they have taken away from the gospel of the Lamb many parts which are plain and most precious**; and **also many covenants** of the Lord have they taken away.

> You may have noticed that covenants (like baptism) are only required to enter the celestial kingdom. Covenants are not required for entrance into terrestrial or telestial glory. Thus, by taking away priesthood and covenants, Satan has done major damage.

27 And **all this have they done** that they might pervert [*change, corrupt*] the right ways of the Lord, **that they might blind the eyes and harden the hearts of the children of men** [*people*].

28 Wherefore, thou seest [*and so you see*] that **after the book** [*the Bible*] **hath gone forth** through the hands of the great and abominable church [*after Satan's kingdom has had their hands on it*], that **there are many plain** [*easy to understand*] **and precious** [*very valuable*] **things taken away** from the book, which is the book of the Lamb of God.

29 And **after these plain and precious things were taken away it goeth forth unto all the nations of the Gentiles**; and after it goeth forth unto all the nations of the Gentiles, yea, even across the many waters [*to the New World, the Americas*] which thou hast seen with the Gentiles which have gone forth out of captivity, thou seest—**because of the many plain and precious things which have been taken out of the book, which were plain unto the understanding of the children of men, according to the plainness which is in the Lamb of God—because of these things which are taken away out of the gospel of the Lamb, an exceedingly great many do stumble, yea, insomuch that Satan hath great power over them.** [*Not knowing or understanding gospel truths and covenants is a terrible disadvantage for people. This is one of the reasons that the Book of Mormon and modern scriptures are so precious. They restore these "plain and precious things" to us.*]

30 Nevertheless, thou beholdest [*But, you can see*] that the Gentiles who have gone forth out of captivity [*the early colonists who escaped their miserable conditions in Europe and came to America*], and have been lifted up [*helped*] by the power of God above

all other nations, upon the face of the land which is choice above all other lands [*America*], which is the land that the Lord God hath covenanted [promised] with thy father that his seed [*descendants*] should have for the land of their inheritance; wherefore, **thou seest that the Lord God will not suffer** [*permit*] **that the Gentiles will utterly destroy the mixture of thy seed, which are among thy brethren.** [*Nephi's surviving descendants, who will have intermixed with the Lamanites, will not be completely destroyed by the influx of immigrants from across the oceans.*]

31 **Neither will he suffer** [*permit*] **that the Gentiles shall destroy the seed of thy brethren** [*the Lamanites*].

Next, the stage will be set in Nephi's mind for him to be shown the Restoration of the gospel through Joseph Smith.

32 **Neither will the Lord God suffer** [*allow*] **that the Gentiles shall forever remain in that awful state of blindness** [*lack of understanding of spiritual things, including the true gospel*], which thou beholdest they are in, because of the plain and most precious parts of the gospel of the Lamb which have been kept back by that abominable church, whose formation thou hast seen.

33 Wherefore saith the Lamb of God [*Christ*]: **I will be merciful unto the Gentiles, unto the visiting of the remnant of the house of Israel** [*Lehi's descendants, in other words, the Lamanites; see verse 34*] **in great judgment.**

"Visited with great judgment" is a scriptural term which basically means to finally get punished for continually rejecting the gospel and God's commandments.

34 And it came to pass that the angel of the Lord spake unto me, saying: Behold, saith the Lamb of God [*listen carefully to what Jesus says*], **after I have visited** [*punished*] **the remnant of the house of Israel—and this remnant of whom I speak is the seed of thy father** [*the Lamanites in the Americas*]—wherefore, after I have visited them in judgment, **and smitten them by the hand of the Gentiles** [*after the American colonists and their descendants have caused misery and destruction among the Lamanites in America*], **and after the Gentiles do stumble exceedingly** [*badly*], **because of the most plain and precious parts of the gospel of the Lamb which have been kept back** [*because of the many clear truths of the gospel taken out of the Bible*] by that abominable church,

which is the mother of harlots
[*which is the most evil of all*], saith the
Lamb—**I will be merciful unto
the Gentiles in that day, inso-
much that I will bring forth
unto them, in mine own power,
much of my gospel, which shall
be plain and precious, saith the
Lamb.** [*In other words, God will restore
His true Church to the earth. This is the
Restoration that began with the Prophet
Joseph Smith.*]

35 For, **behold, saith the Lamb**
[*Christ*]**: I will manifest myself
unto thy seed** [*this would be the visit
of the Resurrected Christ to the Nephites
as recorded in Third Nephi*], that **they
shall write many things which I
shall minister unto them, which
shall be plain and precious; and
after thy seed shall be destroyed**
[*as recorded in Fourth Nephi*], and dwin-
dle in unbelief [*gradually fall away
from living the gospel*], and also the
seed of thy brethren, behold, **these
things shall be hid up** [*Moroni will
hide the gold plates in the Hill Cumorah*],
to come forth unto the Gentiles
[*through Joseph Smith to all of us*], by the
gift and power of the Lamb.

36 And **in them** [*the plates, includ-
ing those from which the Book of Mormon
was translated*] **shall be written my
gospel, saith the Lamb, and my
rock and my salvation.**

37 And **blessed are they** [*including
all faithful Church members today*] **who
shall seek to bring forth my
Zion at that day** [*in the last days*],
for **they shall have the gift and
the power of the Holy Ghost;
and if they endure unto the end
they shall be lifted up** [*exalted*] at
the last day [*on Judgment Day*], and
shall be saved in the everlasting
kingdom of the Lamb [*in the celes-
tial kingdom*]; and whoso shall pub-
lish peace, yea, tidings of great joy,
how beautiful upon the moun-
tains shall they be.

Next, Nephi will be shown how the Restoration of the true gospel of Jesus Christ will take place in the last days.

38 And it came to pass that **I
beheld** [*saw*] the remnant [*those
who will remain*] of the seed of my
brethren [*the Lamanites*], and also
the book [*the Bible*] of the Lamb of
God, which had proceeded forth
from the mouth of the Jew, **that
it came forth from the Gentiles**
[*the colonists, pilgrims, missionaries, and
immigrants, etc., who came to the Americas*]
**unto the remnant of the seed of
my brethren** [*the Lamanites*].

39 And after it [*the Bible*] had come
forth unto them **I beheld other
books** [*such as the Book of Mormon,
Doctrine and Covenants, and the Pearl of
Great Price*], **which came forth by**

the power of the Lamb, from the Gentiles [*Joseph Smith and the members of the Church, including us*] unto them [*the Lamanites*], unto the convincing of the Gentiles [*generally speaking, non-members everywhere*] and the remnant of the seed of my brethren [*specifically speaking of the Lamanites*], and also the Jews who were scattered upon all the face of the earth, **that the records of the prophets** [*contained in the Bible*] **and of the twelve apostles of the Lamb** [*contained in the New Testament*] **are true.**

The Book of Mormon plus the "other books" referred to in verse 39, above, bear witness of the Bible and how important it is. This is particularly needed in our day when so many people no longer consider the Bible to contain the word of God. Rather, they simply think of it as being interesting to read.

40 And the angel spake unto me, saying: **These last records** [*the Book of Mormon plus the "other books" in verse 39*] which thou hast seen among the Gentiles, **shall establish the truth of the first** [*will sustain and support the Bible as being from God*], which are of the twelve apostles of the Lamb, **and shall make known the plain and precious things which have been taken away from them** [*will restore the teachings, doctrines, and covenants which were taken out of the Bible*]; **and shall make known to all kindreds, tongues, and people** [*everyone on earth*], **that the Lamb of God** [*Christ*] **is the Son of the Eternal Father, and the Savior of the world**; and that all men must come unto him, or they cannot be saved.

In verse 41, next, you will see it emphasized again that there is no other way to be saved in heaven, other than coming unto Christ. There is only one path which leads to salvation and exaltation in celestial glory. Many other churches can lead to terrestrial glory, but only one can lead to celestial glory and living with Heavenly Father and Jesus, and that is our church.

41 And **they must come** [*all people must come to Christ, as stated in verse 40*] according to the words which shall be established by the mouth of the Lamb; and **the words of the Lamb shall be made known in the records of thy seed** [*the Book of Mormon*], **as well as in the records of the twelve apostles of the Lamb** [*the Bible*]; wherefore they both shall be established in one [*the Bible and the Book of Mormon will come together, united as witnesses for Christ; see also Ezekiel 37:16–17*]; for there is one God and one Shepherd [*Christ*] over all the earth.

Next, Nephi will be taught that Christ will come to earth and establish His gospel among the Jews and then among the Gentiles (especially through the Apostle Paul). This happened in New Testament times. Nephi is then shown that in the last days—in other words, the time you are now living in—it will be in reverse order. That is, Jesus will manifest Himself first to the Gentiles (through Joseph Smith and the Restoration), and lastly, there will be a large-scale conversion among the Jews.

42 And **the time cometh** [*in about six hundred years from when Nephi is seeing this vision*] that **he** [*Christ*] **shall manifest himself** [*make Himself known*] unto all nations, both **unto the Jews and also unto the Gentiles** [*New Testament times*]; and after he has manifested himself unto the Jews and also unto the Gentiles, then [*in the last days*] **he shall manifest himself unto the Gentiles** [*non-Jews*] **and also unto the Jews**, and the last [*Gentiles who received the gospel "last" in the New Testament, after the Jews*] shall be first, and the first [*the Jews, who were given the gospel first in the New Testament ministry of the Savior*] shall be last [*to receive the gospel in the last days*].

1 NEPHI 14

This chapter is the last chapter of Nephi's vision, in which he was shown the things which his father, Lehi, saw in vision. In it, Nephi will be shown things concerning the last days before the Second Coming of Christ, including the days in which we now live. The angel, mentioned in chapter 13, verse 40, is still his guide and is explaining the things to him that he is seeing and feeling.

In the next several verses, the main issue is the importance of having God on your side because of your personal righteousness, even though living in a wicked world. This is a very important message for each of us.

The main message in verse 1 is that, in the last days before the Second Coming of Christ, the Lord will restore His true gospel. It will come to the Gentiles and will restore the covenants and teachings and ordinances (like true baptism, confirmation to receive the gift of the Holy Ghost, proper sacrament, and so forth) that were taken away from the Bible and the church by the "great and abominable church"—in other words, the church of the devil. We read about that in 1 Nephi 13:26–29.

1 AND it shall come to pass, that **if the Gentiles** [*all people except the Jews*] **shall hearken** [*listen and pay attention*] **unto the Lamb of God** [*Christ*] in that day [*the last days*] that **he shall manifest** [*reveal, show*] **himself unto them in word, and**

also in power, in very deed, unto the taking away of their stumbling blocks [*the the things that stand in their way, keeping them from living the gospel, mentioned in 1 Nephi 13:26–29*]—

2 **And harden not their hearts against the Lamb of God,** [*in other words, if they accept and live the gospel faithfully*] they shall be numbered among the seed of thy father [*they will be among the righteous like Nephi and other righteous descendants of Lehi*]; yea, **they shall be numbered among the house of Israel** [*a scriptural phrase for saying that they will receive all the blessings of Abraham, Isaac, and Jacob, who have already become gods (see D&C 132:37); in other words, this is a way of saying they will receive exaltation*]; and **they shall be a blessed people upon the promised land** [*America*] forever [*they will be greatly blessed as a nation; symbolic of attaining heaven, the celestial glory, and living in the presence of the Father and Christ forever*]; **they shall be no more brought down into captivity** [*Satan will not succeed against them*]; and the house of Israel [*the Lord's covenant people*] shall no more be confounded [*confused, stopped, led astray*].

3 And that great pit [*Satan's trap for us; hell; outer darkness*], which hath been digged for them by that great and abominable church [*the church of the devil; everything Satan tries to do to trap and destroy us; 1 Nephi 14:10*], which was founded by the devil and his children [*Satan's followers*], that he might lead away the souls of men [*people*] down to hell—yea, **that great pit which hath been digged for the destruction of men shall be filled by those who digged it** [*the wicked end up being trapped by their own traps that they set to capture and destroy the righteous*], unto their utter [*complete*] destruction, saith the Lamb of God; **not the destruction of the soul**, save [*except*] it be the casting of it into that hell which hath no end.

"Not the destruction of the soul" in verse 3, above, teaches a very important gospel truth. Such truths are called "doctrines." Nobody can or will ever cease to exist. I had a student once who asked me if I knew of a sin she could commit which would cause her to cease to exist completely. She explained that she knew that after we die, and our mortal body eventually dissolves away, that we still continue to exist until resurrection as spirit beings. She wanted her spirit and intelligence also to cease to exist. I gently explained that this was impossible. Then with the help of her good bishop, problems were resolved and life became worthwhile again. The point here is that we are eternal beings already and that the "destruction of the soul," verse 3, above, means total captivity of the soul by the devil, and being under such captivity forever (see Alma 34:35). This "forever" captivity would only apply to sons of perdition, since all others are eventually out of Satan's reach (see the vision of the three degrees of glory and sons of perdition—outer darkness—in Doctrine and Covenants, section 76).

4 For behold, this is according to the captivity of the devil, and also **according to the justice of God** [*the law of justice*], upon all those who will [*intentionally*] work wickedness and abomination before him [*those who intentionally want to be wicked in spite of God's commandments*].

The prophecy in verses 5–7, next, is what can be termed a "conditional prophecy," meaning that there is an "if-then" relationship involved. In other words, if they do or do not . . . whatever the topic is . . . then thus and such will or will not happen. It is the type of prophecy which reminds us that we have agency, and that by how we use our agency, we are determining our future.

5 And it came to pass that **the angel spake** [*said*] unto me, Nephi, saying: Thou hast beheld that **if the Gentiles repent it shall be well with them; and thou also knowest concerning the covenants of the Lord unto the house of Israel; and thou also hast heard that whoso repenteth not must perish** [*will ultimately be destroyed spiritually or physically or both*].

6 Therefore, wo be [*trouble is coming*] unto the Gentiles **if it so be that they harden their hearts** against the Lamb of God [*reject the teachings of Christ*].

7 For the time cometh, saith the Lamb of God, that **I will work a great and a marvelous work** [*including the Restoration of the true Church by Joseph Smith*] among the children of men [*all people*]; a work which shall be everlasting, either on the one hand or on the other—**either to the convincing** of **them unto peace and life eternal,** [*either convincing them to live the gospel and live with God forever in heaven*] **or unto the deliverance of them to the hardness of their hearts and the blindness of their minds unto their being brought down into captivity, and also into destruction, both temporally** [*being killed, destroyed literally here in mortality*] **and spiritually** [*as far as personal spirituality and righteousness are concerned*], according to the captivity of the devil [*being trapped by Satan*], of which I have spoken.

The above verses are clear reminders of the role that our agency plays in our eventual "placement" for eternity. Our choices have everlasting consequences—in other words, results. In effect, we are now making our final decisions for our eternal placement. We prepared for eons of time in premortality for this final test, and we are now taking it.

The angel asks Nephi another question in verse 8.

8 And it came to pass that when **the angel had spoken these words, he said unto me: Rememberest thou the covenants of the Father unto the house of Israel?** [*By the way, you can review these covenants by reading Abraham 2:9–11, in the Pearl of Great Price.*] **I said unto him, Yea** [*yes*].

9 And it came to pass that **he** [*the angel*] **said unto me: Look, and behold** [*see*] **that great and abominable church, which is the mother of abominations** [*which produces such terrible corruption and wickedness*], whose founder is the devil [*Satan is the one who created it*].

10 And **he said unto me: Behold there are save two churches only; the one is the church of the Lamb of God, and the other is the church of the devil; wherefore, whoso belongeth not to the church of the Lamb of God belongeth to that great church, which is the mother of abominations** [*the source of all evil and wickedness*]; and she is the whore of all the earth.

Verse 10, above, is filled with very strong, basic doctrine. Ultimately, there are just two positions you can take. Either you are with God or you are with the devil. Many people are uncomfortable with boiling it down to such simple terms. Indeed, part of Satan's cunning way of fooling us is trying to make us believe that there is lots of middle ground and that we can put off making decisions as to loyalty to God or the devil for a future time.

Furthermore, there are just two "churches." The Church of Jesus Christ of Latter-day Saints stands alone as the one true Church and stands alone in glory and power to make exaltation available to all who will come unto Christ. All influences which lead people away from the commitments and covenants available in the true Church are part of the other "church," or the "kingdom of the devil" as it is referred to in 1 Nephi 22:22.

We must be careful not to be "down" on all Christian and non-Christian churches as a result of our reading of verse 10, above. Indeed, D&C 10:52 reminds us not to "bash" other churches, rather to understand that our church fills in the gaps in the doctrines and teachings of others and thus builds them up and completes what they have started.

Next, in verse 11, strong language is used to describe Satan's kingdom and power in the last days of the world before the Second Coming of Christ. The term "whore" is a word that means someone who takes that which is pure and holy and good and uses it instead to pollute, make filthy, and destroy. The image of the "whore" (Satan and his evil followers) sitting upon the "many waters" reminds us that filthy water, for example, in the case of a devastating flood causing sewage to get in one's basement, tries to get into everything. Thus, Satan, in the last days, will be very powerful and will be trying to get into every aspect of our lives.

11 And it came to pass that **I looked and beheld the whore of all the earth** [*Satan's kingdom in the last days*], and she sat upon many waters [*symbolic of ability to get into every aspect of society*]; and she had dominion [*great power*] over all the earth, among all nations, kindreds, tongues, and people [*all people*].

Next, Nephi sees that, in the last days, after the Restoration of the gospel through Joseph Smith, the members of the Church, though there are not many of them compared to the populaton of the whole world, have influence throughout the world.

12 And it came to pass that **I beheld the church of the Lamb of God** [*the true Church*], **and its numbers were few, because of the wickedness and abominations of the whore who sat upon many waters** [*because of Satan's power and dominion upon the earth*]; **nevertheless, I beheld that the church of the Lamb, who were the saints of God, were also upon all the face of the earth; and their dominions** [*influence and effectiveness*] upon the face of the earth **were small, because of the wickedness of the great whore whom I saw.**

13 And it came to pass that **I beheld that the great mother of abominations** [*Satan and his evil followers*] **did gather together multitudes upon the face of all the earth, among all the nations of the Gentiles, to fight against the Lamb of God.** [*Satan will have many "allies" or helpers in the last days, as he wages war against the spread of the true gospel of Christ.*]

Verse 14, next, is very comforting and reassuring. It reminds us that we are definitely not alone as we try to be righteous and spread the gospel.

14 And it came to pass that **I, Nephi, beheld the power of the Lamb of God, that it descended** [*came down from heaven*] **upon the saints** [*members*] of the church of the Lamb, and **upon the covenant**

people of the Lord [*often called the house of Israel*], who were scattered upon all the face of the earth; **and they were armed with righteousness and with the power of God in great glory.**

Next, Nephi sees "wars and rumors of war," which are one of the prominent signs of the times or prophecies that will be fulfilled in the last days, showing us that the Second Coming of the Savior is not far off.

15 And it came to pass that **I beheld that the wrath** [*anger*] of God was poured out upon that great and abominable church, insomuch that [*so that*] **there were wars and rumors of wars among all the nations and kindreds of the earth.**

The angel will now emphasize and explain to Nephi some of the main points of this vision.

16 And as there began to be **wars and rumors of wars among all the nations which belonged to the mother of abominations** [*among all the nations which were wicked*], the angel spake unto me, saying: Behold, the wrath of God is upon the mother of harlots [*the anger and punishments of God are coming down upon the wicked; in other words, Satan's kingdom*]; and behold, thou seest all these things.

As stated above, the angel is now reviewing key elements of the vision, including the definition of the "great and abominable church," leading up to the Restoration of the true Church in the last days.

17 And **when the day cometh that the wrath of God is poured out upon the mother of harlots, which is the great and abominable church of all the earth, whose founder is the devil, then, at that day, the work of the Father shall commence, in preparing the way for the fulfilling of his covenants, which he hath made to his people who are of the house of Israel.** [*In other words, when the time arrives, as depicted in the vision, the true Church will be restored, and the long-prophesied gathering of Israel will begin. Nephi is seeing our day.*]

18 And it came to pass **that the angel spake unto me, saying: Look!**

19 And **I looked and beheld** [*saw*] **a man** [*John, the Beloved Apostle, who wrote the book of Revelation in our Bible; see verse 27 in this chapter*]**, and he was dressed in a white robe.**

Just a reminder of scriptural symbolism. John is dressed in white, symbolizing purity and worthiness to be in the presence of God. He is dressed in a robe, symbolizing that he has made and kept covenants, and is thus worthy of exaltation—in other words, of becoming a god.

Next, the angel will tell Nephi more about the man he is seeing in the vision.

20 And **the angel said unto me: Behold one of the twelve apostles of the Lamb.**

21 **Behold, he shall see and write the remainder of these things** [*the next things you, Nephi, will see in this vision*]; yea, and **also many things which have been** [*things about the past, including the premortal council in heaven before any of us were born—see Revelation 5*].

22 And **he shall also write concerning the end of the world** [*including things that will happen shortly before Christ comes, plus details about the millennium, final Judgment Day, and the different degrees of glory after Judgment Day*].

Next, the angel bears his testimony to Nephi that the things that John the Apostle will write are true.

23 Wherefore, **the things which he shall write are just and true**; and behold they are written in the book [*the Bible*] which thou beheld [*which you saw earlier in the vision*] proceeding out of the mouth of the Jew; and at the time they proceeded out of the mouth of the Jew, or, at the time the book proceeded out of the mouth of the Jew, the things which were written were plain and pure, and most precious and easy to the understanding of all men. [*In other words, when the Bible and the book of Revelation were first written, they were clear and easy to understand.*]

24 And behold, the things which this apostle of the Lamb shall write are many things which thou hast seen; and behold, the remainder shalt thou see.

25 **But the things which thou shalt see hereafter thou shalt not write**; for the Lord God hath ordained [*assigned*] the apostle of the Lamb of God that he should write them.

This is a most fascinating instruction given to Nephi. He will now see many more things leading up to the end of the world. But it is not his job to write them. It is the stewardship of the Apostle John, who lived almost seven hundred years after Nephi. He will see the same things Nephi will now see. John is the one who is to write these things for us to read. These writings of John are written in the Bible in the book of Revelation.

26 And also **others** who have been, to them hath he shown all things, and they **have written**

them; and they are sealed up to come forth in their purity, according to the truth which is in the Lamb, in the own due time of the Lord, unto the house of Israel.

Verse 26, above, tells us that there are yet other sealed records or scriptures, which someday will be made available to the people of the Lord by the power of God. This must have been a fascinating verse for Joseph Smith, to realize that others would also be involved someday in bringing ancient records to us like he did the Book of Mormon.

27 And I, Nephi, heard and bear record, that **the name of the apostle of the Lamb was John**, according to the word of the angel.

The Apostle named John, mentioned by Nephi above, was the Apostle who wrote five of the books of the New Testament—namely, the Gospel of John, 1 John, 2 John, 3 John, and the book of Revelation. He was the one who served in the First Presidency of the Church after the Savior went to heaven. It was this presidency—Peter, James, and John—who restored the Melchizedek Priesthood to Joseph Smith and Oliver Cowdery (see D&C 27:12).

Next, Nephi brings his recording of his vision to a close, reminding us that he is simply following the instructions of the angel not to write the rest of what he saw in the vision.

28 And behold, **I, Nephi, am forbidden that I should write the remainder of the things which I saw and heard; wherefore the things which I have written sufficeth me; and I have written but a small part of the things which I saw.** [*It will be interesting to someday be with Nephi when he has time and is permitted to tell us the rest of what he saw.*]

29 And I bear record [*I bear testimony*] that **I saw the things which my father saw, and the angel of the Lord did make them known unto me.**

30 And now I make an end of speaking concerning the things which I saw while I was carried away in the spirit; and if all the things which I saw are not written, the things which I have written are true. And thus it is. Amen.

This is the end of Nephi's vision.

1 NEPHI 15

Nephi has now had the marvelous experience of having a vision in which he was shown the things that his father, Lehi, saw in vision. Imagine what a great testimony-building experience this was for him. Plus, he has seen many things and has been taught much that will help him be a powerful prophet and leader of his people.

He has been what we often refer to as "in the Spirit." Perhaps you have been "in the Spirit" yourself. For example, when you have felt the Holy Ghost strongly in an especially spiritual fireside, or when you have been reading your scriptures, or praying, or whatever. When we are feeling the Spirit so strongly, we are also feeling the love of Heavenly Father and the Savior. Often, we don't want to leave the chapel or classroom because we don't want worldly influences to destroy what we are feeling.

No doubt Nephi was now anxious to share his witness and testimony of the things that his father saw with the others back at camp. As he approaches, however, he sees his brothers arguing. What a letdown! We will now listen to him as he tells this part of his history.

1 AND it came to pass that after I, Nephi, had been carried away in the spirit, and seen all these things, **I returned to the tent of my father.**

2 **And it came to pass that I beheld my brethren, and they were disputing** [*arguing*] **one with another concerning the things which my father had spoken unto them.**

3 **For he truly spake many great things unto them, which were hard to be understood, save a man should inquire of the Lord** [*unless a person prays to God for help in understanding them*]; and they being hard in their hearts [*insensitive and rebellious against religious things*], therefore they did not look unto the Lord as they ought.

We are reminded by Nephi in the previous verse that the things of God can be hard to understand unless we turn to the Lord for help. This is a most important lesson for all of us.

Next, we will see Nephi almost overcome with grief. Knowing that Nephi was inspired as to what to include in the special record contained on the small plates, we can perhaps take comfort in this message from the Lord that even great and highly capable people can have times of depression and sorrow.

4 And now **I, Nephi, was grieved** [*troubled and saddened*] because of the hardness of their hearts, and also, because of the things which I had seen [*remember that he had seen in the vision the downfall and destruction of his own people*], and knew they must unavoidably come to pass because of the great wickedness of the children of men.

The phrase "children of men" as used in verse 4, above, is a term that is used often in the scriptures. It means "people here on earth."

Next, Nephi tells us that he had become very depressed.

5 And it came to pass that **I was overcome because of my afflictions, for I considered that mine afflictions were great above all, because of the destruction of my people, for I had beheld** [*had seen*] their fall.

Next, we will watch Nephi try to help his brethren understand the things of God. When we get to verse 11, we will be given a formula for getting help and counsel from God. It is also a formula for getting a personal testimony.

6 And it came to pass that after I had received strength [*after he got over his depression with help from the Lord*] **I spake** [*spoke*] **unto my brethren, desiring to know of them the cause of their disputations** [*the cause of their arguing among themselves*].

7 And **they said: Behold, we cannot understand the words which our father hath spoken concerning the natural branches of the olive-tree, and also concerning the Gentiles.**

8 **And I said unto them: Have ye inquired of the Lord** [*have you prayed for help*]?

9 And they said unto me: **We have not; for the Lord maketh no such thing known unto us.** [*It may be that there is a touch of sarcasm in their response, in effect saying, "The Lord doesn't talk to us like he does to you, holy little brother."*]

Next, we will see Nephi's teachings about things that can prevent our being sensitive to the Holy Ghost and thus coming to understand the things of God.

10 Behold, I said unto them: **How** [*why*] **is it that ye do not keep the commandments of the Lord?** [*This is a major cause of not being sensitive to the Spirit of the Lord.*] **How is it that ye will perish** [*be destroyed spiritually; in other words, as far as spiritual things are concerned*]**, because of the hardness of your hearts?**

Next, in verse 11, is a formula for receiving help from the Spirit to understand the things of God.

11 Do ye not remember the things which the Lord hath said? —**If ye will not harden your hearts** [*if you will open your hearts to be taught*], and **ask me in faith, believing that ye shall receive, with diligence** [*steadiness and faithfulness*] **in keeping my commandments, surely these things shall be made known unto you.**

Next, Nephi will teach and explain to his brethren the use of the olive-tree symbolism which was shown to Father Lehi and mentioned in 1 Nephi 10:12–14. It deals with the gathering of Israel in the last days, and we have the privilege of watching the fulfillment of this prophecy as it continues to gain momentum in our day. It is a powerful testimony of the truth of the book of Mormon.

12 Behold, I say unto you, that **the house of Israel** [*the Lord's covenant people, in other words, the descendants of Abraham, Isaac, and Jacob*] **was compared unto an olive-tree, by the Spirit of the Lord which was in our father** [*Lehi*]; and behold are we not broken off from the house of Israel [*symbolizing being scattered away from the rest of Israel*], and are we not a branch of the house of Israel [*don't we belong to Israel, the Lord's covenant people*]?

13 And now, **the thing which our father meaneth** [*means*] concerning the grafting in [*being reattached to the main tree*] of the natural branches through the fulness of the Gentiles [*through the fulness of the gospel being restored among the Gentiles by Joseph Smith and the Restoration*], **is, that in the latter days** [*in the last days, before the Second Coming*], **when our seed** [*posterity, descendants*] **shall have dwindled in unbelief** [*will have gradually gone into apostasy, fallen away from the gospel of Christ*], yea, **for the space of many years, and many generations** [*many hundreds of years*] **after the Messiah** [*Christ*] **shall be manifested** [*shown*] **in body unto the children of men** [*many generations after the mortal ministry of the Savior*], **then shall the fulness of the gospel of the Messiah come unto the Gentiles** [*the gospel and the true Church will be restored again, this time to the Gentiles through Joseph Smith and the Restoration*], **and from the Gentiles unto the remnant of our seed** [*and the Lamanites will receive it from the members of our church*]—

It is very important that we know who we are. We must understand that we are children of God, that we can truly become like Him, that we can actually become gods. Knowing this is vital to our self-worth and to our developing desires to be righteous.

Next, Nephi will prophesy that this blessing of knowing who they are will be restored to the Lamanites in the last days.

14 And **at that day** [*after the gospel has been restored in the last days*] **shall the remnant of our seed** [*the Lamanites*] **know that they are of the house of Israel, and that they are the covenant people of the Lord; and then shall they know and come to the knowledge of their forefathers** [*they will know who their ancestors are*], and **also to the knowledge of the gospel of their Redeemer** [*Christ*], which was ministered unto their

fathers [*ancestors*] by him; wherefore [*that is how*], they shall come to the knowledge of their Redeemer **and the very points of his doctrine, that they may know how to come unto him and be saved.**

The message at the end of verse 14, above is most important. It is not enough for people to want to be saved. They must know how to be saved. Perhaps many other Christian as well as non-Christian churches and individuals disagree with us on this. But that is most likely because they do not know what it means to "be saved." They don't realize nor do they accept the fact that, almost always in the scriptures, "being saved" means to be baptized, live the gospel, become like God, and to become gods ourselves.

Thus, with their understanding limited by lack of knowledge ("points of his doctrine," verse 14, above), they believe that to be "saved" a person only needs to be good. This, in fact, is true in reference to obtaining terrestrial glory (see D&C 76:75). But in order to be "saved" and live with God in celestial exaltation, we need knowledge of the gospel. We need "points" of doctrine. We need priesthood authority and ordinances like baptism, confirmation, and temple marriage so that we can make and keep covenants. It is impossible for us to be saved without knowing and living the true gospel.

15 And then **at that day** [*after the true gospel is restored by Joseph Smith*] **will they** [*the Lamanites*] **not rejoice and give-praise unto their everlasting God, their rock and their salvation?** Yea [*yes*], at that day, will they not receive the strength and nourishment from the true vine [*Christ; see John 15:1*]? **Yea, will they not come unto the true fold** [*the true Church; ultimately, celestial exaltation*] **of God?**

The answer to all of the above questions is a very strong yes!

16 **Behold, I say unto you, Yea; they shall be remembered again among the house of Israel; they shall be grafted in** [*gathered in and reattached to the "olive tree," to the "true vine" meaning the true Church*], being a natural branch of the olive-tree [*being bloodline descendants of Israel—Abraham, Isaac, and Jacob*], **into the true olive-tree.**

17 **And this is what our father meaneth; and he meaneth that it will not come to pass** [*the gathering of Israel will not happen*] until after they are scattered by the Gentiles; and he meaneth that it shall come by way of the Gentiles [*it will come to the Lamanites through the church that Joseph Smith will establish among the Gentiles (non-Jews)*], that the Lord may show his power unto the Gentiles, for the very cause that he shall be rejected

of [*by*] the Jews, or of the house of Israel.

You might still be confused a bit as to the difference between the words "**Jews**" and "**Gentiles**" as used in the Book of Mormon. Let's talk about it.

The word "**Jews**" in the Book of Mormon means people who may have come from any or many of the tribes of Israel, who originally lived in the Holy Land. The "Holy Land" means basically where the nation of Israel is today.

The point is that they were "geographically" from the Holy Land.

In the Book of Mormon, "**Gentiles**" are all of the people in the world who don't come from the Holy Land. Many of the Gentiles have the blood of Israel in them but are not "geographically" from the Holy Land recently. Even today, the term "Jew" basically refers to non-Arabic citizens of Israel, plus people elsewhere in the world whose ancestors came from the Holy Land. Most "Jews" have blood from many of the twelve tribes of Israel in their veins.

Also, just a quick note about the term "**house of Israel**." It means the descendants of Abraham, Isaac, and Jacob, or, "the covenant people of the Lord." Almost all of us, including you and me, are from the house of Israel.

Abraham and Sarah had Isaac. Isaac and Rebekah had Jacob. Jacob and his wives had twelve sons. Jacob's name was changed to "Israel." Thus, we have the "house of Israel" or "the family of Israel." The blessings of the gospel and priesthood covenants come to all the world through this lineage.

In summary, we have Abraham, Isaac, and Jacob. God covenanted with Abraham and renewed it with Isaac and with Jacob that through them, all the world would be blessed (see Genesis 12:1–3, 17:4–8, Abraham 2:9–11; Genesis 26:2–5; Genesis 32:24–30).

That is one key reason the designation of lineage in your patriarchal blessing is so important. It tells you which of the tribes of Israel your blessings come through. It reminds you of your responsibilities as a missionary all of your life. It also reminds you that you have the potential to become a god. Abraham, Isaac, and Jacob (and their wives) have all become gods already (see D&C 132:37).

18 Wherefore, **our father hath not spoken of our seed** [*posterity*] **alone, but also of all the house of Israel** [*all of the descendants of Abraham, Isaac, and Jacob*], pointing to the covenant which should be fulfilled in the latter days; which covenant the Lord made to our father [*ancestor*] Abraham, saying: In thy

seed shall all the kindreds [*people*] of the earth be blessed.

19 And it came to pass that I, Nephi, spake much unto them concerning these things; yea, I spake unto them concerning **the restoration of the Jews in the latter days.** [*The Jews will be gathered back to the Holy Land and become a nation. This has happened and is continuing to happen in our day. It is one of the signs of the times that will take place before the Second Coming. There is another "gathering" of the Jews that must yet take place. It is the gathering of them to Christ and to the true Church. Except for a few isolated cases, this appears to be a future occurrence.*]

Next, Nephi will quote from Isaiah, a very important prophet in the Bible, to teach his brothers more about the gathering of Israel in the last days. Remember, our prophets today are talking a lot about our role in gathering Israel too.

20 And **I did rehearse** [*speak*] **unto them the words of Isaiah, who spake** [*spoke*] concerning the restoration of the Jews, or of the house of Israel [*here, the term "Jews" is expanded to mean all the house of Israel, which would include all of us*]; and after they were restored they should [*would*] no more be confounded [*confused; stopped in progressing toward celestial exaltation*], neither should they be scattered again. And it came to pass that I did speak many words unto **my brethren, that they were pacified** [*so that they settled down*] and **did humble themselves before the Lord.** [*This gives us hope, once again, for Laman and Lemuel and the others in the family who have been rebellious.*]

It is quite encouraging at this point to see these rebellious members of the group begin to ask sincere, intelligent questions. It must have done Nephi's heart good to see this happening. In fact, a very helpful question and answer session begins now, which will help us too.

Question

21 And it came to pass that they did speak unto me again, saying: **What meaneth this thing which our father saw in a dream? What meaneth the tree which he saw?**

Answer

22 **And I said unto them: It was a representation of the tree of life.**

Question

23 And they said unto me: **What meaneth the rod of iron which our father saw, that led to the tree?**

Answer

24 And I said unto them that **it was the word of God; and whoso would hearken unto** [*listen*

to and obey] **the word of God, and would hold fast** [*tightly*] **unto it, they would never perish** [*never become lost from God; this is a tremendous promise!*]; **neither could the temptations and the fiery darts of the adversary** [*the devil*] **overpower them unto blindness, to lead them away to destruction**.

25 Wherefore [*this is why*], I, Nephi, did exhort [*strongly urge*] them to give heed unto [*listen to*] the word of the Lord; yea, I did exhort them with all the energies of my soul, and with all the faculty [*ability, skill*] which I possessed, that they would give heed to [*carefully follow*] the word of God and remember to keep his commandments always in all things.

Question

26 And they said unto me: **What meaneth the river of water which our father saw?**

Answer

27 And I said unto them that **the water which my father saw was filthiness**; and so much was his mind swallowed up in [*distracted by*] other things that he beheld not [*didn't notice*] the filthiness of the water.

28 And I said unto them that **it was an awful gulf, which separated the wicked from the tree of life, and also from the saints of God**.

29 And I said unto them that **it was a representation of that awful hell, which the angel said unto me was prepared for the wicked.**

30 And I said unto them that our father also saw that **the justice of God did also divide the wicked from the righteous; and the brightness thereof was like unto the brightness of a flaming fire, which ascendeth** [*goes*] **up unto**

God forever and ever, and hath no end.

Question

31 And they said unto me: **Doth this thing mean the torment** [*pain and torture*] **of the body in the days of probation** [*during our life on earth*], **or doth it mean the final state of the soul** [*our final condition in the next life*] **after the death of the temporal body** [*the physical body*], **or doth it speak of the things which are temporal** [*things which relate to this mortal life*]**?**

Answer

32 And it came to pass that I said unto them that **it was a representation of things both temporal and spiritual; for the day should** [*would*] **come that they must be** [*would be*] **judged of their works, yea, even the works which were done by the temporal body in their days of probation.** [*In other words, we will all face Christ to answer for our choices during this testing period on earth.*]

33 Wherefore, **if they should die in their wickedness they must be cast off also, as to the things which are spiritual, which are pertaining to righteousness** [*they would be kept out of heaven, which is a spiritual and righteous place*]**; wherefore, they must be brought to stand before God** [*Final Judgment Day*]**, to be judged of their works; and if their works have been filthiness they must needs be** [*would be*] **filthy; and if they be filthy it must needs be** [*it has to be*] **that they cannot dwell in the kingdom of God; if so** [*if they were allowed into heaven*]**, the kingdom of God must be** [*would become*] **filthy also.**

In the above verses, Nephi has been answering questions from his brothers and others in the group who have had many chances to know by personal experience that there is a God and that Lehi and Nephi are teaching truth. They will yet have many more such witnesses. If and when they reject the gospel, it will be against knowledge. Thus, how they choose to spend the "days of their probation," in other words, their mortal lives, will likely determine their final judgment. Nephi is clearly teaching this to them.

However, we know that many in this life do not get such a complete set of clear chances to understand and obey the laws of God. God is completely fair. Thus, for such individuals, the completion of their opportunities to understand and accept the gospel laws and covenants will come in the next life in the spirit world mission field, as taught in D&C 138.

However, we would no doubt do well to consider our time on earth to be the determining factor as to whether we will be allowed to continue progressing toward exaltation after we die. If we think this way, it will help us live the gospel more completely on a daily basis.

Next, Nephi continues explaining the logic and reasoning behind the fact that unworthy, unrighteous people cannot return to live forever with God. His brethren asked good, sincere questions, and he is an excellent teacher as he gives them a chance to understand.

34 But behold, I say unto you, **the kingdom of God is not filthy, and there cannot any unclean thing** [*no unworthy, unrighteous people can*] **enter into the kingdom of God**; wherefore [*therefore*] there must needs be a place of filthiness prepared for that which is filthy [*there has to be another place for people who are still not righteous after this life to go to*].

35 **And there is a place prepared**, yea, even **that awful hell** of which I have spoken, **and the devil is the preparator** [*the preparer*] **of it**; wherefore the final state of the souls of men is to dwell in the kingdom of God, or to be cast out because of that justice [*the law of justice*] of which I have spoken.

36 **Wherefore** [*this is why*], **the wicked are rejected** [*ultimately separated*] **from the righteous**, and **also from that tree of life**, whose fruit is most precious and most desirable above all other fruits; yea, and **it** [*exaltation; see D&C 14:7*] **is the greatest of all the gifts of God**. And thus I spake unto my brethren. Amen.

1 NEPHI 16

As you saw, in the last chapter, Nephi's brethren came up with some very good questions in order to try to understand what their father, Lehi, taught them. Although they were apparently sincere, the answers to their questions don't match up well with their attitudes and the way they are living now. And this is a big problem. The answers about personal accountability, final judgment, filthiness, the requirements to be in the presence of God forever, etc., are quite hard for them to accept because they will have to make big changes and do a lot of repenting if they are going to clean up their lives to be righteous consistantly.

Watch now, as Nephi's brethren express their concern that what they have heard is hard on them. But, as you probably know, tough stains generally can't be taken out by gentle soap. This is a lesson clearly taught now by Nephi, and his hopes are raised again by his brethren's responses.

1 AND now it came to pass that after I, Nephi, had made an end of speaking to my brethren, behold **they said unto me: Thou hast declared unto us hard things,**

more than we are able to bear [*more than we can stand*].

2 And it came to pass that **I said unto them that I knew that I had spoken hard things against the wicked**, according to the truth [*but I was just speaking the truth*]; and **the righteous have I justified** [*I have shown that righteousness will pay off eternally*], and testified that they should be lifted up [*exalted*] at the last day [*on Judgment Day*]; wherefore, **the guilty taketh the truth to be hard, for it cutteth them to the very center**.

You can imagine that the last sentence of verse 2, above, was extra unpleasant for the rebellious ones in the group to hear! But it is certainly true!

What Nephi says next is also very true. It contains what we call an "if-then" statement.

3 And now my brethren, **if ye were righteous and were willing to hearken to the truth, and give heed unto it, that ye might walk uprightly before God, then ye would not murmur** [*complain*] **because of the truth**, and say: Thou speakest hard things against us.

4 And it came to pass that I, Nephi, did exhort [*teach and urge*] my brethren, with all diligence, to keep the commandments of the Lord.

5 And it came to pass that **they did humble themselves before the Lord**; insomuch [*so that*] that **I had joy and great hopes of them**, that they would walk in the paths of righteousness.

6 Now, all these things were said and done as my father dwelt in a tent in the valley which he called Lemuel.

Next, Nephi and his brothers, as well as Zoram (who was Laban's servant), get married.

7 And it came to pass that **I, Nephi, took one of the daughters of Ishmael to wife**; and also, **my brethren took of the daughters of Ishmael to wife**; and also **Zoram took the eldest daughter of Ishmael to wife**. [*This must have been quite a ceremony, and quite a time of celebrating and rejoicing!*]

Next, Nephi makes quite a statement about his father, which could be comforting to other parents whose children have not all stayed active in the Church.

8 And thus **my father had fulfilled all the commandments of the Lord which had been given unto him**. And also, I, Nephi, had been blessed of the Lord exceedingly.

It appears that Lehi and his little group of travelers have been camped in the Valley of Lemuel (see 1 Nephi 2:6, 14; 16:6) for some time. Lehi and Sariah waited there while their sons went back to get the brass plates. They remained there while the brothers went back to Jerusalem to get Ishmael and his family to join them so that they could have wives and families. They were camped in this valley when Lehi had his dream of the tree of life, and while Nephi had his visions in which he saw all the things his father saw.

We don't know how much of the eight years they spent in the wilderness, after leaving the Jerusalem area, had already passed when the Lord commanded Lehi to continue their journey into the wilderness. Whatever the case, they will now continue their journey and will eventually arrive at the ocean where they will build a ship and cross the waters to the promised land.

You may be familiar with many of the things we will read about next. Lehi will be given the Liahona (the ball or compass that will guide them on their way and also teach them many things). Nephi will break his bow. Ishmael will die, and there will be a rebellion among some in the group. Laman will plot with others to take Lehi's life and also to kill Nephi.

These rebellious members of the group will have yet another chance to repent and change their attitudes and the direction of their lives when the Lord speaks directly to them and severely scolds them.

9 And it came to pass that the voice of **the Lord spake unto my father** by night, and commanded him that on the morrow [*the next day*] **he should take his journey into the wilderness**.

10 And it came to pass that as **my father** arose in the morning, and went forth to the tent door, to his great astonishment he **beheld upon the ground a round ball** of curious workmanship [*the Liahona; see Alma 37:38*]; and it was of fine brass. And within the ball were two spindles; and the one pointed the way whither [*where*] we should go into the wilderness.

From time to time, the Lord has provided his prophets with physical devices to assist and direct them and their people, including the Liahona, Urim and Thummim, seer stones, and so forth. Since we all know about smart phones, computers, and all kinds of electronic devices, it shouldn't surprise us that the Lord knows about such things too, and has given them to His prophets in times past. Here, Lehi is given a marvelous device of very fine workmanship to assist him and his people as they travel through a dangerous wilderness.

Some symbolism here is quite easy to see. Among other things, this earth can be a rather dangerous place, a "wilderness" so to speak with traps and decoys set up by the devil and his evil followers. We need constant guidance as we journey through life. We receive it through the scriptures and the counsel and teachings of our modern prophets and apostles, as well as from our parents and local leaders. It might even be suggested that we have our "Liahonas" in the form of smart phones and other electronic devices that we can look into and see the scriptures, study the words and teachings of Church leaders, electronically sort through and access many of their messages on specific topics, and so forth.

Next, Lehi and the group prepare to continue their journey into the wilderness by gathering the supplies they will need in order to do so.

11 And it came to pass that we did gather together whatsoever things we should carry into the wilderness, and all the remainder of our provisions [*supplies*] which the Lord had given unto us; and we did take seed of every kind that we might carry into the wilderness.

12 And it came to pass that **we did take our tents and depart into the wilderness**, across the river Laman.

13 And it came to pass that **we traveled for the space of four days**, nearly a south-southeast direction, and we did pitch [*set up*] our tents again; and we did call the name of the place Shazer.

14 And it came to pass that we did take our bows and our arrows, and go forth into the wilderness to slay food for our families; and after we had slain food for our families we did return again to our families in the wilderness, to the place of Shazer. And we did go forth again in the wilderness, following the same direction, keeping in the most fertile parts [*the parts that had the most food available*] of the wilderness, which were in the borders near the Red Sea.

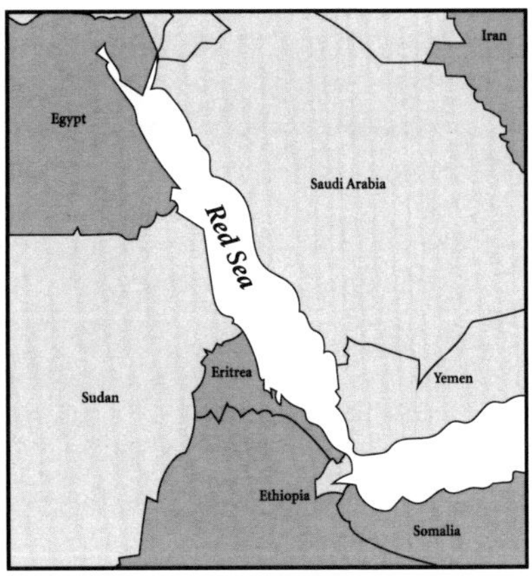

15 And it came to pass that **we did travel for the space of many days**, slaying [*killing*] food by the way, with our bows and our arrows and our stones and our slings.

16 And **we did follow the directions of the ball** [*the Liahona*],

which led us in the more fertile parts of the wilderness.

17 And after we had traveled for the space of many days, **we did pitch our tents for the space of a time** [*for a while*], that we might again rest ourselves and obtain food for our families.

Next, Nephi will break his bow. It is sad that his brethren seem anxious to blame him for all their troubles, when they themselves perhaps have not unstrung their own bows when they should have in order to preserve the spring in them so they would still work for hunting. Whatever the case, it seems to be Satan's way to find someone else to blame for one's own mistakes and sinful behavior.

18 And it came to pass that as **I, Nephi**, went forth to slay food, behold, I **did break my bow**, which was made of fine steel; and **after I did break my bow, behold, my brethren were angry with me** because of the loss of my bow, for we did obtain no food.

19 And it came to pass that we did return without food to our families, and being much fatigued [*very tired*], because of their journeying, they did suffer much for the want of food [*they were very hungry*].

20 And it came to pass that **Laman and Lemuel and the sons of Ishmael did begin to murmur exceedingly** [*complain a lot*], because of their sufferings and afflictions [*troubles*] in the wilderness; and **also my father began to murmur against the Lord his God**; yea, and they were all exceedingly sorrowful, even that **they did murmur against the Lord**.

We have almost come to expect that Laman and Lemuel along with the sons of Ishmael will start to complain and become ugly when things become difficult. But to see Lehi also "murmur against the Lord his God" catches us off guard and can be very disappointing.

However, when we recall from 1 Nephi 1:20 that one of the purposes Nephi stated for writing the things he did was to show us "the tender mercies of the Lord," then we begin to see that perhaps one of the reasons he mentioned this especially difficult time for his father was to show us the kindness of the Lord even to those who definitely know better than to murmur. It reminds us all that forgiveness is still available when we commit sins that we definitely know better than to do.

21 Now it came to pass that I, Nephi, having been afflicted with [*having been troubled along with*] my brethren because of the loss of my bow, and their bows having

lost their springs, it began to be exceedingly difficult, yea, insomuch that **we could obtain no food**.

Next, Nephi's brethren start complaining against God.

22 And it came to pass that I, Nephi, did speak much unto **my brethren**, because they had **hardened their hearts again, even unto complaining against the Lord their God**.

Instead of complaining, Nephi does something to solve their problem. He makes a bow and arrow to hunt with.

This is a good lesson for us. Instead of complaining about a problem, we should do something to solve it.

23 And it came to pass that **I, Nephi, did make out of wood a bow, and out of a straight stick, an arrow**; wherefore, I did arm myself with a bow and an arrow, with a sling and with stones. **And I said unto my father: Whither shall I go to obtain food?** [*Where shall I go to hunt animals for food for us?*]

I had an interesting experience concerning the wood bow and the wooden arrow which Nephi made as mentioned above. Some years ago, a good friend called me one evening and said, "Dave, do you know how true the Book of Mormon is?" I said, "Yes, I think I do." To which he responded, "Yes, but do you know *how* true?" I began to wonder where this was going, so I said, "Tell me. How true is it?" That was the response he had been waiting for.

He asked, "Do you know why Nephi made an arrow out of a stick to use with the wood bow he had just made? Why didn't he simply use one of the arrows he had for his steel bow, which he broke?" I replied that I hadn't ever even thought about that. He went on to say that he had become interested in target practicing with bows and arrows, and upon reading this part of the Book of Mormon again, it occurred to him that the steel bow would use relatively short arrows, but the wooden bow would bend back much farther than a steel bow, thus, the wood bow would require quite a bit longer arrows.

He concluded our conversation by expressing his testimony that Joseph Smith could not possibly have made the Book of Mormon up and that this passage about needing a new arrow for the wood bow was another testimony that Joseph Smith was a true prophet. He felt that there was no way that Joseph Smith could have even known about such things from practical experience in his day, in order to make up such a story.

I thanked my friend for sharing this information with me, and now I, too, marvel even more at the truthfulness of the Book of Mormon each time I read this account of Nephi's broken steel bow.

Another thing: Did you notice in verse 23, above, that even though his father was not perfect and had committed a serious sin by complaining against God, Nephi still honored him and went to him for advice? This is a major lesson for all of us; namely, that we should honor parents in most cases, even though they may not always live up to our hopes and expectations. The effect on Lehi when his son, Nephi, still honored him, despite his negative response to the hardships they were suffering, must have been extremely humbling, yet at the same time, encouraging.

24 And it came to pass that **he did inquire of the Lord**, for they had humbled themselves because of my words; for I did say many things unto them in the energy of my soul.

25 And it came to pass **that the voice of the Lord came unto my father**; and he was truly chastened [*scolded*] because of his murmuring against the Lord, insomuch that he was brought down into the depths of sorrow.

26 And it came to pass that **the voice of the Lord said unto him** [*Lehi*]: **Look upon the ball** [*the Liahona*], **and behold** [*see*] **the things which are written**.

27 And it came to pass that **when my father beheld the things** which were written upon the ball, **he did fear and tremble exceedingly, and also my brethren and the sons of Ishmael and our wives**.

28 And it came to pass that I, Nephi, beheld **the pointers which were in the ball**, that they **did work according to the faith and diligence and heed which we did give unto them**.

There are some strong parallels between how the Liahona worked for Lehi's family and how the Holy Ghost works for us. It has much to do with the "faith and diligence and heed" that we give to it; in other words, how much we follow what He prompts us to do.

29 And **there was also written upon them a new writing**, which was plain to be read, which did give us understanding concerning the ways of the Lord; [*The Lord is constantly striving to teach us if we will listen.*] and it was written and changed from time to time, according to the faith and diligence which we gave unto it. And thus we see that by small means the Lord can bring about great things.

There is much to learn from verse 29, above. For one thing, the value of obedience as a requirement for additional knowledge and revelation is taught. Nephi said that the things on the pointers were plain and were changed from time to time depending on his family's obedience to them.

The basic principle is this: First, we obey, with faith in God and Christ. Then we receive more light and knowledge. If we then obey that, we receive more. If we obey that, we receive yet more, and on and on until, someday, we get to the point that we "shall comprehend even God" (D&C 88:49).

Thus, in this portion of the Book of Mormon, Nephi is teaching us the power and potential of simple faith obedience.

Nephi is a good example of quickly obeying with simple faith. The instructions on the Liahona were for him to go to a certain place on top of the mountain. He did so and his obedience was rewarded. He had a successful hunt and got food for their hungry families.

30 And it came to pass that I, Nephi, did go forth up into the top of the mountain, **according to the directions which were given upon the ball.**

31 **And it came to pass that I did slay wild beasts, insomuch that I did obtain food for our families.**

32 And it came to pass that I did return to our tents, bearing the beasts which I had slain [*carrying the animals that I had killed*]; and now when they beheld that I had obtained food, how great was their joy! And it came to pass that **they did humble themselves before the Lord, and did give thanks unto him.** [*Here, again, they humble themselves, and Nephi's hopes for them are raised.*]

33 And it came to pass that we did again take our journey, traveling nearly the same course as in the beginning; and after **we had traveled for the space of many days we did pitch our tents again, that we might tarry** [*stop; stay in the same place*] for the space of a time [*for a while*].

Perhaps, by now, it makes you a bit nervous when they stop traveling and have time on their hands. Sure enough, there will be trouble, and this time things will get extremely ugly. And this time, Nephi specifically mentions the murmuring of some of the women in the group. It is sometimes said that Satan often has a rather easy time of it when it comes to getting men to turn to evil and wickedness. But as long as women remain true to gospel principles, society remains relatively stable. But when the devil succeeds in getting women to give in also to evil, watch out!

The thing that starts trouble this time is that Ishmael dies.

Remember that his was the family that Nephi and his brothers went back to Jerusalem to get to come back into the wilderness with them, in chapter 4. He was the father of their wives and of Laban's wife.

34 And it came to pass that **Ishmael died**, and was buried in the place which was called Nahom.

35 And it came to pass that **the daughters of Ishmael did mourn exceedingly, because of the loss of their father, and because of their afflictions** [*troubles*] **in the wilderness; and they did murmur against my father, because he had brought them out of the land of Jerusalem, saying: Our father is dead; yea, and we have wandered much in the wilderness, and we have suffered much affliction, hunger, thirst, and fatigue; and after all these sufferings we must perish in the wilderness with hunger.**

36 **And thus they did murmur against my father, and also against me; and they were desirous to** [*they wanted to*] **return again to Jerusalem.** [*Remember that several prophets had already prophesied that Jerusalem would be destroyed. Therefore, in expressing a desire to return to Jerusalem, they were obviously showing lack of faith and openly rebelling.*]

As you will see now, things get really bad.

37 **And Laman said unto Lemuel and also unto the sons of Ishmael: Behold, let us slay our father, and also our brother Nephi, who has taken it upon him to be our ruler and our teacher, who are his elder brethren** [*older brothers*]**.**

38 **Now, he says that the Lord has talked with him, and also that angels have ministered unto him. But behold, we know that he lies unto us; and he tells us these things, and he worketh many things by his cunning arts, that he may deceive our eyes, thinking, perhaps, that he may lead us away into some strange wilderness; and after he has led us away, he has thought to make himself a king and a ruler over us, that he may do with us according to his will and pleasure. And after this manner did my brother Laman stir** [*this is how Laman stirred*] **up their hearts to anger.**

Laman's behavior is becoming more like Satan's. He is now telling absolute lies in order to stir up the others against Lehi and Nephi. He says that Nephi is lying about having angels help him. But we, ourselves, know that both Laman and Lemuel saw the angel who told them to stop beating Nephi and Sam with a rod (1 Nephi 3:28–30).

So, sadly, Laman has been rebellious against God so often now that he has started believing his own lies! This is a real danger for any of us if we keep breaking the commandments of God and lying a lot to try to cover up and becoming more and more wicked.

Next, Laman and the others will be given yet another chance to repent and choose the right. This is another reminder to us of the wonderful patience and love of our Father in Heaven and our Savior, who have infinite love for us. You will notice that as Laman and Lemuel and those who go along with them become more hardened and insensitive, the methods of the Lord, as He tries to reach them, while still respecting their agency, necessarily become stronger and tougher.

39 And it came to pass that the Lord was with us, yea, even **the voice of the Lord came and did speak many words unto them, and did chasten** [*scold*] **them exceedingly; and after they were chastened by the voice of the Lord they did turn away their anger, and did repent of their sins, insomuch that the Lord did bless us again with food, that we did not perish.** [*They respond positively to this stronger approach by a loving God, and our hopes for them are once again raised.*]

1 NEPHI 17

In this chapter, Nephi will be asked to build a ship. Can you imagine being asked by the Lord to build a ship for you and your family to cross the ocean in? Wow! Think of the great faith it would require! Especially if you, like Nephi, had never before built such a thing.

But Nephi has great faith and has already been taught by many experiences to trust and obey the Lord completely. And so, he will do it, getting help and instructions from the Lord as needed.

As you would expect, his brothers and others will make fun of him and refuse to help. In fact, they will actually try to get rid of him by throwing him into the sea. As you read this chapter, you will see what happens to save him and make his brothers and the others help him build the ship.

1 AND it came to pass that **we did again take our journey** [*they started traveling again*] **in the wilderness; and we did travel nearly**

eastward from that time forth. [*Most Book of Mormon scholars believe that they are traveling eastward along the bottom of the Saudi Arabian Penninsula at this point.*] And we did travel and wade through much affliction [*it was a very difficult journey*] in the wilderness; and our women did bear [*have*] children in the wilderness.

We see in verse 2, next, that the Lord gave them many blessings as they went along.

2 **And so great were the blessings of the Lord upon us, that while we did live upon raw meat in the wilderness, our women did give plenty of suck for their children** [*had plenty of milk to nurse their children*], and **were strong, yea, even like unto the men; and they began to bear their journeyings without murmurings.**

3 **And thus we see that the commandments of God must be fulfilled. And if it so be that the children of men keep the commandments of God he doth nourish them, and strengthen them, and provide means whereby they can accomplish the thing which he has commanded them; wherefore, he did provide means for us while we did sojourn** [*live temporarily*] **in the wilderness.**

4 **And we did sojourn for the space of many years, yea, even eight years in the wilderness.**

Next, they finally arrive at the ocean.

5 And we did come to the land which we called Bountiful, because of its much fruit and also wild honey; and all these things were prepared of the Lord that we might not perish [*die*]. And we beheld [*saw*] the sea [*ocean*], which we called Irreantum, which, being interpreted, is many waters.

6 And it came to pass that **we did pitch our tents by the seashore; and notwithstanding** [*even though*] we had suffered many afflictions and much difficulty, yea, even so much that we cannot write them all, **we were exceedingly rejoiced** [*were very happy*] when we came to the seashore; and **we called the place Bountiful, because of its much fruit.**

We again learn much about attitude and simple obedience from Nephi here. Watch his reaction as the Lord asks him to build a ship.

7 And it came to pass that after I, Nephi, had been in the land of Bountiful for the space of many days, **the voice of the Lord came unto me, saying: Arise, and get thee into the mountain. And it**

came to pass that I arose and went up into the mountain, and cried [*prayed*] unto the Lord.

Just a quick comment about some possible symbolism in going up into a mountain to commune with the Lord. It requires effort to climb up a mountain. Similarly, it requires effort for us to live worthy of inspiration and guidance from God. Symbolically, climbing up into a mountain could also represent drawing closer to heaven, or closer to God.

8 And it came to pass that **the Lord spake unto me, saying: Thou shalt construct** [*build*] **a ship, after the manner which I shall show thee** [*according to how I show you*], that I may carry thy people across these waters [*the ocean*].

In verse 9, next, you can see that Nephi has great faith in the Lord. Instead of questioning the Lord about why He was asking him to build a ship when he had no experience in ship building, Nephi simply asks where to find materials to make tools with for building the ship.

9 And I said: Lord, **whither** [*where*] **shall I go that I may find ore** [*rock with metal in it*] **to molten** [*melt so the metal will come out of it*], **that I may make tools to construct the ship after the manner which thou hast shown unto me?**

10 And it came to pass that **the Lord told me whither I should go to find ore, that I might make tools.**

We can learn much from Nephi's reaction to the commandment to build a ship. Think of how much work it would take to make a bellows (a thing to fan the fire with) out of animal skins to blow on the fire to get it hot enough to melt ore in order to have metal with which to make tools for constructing the ship!

First, Nephi would have to go hunting. After a successful hunt, he would have to skin the animal or animals, tan the hides, cut them out, and sew the parts together to form a bellows. Then he would have to dig the ore that the Lord told him about, gather fuel, build a fire, melt the ore, and form the molten metal into tools. All this he did without one complaint. He is earning his way to heaven!

11 And it came to pass that I, Nephi, did make a bellows wherewith to blow the fire, of the skins of beasts; and after I had made a bellows, that I might have wherewith [*what I needed*] to blow the fire, I did smite [*hit*] two stones together that I might make fire.

12 For the Lord had not hitherto suffered [*had not allowed us up to now*] that we should make much fire, as we journeyed in the wilderness;

for he said: I will make thy food become sweet, that ye cook it not;

13 And I will also be your light in the wilderness; and I will prepare the way before you, if it so be that ye shall keep my commandments; wherefore, inasmuch as [*if*] ye shall keep my commandments ye shall be led towards the promised land [*America*]; and ye shall know that it is by me that ye are led.

14 Yea, and the Lord said also that: After ye have arrived in the promised land, **ye shall know that I, the Lord, am God; and that I, the Lord, did deliver you from destruction; yea, that I did bring you out of the land of Jerusalem.**

There is much symbolic teaching in verse 14, above. Right now, as we journey through our mortal lives, we do much on faith. But when we actually arrive in heaven (the "promised land") we will then know positively that the Lord is God, that He exists, and we will become aware of the many times He helped us in our lives while here on earth. We will know that He delivered us from spiritual destruction and bondage through the Atonement of Christ. We will know that He brought us out of the world and worldliness and into heaven.

15 Wherefore [*and so*], I, Nephi, did strive [*try*] to keep the commandments of the Lord, and I did exhort [*strongly encourage*] my brethren to faithfulness and diligence.

16 And it came to pass that **I did make tools of the ore which I did molten** [*melt*] out of the rock [*ore*].

Sadly, in the next verses we will be shown some of the ways Satan discourages the righteous. (Imagine what Noah and Nephi would have to say to each other as they chatted about how they were mocked when they set out to build their ships!)

17 And **when my brethren saw that I was about to build a ship, they began to murmur** [*complain*] against me, saying: **Our brother is a fool, for he thinketh that he can build a ship; yea, and he also thinketh that he can cross these great waters** [*the ocean*].

18 And thus my brethren **did complain against me, and were desirous that they might not labor** [*they didn't want to help build the ship*], for they **did not believe that I could build a ship; neither would they believe that I was instructed of the Lord.**

The attitude of Nephi's brethren caused Nephi much sadness. And, as is usually the case with others who make fun of the righteous, they took great pleasure in the sorrow they were causing him.

19 And now it came to pass that I, Nephi, was exceedingly sorrowful [*very sad*] because of the hardness of their hearts; and now **when they saw that I began to be sorrowful they were glad in their hearts, insomuch that they did rejoice over me, saying: We knew that ye could not construct a ship, for we knew that ye were lacking in judgment** [*you were being foolish*]; wherefore, thou canst not accomplish so great a work.

Satan's way is to blame others for our own shortcomings and mistakes. Next, Laman and Lemuel and the others try to lay the guilt for all their troubles on Lehi. They seem to have very quickly forgotten that when they themselves were faithful and obedient, they were blessed abundantly, even to the point that their women and children prospered and life was very good (see verse 2, above).

20 And **thou art like unto our father, led away by the foolish imaginations** [*foolish ideas*] **of his heart; yea, he hath led us out of the land of Jerusalem, and we have wandered in the wilderness for these many years; and our women have toiled, being big with child; and they have borne children in the wilderness and suffered all things, save it were** [*except*] **death; and it would have been better that they had died before they came out of Jerusalem than to have suffered these afflictions** [*troubles*].

21 Behold, these many years we have suffered in the wilderness, **which time we might have enjoyed our possessions and the land of our inheritance** [*all our money and stuff in Jerusalem*]; yea, **and we might have been happy.**

It is somewhat shocking to see how far off the path these rebellious men have gone and how quickly they gone back to their old spiritual blindness and unrealistic thought. In fact, you may have already noticed that they have not only gone back in their thinking to their old wicked ways, but they have sunk to new lows in lack of reason and lack of awareness of things as they really are. It is once again strongly evident that wickedness does not promote rational thought—in other words, clear thinking!

In the next verse, they think back on Jerusalem and praise its inhabitants as righteous, God-fearing citizens and keepers of the commandments given by the Lord through Moses (remember that they were actually very wicked and ready for destruction). Nephi now teaches us a lesson in how quickly Satan can warp and corrupt the senses and sensibilities of willing students of wickedness. In a sad and rather startling way, Laman, Lemuel, and the others bear testimony that wickedness is actually righteousness. It looks like they have begun to believe their own lies.

Watch what Laman and Lemuel say next about the wicked people back in Jerusalem, many of whom were obviously their friends.

22 And **we know that the people who were in the land of Jerusalem were a righteous people; for they kept the statutes** [*laws*] **and judgments** [*rules*] **of the Lord, and all his commandments, according to the law of Moses; wherefore, we know that they are a righteous people; and our father hath judged them, and hath led us away because we would hearken** [*listen*] unto his words; yea, and **our brother is like unto him. And after this manner** [*type*] of language did my brethren murmur and complain against us.

Next, Nephi will skillfully teach his wayward and rebellious brethren, using scriptures familiar to them. And when he has finished, the Lord will add His testimony in ways that they cannot possibly miss. And once again, they will humble themselves and then they will immediately begin helping Nephi build the ship.

There is a major message here and elsewhere in the Book of Mormon, being repeated over and over. It is this: The Lord loves us. He loves to bless us. He even loves people who are being wicked! And He gives them chance after chance after chance. Even when they rebel and reject Him and His messengers, He gives them additional opportunities to repent and return to Him.

So, now we will watch and learn as Nephi asks several questions and teaches his spiritually needy brethren from the scriptures. He will emphasize past blessings from the Lord and the importance of using those blessings as a basis for being loyal to the Lord now. There is much symbolism in the literal events Nephi uses to teach his people. We will point some of that out as we go along.

23 And it came to pass that **I, Nephi, spake** [*spoke*] **unto them, saying: Do ye believe that our fathers** [*ancestors*], who were the children of Israel, would have been led away out of the hands of the Egyptians if they had not hearkened unto the words of the Lord? [*Symbolism: Do you think we would be rescued from the bondage of sin if we did not listen to the Lord?*]

24 Yea, **do ye suppose that they would have been led out of bondage, if the Lord had not commanded Moses that he should lead them out of bondage?** [*Symbolism: Do you think we would be led out from being slaves to sin if we refuse to listen to our current prophets?*]

25 Now **ye know that the children of Israel were in bondage** [*were slaves in Egypt*]; and **ye know that they were laden** [*burdened*] with tasks, which were grievous to be borne [*very difficult to carry*]; wherefore, **ye know that it must needs be a good thing for them, that they should be brought out of bondage.** [*Symbolism: You know that sin is a terrible task master or slave driver. You know that sin places heavy burdens upon you. So, you know that it is very good to be rescued from sin by the Lord.*]

26 Now **ye know that Moses was commanded of the Lord to do that great work; and ye know that by his word** [*at his command*] the waters of the Red Sea were divided hither and thither [*from one side to the other*], and they passed through on dry ground. [*Symbolism: Our prophets are guided and directed by the Lord, so if we follow them faithfully, we can get through our difficulties and escape the forces of evil also.*]

27 But **ye know that the Egyptians were drowned in the Red Sea, who were the armies of Pharaoh.** [*Symbolism: The day will come when the wicked who fight against the work of the Lord, who refuse to repent, will be destroyed.*]

28 And **ye also know that they were fed with manna** [*a special type of food*] in the wilderness. [*Symbolism: The Lord sustains and helps His people with blessings from above.*]

29 Yea, and **ye also know that Moses, by his word according to the power of God which was in him, smote** [*hit*] the rock, and there came forth water, that the children of Israel might quench their thirst. [*Symbolism: Our thirst for the things of God is quenched by the "living water," which comes from Christ and His Atonement; see John 4:10, 14.*]

30 And notwithstanding they being [*even though they were*] led, the Lord their God, their Redeemer, going before them, leading them by day and giving light unto them by night, and doing all things for them which were expedient [*necessary*] for man to receive, **they hardened their hearts and blinded their minds, and reviled** [*rebelled*] **against Moses and against the true and living God.** [*Symbolism: Even though God does everything possible

to bless His children, some of them still rebel against Him.]

Verse 30, above, especially applies to Laman and Lemuel and the others in their rebellion. It is a strong hint from Nephi that they are being just like the foolish children of Israel who, in the face of such obvious help and witnesses from God, still rebelled against their prophet leader as well as God.

Next, Nephi emphasizes that God always keeps His promises.

31 And it came to pass that according to his word [*promise*] he did destroy them; and according to his word he did lead them; and according to his word he did do all things for them; and **there was not any thing done save it were by his word** [*according to his promises to them*].

32 And after they had crossed the river Jordan **he did make them mighty unto the driving out of the children** [*inhabitants*] of the land, yea, unto the scattering them to destruction.

Symbolism: One can find much symbolism in the crossing of the Jordan River into the promised land. For instance, we must pass through the "water" (baptism) to gain entrance into the "promised land" (the celestial kingdom). Priesthood holders (the priests who carried the ark of the covenant; see Joshua 3:6) enabled the children of Israel to pass through the water (priesthood holders baptize us). Through the help of God, we can drive all "enemies" such as sin, bad habits, etc., out of our lives.

Nephi asks yet more questions as he tries to get his rebellious brethren to repent and keep the commandment of the Lord and help him build the ship.

33 And now, **do ye suppose that the children of this land** [*the inhabitants of Palestine—Canaan—when Joshua led the children of Israel accros the Jordan River into it*], who were in the land of promise, who were driven out by our fathers [*ancestors*], **do ye suppose that they were righteous? Behold, I say unto you, Nay** [*no*].

34 **Do ye suppose that our fathers** [*ancestors*] would have been more choice than they if they had been righteous? I say unto you, Nay. [*Symbolism: It is true that righteousness puts all people, regardless of race or other factors, on an equal footing with God as far as eternal blessings are concerned.*]

35 Behold, **the Lord esteemeth all flesh in one; he that is righteous is favored of God. But behold, this people had rejected every word of God, and they were ripe in iniquity** [*completely wicked*]; and the fulness of the

wrath [*anger*] of God was upon them; and the Lord did curse the land against them, and bless it unto our fathers [*ancestors*]; yea, he did curse it against them unto their destruction, and he did bless it unto our fathers unto their obtaining power over it.

36 Behold, **the Lord hath created the earth that it should be inhabited; and he hath created his children that they should possess it.** [*Message: The purpose of this earth is to be a place where God's children can grow and develop, not to be a place where they come to be destroyed. Hint to Laman and Lemuel: If you get yourselves destroyed because of wickedness, you are wasting the purposes for being sent to earth.*]

37 And **he raiseth up a righteous nation, and destroyeth the nations of the wicked.**

38 And **he leadeth away the righteous into precious lands, and the wicked he destroyeth, and curseth the land unto them for their sakes.** [*Message: God manages things here on earth depending on how people use their agency.*]

39 **He ruleth high in the heavens, for it is his throne, and this earth is his footstool.** [*Symbolism: We are all under God. He has power over all things—including shipbuilding . . . hint, hint.*]

40 And **he loveth those who will have him to be their God. Behold, he loved our fathers, and he covenanted with them, yea, even Abraham, Isaac, and Jacob; and he remembered** [*kept*] the covenants which he had made; wherefore [*that's why*], he did bring them out of the land of Egypt.

The word "loveth," as used in the context of verse 40, above, as well as numerous other scripture references, means, in effect, "is able to bless."

41 And **he did straiten** [*discipline; punish*] them in the wilderness with his rod [*power*]; for they hardened their hearts [*rebelled against Him; refused to keep His commandments*], even as ye have; and the Lord straitened them [*disciplined, punished them*] because of their iniquity [*wickedness*]. He sent fiery flying serpents among them; and after they were bitten he prepared a way that they might be healed; and the labor which they had to perform was to look [*all they had to do was look at the brass serpent Moses made—see Numbers 21:8–9, in the Bible*]; and because of the simpleness of the way, or the easiness of it, there were many who perished. [*Symbolism: The gospel way of life is actually the simplest way. Many consider it to be too simplistic or even simple-minded to believe in God and the Atonement of Christ,*

personal accountability, life after death, etc. Therefore, they refuse the gospel in their lives.]

42 And **they did harden their hearts** from time to time, and **they did revile** against [*criticize; rebel against*] Moses, and also against God; nevertheless, ye know that they were led forth by his matchless power into the land of promise [*what is now basically the country of Israel*].

43 And **now, after all these things, the time has come that they** [*the Jews, meaning the descendants of the children of Israel who dwell in the Jerusalem area at the time of Lehi*] **have become wicked**, yea, nearly unto ripeness [*about ready for destruction*]; and I know not but they are at this day about to be destroyed; for I know that the day must surely come that they must be destroyed, save [*except for*] a few only, who shall be led away into captivity.

44 Wherefore [*this is the reason that*], **the Lord commanded my father** that he should depart into the wilderness; and the Jews also sought [*tried*] to take away his life; yea, **and ye** also **have sought to take away his life**; wherefore, **ye are murderers in your hearts** and ye are like unto them [*the Jews*].

This is strong language and helps explain why Nephi's rebellious brothers and the rebellious others are so insensitive to the Spirit. We are now coming to one of the more famous verses in the Book of Mormon, verse 45. It clearly explains that they have had marvelous manifestations from the Lord which should have strengthened their testimonies and made them firm in the gospel. It explains what is wrong with them now, and it tells why the Lord has to use extreme methods in order to try to save some of His wayward children here on earth.

Next, you will see some of Nephi's words and phrases that seem to indicate that Laman, Lemuel, and the sons of Ishmael are becoming more and more accountable before the Lord for their rebellious behavior.

45 **Ye are swift to do iniquity but slow to remember the Lord** your God. **Ye have seen an angel**, and **he spake unto you**; yea, **ye have heard his voice from time to time**; and **he hath spoken unto you in a still small voice**, **but ye were past feeling, that ye could not feel his words; wherefore, he has spoken unto you like unto the voice of thunder, which did cause the earth to shake as if it were to divide asunder** [*open right up*].

46 And **ye also know that by the power of his almighty word he**

can cause the earth that it shall pass away; yea, and ye know that by his word he can cause the rough places to be made smooth, and smooth places shall be broken up. O, then, why is it, that ye can be so hard in your hearts?

47 **Behold, my soul is rent** [*torn*] with anguish [*worry and pain*] because of you, and my heart is pained; **I fear lest ye shall be cast off forever** [*I am afraid you are going to end up in hell*]. Behold, I am full of the Spirit of God, insomuch that my frame [*body*] has no strength.

Perhaps you've noticed that when the Spirit of the Lord is upon you, you have strong feelings of compassion and love for others. Thus, we understand somewhat why Nephi can care so strongly for his brethren, verse 47, above, in spite of such hateful treatment of him by them.

Watch what they try to do to him now.

48 And now it came to pass that **when I had spoken these words they were angry with me, and were desirous to throw me into the depths of the sea; and as they came forth to lay their hands upon me** [*to grab me*] I spake unto them, saying: In the name of the Almighty God, I command you that ye **touch me not, for I am filled with the power of God, even unto the consuming of my flesh; and whoso shall lay his hands upon me shall wither** [*shrivel up*] **even as a dried reed; and he shall be as naught** [*nothing*] before the power of God, **for God shall smite him.**

49 **And it came to pass that I, Nephi, said unto them that they should murmur no more against their father; neither should they withhold their labor from** [*refuse to help*] **me, for God had commanded me that I should build a ship.**

50 **And I said unto them: If God had commanded me to do all things I could do them. If he should command me that I should say unto this water, be thou earth, it should be** [*would be*] earth; and if I should say it, it would be done.

51 And now, **if the Lord has such great power, and has wrought** [*done*] so many miracles among the children of men, **how is it that he cannot instruct me, that I should build a ship?**

52 **And it came to pass that I, Nephi, said many things unto my brethren, insomuch that they were confounded** [*stopped*] and

could not contend [*fight*] against me; **neither durst they** [*they didn't dare*] **lay their hands upon me nor touch me with their fingers, even for the space of many days. Now they durst not do this lest they should wither before me, so powerful was the Spirit of God; and thus it had wrought** [*worked*] **upon them.**

The gentle approach of the "still small voice" could not humble them. But the threat of physical destruction did. In many ways, such is the case in our day (see D&C 88:88–90). We understand this to be the root cause of so many natural disasters and upheavals in nature in the last days. It is a final attempt by the Lord to people's attention so that they can repent. Otherwise, they will be destroyed by the final wars, etc., or at the actual Second Coming.

Next, we see yet another opportunity given by a loving God for these rebellious ones to repent. While some may look at it as rather harsh, in reality, it is a wonderful kindness.

Imagine how these rebellious men felt when they saw Nephi lift his arm up and point his hand at them.

53 And it came to pass that the Lord said unto me: **Stretch forth thine hand again unto thy brethren, and they shall not wither before thee, but I will shock them, saith the Lord, and this will I do, that they may know that I am the Lord their God.**

54 And it came to pass that **I stretched forth my hand unto my brethren, and they did not wither before me; but the Lord did shake them, even according to the word which he had spoken.**

55 And **now, they said: We know of a surety** [*for sure*] that the Lord is with thee, for **we know that it is the power of the Lord that has shaken us. And they fell down before me, and were about to worship me, but I would not suffer them** [*would not allow them to do so*], saying: I am thy brother, yea, even thy younger brother; wherefore, worship the Lord thy God, **and honor thy father and thy mother, that thy days may be long in the land which the Lord thy God shall give thee.**

Did you notice that Nephi just quoted one of the Ten Commandments to his brethren? It is the fifth commandment. You can read it in the Bible in Exodus 21:12.

1 NEPHI 18

You will notice that the work of building the ship now progresses rapidly, because they are working peacefully with each other and as directed by the Lord as He communicates with Nephi from time to time. They are all busy, and things go well. There is perhaps some interesting and important symbolism, even in the construction of the ship. Notice that their goal is to cross the waters to get to the promised land. Again, water can symbolize baptism, and the promised land can symbolize heaven. The ship can symbolize the help of God to get us back to heaven. Without His help, we cannot make it. The fact that this ship is not "after the manner of men" (verse 2), could symbolize that we can't get to heaven by living the common lifestyle of the "natural man" (Mosiah 3:19). Finally, the fact that Nephi "did pray oft" (verse 3) can remind us of the need for constant prayer and communication with God throughout our lives.

In verse one, notice that they are worshipping the Lord now, which means the rebellious brethren have repented again, at least for a while.

1 AND it came to pass that **they did worship the Lord, and did go forth with me; and we did work timbers of curious workmanship** [*usually means "skillful" or "fine" quality work*]. And **the Lord did show me from time to time after what manner** [*how*] I should work [*make*] the timbers of the ship.

2 Now **I, Nephi, did not work the timbers after the manner which was learned by men** [*I did not form the ship's timbers like men would usually make them*], neither did I build the ship **after the manner of men** [*like other men build ships*]; but I did build it after the manner which the Lord had shown unto me; wherefore, it was not after the manner of men.

3 And **I, Nephi, did go into the mount oft, and I did pray oft unto the Lord; wherefore** [*therefore*] the Lord showed unto me great things. [*Symbolism: When we communicate with the Lord, we are shown great things of the gospel and eternal life, by the Holy Ghost.*]

4 And it came to pass that after I had finished the ship, according to the word of the Lord, my brethren beheld [*saw*] that it was good, and that the workmanship [*quality of work*] thereof was exceedingly fine; wherefore, **they did humble themselves again before the Lord.**

5 And it came to pass that **the voice of the Lord came unto my father, that we should arise and go down into the ship.**

6 **And it came to pass that** on the morrow [*the next day*], **after we had prepared all things, much fruits and meat from the wilderness, and honey in abundance, and provisions according to that which the Lord had commanded us, we did go down into the ship, with all our loading and our seeds, and whatsoever thing we had brought with us, every one according to his age; wherefore, we did all go down into the ship, with our wives and our children.**

Next, Nephi tells us more about his parents' family. In addition to these two more sons, we are told also that Lehi and Sariah had daughters (see 2 Nephi 5:6).

7 And now, my father had begat [*fathered*] two sons in the wilderness [*during the eight years in the wilderness*]; the elder was called **Jacob and the younger Joseph.**

8 **And it came to pass after we had all gone down into the ship, and had taken with us our provisions and things which had been commanded us, we did put forth into the sea** [*we launched the ship*] and were driven forth before the wind towards the promised land. [*Perhaps "wind" in this verse could symbolize the help of the Lord. You can't see it, but you can feel it. And if you use your agency to steer your life in the direction the wind is gently blowing you, you will end up in the "promised land," symbolic of heaven.*]

Perhaps you are already getting a little bit worried because, while they are aboard the ship, they have spare time on their hands. Perhaps one of our most difficult tests in this life is what we do with spare time.

9 And after we had been driven forth before the wind for the space of many days, behold, my brethren and the sons of Ishmael and also their wives began to make themselves merry [*we assume that the word "merry," as used here, means forgetting the Lord and being "noisy, crude, and inappropriate"*], insomuch that **they began to dance, and to sing, and to speak with much rudeness, yea, even that they did forget by what power they had been brought thither** [*they forgot about God*]; yea, they were lifted up unto exceeding rudeness. [*"Rudeness" and its accompanying crudeness are offensive to the Spirit. Unfortunately, our society and, in fact, the whole world have become and are continuing to become ruder and cruder in the last days. We would do well to avoid such behaviors, which often lead to committing serious sins.*]

The singing and dancing mentioned in verse 9, above, had to be inappropriate singing and dancing of some sort, since the Lord obviously approves of appropriate music and dancing. In D&C 136:28, He said: "If thou art merry, praise the Lord with singing, with music, with dancing, and with a prayer of praise and thanksgiving."

Next, we see Nephi become very worried about their rude and offensive behavior.

10 And **I, Nephi, began to fear exceedingly lest the Lord should be angry with us, and smite us because of our iniquity** [*wickedness*], that we should be swallowed up in the depths of the sea; wherefore, **I, Nephi, began to speak to them with much soberness** [*very seriously*]; **but behold they were angry with me, saying: We will not** [*we don't want*] that our younger brother shall be a ruler over us.

11 And it came to pass that **Laman and Lemuel did take me and bind me** [*tie me up*] with cords, and they did treat me with much harshness; **nevertheless, the Lord did suffer it** [*allow it*] that he might show forth his power, unto the fulfilling of his word which he had spoken concerning the wicked.

Verse 11, above, is a very important explanation of some of the suffering which the righteous suffer at the hands of the wicked. Although the righteous often suffer much because of the evil acts of the wicked, they will be fine in eternity, which is what ultimately counts; whereas, the wicked will not "be fine" in the eternities, unless they repent. If the Lord were to stop every cruel act performed against righteous people, soon there would be no real agency, and mortal life as a testing ground would no longer work.

12 And it came to pass that after they had bound me insomuch that I could not move, **the compass** [*the Liahona*], which had been prepared of the Lord, **did cease to work** [*stopped working*].

We find out with these verses that they have been steering the ship and depending on the Liahona for instructions as to what direction to steer it. This can be a reminder that even though we get lots of help from the Lord, He expects us to do our share of the work.

Next, you can see that they are in real trouble now!

13 Wherefore [*because of their wickedness in getting mad at Nephi and tying him up so it really hurt him*], **they knew not whither they should steer the ship, insomuch that there arose a great storm, yea, a great and terrible tempest, and we were driven back upon the waters for the space of three days** [*symbolic of the fact that when we cease to follow the*

Spirit, we lose progress]; and **they began to be frightened exceedingly lest they should be drowned in the sea; nevertheless they did not loose me** [*they still didn't untie my ropes*].

14 And on the fourth day, which we had been driven back, the tempest [*storm*] began to be exceedingly sore [*very bad*].

15 And it came to pass that **we were about to be swallowed up in the depths of the sea** [*the ship was about to sink*]. And after we had been driven back upon the waters for the space of four days, **my brethren began to see that the judgments** [*punishments*] **of God were upon them, and that they must perish** [*they would die*] save that they should [*unless they would*] repent of their iniquities; wherefore, **they came unto me, and loosed the bands** [*untied the ropes*] which were upon my wrists, and behold they had swollen exceedingly; and also mine ankles were much swollen, and great was the soreness thereof [*my wrists and ankles hurt really bad*].

Nephi is a great example of what seeing the big picture of what life is all about and closeness to the Lord can do for a person under extreme trial and tribulation. Such sufferings and hardships are but a "moment in eternity"; yet while going through them, they are "an eternal moment." But with the help of the Lord, they can be "endured well" (D&C 121:8).

Next, Nephi gives clear advise to us about how to endure our troubles well.

16 Nevertheless, **I did look unto my God, and I did praise him all the day long; and I did not murmur** [*complain*] **against the Lord because of mine afflictions** [*troubles*].

Next, we see that Lehi had tried to tell Laman and Lemuel and the sons of Ishmael to stop being rebellious and hurting Nephi, but they threatened him and any others who tried to defend Nephi.

17 **Now my father, Lehi, had said many things unto them, and also unto the sons of Ishmael; but, behold, they did breathe out much threatenings against anyone that should speak for me; and my parents being stricken in years** [*having gotten old*], and having suffered much grief because of their children, they were brought down, yea, even upon their sickbeds. [*The behavior of Laman and Lemuel and the sons of Ishmael almost killed Lehi and Sariah.*]

18 **Because of their grief and much sorrow, and the iniquity** [*wickedness*] **of my brethren, they were brought near even to be carried out of this time to meet**

their God [*the wickedness of Laman and Lemual and the others almost killed Lehi and Sariah*]; yea, their grey hairs were about to be brought down to lie low in the dust; yea, even they were near to be cast with sorrow into a watery grave.

19 **And Jacob and Joseph also, being young** [*neither could have been more than eight years of age*], having need of much nourishment, were grieved [*made very sad*] because of the afflictions of their mother; and **also my wife with her tears and prayers, and also my children** [*Nephi now has his own family*], did not soften the hearts of my brethren that they would loose [*untie*] me.

20 And **there was nothing save it were** [*except*] **the power of God, which threatened them with destruction, could soften their hearts; wherefore, when they saw that they were about to be swallowed up in the depths of the sea they repented of the thing which they had done, insomuch that they loosed** [*untied*] **me.**

Once again, Laman and Lemuel and their rebellious in-laws repented, but only when their own lives were threatened. They seem to be continuing on a downward spiral. Every time they rebel against an earlier "testimony-building experience," it seems to require a more powerful and more personally threatening experience to bring them to their senses. Even in the raging tempest, the love of God was manifest to them, because it was given them to invite them to repent and have a happy, pleasant eternity.

Next, they untie Nephi and he takes over steering the ship according to the directions of the Liahona, which is now working again.

21 And it came to pass after they had loosed me, behold, **I took the compass, and it did work whither I desired it. And it came to pass that I prayed unto the Lord; and after I had prayed the winds did cease, and the storm did cease, and there was a great calm.** [*Symbolic of what happens in our lives when we turn away from evil and return to God.*]

22 And it came to pass that **I, Nephi, did guide the ship, that we sailed again towards the promised land.**

23 **And it came to pass that after we had sailed for the space of many days we did arrive at the promised land** [*America*]; and we went forth upon the land, and did pitch our tents; and we did call it the promised land.

24 And it came to pass that we did begin to till the earth, and **we began to plant seeds; yea, we did put all our seeds into the earth, which we had brought from the land of Jerusalem. And it came to pass that they did grow exceedingly** [*very well*]; wherefore, we were blessed in abundance.

25 And it came to pass that we did find upon the land of promise, as we journeyed in the wilderness, that **there were beasts** [*animals*] **in the forests of every kind, both the cow and the ox, and the ass and the horse, and the goat and the wild goat, and all manner of wild animals, which were for the use of men. And we did find all manner of ore, both of gold, and of silver, and of copper.**

Critics of Joseph Smith and the Book of Mormon have ridiculed the idea that there were horses in the New World. However, solid evidence has since surfaced that horses were indeed in America before Columbus arrived.

The following quote from page 19 of the 1996 *Book of Mormon Student Manual*, used at BYU and in the Institutes of Religion, eliminates the criticism. It reads as follows: "If Joseph Smith had been writing the Book of Mormon instead of translating it from ancient records, he would have been very foolish to have included references to horses on the American continent in Book of Mormon times (1 Nephi 18:25; Enos 21). In 1830, nearly all the historians and scholars were convinced there had been no horses on the American continent before the coming of Columbus. After the Book of Mormon was published, however, archaeological discoveries were made that clearly indicate that horses were in the Americas before Columbus arrived. In the asphalt deposits of Rancho LaBrea in southern California, numerous fossil remains of horses have been found that antedate (predate) Book of Mormon times. Although these discoveries do not absolutely prove horses were in the Americas in the time period covered by the Book of Mormon (about 2600 BC to AD 421), they do prove horses were there before Columbus" (Ludlow, *A Companion to Your Study of the Book of Mormon*, p. 117).

1 NEPHI 19

Nephi will pause here and explain again that he has been commanded to make two sets of records, or plates. As explained in 1 Nephi, chapters 6 and 9, these two sets are referred to as the large plates of Nephi and the small plates of Nephi.

Also, among many other things in this chapter, he will explain why the words of Isaiah are so important and valuable.

1 AND it came to pass that the Lord commanded me, wherefore **I did make plates of ore** [*the large plates of Nephi*] that I might engraven [*write with an engraving tool on thin metal plates*] upon them the record [*history*] of my people. And upon the plates which I made [*the large plates*] I did engraven the record of my father, and also our journeyings in the wilderness, and the prophecies of my father; and also many of mine own prophecies have I engraven upon them.

2 And I knew not at the time when I made them [*the large plates*] that I should be commanded of the Lord to make these plates [*the small plates of Nephi*]; wherefore, the record of my father, and the genealogy of his fathers, and the more part of [*the majority of*] all our proceedings [*what we did*] in the wilderness are engraven upon those first plates [*the large plates*] of which I have spoken; wherefore, the things which transpired [*happened*] before I made these plates [*the small plates*] are, of a truth [*in fact*], more particularly made mention upon [*spoken of with more details in*] the first plates [*the large plates*].

Next, Nephi tells us what kinds of things he was to include on the small plates.

3 And after I had made these plates [*the small plates*] by way of commandment, I, Nephi, received a commandment that **the ministry and the prophecies, the more plain and precious parts of them, should be written upon these plates** [*the small plates*]; and that **the things which were written should be kept for the instruction of my people**, who should possess the land, and **also for other wise purposes** [*including replacing the lost 116 pages of translation previously referred to*], which purposes are known unto the Lord.

4 Wherefore [*this is why*], **I, Nephi, did make a record upon the other plates** [*the large plates*], which gives an account, or which gives **a greater account** [*a more complete account*] **of the wars and contentions and destructions of my people**. And this have I done, and commanded my people what they should do after I was gone; and that these plates [*the small plates*] should be handed down from one generation to another, or from one prophet to another, until further commandments of the Lord.

5 And an account of my making these plates [*the story of how I made the small plates*] shall be given hereafter [*later, in 2 Nephi 5:28–33*]; and then, behold, I proceed according to

that which I have spoken; and this I do that **the more sacred things may be kept** [*on the small plates*] for the knowledge of my people.

6 Nevertheless, I do not write anything upon plates save [*unless*] it be that I think it be sacred. And now, if I do err, even did they err of old; not that I would excuse myself because of other men, but because of the weakness which is in me, according to the flesh, I would excuse myself.

7 For the things which some men esteem to be of great worth, both to the body and soul, others set at naught [*toss aside, ignore*] and trample under their feet. Yea, even the very God of Israel [*Christ; see verse 8*] do men trample under their feet [*walk all over Him*]; I say, trample under their feet but I would speak in other words [*let me say it another way*]—they set him at naught [*ignore Him*], and hearken not to the voice of his counsels [*ignore what He says*].

In verse 7, above, we get a rather strong definition of what it means to ignore the teachings and counsels of the Savior. When we do this, we are, in effect, "walking" on Him!

Next, Nephi gives us some calendar information for when Lehi and his family left Jerusalem.

8 And behold **he** [*Christ*] **cometh**, according to the words of the angel, **in six hundred years from the time my father left Jerusalem**. [*This is how we calculate that Lehi left Jerusalem about 600 BC.*]

9 And the world, because of their iniquity [*wickedness*], shall judge him [*Christ*] to be a thing of naught [*a person of no value*]; wherefore they scourge [*whip*] him [*Matthew 27:26*], and he suffereth [*allows*] it; and they smite [*hit*] him [*Matthew 27:30; Luke 22:63–64*], and he suffereth it. Yea, they spit upon him [*Matthew 27:30*], and he suffereth it, because of his loving kindness and his long-suffering [*patience*] towards the children of men.

In verse 10, next, we have one of the clearest explanations ever given in scripture of the fact that Jesus Christ is the God of the Old Testament.

10 And **the God of our fathers** [*ancestors*], who were led out of Egypt, out of bondage, and also were preserved in the wilderness by him, yea, **the God of Abraham, and of Isaac, and the God of Jacob**, **yieldeth himself** [*surrenders Himself*], according to the words of the angel, as a man, **into the hands of wicked men**, **to be lifted up** [*on the cross*], according to the words of Zenock, and

to be **crucified**, according to the words of Neum, and to be **buried in a sepulchre** [*tomb*], according to the words of Zenos, which he spake concerning the three days of darkness [*at the time of the Savior's Crucifixion*], which should be a sign given of his death unto those who should inhabit the isles of the sea, more especially given unto those who are of the house of Israel.

You probably noticed three prophets spoken of in verse 10, whose names are not mentioned anywhere else other than the Book of Mormon. They are Zenock, Neum, and Zenos. They were apparently Old Testament prophets, whose writings have been left out of or lost from the Bible. This is one way we know that the Bible does not have all of the words of God; in other words, all of the scriptures. For example, God has given us other scriptures, such as the Book of Mormon, the Doctrine and Covenants, and the Pearl of Great Price.

Next, Nephi quotes one of the prophets (possibly Zenos, but we don't know for sure) as he prophesies about the conditions on the American continent at the time of the Savior's Crucifixion and Resurrection. Notice that, according to the prophecy, the more righteous in America at the time of the Savior's Crucifixion and Resurrection will hear the Savior personally, but the others will meet with destruction because of their wickedness.

11 For thus spake the prophet: **The Lord God surely shall visit all the house of Israel at that day, some with his voice, because of their righteousness, unto their great joy and salvation**, **and others with the thunderings and the lightnings of his power, by tempest, by fire, and by smoke, and vapor of darkness, and by the opening of the earth, and by mountains which shall be carried up**.

12 And all these things must surely come, saith the prophet Zenos. And **the rocks of the earth must rend** [*will be torn apart*]; and because of the groanings of the earth, many of the kings of the isles of the sea shall be wrought upon [*influenced*] by the Spirit of God, to exclaim: The God of nature suffers.

The prophecy continues and tells us what will happen to the Jews, after they crucify Christ.

13 And as for those who are at Jerusalem, saith the prophet, **they shall be scourged** [*beaten; badly treated*] **by all people, because they crucify the God of Israel** [*Christ*], **and turn their hearts aside** [*shut their hearts to Him*], **rejecting signs and wonders** [*including*

the miracles performed by the Savior], **and the power and glory of the God of Israel.**

14 And **because they turn their hearts aside** [*because they refuse to believe in Christ and His gospel*], saith the prophet, **and have despised the Holy One of Israel** [*Christ*], **they shall wander in the flesh** [*they will wander here and there on the earth*], **and perish** [*die*], **and become a hiss and a byword** [*and become a cuss word; become looked down upon*], **and be hated among all nations.**

Next, we see that the day will come, according to this prophecy, that the Jews will come unto Christ and receive the blessings promised to the righteous.

15 Nevertheless, **when** that day cometh, saith the prophet, that **they no more turn aside their hearts against the Holy One of Israel** [*when they repent and come unto Christ*], then will he remember [*be able to keep*] the covenants which he made to their fathers [*ancestors*].

Here, Nephi is teaching us about the gathering of Israel when the gospel is restored in the last days. The gospel will go to all the earth in the last days, meaning the day we live in. No doubt you have heard our prophets today speak often of the gathering of Israel. All members of the Church are invited and asked to help bring people to Christ.

16 Yea, then will he remember [*bring His gospel and its covenants to*] the isles of the sea [*the other lands and continents of the earth, including the Americas*]; yea, and **all the people who are of the house of Israel, will I gather in**, saith the Lord, according to the words of the prophet Zenos, from the four quarters of the earth [*from all the earth*].

17 Yea, and all the earth [*all people*] shall see the salvation of the Lord, saith the prophet; every nation, kindred, tongue and people shall be blessed.

It is important to keep in mind, as we speak of the gathering of Israel in the last days, that we must all be "gathered" spiritually. In other words, while there are many physical "gatherings" to various lands, such as the Jews being gathered back to the Holy Land, all who desire salvation in celestial exaltation must allow themselves to be "gathered" to the Savior and ultimately to Heavenly Father.

By faithfully attending church, saying your prayers, reading the scriptures, serving others, being a good example to your friends, and so forth, you are making sure that you, yourself, are being "gathered" with the rest of covenant Israel.

18 And **I, Nephi, have written these things unto my people, that perhaps I might persuade them that they would remember the Lord their Redeemer.**

19 **Wherefore** [*this is the reason*], I speak unto all the house of Israel, if it so be that they should obtain these things [*my writings; the scriptures*].

Next, Nephi tells us that he worrys a lot about the people back in Jerusalem. You can tell that he is a righteous man. Otherwise, he would not even worry about them because of how they treated his father and the family. In fact, he would probably be glad that they were being destroyed by enemy armies.

One way you can tell if you have the Holy Ghost with you is that you tend to love all people like the Savior loves all people.

20 For behold, **I have workings in the spirit** [*I have great cause for concern in my mind and soul*], which doth weary me even that all my joints are weak, **for those who are at Jerusalem; for had not the Lord been merciful, to show unto me concerning them, even as he had prophets of old, I should have** [*would have*] perished also.

21 And he surely did show unto the prophets of old all things concerning them; and also he did show unto many concerning us; wherefore, it must needs be [*it is very important*] that we know concerning them for **they are written upon the plates of brass.**

At this point, Nephi explains to us why it was so important that he and his people had access to the scriptures written upon the brass plates.

22 Now it came to pass that **I, Nephi, did teach my brethren these things** [*about the gathering of Israel spoken of in the previous verses*]; and it came to pass that **I did read many things to them, which were engraven upon the plates of brass, that they might know concerning the doings of the Lord in other lands, among people of old.**

Next, Nephi tells us why he especially likes to read the words of the prophet Isaiah to his people.

23 And I did read many things unto them which were written in the books of Moses [*the first five books of the Old Testament, written by Moses—namely, Genesis, Exodus, Leviticus, Numbers, and Deuteronomy*]; **but that I might more fully persuade them to believe in the Lord their Redeemer I did read unto them that which was written by the prophet Isaiah; for I did liken** [*compare, show how they apply*] all

scriptures unto us, that it might be for our profit and learning.

Did you see why Nephi likes to read Isaiah to his family? It is to give them more reasons to believe in Jesus Christ, their Redeemer.

Also, above, in verse 23, we find a great key to understanding and applying the scriptures in our lives. We must "liken all scriptures unto us." We need to develop the ability to see applications in the scriptures that would apply to situations in our own lives. Then the scriptures come to life.

For example, Nephi's brothers badly mistreat him, yet he then "frankly" forgives them (1 Nephi 7:21). It is likely that each of us has encountered, or yet will encounter, situations in which people treat us badly. If we are successful in "likening the scriptures unto us," we will frankly forgive too. We will thus free ourselves from the bondage of bitterness and hatred.

Next, in versae 24, Nephi gives us another important reason for reading and studying the writings of Isaiah.

24 Wherefore I spake unto them, saying: Hear ye the words of the prophet [*Isaiah*], ye who are a remnant of the house of Israel, a branch who have been broken off; **hear ye the words of the prophet, which were written unto all the house of Israel, and liken them unto yourselves, that ye may have hope as well as your brethren from whom ye have been broken off; for after this manner has the prophet written.**

Did you catch this reason? It is to give us increased hope that we can make it back home to Heavenly Father after we die, if we have faith in Christ and use His Atonement.

Just a few more thoughts and comments about understanding Isaiah before we go to the next two chapters of First Nephi.

For many members of the Church, Isaiah is difficult to understand. Just knowing what Nephi said in verses 23 and 24, above, is motivation for a renewed effort at understanding Isaiah's writings. If we succeed, we will have a stronger testimony and understanding of Christ as our Redeemer. This, in turn, will give us wonderful "hope" that we will have a pleasant Judgment Day. The word "hope," as used in the Book of Mormon, is not the same as in common English usage today. In the Book of Mormon, "hope" means "assurance" (see Alma 57:11). Thus, in 2 Nephi 31:20, Nephi speaks of "steadfastness in Christ," which brings "a perfect brightness of hope," which leads to eternal life (exaltation). There is nothing "wishy-washy" or "maybe-ish" about this type of hope.

Isaiah, then, when adequately understood, bears witness of Christ. As this witness is confirmed into our souls by the Holy Ghost, we can be strengthened to the point in our attitudes and behaviors that we can plan on eternal life. This planning on eternal life is not arrogant. It is not prideful, nor is it unwise. It is simply the true state of the humble followers of Christ. It is the "perfect brightness of hope" to which we are invited by Isaiah.

If you will pay the price to study the next two chapters and accompanying notes carefully and prayerfully, you will begin to understand Isaiah. You will see that he uses rich symbolism. You will see that he paints pictures with words. We will use many notes within the verses to help you get the feel for Isaiah's writing style and message. Be aware that the Savior quoted Isaiah more than He quoted any other prophet. In fact, in 3 Nephi 23:1, Jesus commanded His people to study Isaiah. He said, "Ye ought to search these things [*Isaiah's writings*]. Yea, a commandment I give unto you that ye search these things diligently; for great are the words of Isaiah."

One last suggestion before we get into these next two chapters. Nephi said that his people had difficulty understanding Isaiah because "they know not concerning the manner of prophesying among the Jews" (see 2 Nephi 25:1). This can make it difficult for us also. It may help to note a few characteristics of Isaiah's "manner of prophesying." For instance:

Isaiah uses much symbolism. He uses many phrases peculiar to his time and people. These are known as idioms.

Example

"Thy neck is an iron sinew, and thy brow brass" (1 Nephi 20:4). This is, in effect, saying, "You have iron in your neck and you are thick-skulled." In other words, you are not humble; you won't bow your heads in humility before God, and it is hard for Him to get anything into your heads.

Isaiah deliberately repeats for emphasis. Because of this writing and teaching technique, some people begin to think they have missed something, because they don't believe that Isaiah would constantly repeat things.

Example

"Go ye forth of Babylon, flee ye from the Chaldeans [*the inhabitants of southern Babylon*]" (1 Nephi 20:20). In other words, flee, run away from evil!

Example

Isaiah repeats the same concept in two different ways in

the following: "The Lord hath called me from the womb; from the bowels of my mother hath he made mention of my name" (1 Nephi 21:1). In other words, Israel was foreordained in the life before we came to earth to be God's covenant people.

Many of the things Isaiah teaches can have more than one meaning and more than one fulfillment. Therefore, it is usually unwise to limit what he teaches to only one specific meaning, unless the context warrants it.

Example

"And they thirsted not; he led them through the deserts; he caused the waters to flow out of the rock for them; he clave the rock also and the waters gushed out" (1 Nephi 20:21). While the Lord literally led the children of Israel through the wilderness as they escaped from Egyptian slavery, and literally caused water to flow out of the rock to quench their thirst and save their lives, there is much symbolic meaning also. For instance, He leads us through the wilderness of sin and wickedness. He provides "living water" (John 4:10) and quenches our spiritual thirst eternally.

1 NEPHI 20

As mentioned before, many members of the Church find Isaiah difficult to understand. If you will stick with it, and perhaps pray a little harder than usual for the help of the Holy Ghost to understand these next two chapters, and even study a little harder with the help of the notes I have included, you will likely come out understanding and appreciating Isaiah more than you thought you could.

1 Hearken and hear this, O house of Jacob [*Listen carefully, Jacob's children; in other words, the twelve tribes of Israel*], who are called by the name of Israel [*Jacob*], and are come forth out of the waters of Judah, or out of the waters of baptism [*who have been baptized and thus are my covenant people*], who swear [*make covenants*] by the name of the Lord [*just as we, today, make covenants in the name of Jesus Christ*], and make mention of [*pray to and talk about*] the God of Israel, yet they swear [*make covenants*] not in truth nor in righteousness [*the problem is that they claim to be the Lord's people but break covenants, don't live the gospel*].

2 Nevertheless, they call themselves of the holy city [*they claim to be the Lord's people*], but they do not stay themselves [*do not rely*] upon the God of Israel, who is the Lord of Hosts [*the God of all*]; yea, the Lord of Hosts is his name.

In the next several verses, Isaiah reminds Israel that there is no lack of obvious evidence that the true God exists.

In verse 3, next, the Lord tells the people that He has given them many prophecies, then fulfilled them so they can know that He exists.

3 Behold, I [*the Lord*] have declared the former things [*prophecies*] from the beginning [*so you would have plenty of evidence that I exist*]; and they [*prophecies*] went forth out of my mouth [*through what My prophets taught*], and I showed [*fulfilled*] them. I did show them suddenly [*when you did not expect them to take place, so you can know I really am your God, and your idols are false; see Isaiah 42:9*].

Next, the Lord tells His covenant people that they are prideful and stubborn and that's why He had to give them such obvious evidence that He exists.

4 And I [*the Lord*] did it [*gave and fulfilled prophecies*] because I knew that thou art obstinate [*prideful, stubborn*], and thy neck is an iron sinew [*your necks are as if they have iron in them; you are not humble, won't bend your neck in humility*], and thy brow brass [*you are thick-headed; it is hard to get anything through your thick skulls*];

Next, through Isaiah, the Lord tells covenant Israel that from the very beginning He has placed obvious evidence that He exists in the form of prophecies of the future. He has then fulfilled these prophecies so that His people have every chance of gaining and keeping testimonies of His existence and love and concern for them. This is similar to the prophecies of the last days, or signs of the times, which are being fulfilled all around us now.

Notice that Isaiah is saying the same thing over and over here with different words, for emphasis. As I mentioned in the notes at the end of chapter 19, repetition is one of Isaiah's main teaching methods.

5 And I have even from the beginning declared to thee [*I prophesied things*]; before it [*the prophesied events*] came to pass I showed them thee [*I prophesied them to you*]; and I showed them for fear lest thou shouldst say—mine idol hath done them, and my graven image [*idol*], and my molten image [*idol*] hath commanded them [*I have shown you my power via prophecies, so you couldn't claim your idols have power*].

6 Thou hast seen and heard all this [*all this obvious evidence that I exist*]; and will ye not declare [*acknowledge*] them? And that I have showed thee new things [*things you couldn't possibly have known in advance*] from this time, even hidden things, and thou didst not know them [*didn't pay attention; didn't acknowledge them*].

7 They are created now [*the prophesied events are taking place now*], and

not from the beginning [*you couldn't have guessed they were going to happen back then when the prophecies were given*], even before the day when thou heardest them not [*back then when there was no clue that the prophesied events would take place*] they were declared unto thee [*I told you in advance*], lest thou shouldst say—Behold I knew them.

8 Yea, and thou heardest not [*you ignored the prophecies*]; yea, thou knewest not [*you would not acknowledge them*]; yea, from that time thine ear was not opened [*you refused to listen*]; for I knew that thou wouldst deal very treacherously [*I knew that you would be dangerously dishonest*], and wast called a transgressor from the womb [*I've had trouble with you Israelites right from the start!*].

Next, the Lord reminds all of us that if it were not for His mercy, Israel would have been cut off long ago.

9 Nevertheless [*however*], for my name's sake [*I, the Lord, have a reputation to uphold of being merciful*] will I defer [*delay*] mine anger, and for my praise [*glory, honor, reputation*] will I refrain [*hold back*] from thee, that I cut thee not off [*I'll not destroy you completely even though you deserve it*].

Next, the Lord prophesies of the future, through Isaiah, the prophet, saying that the time will yet come that He will make His covenant people, Israel, pure and clean and righteous.

10 For, behold, I [*the Lord*] have refined thee [*Israel*], I have chosen thee [*I will make you*] in the furnace of affliction [*I will purify you in the refiner's fire*].

"The refiner's fire" makes us think of a skillful craftsman carefully applying fire to gold ore in order to remove all the impurities and thus produce pure gold.

Next, in verse 11, we are reminded that the Lord doesn't help us only because it is His calling as the Redeemer and Savior. Rather, He helps us and works patiently with us because He loves us.

11 For mine own sake [*because I love you; see verse 14*], yea, for mine own sake [*because I want to*] will I do this [*refine and purify you by allowing troubles to come into your lives*], for I will not suffer [*allow*] my name to be polluted [*so that people can't say that I don't keep my promises to Israel*], and I will not give my glory unto another [*I will remain true to you; see Jeremiah 3:14. By the way, this can be good advice for marriage partners*].

The main theme of verses 12–17 is that Israel was called and foreordained in the premortal life to serve and bring others to Christ.

12 Hearken [*listen carefully*] unto me, O Jacob, and Israel my called [*you have a calling; see Abr. 2:9–11*], for I am he [*Christ*]; I am the first, and I am also the last [*I am your Savior; Jesus was there at the Creation and will be there at Final Judgment*].

13 Mine hand hath also laid the foundation of the earth [*I am the Creator of the earth*], and my right hand [*covenant hand; hand of power*] hath spanned the heavens [*spread out; created the skies*]. I call unto them [*Israel in verses 12 and 14*] and they stand up together [*let them, Israel, all stand up and listen; this goes with the first part of verse 14*].

14 All ye, assemble yourselves, and hear; who among them [*seems to be referring to Israel's idols; see verse 5*] hath declared these things [*prophecies; see verses 3, 6, etc.*] unto them [*Israel*]? The Lord hath loved him [*Israel*]; yea, and he [*the Lord*] will fulfill his word which he hath declared by them [*the prophets*]; and he will do his pleasure on Babylon [*symbolic of the wicked; in other words, God will punish the wicked*], and his arm [*symbolic of power*] shall come upon the Chaldeans [*southern Babylon; Babylon will eventually be destroyed, just as has been prophesied*].

15 Also, saith the Lord; I the Lord, yea, I have spoken; yea, I have called him [*Israel*] to declare [*Israel has a job to do*], I have brought him, and he shall make his way prosperous [*God will help; could also mean that Heavenly Father called Christ to prophesy; also, that Christ called Isaiah to prophesy*].

Verse 15, above, is an example of where Isaiah's writing can have more than one meaning.

Next, the Lord invites the people of Israel to come close to Him.

16 Come ye [*Israel*] near unto me; I have not spoken in secret [*I have been very open about the gospel, etc.*]; from the beginning, from the time that it was declared have I spoken; and the Lord God, and his Spirit, hath sent me [*the Father sent Christ; or could also mean that Christ sent Isaiah*].

17 And thus saith the Lord, thy Redeemer [*Christ*], the Holy One of Israel; I have sent him [*Israel; see verses 12 and 19; or, dualistically, this could refer to Isaiah*], the Lord thy God who teacheth thee to profit [*for your profit, benefit*], who leadeth thee by the way thou shouldst go, hath done it.

18 O that thou hadst hearkened [*I wish that you had listened*] to my commandments [*can apply directly to Laman and Lemuel; no doubt this is one reason Nephi is quoting Isaiah to them*]—then had thy peace been as a river [*you*

could have had peace flowing constantly like a river into your lives], and thy righteousness as the waves of the sea [*your righteousness would have been steady and constant, like the waves of the sea*].

Next, Isaiah says, in effect, that Israel has the potential to become a truly large and great nation, if they would just make and keep covenants with God. As it is, though, Isaiah goes into what can be termed "future perfect tense" in which he treats the future as if it has already happened and prophetically tells the Israelites that they could have become a great nation, if only they had learned to be obedient to God's commandments.

19 Thy seed [*Israel's posterity*] also had been as the sand [*would have been as many as the sands of the seashore*]; the offspring of thy bowels [*your descendants*] like the gravel [*grains of sand*] thereof; his [*Israel's*] name should not [*would not*] have been cut off nor destroyed from before me [*Israel could have had it very good, and could have avoided such great destruction*].

Next, Isaiah warns all of us to run away from wickedness. He says it twice, then tells us to be happy as we live the gospel.

20 Go ye forth of Babylon [*flee wickedness; stop being wicked*], flee ye from the Chaldeans [*wickedness; Chaldeans were residents of southern Babylon, which was a wicked country in Isaiah's day*], with a voice of singing [*be happy about being righteous*] declare ye [*preach this*], tell this, utter to the end of the earth; say ye: The Lord hath redeemed his servant Jacob [*Israel can be saved—including Laman and Lemuel—if they will repent*].

"Babylon," as used in verse 20, above, is very symbolic. Anciently, it was an actual country and city, basically where Iraq is today. Isaiah as well as many other prophets use Babylon to symbolize wickedness and to represent Satan's kingdom. The imagery is fascinating, because Babylon was a fearsome enemy of Israel.

The huge city of Babylon was so enormous that it took 56 miles of walls to surround and protect it. The walls were 335 feet high and 85 feet wide (see Bible Dictionary, under "Babylon"). It was a center of wickedness, and thus in many scriptures it came to symbolize general wickedness and the devil's domain.

In fact, part of the imagery of Babylon is that it seemed indestructible, just as Satan's kingdom and domain on earth seems powerful and indestructible. However, Babylon fell in 538 BC and was never rebuilt, just as Satan's kingdom will eventually fall, and never be rebuilt as he and his evil followers are cast into outer darkness (see D&C 1:16; 88:111–15).

Next, Isaiah reminds us what the Lord can do for righteous people, just like He did for the children of Israel when they escaped Egyptian captivity by fleeing into the desert.

21 And they thirsted not; he led them through the deserts; he caused the waters to flow out of the rock for them; he clave [*broke open*] the rock also and the waters gushed out [*just look what the Lord can do for those who trust in him!*].

Finally, Isaiah warns the wicked that wickedness does not bring peace.

22 And notwithstanding [*even though*] he hath done all this, and greater also, **there is no peace, saith the Lord, unto the wicked** [*a major message for Laman and Lemuel and all of us*].

1 NEPHI 21

You have no doubt heard our prophets today say a lot about the gathering of Israel. The word "Israel," in this context or setting, means the Lord's covenant people, meaning people who are related to the twelve tribes of Israel. Your patriarchal blessing will tell you which of the tribes of Israel your blessings and responsibilities come through. All members of covenant Israel, who try to live the gospel, will ultimately receive all of the blessings promised to Abraham, Isaac, and Jacob, who were the ancestors of the twelve tribes of Israel. These promised blessings include the blessing of exaltation, which means living in our own family units forever and becoming gods. These promised blessings also include the responsibility of spreading the gospel and helping to bring people to Christ.

In this chapter, Isaiah continues his prophecy about the Savior and of the gathering of Israel in the last days. The prophecy includes the fact that the governments of many nations will assist in this gathering. In the last days, Israel will finally do the work she was originally called to do but failed to accomplish in the past.

Beginning with verse 1, we will be taught about the foreordination of covenant Israel and the responsibilities we have as the Lord's chosen people. Remember that "chosen" includes the concept that we are chosen to carry whatever burdens are necessary in order to spread the gospel and the priesthood throughout the earth.

By the way, "foreordination" means that, in our premortal existence, we were chosen, selected and blessed by God to fulfill certain missions, responsibilities, and callings during our mortal lives here on earth.

Isaiah sets the stage for this prophecy about the gathering of Israel in the last days by having us think of Israel as a person who is thinking about her past and feels like she has been a failure as far as her calling and mission from the Lord is concerned.

Then she is startled by her success in the last days.

You will see that Isaiah repeats many things many times for emphasis as he teaches us about the important role of the people of covenant Israel (including you and me) in helping gather people back to God.

1 And again: Hearken [*listen carefully*], O ye house of Israel, all ye that are broken off and are driven out [*scattered Israel; Isaiah is speaking prophetically to scattered Israel*] because of the wickedness of the pastors [*leaders and teachers*] of my people; yea, all ye that are broken off, that are scattered abroad, who are of my people, O house of Israel. Listen, O isles [*faraway nations and lands, including those across the sea*], unto me [*Israel*], and hearken ye people from far; the Lord hath called me [*Israel*] from the womb [*from before I was born, in other words, foreordination*]; from the bowels of my mother hath he [*the Lord*] made mention of my name [*Israel has had a job to do since the beginning*].

2 And he hath made my mouth like a sharp sword [*Israel is to spread the true gospel, which helps people cut through false ideas and teachings like a sharp sword*]; in the shadow [*shade; protection*] of his hand hath he hid me, and made me a polished shaft [*like a polished arrow; in other words, an effective servant of the Lord, such as Joseph Smith, Isaiah, or any faithful Israelite*]; in his quiver hath he hid me;

3 And said unto me [*Israel*]: Thou art my servant, O Israel, in whom I will be glorified [*Israel will yet do its job to gather the rest of Israel*].

In verses 4–12 and beyond, Isaiah portrays the loneliness of Israel waiting for the Restoration. It is almost as if Isaiah were writing a stage play with one lone character on the stage, representing Israel, speaking in a sad, lonely, remorseful voice and recounting the missed and seemingly lost opportunities to fulfill her mission and God-given destiny.

4 Then I [*Israel*] said, I have labored in vain [*I haven't been a very good servant; I have wasted my efforts*], I have spent my strength for naught [*for nothing*] and in vain [*in false religions and wicked living*]; surely my judgment is with the Lord, and my work with my God [*in other words, my fate rests with the Lord; it is up to God what He wants to do with me now that I have failed to do what He asked me to do*].

5 And now, saith the Lord—that formed me from the womb [*who foreordained me*] that I should be his servant, to bring Jacob [*Israel*] again to him—though Israel be not gathered, yet shall I be glorious in the eyes of the Lord [*if I do my best, I'll be okay, even if people reject my*

message], and my God shall be my strength.

Next, the Lord, in effect, tells Israel that it is too easy of a calling to merely work at bringing scattered Israel back to God. Israel needs to have something more challenging to do—namely, to bring the gospel to all peoples of the earth.

6 And he [*the Lord*] said: It is a light thing [*not enough*] that thou [*Israel*] shouldst be my servant to raise up [*restore the gospel to*] the tribes of Jacob [*Israel*], and to restore the preserved [*remaining people*] of Israel [*the job of the Church today*]. I will also give thee for [*another assignment; namely, to be*] a light to the Gentiles, that thou mayest be my salvation unto the ends of the earth [*a calling to bring the gospel to everyone on earth*].

Abraham 2:9–11 clearly teaches this responsibility that Israel has, to bring the gospel and the priesthood blessings to all the earth. In fact, in your patriarchal blessing, your lineage is declared. This is a most important part of your blessing because it reminds you of your sacred duty to help bring the gospel to all the world throughout your life.

Next, Isaiah prophesies that the day will come when Israel will become a powerful force in the world, whereas, in the past, Israel was walked on almost at will by nation after nation.

7 Thus saith the Lord, the Redeemer of Israel [*Christ*], his [*Israel's*] Holy One, to him [*Israel*] whom man despiseth, to him whom the nation abhorreth [*to the nation hated by others*], to servant of rulers [*for much of past history, Israel has been a servant and slave to many nations*]: Kings shall see and arise [*out of respect for Israel*], princes [*leaders of nations*] also shall worship, because of the Lord that is faithful [*because the Lord will keep His promises to you*].

8 Thus saith the Lord: In an acceptable time [*when the time is right, beginning with the Restoration and Joseph Smith*] have I heard thee [*I will have answered your cries for help*], O isles of the sea [*far continents beyond Asia and Africa, such as America, etc.*], and in a day of salvation have I helped thee [*here, Isaiah is speaking of the future as if it had already happened*]; and I will preserve thee, and give thee my servant [*prophets, including Joseph Smith*] for a covenant of the people, to establish the earth [*to reestablish the gospel upon the earth*], to cause to inherit the desolate heritages [*to restore Israel to the lands of her inheritance. In other words, the gathering will definitely take place; see verse 19*];

9 That thou mayest say to the prisoners [*the living and the dead in spiritual darkness*]: Go forth [*go free from spiritual bondage*]; to them that sit in darkness: Show yourselves [*come out of prison*]. They shall feed in the ways [*their "Shepherd," Christ, will lead them to the gospel path where they will get fed the gospel*], and their pastures shall be in all high places [*they will partake of the best, the highest, the gospel of Christ*].

10 They shall not hunger nor thirst [*for the true gospel anymore, because they will have it*], neither shall the heat nor the sun smite them; for he [*Christ*] that hath mercy on them shall lead them, even by the springs of water [*symbolic of living water; see John 4:10*] shall he guide them [*benefits of accepting and living the gospel*].

As mentioned at the beginning of chapter 20, Isaiah is very thorough. He repeats, then repeats the message, and then repeats it again, and yet again. In these verses, we are seeing this method employed by Isaiah to emphasize the wonderful benefits of the restored gospel and following Christ to the "high places" where the best "pasture" is to be found—namely, eternal exaltation.

11 And I will make all my mountains [*"mountains" are often symbolic of temples*] a way [*a path, a means of arriving at a destination*], and my highways shall be exalted [*I will prepare "gospel highways" in all parts of the world, through the Restoration of the gospel and the gathering in the last days, which will lead the faithful Saints to exaltation*].

12 And then [*in the last days gathering*], O house of Israel, behold, these [*Israel*] shall come from far; and lo, these from the north and from the west; and these from the land of Sinim [*from everywhere*].

Next, Isaiah teaches that people everywhere will have great happiness and joy when the gospel is restored and Israel is gathered in to God.

13 **Sing, O heavens; and be joyful, O earth**; for the feet of those who are in the east shall be established; and **break forth into singing**, O mountains; for they shall be smitten no more; for the Lord hath comforted his people [*speaking prophetically of the future, as if it has already happened*], and will have mercy upon his afflicted [*the Lord will eventually redeem Israel*].

Remember, after verse 3, above, we suggested that verses 4–12 (and beyond) could be like a stage play, with Israel as the only actor or actress, lamenting her failure to do what the Lord called her to do. In verse 14, next, Israel, in effect, rejects the prophetic encouragement given in verse 13.

14 But, behold, Zion [*Israel*] hath said: **The Lord hath forsaken me, and my Lord hath forgotten me** [*wicked Israel's complaint*]—but he will show that he hath not.

In verse 15, next, the Lord strongly says that He has not forgotten Israel!

15 For can a woman forget her sucking [*nursing*] child, that she should not have compassion on the son of her womb? Yea, they may forget [*yes, even that happens among mortals*], **yet will I not forget thee, O house of Israel** [*a promise! I will keep my promise to restore the gospel and to gather Israel again*].

Verse 16, next, contains some of the most beautiful Atonement symbolism in scripture. Just as a workman's hands bear witness of his work, such as a carpenter with callouses and blisters, so shall the nail prints in the Savior's hands bear witness of His work for us.

16 **Behold, I have graven thee upon the palms of my hands** [*each of us is "engraved," so to speak, upon the Savior's hands where the nails pierced His flesh; in other words, the wounds on the palms of His hands bear witness of His work for us*]; **thy walls are continually before me** [*"walls" would represent a person's house; in other words, I know where you live and always know what help you need*].

Next, Isaiah prophesies that things will be turned around in the last days such that the enemies of Israel, who once caused he great trouble, will now flee from her.

17 Thy children shall make haste against thy destroyers [*your descendants will finally start winning against your enemies*]; and they that made thee waste [*those who caused you great trouble*] shall go forth of thee [*will flee from you*].

18 Lift up thine eyes round about and behold [*let me show you (complaining Israel in verse 14) the future*]; all these [*righteous, faithful descendants in the last days*] gather themselves together [*You thought you were going to be wiped out completely, but look at all your descendants in the future!*], and they shall come to thee. And as I live, saith the Lord, thou shalt surely clothe thee with them all, as with an ornament, and bind them on even as a bride [*a bride puts on her finest clothing for the occasion; Israel will have her finest descendants in the last days*].

19 For thy waste and thy desolate places, and the land of thy destruction [*you've been trodden down for centuries*], shall even now be too narrow by reason of the inhabitants [*you will have so many descendants you'll seem to be running out of room; latter-day gathering of Israel*]; and they [*your

former enemies] that swallowed thee up shall be far away.

20 The children [*converts to the true gospel*] whom thou shalt have, after thou hast lost the first [*via apostasy, war, etc.*], shall again in thine ears say: The place is too strait for me [*there's not enough room for us all*]; give place to me that I may dwell.

The fulfillment of the above prophecy that, in the last days before the Second Coming of Christ, there will be a great increase in faithful members of the Church is happening in our day. Just consider the vast building program of the Church as we build temples and chapels to try to keep up with the increase in the number of members of the Church.

Next, Isaiah once again tells us that, in the last days, there will be a lot of people joining the Church, as Israel is gathered.

21 Then [*in the last days*] shalt thou [*Israel*] say in thine heart: Who hath begotten me these [*where in the world did all these Israelites come from?*], seeing I have lost my children, and am desolate, a captive, and removing to and fro [*scattered*]? And who hath brought up these? Behold, I was left alone [*I thought I had completely failed in my foreordination to take the gospel to all the world*]; these, where have they been?

I hope you are beginning to appreciate Isaiah's inspired ability to create pictures and feelings, indeed drama, with words as he teaches. Perhaps you have now felt Israel's discouragement and maybe even caught a slight touch of self-pity on her part as Isaiah has portrayed her in this chapter. Isaiah thus skillfully set the stage for her astonishment at the fulfillment of the Lord's promises to her in the last days. This could be symbolic of skeptics in all ages of the world who are bound to be caught off guard as the prophesied miracles of gathering take place.

Next, the Lord answers Israel's question, "Where did all these come from?" He tells us how He will accomplish this great gathering of Israel in the last days. As you will see, He, the Lord, will cause it to happen. That is why it will happen!

22 Thus saith the Lord God: Behold, I will lift up mine hand [*I will signal*] to the Gentiles, and set up my standard [*the Church, true gospel of Christ*] to the people; and they [*the Gentiles*] shall bring thy sons in their arms, and thy daughters shall be carried upon their shoulders [*Gentile nations will help gather Israel*].

23 And kings shall be thy nursing fathers, and their queens thy nursing mothers [*example: Great Britain was*

very influential in establishing a homeland for the Jews in Palestine, after World War I, and helped sponsor the establishment of the Nation of Israel, in the United Nations in 1948]; they [*the leaders of nations*] shall bow down to thee with their face towards the earth, and lick up the dust of thy feet [*many nations will help gather Israel in the last days*]; and thou shalt know that I am the Lord; for they shall not be ashamed that wait for [*trust in*] me.

Just a bit more about the fulfillment of the marvelous prophecy in verse 23, above, about the gathering of the Jews in the last days. In 1830, when the Church was officially organized, the Jewish population in the Holy Land was about seven thousand. Now, it is over three million!

Next, in verse 24, Isaiah portrays Israel as asking, in effect, "How could we, who have virtually always been victims (prey) of such powerful enemies, ever be rescued from them and set free?" The Lord will answer their question in verse 25.

24 For shall the prey [*Israel*] be taken [*set free*] from the mighty [*powerful enemies*], or the lawful [*the Lord's covenant people*] captives delivered [*be set free*]?

As you will see, in verse 25, the answer to the question in verse 24, is "Yes!")

25 But thus saith the Lord, even the captives [*Israel*] of the mighty [*powerful enemies*] shall be taken away [*rescued*], and the prey [*victims*] of the terrible [*tyrants*] shall be delivered [*set free*]; for I [*the Lord*] will contend [*fight*] with him that contendeth with thee [*Israel*], and I will save thy children [*the answer to Israel's question in verse 24 is that the Lord will rescue them and set them free*].

26 And I will feed them [*Israel's enemies*] that oppress thee [*treat you badly*] with their own flesh; they shall be drunken [*out of control*] with their own blood as with sweet wine [*your enemies will turn against each other and destroy themselves*]; and all flesh [*all people*] shall know that I, the Lord, am thy Savior and thy Redeemer, the Mighty One of Jacob.

1 NEPHI 22

One of the great blessings of having the Book of Mormon is that Nephi explains many chapters of Isaiah for us. This gives us a great advantage over all other people on earth as far as understanding Isaiah is concerned. In this case, Nephi will explain what Isaiah said in the two chapters of Isaiah that we just read, namely 1 Nephi, chapters 20–21. Having Nephi as our teacher will greatly increase our ability to understand other chapters of Isaiah also.

By the way, since Nephi would likely have been reading Isaiah to his brethren from the brass plates of Laban, and since the brass plates were likely produced approximately one hundred years (or less) after Isaiah lived, the writings of Isaiah on thesae plates would be a much more original source than the earliest manuscripts for the Bible. In fact, the brass plates even had three verses which our Bible doesn't have. These three verses appear as 1 Nephi 22:15–17. Nephi quotes them as he explains this segment of Isaiah.

As we continue now, Nephi's brethren will ask good questions about understanding Isaiah. Nephi's answers will be helpful to us too.

1 AND now it came to pass that after I, Nephi, had read these things [*some of Isaiah's writings*] which were engraven upon the plates of brass, my brethren came unto me and said unto me: [*Question:*] **What meaneth these things which ye have read?** Behold, **are they to be understood according to things which are spiritual, which shall come to pass according to the spirit and not the flesh** [*are they spiritual or literal*]?

2 And I, Nephi, said unto them: Behold they were manifest [*told*] unto the prophet by the voice of the Spirit; for by the Spirit are all things made known unto the prophets, which shall come upon the children of men according to the flesh [*during mortality*].

3 Wherefore [*therefore*], [*Answer:*] **the things of which I have read are things pertaining to things both temporal and spiritual** [*they are things that will actually happen to the house of Israel, as well as things with spiritual meanings*]; for it appears that **the house of Israel** [*the descendants of Abraham, Isaac, and Jacob; in other words, the twelve tribes of Israel*], sooner or later, **will be scattered upon all the face of the earth**, and also among all nations.

4 And behold, there are many who are already lost from the knowledge of those who are at Jerusalem [*such as the ten lost tribes who were carried away about 721 BC*]. Yea, the more part [*the majority*] of all the tribes have been led away; and they are scattered to and fro upon the isles of the sea [*all over the world*]; and whither they are none of us knoweth, save that [*except that*] we know that they have been led away.

5 And since they have been led away, these things [*the words of Isaiah*] have been prophesied concerning them, and also concerning all those who shall hereafter be scattered and be confounded [*confused; stopped in their progression*], because of

the Holy One of Israel; for against him [*Christ*] will they harden their hearts; wherefore, they [*Israel*] shall be scattered among all nations and shall be hated of all men.

6 Nevertheless, after they [*scattered Israel*] shall be nursed [*helped to gather*] by the Gentiles, and the Lord has lifted up his hand upon the Gentiles [*has blessed them with the restored gospel*] and set them up for a standard [*after the gospel has been restored among the Gentiles through the Prophet Joseph Smith*], and their children [*Israel's descendants*] have been carried in their [*the Gentiles'*] arms, and their daughters [*descendants*] have been carried upon their [*the Gentiles'*] shoulders, behold **these things of which are spoken are temporal** [*literal; they will actually happen, physically, to Israel*]; for thus [*such*] are the covenants of the Lord with our fathers [*ancestors*]; and it meaneth us [*the Lamanites*] in the days to come [*in the future*], and also all our brethren who are of the house of Israel. [*In other words, all who are willing will be gathered in to God.*]

7 And it meaneth that the time cometh that after all the house of Israel have been scattered and confounded [*stopped in progressing, including making progress in returning to God*], that the Lord God will raise up a mighty nation [*the United States of America*] among the Gentiles, yea, even upon the face of this land [*America*]; and by them [*the Gentiles who came from Europe, etc. and settled America*] shall our seed [*the Lamanites*] be scattered.

Next, Nephi will explain and apply Isaiah's prophecy specifically to the Lamanites.

8 And after our seed is scattered the Lord God will proceed to do a marvelous work among the Gentiles [*the Restoration of the gospel through Joseph Smith*], which shall be of great worth unto our seed [*the Lamanites*]; wherefore [*and so*], it is likened unto [*compared to*] their being nourished by the Gentiles [*the members of the Church*] and being carried in their arms and upon their shoulders.

9 And it [*the restored gospel, the true Church*] shall also be of worth unto the Gentiles; and not only unto the Gentiles but unto all the house of Israel [*which will eventually include all who join the Church and live the gospel*], unto the making known of the covenants of the Father of heaven unto Abraham, saying: In thy seed shall all the kindreds [*people*] of the earth be blessed.

Remember, as noted previously, the word "Gentiles" has many different meanings, all of which are context sensitive. In verses 8 and

9, above, it means people who have the blood of Israel in them, but whose ancestors did not specifically come from the Holy Land in recent generations (see Bible Dictionary, under the topic "Gentiles").

10 And I would, my brethren, that ye should know [*I want you to know*] that all the kindreds [*all peoples*] of the earth cannot be blessed unless he [*the Lord*] shall make bare his arm [*show forth His power*] in the eyes of the nations. [*In other words, it will take obvious help from God to cause the prophesied gathering of Israel to take place.*]

11 Wherefore [*therefore*], the Lord God will proceed to make bare his arm in the eyes of all the nations, in bringing about his covenants [*including priesthood ordinances such as baptism, confirmation, temple marriage, and so forth*] and his gospel unto those who are of the house of Israel.

While the strict literal definition of Israel is anyone who has the blood of Abraham, Isaac, Jacob (Israel), and the twelve tribes of Israel in their veins, in our day virtually all people have the blood of Israel because of the widespread scattering of Israel to all the earth over thousands of years.

Therefore, all who join the Church are considered to be covenant Israel with all the responsibilities and blessings of descendants of Abraham, Isaac, and Jacob.

12 Wherefore [*therefore*], he will bring them again out of captivity [*actual physical bondage as well as spiritual bondage*], and they shall be gathered together to the lands [*not just one land, rather many lands*] of their inheritance; and they shall be brought out of obscurity [*where nobody hardly even knows about them*] and out of darkness [*spiritual darkness*]; and they shall know that the Lord is their Savior and their Redeemer, the Mighty One of Israel.

13 And the blood of [*all the bad, evil things done by*] that great and abominable church, which is the whore of all the earth [*Satan's kingdom, including all the bad things he does and all the wicked who follow his evil ways; see verse 22*], shall turn upon their own heads [*will come back to destroy them*]; for they shall war among themselves, and the sword of their own hands shall fall upon their own heads, and they shall be drunken with their own blood. [*A description of conditions among the wicked, especially in the last days before the Second Coming.*]

14 And every nation which shall war against thee, O house of Israel, shall be turned one against another [*this is a very specific prophecy, which we are watching now as it proceeds into fulfillment*], and they shall fall into the pit [*the trap*] which they digged to ensnare [*trap*] the people

of the Lord. And all that fight against Zion [*God's work*] shall be destroyed, and that great whore [*Satan's kingdom; the wicked*], who hath perverted [*polluted and twisted to satisfy their own lusts*] the right ways of the Lord, yea, that great and abominable church [*the church of the devil—see 1 Nephi 14:10—and everything that goes along with it*], shall tumble to the dust and great shall be the fall of it.

> In verses 15–17, next, it appears that Nephi is quoting three verses from Isaiah's writings that are found nowhere else in scripture. We understand that these verses were on the brass plates but were left out of the Bible somewhere along the way. They seem to fit at the end of 1 Nephi, chapter 21. They would fit between Isaiah, chapter 49 and Isaiah, chapter 50 in the Bible. (See *Old Testament Student Manual, 1 Kings through Malachi*, p. 194.)
>
> These three verses look ahead to the future and prophesy about the Second Coming of the Savior and things that will happen right before it. So it should be especially interesting to us.

15 For behold, saith the prophet [*Isaiah*], **the time cometh speedily that Satan shall have no more power over the hearts of the children of men** [*this refers to the millennium*]; **for the day soon cometh that all the proud and they who do wickedly shall be as stubble** [*dry straw, which burns easily*]; and the day cometh that they must be burned. [*They will be burned by the glory of Christ when He comes; see D&C 5:19 plus 2 Nephi 12:10, 19, 21.*]

16 For **the time soon cometh that the fulness of the wrath** [*anger*] **of God shall be poured out upon all the children of men** [*all wicked people*]; for he will not suffer [*allow*] that the wicked shall destroy the righteous.

17 Wherefore, **he will preserve** [*save*] **the righteous by his power**, even if it so be that the fulness of his wrath must come, and the righteous be preserved, **even unto** [*even if it requires*] **the destruction of their enemies by fire**. Wherefore, the righteous need not fear [*a major message for those who are striving to live the gospel*]; for thus saith the prophet [*Isaiah*], **they shall be saved**, even if it so be as by fire.

> Next, Nephi will explain what he just quoted from Isaiah in verses 15–17, above. Remember, he is still answering the questions his brethren asked in verse 1 as to which prophecies of Isaiah are literal physically and which ones are symbolic or spiritual.

18 Behold, my brethren, I say unto you, that **these things must**

shortly come [*will occur shortly after the Restoration of the gospel*]; yea, even **blood, and fire, and vapor of smoke** must come [*meaning that there will be terrible disasters and troubles throughout the world in the last days; these are called "signs of the times" in the last days*]; and it must needs be **upon the face of this earth** [*it will literally happen upon the earth*]; and it cometh unto men according to the flesh if it so be that they will harden their hearts against the Holy One of Israel [*Christ*]. [*It will literally happen to people who work to destroy righteousness on earth.*]

19 For behold, **the righteous shall not perish; for the time surely must come that all they who fight against Zion shall be cut off.**

20 And the Lord will surely prepare a way for his people, unto the fulfilling of the words of Moses, which he spake, saying: A prophet [*Christ*] shall the Lord your God raise up unto you, like unto me [*Moses*]; him shall ye hear in all things whatsoever he shall say unto you. And it shall come to pass that all those who will not hear that prophet [*Christ*] shall be cut off from among the people [*will be separated from the people of the Lord*].

Next, Nephi tells us who the prophet was that Moses prophesied about.

21 And now I, Nephi, declare unto you, that **this prophet of whom Moses spake was the Holy One of Israel** [*the Savior*]; wherefore, he [*Christ*] shall execute [*carry out*] judgment in righteousness.

22 And **the righteous need not fear, for they are those who shall not be confounded** [*will not be stopped in their progress toward exaltation*]. **But it is the kingdom of the devil** [*everything the devil has and is trying to do against God and His people; the "church of the devil" in 1 Nephi 14:10*], which shall be built up among the children of men [*which will become powerful upon the earth*], which kingdom is established among them which are in the flesh. [*In other words, it is literal that Satan will gain tremendous power among the wicked in the last days upon the earth.*]

Nephi mentioned that the righteous do not need to fear, three times in the above verses (verses 17, 19, and 22). This indeed is a major message to us from Isaiah, Nephi, and the Savior.

Nephi will now describe motives of wicked people and organizations. We would do well to avoid such motives in our own thinking and behaviors.

23 For the time speedily shall come that all churches [*organizations, whether they be religious, political, secret combinations, or whatever*] which are built up **to get gain** [*wealth*], and all those who are built up **to get power over the flesh** [*to exercise unrighteous dominion over people*], and those who are built up **to become popular in the eyes of the world, and those who seek the lusts of the flesh** [*sexual immorality*] **and the things of the world** [*materialism*], and **to do all manner of iniquity** [*all kinds of wickedness*]; yea, in fine [*in summary*], **all those who belong to the kingdom of the devil are they who need fear, and tremble, and quake; they are those who must** [*because of the law of justice*] be brought low in the dust; they are those who must be consumed as stubble [*who will be burned like dry grain stalks*]; and this is according to the words of the prophet [*Isaiah*].

Next, Nephi describes conditions of the world during the Millennium (the 1,000 years of peace after Christ comes for His Second Coming).

24 And the time cometh speedily that **the righteous must be led up as calves of the stall** [*will have peace and protection like new calves who have their own little shed where they are protected from coyotes, wolves, dogs, etc.*]**, and the Holy One of Israel** [*Christ*] **must reign** [*will rule*] **in dominion, and might, and power, and great glory** [*Christ will rule and reign on earth during the Millennium*].

25 And **he gathereth his children** from the four quarters of the earth [*those who are willing to follow Christ will be gathered from throughout the earth*]; and he numbereth his sheep [*His faithful followers*], and they know him; and there shall be one fold and one shepherd; **and he shall feed his sheep**, and in him they shall find pasture.

26 And **because of the righteousness of his people, Satan has no power**; wherefore, he cannot be loosed for the space of many years [*Satan will be bound at the beginning of the millennium and won't be let loose until the end of the millennium*]; for he hath no power over the hearts of the people, for they dwell in righteousness, and the Holy One of Israel reigneth.

Some people consider that the "righteousness of his people" (verse 26, above) during the Millennium will be the only way of binding Satan so he has no power to tempt people during the Millennium. This is not the case. D&C 101:28 teaches that Satan will not even have the power to tempt during the Millennium. While we can certainly limit his power over us by not yielding to his temptations, we know we cannot stop him from tempting us. Christ is the only one who can stop him completely. And He will do so when He comes again. This doctrine is clearly taught in the 1981 Institute of Religion *Doctrine and Covenants Student Manual*, page 89, as follows:

"In speaking of the millennial era, Nephi said that 'because of the righteousness of his—the Lord's—people, Satan has no power; wherefore, he cannot be loosed for the space of many years; for he hath no power over the hearts of the people, for they dwell in righteousness, and the Holy One of Israel reigneth' (1 Nephi 22:26).

"President Joseph Fielding Smith taught concerning the binding of Satan: 'There are many among us who teach that the binding of Satan will be merely the binding which those dwelling on the earth will place upon him by their refusal to hear his enticings. This is not so. He will not have the privilege during that period of time to tempt any man (D&C 101:28)'" (Smith, *Church History and Modern Revelation*, 1:192).

"These two statements at first may seem to be at variance, but in reality they are not. It is true that the result of the righteousness of the Saints is that Satan cannot exert power over them. The restrictions that will come upon Satan will be a result of two important actions by the Lord: (1) he will destroy telestial wickedness from the earth at his second coming; and (2) as a reward for heeding his counsels, the Lord will pour out his Spirit upon the righteous who remain to the extent that Satan's power will be overwhelmed.

"Thus, Satan will not have the power to tempt or negatively influence the Lord's people. Both the righteousness of the Saints and the operation of the Lord's power are necessary to bind Satan: if the Saints do not give heed to God's word, he will not impart of his Spirit; and if the Lord's influence is not brought to bear to aid the Saints, they, on their own power, cannot withstand the force of the adversary" (*Doctrine and Covenants Student Manual*, p. 89).

Remember that Nephi is still answering the questions of his brethren as to which things Isaiah taught are literal and which are spiritual.

27 And now behold, I, Nephi, say unto you **that all these things must come according to the flesh** [*all these things will be literally fulfilled*].

28 But, behold, **all nations, kindreds, tongues, and people shall dwell safely in the Holy One of Israel if it so be that they will repent.** [*The peace and safety brought by the Atonement of Christ and His gospel are*

available to all people, regardless of their lineage or any other factors, if they are willing to repent and live the gospel.]

> Remember that God is completely fair to all His children, therefore, ultimately, whether in this life or in the spirit world that follows, everyone will receive a completely fair set of opportunities to use their agency to follow Christ (see D&C 138). Therefore, all "shall dwell safely in the Holy One of Israel" if they so choose (see verse 28, above).

29 And now I, Nephi, make an end; for I durst not speak further as yet concerning these things [*this was all that I dared to say to my brethren at this time*].

> Next, Nephi will bear his testimony that the things written on the brass plates are true.

30 Wherefore, my brethren, I would that ye should consider that **the things** [*particularly Isaiah*] **which have been written upon the plates of brass are true**; and **they testify that a man must be obedient to the commandments of God**.

31 Wherefore, ye need not suppose that I and my father are the only ones that have testified, and also taught them. [*Isaiah and others have taught them too.*] **Wherefore, if ye shall be obedient to the commandments, and endure to the end, ye shall be saved at the last day** [*on Judgment Day*]. And thus it is. Amen.

THE SECOND BOOK OF NEPHI

2 NEPHI 1

Remember that Lehi and Sariah and their family have now been in America for quite a while. Their sons, including Nephi, have married and now have families of their own. It won't be too long before Father Lehi dies. In chapters 1–3, he will give his final messages to his people. He will teach, review, prophesy, and bless his posterity.

1 AND now it came to pass that after I, Nephi, had made an end of teaching my brethren, our father, **Lehi, also spake** [*spoke, said*] **many things unto them, and rehearsed unto them** [*reviewed with them*], how great things [*what great things*] the Lord had done for them in bringing them out of the land of Jerusalem.

2 And he spake unto them concerning their rebellions upon the waters [*while they were on the ocean in their ship*], and the mercies of God in sparing their lives, that they were not swallowed up in the sea.

3 And he also spake unto them concerning the land of promise [*America*], which they had obtained—how merciful the Lord had been in warning us that we should flee out of the land of Jerusalem.

In verses 1–3, above, Lehi tries again to strengthen the testimonies of his rebellious sons by reminding them of the mercies of the Lord. He encourages them to remember these things. Remembering past blessings from the Lord is a very powerful way to strengthen our testimonies and keep us faithful through difficult times in our lives.

4 For, behold, said he, **I have seen a vision, in which I know that Jerusalem is destroyed; and had we remained in Jerusalem we should** [*would*] also have perished [*died*].

5 But, said he, notwithstanding [*in spite of*] our afflictions [*troubles*], **we have obtained a land of promise, a land which is choice above all other lands** [*literal; also symbolic of attaining heaven, despite hardships and trials during our lives on earth*]; a land which the Lord God hath covenanted

with me should be a land for the inheritance of my seed [*descendants*]. Yea, the Lord hath covenanted [*promised*] this land unto me, and to my children forever, and also all those who should be led out of other countries by the hand of the Lord.

Symbolism: We must be led by the Lord in order to enter celestial glory; covenants are required for entrance into the celestial kingdom—except for children who die before the age of accountability (see D&C 137:10), and the intellectually handicapped (see D&C 29:50).

6 Wherefore, **I, Lehi, prophesy** according to the workings of the Spirit which is in me, that there shall none come into this land save they shall be brought by the hand of the Lord.

Verse 6, above, is a fascinating prophecy. It is important to realize that the New World remained undiscovered for all practical purposes, for many centuries until Columbus, and this despite the fact that numerous adventurers such as Vikings had come temporarily. It is a testimony that the Lord held others back from settling the Americas until the time was right for it to be discovered to the whole world (see verse 8, below).

In verse 7, next, we find the formula for retaining freedom and liberty in this land. It is also a formula for retaining personal freedom from spiritual bondage.

7 Wherefore [*therefore*], this land is consecrated unto [*set aside for*] him whom he [*the Lord*] shall bring. And **if it so be that they** [*the inhabitants of this land*] shall **serve him according to the commandments which he hath given, it shall be a land of liberty unto them; wherefore, they shall never be brought down into captivity; if so** [*if they are conquered by foreign nations*], it shall be because of iniquity [*wickedness*]; for **if iniquity shall abound** [*if lots of people in America become wicked*] **cursed shall be the land for their sakes** [*because of them*], but unto the righteous it shall be blessed forever.

Next, Lehi explains the wisdom of the Lord in keeping others from discovering the Americas for the time being.

8 And behold, it is wisdom that this land should be kept as yet from the knowledge of other nations; for behold, **many nations would overrun the land, that there would be no place for an inheritance.**

Next, Lehi tells the inhabitants of the promised land how they can keep from being conquered by other nations.

9 Wherefore, I, Lehi, have obtained a promise, that **inasmuch as** [*if*] **those** [*including the Mulekites (Mosiah 25:2) and Lehi's people*] **whom the Lord God shall bring out of the land of Jerusalem shall keep his commandments, they shall prosper upon the face of this land; and they shall be kept from all other nations, that they may possess this land unto themselves. And if it so be that they shall keep his commandments they shall be blessed upon the face of this land, and there shall be none to molest them, nor to take away the land of their inheritance; and they shall dwell safely forever.**

Next, Lehi tells how inhabitants of the promised land could stop receiving protection from the Lord.

10 **But behold, when the time cometh that they** [*including the Lamanites*] shall **dwindle in unbelief** [*gradually stop believing in God; apostatize*], after they have received so great blessings from the hand of the Lord—having a knowledge of the creation of the earth, and all men, knowing the great and marvelous works of the Lord from the creation of the world; having power given them to do all things by faith; having all the commandments from the beginning, and having been brought by his infinite goodness into this precious land of promise—behold, I say, **if the day shall come that they will reject the Holy One of Israel, the true Messiah, their Redeemer and their God, behold, the judgments of him that is just** [*the punishments of God*] **shall rest upon them.**

11 Yea, **he will bring other nations unto them, and he will give unto them** [*the other nations*] power, and he will take away from them [*the Lamanites*] the lands of their possessions, and he will cause them to be scattered and smitten [*badly treated*].

12 Yea, as one generation passeth to another there shall be bloodsheds, and great visitations [*troubles and punishments*] among them; **wherefore** [*therefore*], my sons, **I would** [*I desire*] **that ye would remember; yea, I would that ye would hearken** [*listen seriously*] **unto my words.**

Next, you can see that Lehi is very worried that Laman and Lemuel are spiritually asleep. He is afraid that they have rebelled against God so much that they no longer have the ability to recognize the great value of living the gospel, keeping the commandments of God and receiving inspiration and promptings from the Holy Ghost.

13 **O that ye would awake** [*o how I wish that you would wake up*]; awake from a deep sleep [*spiritually asleep*], yea, even **from the sleep of hell, and shake off the awful chains by which ye are bound, which are the chains which bind the children of men** [*people*], that they are carried away captive down to the eternal gulf of misery and woe [*hell*].

As Lehi continues to plead with Laman and Lemuel to repent and seek to keep the commandments of God, we learn an obvious and comforting truth; namely, that righteous parents (like Lehi and Sariah) of rebellious children, who have tried to teach and guide them in the paths of righteousness, will themselves be saved. You will see this in verse 15.

14 Awake! and arise from the dust, and hear the words of a trembling parent, whose limbs [*body*] ye must soon lay down in the cold and silent grave [*who is going to die soon*], from whence [*where*] no traveler can return; a few more days and I go the way of all the earth [*I will soon die, just as everyone must die*].

15 But behold, **the Lord hath redeemed my soul from hell; I have beheld** [*seen*] **his glory, and I am encircled about eternally in the arms of his love.**

Next, Lehi explains how he has been very worried about Laman and Lemuel all along.

16 And I desire that ye should remember to observe the statutes [*laws and commandments*] and the judgments [*rules*] of the Lord; **behold, this hath been the anxiety of my soul** [*this is why I have been so worried about you*] **from the beginning.**

17 **My heart hath been weighed down with sorrow from time to time, for I have feared, lest for the hardness of your hearts** [*because of the rebelliousness of your hearts*] **the Lord your God should come out in the fulness of his wrath** [*anger*] **upon you, that ye be cut off and destroyed forever;**

18 **Or, that a cursing should come upon you for the space of many generations** [*hundreds of years*]**; and ye are visited** [*punished*] **by sword, and by famine, and are hated, and are led according to the will and captivity of the devil** [*according to how Satan treats wicked people under his influence and captivity*].

19 **O my sons, that these things might not come upon you, but that ye might be a choice and a**

favored people of the Lord. But behold, his will be done; for his ways are righteousness forever.

Next, Lehi gives us a simple formula for being happy or being miserable.

20 And he [*the Lord*] hath said that: **Inasmuch as ye** [*if you*] **shall keep my commandments ye shall prosper** [*have happiness and grow and progress*] **in the land; but inasmuch as ye will not keep my commandments ye shall be cut off from my presence** [*a simple statement of eternal fact*].

Next, Lehi pleads with Laman and Lemuel to rise up and be real men, righteous and united.

21 And now that my soul might have joy in you, and that my heart might leave this world with gladness because of you, that I might not be brought down with grief and sorrow to the grave, **arise from the dust, my sons, and be men, and be determined in one mind and in one heart, united in all things, that ye may not come down into captivity** [*literal and spiritual*];

Next, Lehi defines the word "cursed" in the ultimate sense of the word. It means to be stopped in eternal progress and to be subject to Satan eternally.

22 That ye may not be **cursed with a sore** [*very severe*] **cursing; and also, that ye may not incur** [*cause*] the displeasure of a just [*righteous, fair*] God upon you, unto the destruction, yea, **the eternal destruction of both soul** [*spirit*] **and body.**

We know that we cannot ever be destroyed in the sense that we will no longer exist. We know that all will be resurrected, including even sons of perdition (see D&C 88:28–32 and 97–102). Thus, the spirit and body will continue inseparably forever after the resurrection and cannot be destroyed in the sense of ceasing to exist, as stated above. Therefore, the "eternal destruction of both soul and body," at the end of verse 22, above, has to refer to never again being privileged to dwell in the presence of God in celestial glory (see D&C 76:112).

23 **Awake, my sons; put on the armor** [*protection*] **of righteousness. Shake off the chains** [*of rebellion and wickedness*] with which ye are bound [*all tied up*], and come forth out of obscurity [*being less and less influential in doing good*], and arise from the dust.

24 **Rebel no more against your brother** [*Nephi*], whose views have been glorious, and who hath [*has*] kept the commandments from the time that we left Jerusalem;

and who hath been an instrument [*tool*] in the hands of God, in bringing us forth into the land of promise; for were it not for him, we must have [*would have*] perished with hunger in the wilderness; nevertheless, ye sought [*tried*] to take away his life; yea, and he hath suffered much sorrow because of you.

Lehi is still very worried about how Laman and Lemuel will treat Nephi after Lehi dies.

25 And I exceedingly fear and tremble because of you, lest he shall suffer again; for behold, **ye have accused him that he sought power and authority over you** [*you accused him of wanting to rule over you*]; but I know that he hath not sought for power nor authority over you, **but he hath sought the glory of God** [*he just wanted to do what God wants*], and your own eternal welfare [*what is best for you forever*].

Next, we are given an excellent lesson in understanding that how the wicked see things is much different than reality. It is difficult but important to realize that wicked people do not think like the righteous do.

26 And ye have murmured [*complained*] because he [*Nephi*] hath been plain unto you. **Ye say that he hath used sharpness; ye say that he hath been angry with you; but behold, his sharpness was the sharpness of the power of the word of God, which was in him; and that which ye call anger was the truth, according to that which is in God, which he could not restrain** [*hold back*], manifesting boldly concerning [*showing very clearly*] your iniquities [*sins*].

27 And it must needs be [*it is necessary*] that the power of God must be with him, even unto his commanding you that ye must obey. But behold, **it was not he, but it was the Spirit of the Lord which was in him, which opened his mouth to utterance that he could not shut it.**

Next, Lehi offers his "first" blessing, in other words, his best possible blessing to his sons and sons-in-law. The choice is up to them. This is a clear example of the fact that we each have moral agency and that we truly are free to choose what happens to us in the next life and throughout eternity.

28 And now my son, Laman, and also Lemuel and Sam, and also my sons who are the sons of Ishmael, behold, **if ye will hearken unto** [*listen to and obey*] **the voice of Nephi ye shall not perish. And if ye will hearken unto him I leave**

unto you a blessing, yea, even my first blessing [*the choicest blessing, the blessings that will come from living the gospel; perhaps, in this case, it could be called the "birthright" blessing*].

Each of us, regardless of birth order, is entitled to inherit all that the Father has—in other words, exaltation. This would be the "first blessing" or "birthright blessing" in the eternal gospel sense. It will come to each of us if we choose to keep the commandments.

29 **But if ye will not hearken unto him I take away my first blessing** [*you will lose your spiritual inheritance, including the right to lead our people*], yea, even my blessing, and it shall rest upon him [*Nephi*].

Next, we see that Zoram, the servant of Laban who got the brass plates for Nephi and his brothers and then went with them into the wilderness, was a good man and had not joined Laman and Lemuel in rebelling against Nephi and his father.

30 **And now, Zoram, I speak unto you: Behold, thou art the servant of Laban; nevertheless, thou hast been brought out of the land of Jerusalem, and I know that thou art a true friend unto my son, Nephi, forever.**

31 Wherefore [*therefore*], **because thou hast been faithful thy seed** [*your children and their children on down through time; posterity*] **shall be blessed with his seed, that they dwell in prosperity** [*that they will have many blessings and will get along very well*] long upon the face of this land [*America*]; and nothing, save [*except*] it shall be iniquity [*wickedness*] among them, shall harm or disturb their prosperity upon the face of this land forever.

Zoram has been made a full family member in Lehi's family, just as promised by Nephi in 1 Nephi 4:31–37. This is certainly symbolic of the fact that anyone, regardless of race and national origin, can be made a full citizen in the household of God by making and keeping covenants.

Finally, Lehi blesses Zoram that he and his family and descendants will have the security of living upon this land along with Nephi and his descendants, if they keep the commandments of the Lord. This is truly a wonderful example of the power of a father's blessing.

32 Wherefore, if ye shall keep the commandments of the Lord, the Lord hath consecrated [*blessed and set aside*] this land for the security of thy seed [*posterity*] with the seed of my son [*Nephi*].

2 NEPHI 2

This chapter contains one of the finest and most complete sermons anywhere in scripture on some very basic doctrines and teachings of the gospel. If you get a basic understanding and testimony of these doctrines, you will be well on your way to having a good understanding of the true gospel of Jesus Christ. These doctrines are

- The Fall of Adam and Eve
- Justice
- Mercy
- The Atonement of Jesus Christ
- Agency

This chapter describes the interrelationship of each of these elements with the others. It ties in very closely with 2 Nephi 9. In fact, you may wish to make a note in the heading of 2 Nephi 2 in your own scriptures, to the effect that chapters 2 and 9 go together.

Since the teachings in these two chapters are so vital to our understanding of the gospel of Jesus Christ, I will pause for a few moments here and depart from my usual format in order to invite you to check your knowledge about the Fall, the Atonement, and related topics. It is in the form of a true/false quiz. I will provide an answer key for you at the end of the quiz.

True or False Quiz for 2 Nephi 2 and 9

Questions

1. True or False
Because of the Savior's Atonement, everyone but the very most wicked will be resurrected.

2. True or False
In a way, it is too bad Adam and Eve partook of the forbidden fruit, because our lives would have been much easier if they hadn't.

3. True or False
If Adam and Eve had not transgressed in the Garden of Eden, they and their children would never have become mortal and progressed.

4. True or False
Because of their transgression and the resulting Fall, Adam was cursed severely by God, but Eve got an even worse cursing.

5. True or False
Because of Christ's Atonement, people can be forgiven of all but two types of sin.

6. True or False
Bishops can forgive sins.

7. True or False
The only sins we have to confess to a bishop are sins listed in the temple recommend interview.

8. True or False
If you have a problem confessing your sins to your own bishop, it is

sometimes permissible to confess to another bishop.

9. True or False
Part of the punishment for sinning is having to confess to the bishop.

10. True or False
It is not possible in this life to know for sure if you have been forgiven, but you can have a feeling of peace that gives you hope.

11. True or False
One way we can tell if we have been forgiven is that we won't remember the sin anymore.

12. True or False
If we repent of our sins, they will be taken off the records in heaven.

13. True or False
There is much, much more to repenting than the act of confessing.

14. True or False
It was a good thing that Adam and Eve ate the forbidden fruit.

15. True or False
Many people will have a very enjoyable Judgment Day.

16. True or False
Without the Savior's Atonement, we could not be resurrected and thus would have become like the devil.

17. True or False
It is okay to plan on making it to the highest part of heaven.

Answers

1. False.
Everyone will get resurrected (2 Nephi 9:22).

2. False.
The Fall was good, plus it was absolutely necessary (2 Nephi 2:22–25).

3. False.
They would not have had children (2 Nephi 2:22–23).

4. False.
Neither of them was cursed. Satan was the one who was cursed. The Fall was a great blessing, and it gave Adam and Eve ownership of the consequences, which brought great joy along with hardships, which promoted growth (see Moses 5:10–11). The ground was cursed for Adam's sake (Genesis 3:14–17).

5. True.
Denying the Holy Ghost (D&C 76:31–35) and first degree murder (D&C 42:18) are unforgivable. All other sins can be forgiven (Isaiah 1:18).

6. True or false, depending on how you are thinking.
Only God can forgive sins, but the bishop can forgive sins for the Church in terms of allowing people to go to the temple, etc.

7. Basically true.
This is because there is a question in the temple recommend interview that asks if there is any sin that should have been confessed to a bishop but that hasn't been. However, you could answer "false,"

since not every possible sin is mentioned in the interview.

8. False.
Your bishop is the only one who has the keys of authority over you (except in the case of students who may have a campus ward plus a home ward). The issue here is the priesthood keys of authority and accompanying stewardship. If members have valid difficulty talking to their own bishops, they may confess to their stake president.

9. Absolutely false.
It is not punishment to be helped in overcoming sins.

10. False.
The Holy Ghost can give you a good feeling, which lets you know you are on the path to exaltation. We are counseled in 2 Nephi 31:20 to press forward with a "perfect brightness of hope."

11. False.
Alma could remember his sins, but they pained him no more (Alma 36). Sometimes people seem to get D&C 58:42–43 mixed up where the Lord "remembers them no more," referring to Judgment Day, and they think that applies to us in terms of remembering them no more.

12. True.
D&C 58:42. However, if a student is being very observant, he or she might refer to D&C 82:7, where the Lord warns that "former sins return" if the sin is repeated again, and thus say correctly that, in this context, the answer is "false." The important result of the discussion for this question is that, upon deep and sincere repentance, our sins are forgiven and gone forever (Isaiah 1:18).

13. True.
D&C 58:42–43, and many more scriptures.

14. True.
See 2 Nephi 2:22–25 and Moses 5:10–11, among others.

15. True.
See 2 Nephi 9:14, second half of verse.

16. True.
See 2 Nephi 9:7–9.

17. True.
See 2 Nephi 31:20 and many other references. If we don't plan on it, we are less determined in our quest for exaltation.

Now that you have taken the above pretest, we will continue with Lehi's powerful teachings about agency, the Fall, the Atonement, justice, and mercy.

Lehi is speaking to his son Jacob, who may be in his late teens to early twenties by now. Jacob was the first of two sons born in the wilderness to Lehi and Sariah. Joseph was born after Jacob.

1 AND now, Jacob, I speak unto you: Thou art my first-born in the days of my tribulation in the

wilderness. And behold, in thy childhood thou hast suffered afflictions and much sorrow, because of the rudeness of thy brethren.

"Rudeness" as used in verse 1, above, seems to be a much stronger word than the word "rudeness" today. It appears to include cruelty and wickedness.

2 Nevertheless, Jacob, my first-born in the wilderness, thou knowest the greatness of God; and **he shall consecrate thine afflictions for thy gain** [*bless you so that the problems you have will actually strengthen you*].

Those who remain true and faithful to God through difficult trials and tribulations enable Him to bless them and strengthen them tremendously.

3 Wherefore, thy soul [*you*] shall be blessed, and thou shalt [*you will*] dwell [*live*] safely with thy brother, Nephi; and thy days shall be spent in the service of thy God. Wherefore, **I know that thou art redeemed, because of the righteousness** [*the Atonement*] **of thy Redeemer; for thou hast beheld that in the fulness of time** [*the time appointed by the Father*] he [*Christ*] cometh to bring salvation unto men.

There is something I would like to point out to you, based on verse 3, above. The Atonement of Christ worked before it was actually performed by the Savior here on earth. Lehi says that it worked for Jacob, and Jacob and countless others lived before Christ. In fact, it even worked in premortality as we exercised our agency there. Elder Jeffrey R. Holland taught it as follows:

"We could remember that even in the Grand Council of Heaven He loved us and was wonderfully strong, that we triumphed even there by the power of Christ and our faith in the blood of the Lamb" (Holland, "'This Do in Remembrance of Me,'" p. 67).

It even worked for us in our premortal life. The Institute of Religion New Testament Student Manual, *The Life and Teachings of Jesus and His Apostles*, teaches: "We were given laws and agency, and commandments to have faith and repent from the wrongs that we could do there. '. . . Man could and did in many instances, sin before he was born'" (*The Life and Teachings of Jesus and His Disciples*, 1979 Edition, pp. 336–37).

The point is that the Atonement has been blessing our lives for countless eons of time already and will continue to do so if we try to do our best to keep the commandments.

4 And **thou hast beheld in thy youth his glory** [*it appears that Jacob saw the Savior while still relatively young*]; wherefore [*that's why*], thou art blessed even as they unto whom he shall minister in the flesh [*you are blessed just like the people who will see Him on earth during His mortal or earthly mission*]; for the Spirit is the same, yesterday, today, and forever [*The same plan of salvation has been and always will be used to bring people to Christ.*] And **the way is prepared** [*the Father's plan of salvation prepares the way*] **from the fall of man** [*the Fall of Adam and Eve*], **and salvation is free** [*is available to all*].

Watch now, and notice how skillfully Lehi builds one principle upon another as he teaches the basic plan of salvation. The "plan of salvation" means the stages and steps that Heavenly Father is sending us through, all the way from our premortal existence to the time that we can return to live with Him forever. First, he teaches that in order to have and use agency, we must have sufficient knowledge of the gospel.

5 And **men are instructed sufficiently that they know good from evil. And the law** [*the laws and rules Moses gave to his people*] is given unto men. And by the law no flesh is justified [*no one can be saved by the law of Moses*]; or, by the law [*of Moses*] men are cut off [*cannot return to the presence of God*]. Yea, **by the temporal law** [*the law of Moses which had lots of things people had to do, such as offer sacrifices*] **they were cut off** [*couldn't get back to heaven*]; and also, by the **spiritual law they perish from that which is good, and become miserable forever.**

We understand the spiritual law in verse 5, above, to be the law governing spiritual death. In other words, wickedness leads to spiritual death, meaning the death of our spirituality. We are kept out of God's presence in celestial glory.

Now that he has laid the doctrinal foundation, he teaches us that we must use the Atonement of Christ to avoid spiritual death.

6 Wherefore, **redemption** [*freedom from spiritual death*] **cometh in and through the Holy Messiah** [*Christ*]; for he is full of grace and truth [*fully capable of saving us*].

7 Behold, **he** [*Christ*] **offereth himself a sacrifice for sin, to answer the ends of the law** [*to satisfy the law of justice*], **unto all those who have a broken** [*humble; under proper control*] **heart and a contrite spirit** [*"contrite" means "desiring correction as needed"*]; and unto none else can the ends [*requirements*] of the law [*of justice*] be answered.

8 Wherefore, how great the importance to make these things known

unto the inhabitants of the earth [*this is why the gospel must be taught to everyone*], that they may know that **there is no flesh** [*there are no resurrected people*] **that can dwell** [*live*] **in the presence of God, save it be through the merits, and mercy, and grace of the Holy Messiah** [*except through the power of the Atonement*], who layeth down his life according to the flesh [*as a mortal*], and taketh it again [*is resurrected*] by the power of the Spirit, that he may bring to pass the resurrection of the dead, being the first that should rise. [*Christ will be the first one from this earth to be resurrected.*]

9 Wherefore, he is the firstfruits [*the first resurrected*] unto God [*the Father*], inasmuch as he shall make intercession for all the children of men [*His Atonement will be available to all people*]; and **they that believe in him shall be saved** [*exalted in the celestial kingdom*].

Next, Lehi will teach about the laws of justice and mercy. These two eternal laws work together with the Atonement of Jesus Christ to make it so that we are accountable and can truly use our agency to choose whether or not we return back into the presence of God. If we choose to try our best to live the gospel and repent as needed, we get mercy, and the Atonement makes us clean and free from sin so that we can return to live with God. This is the result of what is called the law of mercy.

If we choose not to live the gospel and not to repent, we get justice, in other words, punishment, for our sins and won't be allowed to return to live with God. This is the result of what is called the law of justice.

10 And **because of the intercession** [*Christ's Atonement*] **for all, all men come unto God** [*all will ultimately be accountable*]; wherefore, **they stand in the presence of him, to be judged of him according to the truth and holiness which is in him** [*Christ's judgment will be completely fair*]. Wherefore, the ends of the law [*the purposes of the law of justice*] which the Holy One [*Christ*] hath given, unto the inflicting [*applying*] of the punishment which is affixed [*which is attached to violating the laws of God*], which punishment that is affixed is in opposition to that of the happiness [*the law of mercy*] which is affixed, to answer the ends [*to fulfill the purposes and goals*] of the atonement—

Lehi now explains that in order for our agency to be true agency, we must have choices. In order to have true choices, we must have opposites. In order to have opposites, we must be in an environment where opposition exists.

For example, you might have to choose between going to church or hanging out with friends and watching a video. Or, you might have to choose between paying your tithing or buying a game for your electronic device. These are examples of opposition in real life.

Watch now as Lehi gives several major examples of types of opposition that we may face in our lives.

11 For **it must needs be** [*it is necessary*], **that there is an opposition in all things**. If not so, my first-born in the wilderness [*Jacob*], righteousness could not be brought to pass [*the Atonement of Christ would not be able to work*], neither **wickedness**, neither **holiness** nor **misery**, neither **good** nor **bad**. Wherefore, all things must needs be a compound in one [*everything would be the same; nothing would work as far as personal progress is concerned*]; wherefore, if it should be one body [*if everything were the same, without opposites*] it must needs remain as dead [*nothing would happen*], having no **life** neither **death**, nor **corruption** nor **incorruption**, **happiness** nor **misery**, neither **sense** [*feeling*] nor **insensibility** [*lack of feeling*].

12 Wherefore, **it must needs have been created for a thing of naught** [*nothing in life would have purpose*]; wherefore **there would have been no purpose in the end** [*goal, purpose*] **of its creation**. Wherefore, **this thing must** needs [*if there were no opposites, which require agency choices, it would*] **destroy** the wisdom of God and his eternal purposes, and also the power, and the **mercy**, and the **justice** of God.

Next, you will see one of the greatest series of logical statements ever written!

13 And if ye shall say there is **no law**, ye shall also say there is **no sin**. If ye shall say there is **no sin,** ye shall also say there is **no righteousness**. And if there be **no righteousness** there be **no happiness**. And if there be **no righteousness nor happiness** there be **no punishment nor misery**. And if these things are not there is **no God. And if there is no God we are not** [*we don't exist*]**, neither the earth**; for there could have been no creation of things, neither to act nor to be acted upon [*there would be no opportunity for choice*]; wherefore, all things must have vanished away [*there would be no existence at all!*].

Having taught the necessary roles of justice and mercy, agency and opposition, Lehi will now bear his testimony of God and that we do indeed have agency to choose.

14 And now, my sons, I speak unto you these things for your

profit and learning [*to help you*]; for **there is a God**, and **he hath created all things**, both the heavens and the earth, and all things that in them are, **both things to act and things to be acted upon** [*so we can have true agency*].

Next, Lehi will explain why Adam and Eve were faced with the opposing choices of the two trees in the Garden of Eden.

15 And to bring about his eternal purposes in the end of man [*His goals for His children*], after he had created our first parents [*Adam and Eve*], and the beasts [*animals*] of the field and the fowls [*birds*] of the air, and in fine [*in summary*], all things which are created, it must needs be [*it is absolutely necessary*] that there was an opposition; even **the forbidden fruit in opposition to the tree of life**; the **one** being **sweet** and **the other bitter**.

Next, Lehi ties moral agency in with what he has taught above, and explains the absolute necessity for opposition in order to exercise agency.

16 Wherefore [*this is why*], **the Lord God gave unto man that he should act for himself**. Wherefore, **man could not act for himself save it should be that he was enticed** [*attracted*] **by the one or the other**.

Next, Lehi explains how Lucifer became the devil and why he tries to get us to follow him. He also tells us that Satan tempted Eve in the Garden of Eden and that after Adam and Eve ate the forbidden fruit, they were cast out of the Garden of Eden.

17 And I, Lehi, according to the things which I have read, must needs suppose that **an angel of God** [*Lucifer*], according to that which is written, **had fallen from heaven**; wherefore, **he became a devil**, having sought that which was evil before God [*he rebelled against God*].

18 And **because he had fallen from heaven, and had become miserable** forever, **he sought** [*wanted*] **also the misery of all mankind** [*all people*]. Wherefore [*that's why*], he said unto Eve, yea, even that old serpent [*one of Satan's nicknames*], who is the devil, who is the father of [*the originator of*] all lies, wherefore he said: Partake [*eat*] of the forbidden fruit [*the fruit of the tree of good and evil, in the Garden of Eden*], and ye shall not die, but ye shall be as God, knowing good and evil.

Satan only told one lie in the Garden of Eden: namely, that they would not die. Otherwise, everything he said was true. This is a reminder that he is a master at mixing enough truth into his temptations that it makes them seem okay.

19 And after Adam and Eve had partaken of the forbidden fruit they were driven out of the garden of Eden, to till [*farm*] the earth.

20 And they have brought forth [*have had*] children; yea, even the family of all the earth. [*Adam and Eve started people on this earth.*]

Now, Lehi will teach that we need enough time in this life on earth to exercise our agency among the many choices we have between good and evil. That way we have personal ownership of our final judgment. For those over age eight, who die before they have had sufficient time to be taught the gospel and exercise their agency, there is a great missionary work going on in the spirit world (see D&C 138).

21 And the **days of the children of men** [*people*] **were prolonged**, according to the will of God, **that they might repent while in the flesh** [*during life on earth, in other words, during mortality*]; wherefore, their state [*mortal lives*] became **a state of probation** [*a time of testing and learning*], and their time was lengthened [*they were given enough time*], according to the commandments which the Lord God gave unto the children of men. For **he gave commandment that all men must repent**; for he showed unto all men that they were lost, because of the transgression of their parents [*the Fall of Adam and Eve*].

Next, Lehi continues by teaching us what would have happened if Adam and Eve had not partaken of the forbidden fruit.

22 And now, behold, **if Adam had not transgressed he would not have fallen**, but **he would have remained in the garden of Eden**. And **all things** which were created **must have** [*would have*] **remained in the same state** in which they were after they were created; **and they must have remained forever, and had no end**.

The word "end" in verse 22, above, can have two meanings in this verse, both of which make sense. One meaning is "never ending" and the other is "no purpose."

23 And **they would have had no children**; wherefore they would have remained in a state of innocence, having **no joy**, for they knew **no misery**; **doing no good**, for they knew **no sin**.

Next, Lehi answers a question that many members of the Church ask—namely, "Was God surprised when they ate the fruit? Was there a 'plan B' in case Adam and Eve did not partake of the forbidden fruit?" The answer is "No," because God knows all things as explained in verse 24, next.

24 But behold, **all things have been done in the wisdom of him who knoweth all things**.

Brigham Young taught that there was no "plan B" as follows:

"The Lord knew they would do this, and he had designed that they should" [*Young, Discourses of Brigham Young, p. 103*].

Furthermore, Joseph Smith said the following: "Adam did not commit sin in eating the fruits, for God had decreed that he should eat and fall" (*The Words of Joseph Smith*, p. 63).

Next comes one of the most beautiful quotes from the Book of Mormon. You may have already heard it many times. It reminds us that our lives on earth are designed to be mostly enjoyable.

25 **Adam fell that men might be; and men are, that they might have joy.**

Next, in verses 26 through 29, Lehi emphasizes the role of the Atonement of Christ in overcoming the effects of the Fall of Adam and Eve. If you study this enough to understand it quite well, you will have a good head start in understanding the basic teachings of the Church and will be better able to teach others.

26 And **the Messiah cometh** in the fulness of time [*Jesus will be born and will fulfill His mission on earth when Heavenly Father says it is time to.*], **that he may redeem the children of men from the fall** [*so that He can set mortals free from the results of the Fall of Adam and Eve*]. And **because that they are redeemed from the fall** they **have become free forever, knowing good from evil; to act for themselves and not to be acted upon**, save [*except*] it be by the punishment of the law [*the law of justice*] at the great and last day [*on Judgment Day*], according to the commandments which God hath given.

We find a very interesting and significant teaching near the end of verse 26, above. Many students of the gospel wonder why the wicked don't get "caught up with." In other words, why does the Lord let them get away with so much for so long? In verse 26, plus in previous verses, Lehi teaches that everyone's days were prolonged in order to give them plenty of time to exercise their agency wisely. And here he teaches basically that (at least for most people) they won't get caught up with until the final day of judgment.

27 Wherefore, **men are free according to the flesh** [*people are free to choose during their entire mortal*

lives]; and all things are given them which are expedient [*necessary*] unto man [*ultimately, all people will get everything necessary to exercise their agency wisely, whether in mortality or in the spirit world; see D&C 138*]. And **they are free to choose liberty and eternal life** [*free to choose freedom from the effects of sin and to live with God forever*], **through the great Mediator of all men** [*through the Atonement of Christ*], **or to choose captivity and death** [*or choose to live wickedly and not repent and thus, be caught in Satan's traps and not be able to return to live with God*], according to the captivity and power of the devil; for he seeketh that all men might be miserable like unto himself.

28 And now, my sons, I would that ye should [*I want you to*] **look to the great Mediator** [*have faith in Christ*], and **hearken unto his great commandments** [*keep His commandments*]; and **be faithful unto his words, and choose eternal life** [*"eternal life" means means going to the highest degree of glory in the celestial kingdom, which is called "exaltation."*] according to the will of his Holy Spirit [*the Holy Ghost will help you*];

29 And **not choose eternal death** [*"spiritual death"; means being cut off forever from returning to live with God*], **according to the will of the flesh** [*by giving in to physical temptation*] and the evil which is therein, **which giveth the spirit of the devil power to captivate** [*capture*], **to bring you down to hell, that he may reign** [*rule*] over you in his own kingdom.

30 **I have spoken these few words unto you all, my sons, in the last days of my probation** [*shortly before I die*]; **and I have chosen the good part** [*I have chosen eternal life*], according to the words of the prophet [*as taught by the prophets*]. And **I have none other object save it be the everlasting welfare of your souls** [*I have no other goal except helping you to get to heaven*]. Amen.

2 NEPHI 3

In this chapter, Lehi tells us of a great prophecy given by Joseph, who was sold into Egypt. This prophecy is not in the Bible. We learn from 2 Nephi 4:2 that it was on the brass plates. So, Lehi was able to study it and Nephi was able to write it onto the small plates of Nephi, which we are reading from now in the Book of Mormon.

You may remember that Joseph in Egypt is one of our favorite Bible stories from the Old Testament. Joseph had ten older brothers who didn't like him. They were jealous of how their father treated him so extra special, including giving him a beautiful coat of many colors. One day when the brothers were far away from home tending their flocks, young Joseph came to visit them. When they saw him coming, they decided to kill him and toss his body into a deep pit and then tell their father that he was killed by some wild animal. But they changed their minds and decided to sell him as a slave to some merchants who were traveling to Egypt. So, Joseph ended up as a slave in Egypt. You can read the details about this in Genesis, chapter 37, in the Bible.

In Egypt, Joseph still kept the commandments of God and, over many years, became a mighty leader and a prophet of God. As mentioned above, we have one of his prophecys here in this chapter of the Book of Mormon.

He prophesies about one of his descendants—namely, the Prophet Joseph Smith. Perhaps you will recall that the angel told Nephi during his vision that the brass plates contained more information than we have in the Old Testament (see 1 Nephi 13:23). It appears that this prophecy given by Joseph in Egypt is one example of this fact.

1 AND **now I** [*Lehi*] **speak unto you, Joseph, my last-born. Thou wast** [*you were*] born in the wilderness of mine afflictions [*during the eight years of trials and troubles in the wilderness, after they left Jerusalem*]; yea, in the days of my greatest sorrow did thy mother bear thee [*give birth to you*].

2 And may the Lord consecrate also unto thee [*give you*] this land [*America*], which is a most precious land, for thine inheritance [*for you to have and to keep*] and the inheritance of thy seed [*posterity, descendants*] with thy brethren, for thy security forever, **if it so be that ye shall keep the commandments of the Holy One of Israel** [*Christ*].

3 And now, Joseph, my last-born, whom I have brought out of the wilderness of mine afflictions, **may the Lord bless thee forever, for thy seed** [*descendants*] shall not utterly be destroyed [*killed off completely*].

Next, Lehi tells his son, Joseph, what his own lineage is. Lineage, as used here, means which of the twelve tribes of Israel you are from. Your patriarchal blessing will tell you your lineage. The lineage of the twelve tribes includes great blessings and responsibilities given by the Lord to Abraham, Isaac, and Jacob. As you will see, in verse 4, Lehi is from the tribe of Joseph, who was one of the twelve sons of Jacob, in other words, one of the twelve tribes of Israel.

4 For behold, thou art the fruit of my loins [*you are my child, my offspring*]; and **I am a descendant of Joseph who was carried captive into Egypt** [*Joseph who was sold*

into Egypt]. And great were the covenants [*promises*] of the Lord which he made unto Joseph.

It will be helpful for what comes next if we take a moment and point out the four "Josephs" who will be involved in Lehi's teachings to his son Joseph in this chapter. We will number them:

1. **Joseph who was sold into Egypt.** Jacob's son, Isaac's grandson, Abraham's great-grandson.

2. **Joseph, Lehi's son**, spoken to in this chapter.

3. **Joseph Smith Sr.**, the father of the Prophet Joseph Smith.

4. **Joseph Smith Jr.**, the prophet of the Restoration who restored Christ's true Church in the latter days.

5 Wherefore, **Joseph** [*who was sold into Egypt*] **truly saw our day. And he obtained a promise of the Lord, that out of the fruit of his loins** [*out of his posterity*] the Lord God would raise up a righteous branch [*a righteous people*] unto the house of Israel; not the Messiah, but a branch which was to be broken off [*scattered away from the other tribes of Israel*], nevertheless, to be remembered in the covenants of the Lord that the Messiah [*Christ*] should be made manifest unto them [*Israel?*] in the latter days, in the spirit of power, unto the bringing of them out of darkness unto light—yea, out of hidden darkness [*many who are in spiritual darkness think they are "enlightened" or living in the light; therefore, their spiritual darkness is "hidden" to them*] and out of captivity unto freedom [*the Restoration of the gospel*].

6 For **Joseph** [*in Egypt*] **truly testified, saying: A seer** [*Joseph Smith Jr.*] **shall the Lord my God raise up, who shall be a choice seer unto the fruit of my loins** [*my posterity*].

Next, Lehi tells his son Joseph what the exact words were in Joseph in Egypt's prophecy.

Imagine how Joseph Smith must have felt as he was translating the Book of Mormon from the gold plates and came across this prophecy about himself! Remember that a "seer" is a prophet.

7 Yea, **Joseph** [*in Egypt*] **truly said: Thus saith the Lord unto me** [*this is what the Lord said to me*]**: A choice seer** [*Joseph Smith Jr.*] **will I raise up out of the fruit of thy loins** [*will I call to be a prophet from your posterity*]; **and he shall be esteemed highly among the fruit of thy loins** [*he will be highly respected among your posterity*]. And **unto him will I give commandment that he shall do a work** [*restore the true Church of Jesus*

Christ in the last days] **for the fruit of thy loins, his brethren** [*his fellow Israelites*], **which shall be of great worth unto them** [*which will be very valuable to them*], **even to the bringing of them to the knowledge of the covenants which I have made with thy fathers** [*which will teach them about the promises I made to Abraham, Isaac, and Jacob*].

8 And **I will give unto him** [*Joseph Smith Jr.*] **a commandment that he shall do none other work, save** [*except*] **the work which I shall command him** [*Joseph Smith Jr. will be commanded not to get distracted by other things*]. And **I will make him great in mine eyes; for he shall do my work.**

9 And he [*Joseph Smith Jr.*] **shall be great like unto Moses, whom I have said I would raise up unto you** [*the children of Israel in Egypt*], to deliver my people [*out from Egyptian slavery*], O house of Israel.

10 And Moses will I raise up, to deliver thy people out of the land of Egypt.

11 **But a seer** [*Joseph Smith Jr.*] **will I raise up out of the fruit of thy** [*Joseph in Egypt*] **loins; and unto him** [*Joseph Smith Jr.*] **will I give power to bring forth my word** [*to restore the true gospel*] unto the seed of thy loins [*Ephraim and Manasseh*]—and **not to the bringing forth my word only, saith the Lord, but to the convincing them of my word, which shall have already gone forth among them** [*the Book of Mormon will bear witness of the truth of the Bible*].

12 Wherefore, **the fruit of thy loins** [*the posterity of Joseph in Egypt*] **shall write** [*the Book of Mormon*]; **and the fruit of the loins of Judah** [*the Jews*] **shall write** [*the Bible*]; **and that which shall be written by the fruit of thy loins** [*the Book of Mormon*], **and also that which shall be written by the fruit of the loins of Judah** [*the Bible*], **shall grow together, unto the confounding** [*stopping*] of false doctrines and laying down of contentions [*arguing about God and His teachings*], and establishing peace among the fruit of thy loins, and bringing them to the knowledge of their fathers [*ancestors*] in the latter days [*the last days before the Second Coming of Christ*], and also to the knowledge of my covenants [*My promises to covenant Israel*], saith the Lord.

13 And **out of weakness he** [*Joseph Smith Jr.*] **shall be made strong**, in that day when my work shall commence [*begin*] among all my people, unto the restoring thee, O house of Israel, saith the Lord. [*The*

work Joseph Smith Jr. does will start the gathering of Israel back to Christ in the last days.]

14 And **thus prophesied Joseph** [*this is what Joseph in Egypt prophesied*], saying: Behold, **that seer** [*Joseph Smith Jr.*] **will the Lord bless; and they that seek to destroy him shall be confounded** [*those who try to stop the work Joseph Smith does will be unsuccessful*]; for this promise, which I [*Joseph in Egypt*] have obtained of the Lord, of the fruit of my loins, shall be fulfilled. Behold, I [*Joseph in Egypt*] am sure of the fulfilling of this promise;

The prophecy you see next is amazing! Joseph in Egypt was inspired about 3600 years before it happened to prophesy that the prophet who would restore the true Church of Jesus Christ in the last days would be named Joseph and that his father would also be named Joseph.

And that is exactly what happened. The father, Joseph Smith, and the mother, Lucy Mack Smith, had a baby boy born to them on December 23, 1805, and they decided to name him Joseph Smith. This was Joseph Smith Jr., the prophet who restored our church.

15 And **his name shall be called after me** [*Joseph Smith Jr. will be named "Joseph," like I am*]; **and it shall be after the name of his father** [*Joseph Smith Sr.*]. And he shall be like unto me [*a prophet and seer*]; for the thing, which the Lord shall bring forth by his hand, by the power of the Lord [*the Restoration of the gospel, the true Church of Jesus Christ*] shall bring my people unto salvation.

16 Yea, **thus prophesied Joseph** [*Joseph in Egypt*]: I am sure of this thing, even as I am sure of the promise of Moses; for the Lord hath said unto me, I will preserve thy seed forever.

Next, Joseph in Egypt prophesies that in the future the Lord would call a great prophet, who would be named Moses, to lead the children of Israel out of Egypt and to the promised land.

17 And the Lord hath said: **I will raise up a Moses**; and I will give power unto him in a rod [*he will be a great leader with authority*]; and I will give judgment unto him in writing [*Moses will be a skilled writer—he wrote Genesis, Exodus, Leviticus, Numbers, and Deuteronomy*]. Yet I will not loose his tongue [*Moses won't be a great speaker; see Exodus 4:10*], that he shall speak much, for I will not make him mighty in speaking. But I [*Jehovah, the Old Testament name of the premortal Jesus Christ who was still a spirit at that time because he had not yet been born to Mary*] will write unto him my law, by the finger of mine own hand [*the stone

tablets containing the Ten Commandments plus other things]; and **I will make a spokesman for him** [*a man to speak for Moses, namely his brother, Aaron; Exodus 4:14–16*].

18 And the Lord said unto me [*Joseph in Egypt*] also: I will raise up unto the fruit of thy loins [*your posterity*]; and I will make for him [*Joseph Smith Jr.*] a spokesman [*perhaps Sidney Rigdon; see D&C 100:9*]. And I, behold, **I** [*the Lord*] **will give unto him** [*Joseph Smith Jr.*] **that he shall write** [*translate*] **the writing of the fruit of thy loins** [*the golden plates*], unto the fruit of thy loins [*so that my gospel can come to your descendants*]; and the spokesman of thy loins shall declare it.

19 And the words [*from the golden plates*] which he [*Joseph Smith Jr.*] shall write [*translate*] shall be the words which are expedient [*essential, necessary*] in my wisdom should go forth unto the fruit of thy loins. And it shall be as if the fruit of thy loins [*the Book of Mormon prophets and people*] had cried unto them from the dust [*had spoken to them from the ground; in other words, from the spot in the Hill Cumorah where they were buried*]; for I know their faith.

20 And **they** [*the Book of Mormon prophets*] **shall cry** from the dust [*shall speak from the past from the ground*]; yea, even **repentance unto their brethren**, even after many generations have gone by them. And it shall come to pass that their cry shall go, even according to the simpleness of their words. [*The Book of Mormon will be instrumental in restoring the gospel's "plain and precious" truths.*]

21 Because of their [*prophets of the Book of Mormon*] faith their words shall proceed forth out of my [*the Lord's*] mouth unto their brethren who are the fruit of thy loins [*descendants of Joseph in Egypt*]; and the weakness of their words will I make strong in their faith, unto the remembering of my covenant [*keeping of my promise*] which I made unto thy [*Joseph in Egypt*] fathers [*ancestors*].

Lehi now briefly summarizes to his son, Joseph, the prophecies of Joseph in Egypt.

22 And now, behold, my son Joseph [*Lehi's son*], after this manner did my father [*my ancestor, Joseph in Egypt*] of old prophesy.

23 Wherefore, because of this covenant thou [*Joseph, Lehi's son*] art blessed; for **thy seed** [*your posterity*] **shall not be destroyed, for they shall hearken unto the words of the book**.

24 And **there shall rise up one mighty among them** [*Joseph Smith*

Jr.; see 2 Nephi 3:24, footnote 24a], **who shall do much good, both in word and in deed** [*in teaching and actions*], being an instrument [*a tool*] in the hands of God, with exceeding faith, to work mighty wonders, and do that thing which is great in the sight of God, unto **the bringing to pass much restoration** [*the Restoration of the gospel and true Church*] unto the house of Israel, and unto the seed of thy brethren.

25 And now, blessed art thou, Joseph [*Lehi's son*]. Behold, thou art little; wherefore hearken unto [*listen to and follow*] the words of thy brother, Nephi, and it shall be done unto thee even according to the words which I have spoken. Remember the words of thy dying father. Amen.

2 NEPHI 4

In this chapter, Lehi gives his final blessings to his posterity and then grows older and dies. These blessings are like the patriarchal blessings we get today. As we listen in on Lehi's words, we will gain some very important doctrinal insights as to what happens to children whose parents are not faithful to the Lord. We will point these out when we get to them.

First, Nephi will review some of the words of his father and teach us, and then he will humbly express concern for his own shortcomings. We must pay close attention to all his conclusions about his inadequacies or we will miss an important lesson for ourselves.

1 AND **now, I, Nephi, speak concerning the prophecies of which my father hath spoken, concerning Joseph, who was carried into Egypt.**

2 For behold, he [*Joseph in Egypt*] truly prophesied concerning all his seed [*posterity; Ephraim and Manasseh*]. And the prophecies which he wrote, there are not many greater. [*"Greater" can mean "more important." But it can also mean "which cover more territory about the subject."*] And **he prophesied concerning us, and our future generations; and they are written upon the plates of brass.**

Now, pay careful attention to what Lehi says as he blesses Laman's children, who will not have the same opportunities on earth to understand the gospel as Nephi's children will. This is because Laman refuses to live the gospel so his children don't get a good chance to live it. He is a bad example for them. You will see a major message about God's fairness.

3 Wherefore, after my father had made an end of speaking concerning the prophecies of Joseph, **he called the children of Laman, his sons, and his daughters,**

and said unto them: Behold, my sons, and my daughters, who are the sons and the daughters of my first-born [*Laman*], I would that ye should give ear unto my words [*please listen carefully to what I say*].

4 For the Lord God hath said that: **Inasmuch as** [*if*] **ye shall keep my commandments ye shall prosper** [*do well*] **in the land; and inasmuch as ye will not keep my commandments ye shall be cut off from my presence** [*you can't come and live with Me in heaven*]**.**

5 **But** behold, my sons and my daughters, **I cannot go down to my grave save I should leave a blessing upon you** [*I cannot die without giving you a blessing first*]; for behold, **I know that if ye are brought up in the way ye should go ye will not depart from it.**

The last phrase in verse 5, above, is a most important doctrine concerning those who do not get a fair set of opportunities to learn about and accept the gospel while on earth, because of bad examples by their parents or whatever. Lehi says that he knows that if they had been given a proper gospel upbringing, they would have remained faithful to it.

A similar doctrine is taught in the Doctrine and Covenants as follows:

D&C 137:7–8

7 Thus came the voice of the Lord unto me, saying: All who have died without a knowledge of this gospel, who would have received it if they had been permitted to tarry [live long enough on earth], *shall be heirs of the celestial kingdom of God;*

8 Also all that shall die henceforth [from here on] *without a knowledge of it, who would have received it with all their hearts, shall be heirs of that kingdom;*

Thus, we see that God is completely fair, and that all His children will get a completely fair set of opportunities to accept and live the gospel before Final Judgment, even if it means getting that opportunity in the spirit world (see D&C 138) and during the Millennium. Now, we will continue with Lehi's blessing to Laman's children.

6 **Wherefore** [*therefore*], **if ye are cursed** [*stopped in gospel progression because you haven't been taught properly*], behold, **I leave my blessing upon you, that the cursing may be taken from you and be answered upon the heads of your parents** [*your parents will be held accountable instead of you*].

What about parents who repent, but it is too late for them to reclaim their wayward children? Answer: That is what the Atonement is all about—namely, to lift sins and burdens off our shoulders which we cannot fix ourselves. In other words, parents can be forgiven too, and God will make sure that their children do get a fair chance before Judgment Day, as stated in the above quotes.

7 **Wherefore** [*therefore*], **because of my blessing the Lord God will not suffer** [*allow*] **that ye shall perish** [*spiritually*]; wherefore, he will be merciful unto you and unto your seed forever.

8 And it came to pass that after my father had made an end of [*finished*] speaking to the sons and daughters of Laman, **he caused the sons and daughters of Lemuel to be brought before him** [*in front of him*].

9 And he spake [*spoke*] unto them, saying: Behold, my sons and my daughters, who are the sons and the daughters of my second son [*Lemuel*]; behold **I leave unto you the same blessing which I left unto the sons and daughters of Laman; wherefore, thou shalt not utterly be destroyed; but in the end** [*ultimately*] **thy seed shall be blessed.** [*Ultimately, you will have the opportunity to receive the full blessings of the gospel. This is another clear statement that God is completely fair to all His children.*]

10 And it came to pass that when my father had made an end of [*finished*] speaking unto them, behold, **he spake unto the sons of Ishmael, yea, and even all his household** [*all of Ishmael's descendants*].

11 And after he had made an end of speaking unto them, **he spake unto Sam, saying: Blessed art thou, and thy seed; for thou shalt inherit the land like unto thy brother Nephi. And thy seed shall be numbered with his seed; and thou shalt be even like unto thy brother, and thy seed like unto his seed; and thou shalt be blessed in all thy days.**

Now, we will say goodbye to Lehi, at least for a while until we meet him in the next life. Hopefully, you have a strong feeling of appreciation for this great prophet and father.

12 And it came to pass after my father, **Lehi,** had spoken unto all his household [*his whole family*], according to the feelings of his heart and the Spirit of the Lord which was in him, he waxed [*grew*] old. And it came to pass that he **died**, and was buried.

Sadly, a little while after Lehi dies, Laman and Lemuel and the sons of Ishmael start rebelling again. They just don't seem to want to live the gospel. And they blame Nephi for their troubles because he and their father were always preaching the gospel to them.

This is going to be very hard on Nephi and the ones who want to be righteous and live the gospel.

13 And it came to pass that **not many days after his death, Laman and Lemuel and the sons of Ishmael were angry with me** because of the admonitions [*warnings and counsels*] of the Lord.

14 For I, Nephi, was constrained [*required by the Holy Ghost*] to speak unto them, according to his word; for I had spoken many things unto them, and also my father, before his death; many of which sayings are written upon mine other plates [*the large plates of Nephi*]; for a more history part are written upon mine other plates.

15 And upon these [*the small plates of Nephi*] I write the things of my soul, and many of the scriptures [*the written words of God*] which are engraven upon the plates of brass. For **my soul delighteth in the scriptures, and my heart pondereth them, and writeth them for the learning and the profit of my children**.

Verses 15–35 are known as "The Psalm of Nephi." In these verses, he both rejoices in the scriptures and the things of the Lord, while at the same time expressing concern for his mortal frailties and shortcomings. Certainly, we can relate to him. You may wish to underline or highlight some of the things we **bold** in your own Book of Mormon by way of emphasis and learning.

16 Behold, **my soul delighteth in the things of the Lord; and my heart pondereth** [*thinks and analyzes*] **continually upon the things which I have seen and heard**.

17 **Nevertheless,** notwithstanding [*in spite of*] the great goodness of the Lord, in showing me his great and marvelous works, my heart exclaimeth: **O wretched man that I am!** Yea, my heart sorroweth because of my flesh [*my mortal weaknesses*]; my soul grieveth [*is made sad*] because of mine iniquities [*my sins and shortcomings*].

18 I am encompassed about [*surrounded*], because of the temptations and the sins which do so easily beset [*act on*] me.

There is certainly comfort for us in the fact that even great and righteous people, such as Nephi, have feelings of being overwhelmed by their weaknesses. Isaiah expresses similar feelings in Isaiah 6:5.

We might ask a question here: why would such a righteous man as Nephi be so concerned, when we know that he is solidly on the strait and narrow path leading to exaltation? Perhaps the answer is found in the fact that the more righteous people become, the more little imperfections glare at them in the light of truth. Things bother them now that formerly hardly registered in their minds. Actually, such people can rejoice that they are noticing such things in their lives now. It is a witness that they are well along on the path back to God. You will see Nephi teaching us this principle of rejoicing in verses 28 and 30. This rejoicing is possible because of the Atonement of Christ.

Now back to Nephi's teaching. Pay careful attention to the steps that he takes from being weighed down with feelings of falling short on through to the rejoicing that comes from relying completely upon the "Rock of our salvation," who is Christ the Lord.

19 And when I desire to rejoice, **my heart groaneth** because of my sins; **nevertheless, I know in whom I have trusted.**

20 **My God hath been my support**; he hath led me through mine afflictions [*troubles and trials*] in the wilderness; and he hath preserved me upon the waters of the great deep [*when they were crossing the ocean on their ship*].

21 **He hath filled me with his love**, even unto the consuming of my flesh.

22 **He hath confounded** [*stopped*] **mine enemies, unto the causing of them to quake before me.**

23 Behold, **he hath heard my cry by day, and he hath given me knowledge by visions in the night-time.**

24 **And by day have I waxed** [*grown*] **bold in mighty prayer before him; yea, my voice have I sent up on high; and angels came down and ministered unto me.**

25 **And upon the wings of his Spirit hath my body been carried away upon exceedingly high mountains** [*I have been given mighty perspectives, in order to see things as God sees them*]. And mine eyes have beheld [*seen*] great things, yea, even too great for man; therefore I was bidden [*told*] that I should not write them.

26 O then, if I have seen so [*such*] great things, if the Lord in his condescension [*humility*] unto the children of men hath visited men in so much mercy, **why should my heart weep and my soul linger in the valley of sorrow** [*why should I keep holding on to the past*], and my flesh waste away, and my strength slacken [*become weak*], because of mine afflictions?

27 And **why should I yield to sin, because of my flesh? Yea, why should I give way to temptations, that the evil one** [*Satan*] have place in my heart to destroy my peace and afflict my soul? **Why am I angry because of mine enemy?** [*Why am I so human?*]

> Pay close attention now to where this goes. If we fail to see and feel and accept this next teaching of Nephi, we will likely fall into the carefully laid trap of low self-esteem, discouragement, and depression.

28 **Awake, my soul! No longer droop in sin. Rejoice, O my heart** [*the center of feelings; allow yourself to feel good about you*], and give place no more for the enemy of my soul.

29 **Do not anger again because of mine enemies. Do not slacken my strength because of mine afflictions.**

30 **Rejoice, O my heart, and cry** [*pray*] unto the Lord, and say: O Lord, I will **praise thee forever; yea, my soul will rejoice in thee, my God, and the rock of my salvation.** [*Rejoice and be happy because you know you can make it because of the Savior!*]

31 **O Lord, wilt thou redeem my soul? Wilt thou deliver me out of the hands of mine enemies? Wilt thou make me that I may shake at the appearance of sin?** [*The answer is "Yes!"*]

32 **May the gates of hell be shut continually before me, because that my heart is broken and my spirit is contrite!** [*"Contrite" means "I want to be corrected."*] O Lord, wilt thou not shut the gates of thy righteousness before me, **that I may walk in the path of the low valley, that I may be strict in the plain road!**

> The final phrase in verse 32, above, is a pure Bedouin term still used in the Near East. It is another internal evidence that the Book of Mormon has its origins in the Holy Land.

33 O Lord, **wilt thou encircle me around in the robe of thy righteousness! O Lord, wilt thou make a way for mine escape before mine enemies! Wilt thou make my path straight before me! Wilt thou not place a stumbling block in my way—but that thou wouldst clear my way before me, and hedge not up** [*don't block*] my way, but the ways of mine enemy.

34 O Lord, **I have trusted in thee, and I will trust in thee forever** [*one hundred percent commitment*]. **I will not put my trust in the arm of flesh** [*I will not place my trust in man*]; for I know that cursed

is he that putteth his trust in the arm of flesh. Yea, cursed [*stopped*] is he that putteth his trust in man or maketh flesh his arm [*those who rely on the philosophies and counsels of men, rather than using God as their standard*].

35 Yea, I know that **God will give liberally** [*generously*] **to him that asketh. Yea, my God will give me, if I ask not amiss** [*if I do not ask for inappropriate things; compare with D&C 46:30 and 50:30*]; therefore **I will lift up my voice unto thee; yea, I will cry unto thee, my God, the rock of my righteousness. Behold, my voice shall forever ascend** [*go*] **up unto thee, my rock and mine everlasting God. Amen.**

You watched as Nephi moved from potential overwhelming discouragement to solid and firm confidence in his future with God. This Psalm of Nephi is one of the most beautiful and powerful in all scripture. It applies to every one of us, and has power to lift each of us from discouragement.

2 NEPHI 5

Chapter 5 is a pivotal chapter. In it we will see the separation of Nephi and his righteous followers from Laman and Lemuel and the wicked who go with them. We will be taught many principles of spiritual survival, including the fact that you sometimes have to get away from those you have tried so hard to save, for fear of being destroyed spiritually or literally yourself.

1 BEHOLD, it came to pass that **I, Nephi, did cry** [*pray*] **much unto the Lord my God, because of the anger of my brethren.**

What do you think Nephi asked for in his prayers to God on behalf of his wicked brothers? What do you think he hoped for? No doubt he asked that their hearts be softened, as had happened many times before. But—and here is an important lesson—God respects agency and the likelihood that they will change their ways and choose righteousness, seem to be getting less and less. In fact, they are once again thinking about killing Nephi.

2 **But behold, their anger did increase against me, insomuch that they did seek to take away my life.**

Watch how they blame their wicked behavior on Nephi.

3 Yea, **they did murmur against me, saying: Our younger brother thinks to rule over us; and we have had much trial because of him; wherefore** [*therefore*], **now let us slay** [*kill*] **him, that we may not be afflicted more** [*so that we will not have more problems*] because of his words. For behold, we will not

have him to be our ruler; for it belongs unto us, who are the elder brethren, to rule over this people.

Verse 3, above, points out one of Satan's much-used tools—namely, blame others for your own bad behavior. Many people spend years trying to find out whom to blame for their present sinful behavior. They would be best served by forgiving, fleeing if necessary, and repenting and changing their own behavior.

4 Now I [*Nephi*] do not write upon these plates [*the small plates*] all the words which they murmured against me. But it sufficeth me [*it is enough*] to say, that **they did seek to take away my life.**

5 And it came to pass that **the Lord did warn me, that I, Nephi, should depart from them and flee into the wilderness, and all those who would go with me.**

A young lady once came to me in tears because her friends were getting deeper and deeper involved in sinful behaviors and associations, and her efforts to save them were not working. She now feared that she was on the verge of being corrupted herself. In fact, she was now hanging her clothing, which smelled of tobacco and some drugs, out on the deck of her home so they would not transfer the smells to her Sunday clothes that she wore to church.

She had hung out with these friends for years and had initially felt that she was strong enough in the gospel to weather the storms of evil influence and still be available to them to drive if they were drunk. She wanted to be around to try to talk them out of viewing the videos they chose, or at least to chat about gospel values and standards if and when they might be receptive. But now her own mind and spirit were being negatively influenced, and it scared her. Her biggest fear was that if she no longer associated with them, they would have no one to rescue them. As she contemplated leaving the group, she felt like a deserter.

When we talked, I asked her if she had read the Book of Mormon. She said, "Yes, several times." Then I said, "Do you remember what Nephi had to do when it got too dangerous for him?" And with visible relief, she said, "Yes. He had to flee from Laman and Lemuel." And then, with even more relief, she said, "Then, it would be okay with God if I left the group? I wouldn't be responsible for their souls? I wouldn't be a deserter?" Verse 5 answered her concerns and solved her dilemma.

She left the group, though they tried to get her to come back. She went on to serve a mission and is happily married, a mother of five children, and is a Young Women president at the time of the writing of this book.

Nephi obeyed the Lord and fled away from the environment and people who could destroy him and his people. He took all the people with him who still believed in God and wanted to live the gospel.

6 Wherefore, it came to pass that I, Nephi, did take my family, and also Zoram and his family, and Sam, mine elder brother and his family, and Jacob and Joseph, my younger brethren, and also my sisters [*he apparently had sisters who were not yet married*], and all those who would go with me. And **all those who would go with me were those who believed in the warnings and the revelations of God; wherefore, they did hearken unto my words.**

7 And we did take our tents and whatsoever things were possible for us, and did journey in the wilderness for the space of many days. And after we had journeyed for the space of many days **we did pitch our tents** [*we settled there*].

8 And my people would [*wanted*] that we should call the name of the place Nephi; wherefore, **we did call it Nephi**.

9 And all those who were with me did take upon them to call themselves the people of Nephi.

Next, Nephi tells us that he and his people were still living according to the law of Moses. They knew of Christ and that He would be born six hundred years from the time Lehi left Jerusalem. The law of Moses was given to the children of Israel by the Lord after they were led out of Egyptian captivity. It was designed to point toward Christ and to prepare people for the full gospel of Christ. Following it properly allowed Nephi and his people to live "after the manner of happiness" (see verse 27). This is a reminder that the law of Moses was actually a rather high law, compared to the ways of the world. (You may wish to take time to read Exodus, chapters 20, 22:1–9; 23:1–9, and others, for a quick reminder that the laws that Moses gave his people, under the direction of the Lord, were much higher than most in our society today live.)

10 And **we did observe to keep the judgments** [*laws*], and the **statutes** [*rules*], and the **commandments** of the Lord in all things, **according to the law of Moses**.

11 **And the Lord was with us**; and we did prosper exceedingly; for we did sow [*plant*] seed, and we did reap [*harvest*] again in abundance [*lots of it*]. And we began to

raise flocks, and herds, and animals of every kind.

12 And I, Nephi, had also brought the records which were engraven upon the plates of brass [*their scriptures*]; and also the ball [*Liahona*], or compass, which was prepared for my father by the hand of the Lord, according to that which is written.

13 And it came to pass that we began to **prosper exceedingly, and to multiply in the land** [*the result of living the gospel as a society*].

Some people wonder whether or not it is proper and righteous to make military preparations for self-defense. In fact, protesters often make much of their opposition to this practice. Here again we see that the Book of Mormon is written to help us in our day. Verse 14, next, reminds us that there is wisdom in making such preparations.

14 And **I, Nephi**, did take the sword of Laban, and after the manner of it [*using it for a pattern*] **did make many swords, lest by any means the people who were now called Lamanites should come upon us and destroy us**; for I knew their hatred towards me and my children and those who were called my people.

15 And I did teach my people to build buildings, and to work in all manner of wood, and of iron, and of copper, and of brass, and of steel, and of gold, and of silver, and of precious ores, which were in great abundance. [*Education and working hard go together with living the gospel.*]

16 And **I, Nephi, did build a temple**; and I did construct it after the manner of [*like*] the temple of Solomon [*ninety feet long by thirty feet wide by thirty feet high; see 1 Kings 6:2*] save [*except*] it were not built of so many precious things; for they were not to be found upon the land, wherefore, it could not be built like unto Solomon's temple. But the manner of the construction [*the way it was built*] was like unto the temple of Solomon; and the workmanship thereof was exceedingly fine.

Some people criticize us and the Church for spending so much money on temples and making them so beautiful, as opposed to giving to the poor. We do both. There is simple symbolism in putting our finest materials into the building of our temples, as did Nephi and his people. The putting of our finest work and efforts into temple building is symbolic of putting our best efforts and resources into worshipping God and living worthy of exaltation.

17 And it came to pass that I, Nephi, did cause my people to be industrious [*to stay busy and work hard*], and to labor [*work*] with their hands.

Next, the people want Nephi to be their king, but he doesn't want to be a king but rather to serve and help them as much as possible.

18 And it came to pass that **they would that I should be their king**. But I, Nephi, was desirous that they should have no king; nevertheless, I did for them according to that which was in my power.

Next, Nephi points out two times that the prophecies of the Lord had now been fulfilled, concerning them.

19 And behold, **the words of the Lord had been fulfilled unto my brethren, which he spake concerning them** [*see 1 Nephi 2:21– 22*], that I should be their ruler and their teacher. Wherefore, I had been their ruler and their teacher, according to the commandments of the Lord, until the time they sought to take away my life.

20 Wherefore, **the word of the Lord was fulfilled which he spake unto me, saying that: Inasmuch as** [*if*] they will not hearken unto [*listen to and obey*] thy words they shall be cut off from the presence of the Lord. And behold, **they were cut off from his presence.** [*The prophecy had been fulfilled. Symbolism: The day will come that the wicked are cut off from ever returning to the presence of God, if they continually ignore His invitations to repent and be happy eternally.*]

Next, the topic of people's being cursed comes up. It is important to understand that the "curse" spoken of is when the Spirit of the Lord withdraws. Thus, we can "curse" ourselves as far as present and eternal blessings are concerned. People have agency, and when they continually ignore the light of Christ and the invitations that the Lord sends out to live the gospel and come unto Him, they are "cursed" or stopped in spiritual progression by their own choices.

21 And **he had caused the cursing to come upon them** [*He had withdrawn His Spirit*], yea, even a sore [*very severe*] cursing, because of their iniquity [*wickedness*]. For behold, **they had hardened their hearts against him, that they had become like unto a flint** [*unyielding in their evil ways*]; wherefore, as they were white, and exceedingly fair and delightsome, that they might not be enticing unto my people the Lord God did cause a

skin of blackness to come upon them.

The skin of blackness in verse 21, above, is a sensitive subject and must be kept absolutely within the context here. The curse is the withdrawal of the Lord's Spirit. Joseph Fielding Smith explained it as follows:

"The dark skin was placed upon the Lamanites so that they could be distinguished from the Nephites and to keep the two peoples from mixing. The dark skin was the sign of the curse. **The curse was the withdrawal of the Spirit of the Lord** and the (withdrawal of the Spirit was the cause of the) Lamanites becoming a 'loathsome and filthy people, full of idleness and all manner of abominations' (I Nephi 12:23). The Lord commanded the Nephites not to intermarry with them, for if they did they would partake of the curse (they would also become spiritually dead). The dark skin of those who have come into the Church is no longer to be considered a sign of the curse" (Smith, *Answers to Gospel Questions*, 3:123–24).

22 And thus saith the Lord God: I will cause that they shall be loathsome [*not attractive*] unto thy people, save [*unless*] they shall repent of their iniquities [*wickedness*].

23 And cursed shall be the seed [*children; posterity*] of him that mixeth with their seed; for they shall be cursed even with the same cursing [*because of their choices, the Spirit of the Lord will have to withdraw from them too*]. **And the Lord spake it, and it was done.**

24 And **because of their cursing** [*because the Spirit of the Lord had withdrawn*] which was upon them **they did become an idle people, full of mischief and subtlety** [*were sly*], and did seek in the wilderness for beasts of prey.

Next, the Lord tells Nephi why He, the Lord, would allow the Lamanites to continue being a source of trouble and worry to Nephi's people. It was so that the people of Nephi would be reminded to live the gospel and stay close to the Lord.

25 And the Lord God said unto me: **They shall be a scourge** [*trouble, problem*] **unto thy seed** [*posterity*], **to stir them up in remembrance of me**; and inasmuch as [*if*] they will not remember me, and hearken unto my words, they [*the Lamanites*] shall scourge [*trouble*] them even unto destruction.

Next, Nephi consecrates or sets apart his younger brothers, Jacob and Joseph, to be leaders and teachers in the Church. Based on what we know, these would be priesthood callings in the Church to help lead the people.

By now, Jacob and Joseph would no doubt be full grown men and probably had their own families.

26 And it came to pass that **I, Nephi, did consecrate Jacob and Joseph, that they should be priests and teachers over the land of my people**.

27 And it came to pass that **we lived after the manner of happiness**.

28 And **thirty years had passed away from the time we left Jerusalem**.

29 **And I, Nephi, had kept the records upon my plates** [*the large plates of Nephi*], which I had made, of my people thus far.

30 And it came to pass that **the Lord God said unto me: Make other plates** [*the small plates of Nephi, the translation of which we are reading now*]; and thou shalt engraven many things upon them [*the small plates*] which are good in my sight, for the profit [*benefit*] of thy people.

31 Wherefore [*and so*], I, Nephi, to be obedient to the commandments of the Lord, went and made these plates [*the small plates*] upon which I have engraven these things [*the things we have been reading so far in the Book of Mormon*].

32 **And I engraved that which is pleasing unto God. And if my people are pleased with the things of God they will be pleased with mine engravings which are upon these plates**.

33 And if my people desire to know the more particular part [*more details*] of the history of my people they must search mine other plates [*the large plates of Nephi*].

34 And it sufficeth me to say that **forty years had passed away, and we had already had wars and contentions with our brethren**.

2 NEPHI 6

Remember Nephi's younger brother, Jacob? He was born to Lehi and Sariah during their eight years in the wilderness, between the time the family fled from Jerusalem and the time they boarded their ship to sail to America.

Nephi now records some teachings of his brother, Jacob, as Jacob teaches Nephi's people. Jacob is probably thirty-five to forty-five years old by now. He will review Jewish history and in so doing will remind all of us that we, Israel, have much to do and that we must come unto Christ and remain faithful in order to return to God.

1 **THE words of Jacob, the brother of Nephi, which he spake unto the people of Nephi:**

2 Behold, my beloved brethren, I, Jacob, having been called of God, and ordained after the manner of his holy order [*I hold the Melchizedek Priesthood*], and having been consecrated [*ordained and set apart*] by my brother Nephi, unto whom ye look as a king or a protector, and on whom ye depend for safety, behold ye know that I have spoken unto you exceedingly many things [*I have already taught you many things*].

3 Nevertheless, I speak unto you again; for I am desirous for the welfare of your souls [*I want you to live the gospel and be saved and return to live with God*]. Yea, mine anxiety is great for you [*I worry a lot about you*]; and ye yourselves know that it ever has been. For I have exhorted you with all diligence [*I have taught and warned you faithfully*]; and I have taught you the words of my father [*Lehi*]; and **I have spoken unto you concerning all things which are written, from the creation of the world**.

Just as Nephi turned to the words of Isaiah to teach his people (see 1 Nephi 20–21), so also will Jacob use Isaiah. The last sentence of verse 4, next, summarizes what studying Isaiah will do for us. It will help us glorify God by living worthy of returning to Him and becoming gods ourselves (compare with Moses 1:39).

4 And now, behold, **I would** [*I want to*] **speak unto you concerning things which are, and which are to come** [*the future*]; **wherefore** [*in order to do this*], **I will read you the words of Isaiah**. And they are the words which my brother [*Nephi*] has desired that I should speak unto you. And I speak unto you for your sakes, **that ye may learn and glorify the name of your God**.

5 And now, **the words which I shall read are they which Isaiah spake concerning all the house of Israel** [*this includes us*]; wherefore, they may be likened unto [*compared to*] you, for ye are of the house of Israel [*you are descendants of the twelve tribes of Israel*]. And **there are many things which have been spoken by Isaiah which may be likened unto you** [*which apply to you*], **because ye are of** [*from*] **the house of Israel**.

Jacob basically quotes the same portions of Isaiah that Nephi used in 1 Nephi 20–21. First, he quotes Isaiah in verses 6 and 7; then he explains how these verses apply to the Jews.

6 And now, these are the words [*of Isaiah*]: Thus saith the Lord God: Behold, I will lift up mine hand to the Gentiles [*people who are not Jews*], and set up my standard [*the gospel; the true Church*] to the people; and they shall bring thy sons in their arms, and thy daughters shall be carried upon their shoulders [*leaders of nations will help with the last days gathering of Israel*].

7 And kings [*leaders of nations*] shall be thy nursing fathers [*will help you gather*], and their queens thy nursing mothers; they shall bow down to thee with their faces towards the earth [*they will be humbled in your presence*], and lick up the dust of thy feet [*and serve you and feel that you are awsome*]; **and thou shalt know that I am the Lord** [*and then you will see that My promises are fulfilled*]; for they shall not be ashamed [*disappointed*] that wait for me [*who trust in Me*].

8 And now I, Jacob, would speak somewhat concerning these words [*I will now explain what Isaiah said here*]. For behold, the Lord has shown me that those who were at Jerusalem [*the Jews*], from whence [*where*] we came, have been slain and carried away captive [*by the nation of Babylon*].

9 Nevertheless [*even though this has happened*], **the Lord has shown unto me** that they [*the Jews*] should [*will*] return again. [*They did, in about 538 BC when Cyrus the Persian easily conquered Babylon and allowed the Jewish captives to return back home to Jerusalem.*] And he also has shown unto me that the Lord God, the Holy One of Israel [*Christ*], should manifest [*show*] himself unto them in the flesh [*Jesus will show Himself to the Jews and live among them as a mortal*]; and **after he should manifest himself they** [*the Jews*] **should** [*will*] **scourge Him** [*whip Him with a whip with bone and metal bits in the leather thongs at the end of it*] **and crucify him**, according to the words of the angel who spake it unto me.

10 **And after they** [*the Jews*] **have hardened their hearts and stiffened their necks** [*rebelled*] **against the Holy One of Israel** [*against the Savior*], behold, the judgments [*punishments*] of the Holy One of Israel shall come upon them. And the day cometh that **they** [*the Jews*] **shall be smitten and afflicted** [*beaten and treated badly*].

11 Wherefore [*therefore*], **after they are driven to and fro** [*everywhere*], for thus saith the angel [*this is what the angel explained to me*], **many shall be afflicted in the flesh** [*they shall suffer much physical suffering*], **and shall not be suffered to perish** [*the Jews will not be destroyed completely*], because

of the prayers of the faithful; **they shall be scattered, and smitten, and hated;** nevertheless, **the Lord will be merciful unto them, that when they shall come to the knowledge of their Redeemer, they shall be gathered together again to the lands of their inheritance.**

The Lord's promise to the Jews, given at the end of verse 11, above, is already taking place in our day. It is one of the signs of the times (prophecies that will be fulfilled in the last days, letting us know that the Second Coming of Christ is getting close).

12 **And blessed are the Gentiles** [*in this context, people who are not Jews; this basically includes most of us*], they of whom the prophet has written; for behold, **if it so be that they shall repent and fight not against Zion** [*the work of the Lord*], **and do not unite themselves to that great and abominable church** [*the church of the devil, meaning Satan's kingdom, evil, wickedness, etc.; see 1 Nephi 22:23*], **they shall be saved; for the Lord God will fulfill his covenants** [*promises*] which he has made unto his children; and **for this cause the prophet has written these things** [*this is why Isaiah wrote these things*].

13 Wherefore, **they that fight against Zion and the covenant people of the Lord shall lick up the dust of their feet** [*the righteous will ultimately win against the wicked*]; **and the people of the Lord shall not be ashamed** [*will not be disappointed or stopped in living the gospel*]. For the people of the Lord are they who wait for him [*who trust Him and keep worshipping Him*]; for they still wait for the coming of the Messiah.

In verse 14, next, Jacob explains that Isaiah referred to the "second time" when the Jews would return to their home country, Israel. This implies that there would be two major times when they would return. The first was when they returned from Babylonian captivity in two major waves, 538 BC (before Christ's birth) and 520 BC (see 2 Kings 24). The second major return of the Jews will occur in the last days. We are watching the fulfillment of this prophecy now. However, that part of the gathering, meaning to their homelands, is underway, but that the most important "gathering" prophesied—namely, being gathered to Christ—has not really made much headway among the Jews today. Joseph Fielding Smith (who was an Apostle and became one of the Presidents of the Church) speaks of this as follows:

"Not many of the Jews, I take it from my reading of the scriptures, will believe in Christ before he comes. The Book of Mormon tells us that they shall begin to believe in him (see 2 Nephi 30:7). They are now beginning to believe in him. The Jews today look upon Christ as a great Rabbi. They have accepted him as one of their great teachers; they have said that, 'He is Jew of Jew, the greatest Rabbi of them all,' as one has stated it. When the gospel was restored in 1830, if a Jew had mentioned the name of Christ in one of the synagogues, he would have been rebuked. Had a rabbi referred to him, the congregation would have arisen and left the building. And so, we see the sentiment has changed. Now I state this on Jewish authority that they are beginning to believe in Christ, and some of them are accepting the gospel.

"But in the main they will gather to Jerusalem in their unbelief; the gospel will be preached to them; some of them will believe. Not all of the Gentiles have believed when the gospel has been proclaimed to them, but the great body of the Jews who are there assembled will not receive Christ as their Redeemer until he comes himself and makes himself manifest unto them" (Smith, *Doctrines of Salvation*, 3:9; *Book of Mormon Student Manual*, p. 27).

14 And behold, **according to the words of the prophet** [*Isaiah*], **the Messiah** [*Christ*] **will set himself again the second time to recover them** [*the return of the Jews in the last days*]; wherefore, he will manifest himself unto them in power and great glory [*perhaps referring, among other things, to the appearance of the Savior on the Mount of Olives*], unto the destruction of their enemies, when that day cometh when they shall believe in him; and none will he destroy that believe in him.

Some of the signs of the times are mentioned next.

15 And they that believe not in him shall be destroyed, both by **fire**, and by **tempest** [*terrible storms with high winds*], and by **earthquakes**, and by **bloodsheds**, and by **pestilence** [*terrible diseases, plagues, and other miserable troubles*], and by **famine**. And they shall know that the Lord is God, the Holy One of Israel.

Next, Jacob quotes Isaiah as he asks a most significant question. In this context, since Jacob is prophesying about the Jews, we will add notes that refer to the Jews. He basically asks, "How will the Jews ever survive and be set free from such terrible troubles?"

16 For **shall the prey** [*the Jews, who have been victims over the centuries*] **be taken from the mighty** [*be set free from their mighty enemies*], **or the**

lawful captive [*the covenant people of the Lord*] **delivered** [*be set free from their enemies*]? [*The answer is "Yes!" as emphasized in verse 17, next.*]

17 But thus saith the Lord: **Even the captives of the mighty** [*the Jews who have been so terribly persecuted by powerful enemies*] **shall be taken away** [*set free*], and the prey [*victims*] of the terrible [*tyrants*] **shall be delivered** [*set free*]; [*and this is how:*] for **the Mighty God shall deliver** [*save*] **his covenant people**. For thus saith the Lord: **I will contend** [*fight*] **with them that contendeth with thee** [*I, the Lord, will fight your battles*]—

18 **And I will feed them that oppress thee** [*treat you badly*], **with their own flesh** [*I will turn your enemies against each other*]; and they shall be drunken with their own blood as with sweet wine [*they will fight against each other*]; **and all flesh** [*all people*] **shall know that I the Lord am thy Savior and thy Redeemer**, the Mighty One of Jacob [*because the prophecies about the gathering of the Jews will be so obviously fulfilled*].

2 NEPHI 7

Since Isaiah uses a lot of symbolism, and since the Lord uses symbolism in many settings, including the temple, to teach us, I will include here a list of several items of symbolism commonly used in the scriptures. You may find it useful in your scripture study, especially when you study Isaiah and also the book of Revelation in the Bible.

Symbolism Often Used in the Scriptures

Colors

White	purity; righteousness; exaltation (Example: Rev. 3:4–5)
Black	evil; famine; darkness (Example: Rev. 6:5–6)
Red	sins; bloodshed (Example: Rev. 6:4; D&C 133:51)
Blue	heaven; godliness; remembering and keeping God's commandments (Example: Num. 15:37–40)
Green	life; nature (Example: Rev. 8:7)
Amber	sun; light; divine glory (Example: D&C 110:2; Rev. 1:15; Ezek. 1:4, 27; 8:2)
Scarlet	royalty (Example: Dan. 5:29; Matt. 27:28–29)

Silver	worth, but less than gold (Example: Ridges, *Isaiah Made Easier*, Isa. 48:10 notes)
Gold	the best; exaltation (Example: Rev. 4:4)

Body Parts

Eye	perception; light and knowledge
Head	governing
Ears	obedience; hearing
Mouth	speaking
Hair	modesty; covering
Members	offices and callings
Heart	inner man; courage
Hands	action, acting
Right Hand	covenant hand; making covenants
Bowels	center of emotion; whole being
Loins	posterity; preparing for action (gird up your loins)
Liver	center of feeling
Reins	kidneys; center of desires, thoughts
Arm	power
Foot	mobility; foundation
Toe	associated with cleansing rites (Example: Lev. 14:17)
Nose	anger (Example: 2 Sam. 22:16; Job 4:9)
Tongue	speaking
Blood	life of the body
Knee	humility; submission
Shoulder	strength; effort
Forehead	total dedication, loyalty (Example: Rev. 14:1—loyalty to God; Rev. 13:16—loyalty to wickedness, Satan)

Numbers

1	unity; God

3	God; Godhead; A word repeated three times means superlative, "the most" or "the best" (see Isaiah 6:3)
4	mankind; earth (see Smith's Bible Dictionary, p. 456) (Example: Rev. 7:1. Four angels over four parts of the earth)
7	completeness; perfection. When man lets God help , it leads to perfection. (man + God = perfection) 4 + 3 = 7
10	numerical perfection; well-organized (Example: Ten Commendments, tithing) (Example: Satan is well-organized, Rev. 13:1)
12	divine government; God's organization (Example: JST Rev. 5:6)
40 days	literal; sometimes means "a long time" as in 1 Samuel 17:16
Forever endless	can sometimes be a specific period or age, not endless

(see BYU Religious Studies Center Newsletter, Vol. 8, No. 3, May 1994)

Other

Horse	victory; power to conquer (Example: Rev. 19:11; Jer. 8:16)
Donkey	peace (Example: Christ came in peace at the Triumphal Entry)
Palms	joy; tiumph, victory (Example: John 12:13; Rev. 7:9)
Wings	power to move, act, etc. (Example: Rev. 4:8; D&C 77:4)
Crown	power; dominion; exaltation (Example: Rev. 2:10; 4:4)
Robes	royalty; kings, queens; exaltation (Example: Rev. 6:11; 7:14; 2 Ne. 9:14; D&C 109:76; 3 Ne. 11:8)

As we continue with 2 Nephi 7, Jacob now quotes what is basically known as Isaiah, chapter 50, in the Bible.

As you will see, Isaiah asks the question, "Did I leave you, or did you leave Me?" The answer, of course, is "You left me." We know that God never leaves His children. They leave Him when they rebel and quit living the gospel. The real question He is asking is "Did I break My promises to you or did you break your promises with Me?" (Such as the promises you made when your were baptized.)

Another question that Isaiah asks is, basically, "Why don't you come unto Christ? Has He lost His power to save you?"

In this chapter we also learn that one of the terrible tortures inflicted upon the Savior during His trial and Crucifixion was the pulling out of His whiskers.

In this chapter, Isaiah speaks of the future as if it had already happened. This sometimes makes his writings hard for people to understand. He is prophesying some details of the Savior's trial and Crucifixion over 700 years before those things took place.

Watch, now, as the Lord asks the rebellious and wicked people of Israel who divorced whom. He is comparing Israel's rebelling and leaving God to a married couple who is getting a divorce. In other words, who left whom?

Notice that Isaiah repeats things several times to emphasize what he is teaching.

1 Yea, for thus saith the Lord: **Have I put thee away** [*Have I divorced you*], **or have I cast thee off forever? For thus saith the Lord: Where is the bill of your mother's divorcement** [*where are the divorce papers*]? To whom have I put thee away, or to which of my creditors have I sold you [*Was it I who sold you, or did you sell yourselves into trouble and misery*]? Yea, **to whom have I sold you? Behold, for your iniquities** [*Answer: because of your wickedness*] **have ye sold yourselves** [*you brought it upon yourselves!*], and for your transgressions is your mother [*your apostate nation; Hosea 2:2*] put away [*scattered and smitten*].

Next, Isaiah answers his own question by telling the wicked people of covenant Israel how they would leave God by rejecting the Savior when He came to earth. Remember that Isaiah is speaking of the future as if it had already happened.

2 Wherefore [*this is why*], **when I** [*Jesus*] **came, there was no man** [*who received me as the Savior, the Messiah*]; **when I called, yea, there was none to answer** [*nobody responded and accepted my teachings*]. O house of Israel, **is my hand shortened at all that it cannot redeem, or have I no power to deliver** [*have I lost my power to save you*]? Behold, at my rebuke [*command*] I dry up the sea [*like I did when I parted the Red Sea for the children of Israel so they could cross it on dry ground to escape Pharaoh's Egyptian soldiers*], I make their rivers a wilderness and their fish to stink because the waters are dried up, and they die because of thirst [*I haven't lost my power*].

3 **I clothe the heavens with blackness, and I make sackcloth their covering** [*I can cause the sky to be dark during the day as if it were mourning the dead. In fact, it will at Jesus's Crucifixion; see Matt 27:45*].

4 **The Lord God** [*Heavenly Father*] **hath given me** [*Jesus; see verse 6*] **the tongue of the learned** [*Father taught Me well*], that I should know how to speak a word [*a strengthening and comforting word*] in season unto

thee, O house of Israel. When ye are weary he waketh morning by morning. **He waketh mine ear to hear as the learned** [*German Bible, Luther edition says: "He, the Father, is constantly communicating with me and I hear as his disciple"*].

5 The Lord God [*the Father*] hath opened mine ear, and I was not rebellious, neither turned away back [*I accomplished my calling, the Atonement; you should do your job to live the gospel and take it to all the world*].

Isaiah now prophesies some very specific details about what the Roman soldiers did to the Savior as they tortured Him before His Crucifixion. Remember, this will take place about 700 years from the time that Isaiah is prophesying it. God really does know the future, doesn't He!

6 **I gave my back to the smiter** [*I allowed the Roman soldiers to scourge Me; see note about scourging in 2 Nephi 6:9 in this book*], **and my cheeks to them that plucked off the hair** [*pulled out the whiskers of my beard*]. **I hid not my face from shame and spitting** [*as My time for crucifixion came*].

7 For **the Lord God** [*Heavenly Father*] **will help me, therefore shall I not be confounded** [*I'll not be stopped from performing the Atonement*]. **Therefore** [*this is why*] **have I set my face like a flint** [*I have braced Myself for the ordeal*], **and I know that I shall not be ashamed** [*I will not fail*].

8 And **the Lord** [*the Father; see verse 9*] **is near, and he justifieth me** [*approves of everything I do; could refer to Isaiah too*]. Who will contend with me [*who is willing to go against such odds*]? Let us stand together [*go to court, as in a court of law*]. Who is mine adversary? Let him come near me [*face me*], and I will smite him with the strength of my mouth [*the truth from My mouth will ultimately win*].

The phrase "and I will smite him with the strength of my mouth," in verse 8, above, is not in our Bible, thus showing us that the brass plates contained a more accurate record of Isaiah's teachings.

9 For **the Lord God** [*the Father*] **will help me. And all they who shall condemn** [*fight against*] me, behold, all they shall wax old as a garment [*grow old like an old, rotten rag*], and the moth shall eat them up [*the wicked will have their day of power, then receive their punishment*].

Next, the Lord, speaking through Isaiah, asks, "Who is there among you who loves the Lord and strives to live the gospel but does not receive any light and help from Him?"

10 Who is among you that feareth [*respects*] the Lord, that obeyeth the

voice of his servant [*prophets*], that walketh in darkness [*spiritual darkness*] and hath no light? [*Answer. Nobody, because the Lord blesses His followers with light.*]

11 Behold all ye [*the wicked*] that kindle fire, that compass [*surround*] yourselves about with sparks, walk in the light of your fire and in the sparks which ye have kindled [*all of you who try to live without God, according to your own "light" and philosophies, are like someone walking on a dark night trying to make sparks to light their way*]. This shall ye have of mine hand—ye shall lie down in sorrow [*Misery awaits those who try to live without God*].

2 NEPHI 8

Next, Isaiah first speaks to people who are trying to live righteously and teaches us to see the big picture and who we really are and where we fit in to God's plans. He reminds all of us not to think negatively about ourselves, rather, to remember that we are children of God and to strive to fulfill our true potential to become like Him.

First, he reminds us that we are covenant Israel; in other words, we are descendants of Abraham and his wife, Sarah. The Lord said that He would bless the whole world by having the descendants of Abraham and Sarah take the gospel to everybody. That is our job today.

1 **Hearken unto me, ye that follow after righteousness** [*the Lord is now speaking to the righteous*]. **Look unto the rock** [*the good, solid rock—Abraham and Sarah*] **from whence ye are hewn** [*from which you are cut*], **and to the hole of the pit** [*the rock quarry*] **from whence ye are digged** [*consider where you come from; you are God's covenant people!*].

2 **Look unto Abraham, your father** [*ancestor*], **and unto Sarah**, she that bare you [*Sarah is side by side with Abraham in importance*]; for I called him alone [*when he was childless*], and blessed him [*see Abraham 2:9–11*].

3 For **the Lord shall comfort Zion** [*the Lord will bless His covenant people and help them fulfill their calling*], he will comfort all her waste places [*Israel will be gathered and restored*]; and he will make her wilderness like Eden, and her desert like the garden of the Lord [*the Garden of Eden*]. **Joy and gladness shall be found therein**, thanksgiving and the voice of melody [*there will be happiness and singing when the Lord gathers Israel. The righteous will get a wonderful reward*].

4 **Hearken** [*listen*] **unto me** [*Christ*], my people; and give ear unto me [*listen to Me*], O my nation; for **a law shall proceed from me** [*the

teachings and doctrines of the true gospel; see Isaiah 51:4, footnote a], **and I will make my judgment to rest for a light for the people** [*My laws will bring light to the nations*].

The Lord reminds the righteous that His Atonement and His gospel are always nearby and available to them.

5 **My righteousness** [*My ability to save you; triumph*] **is near** [*is close to you; is available to you*]; my salvation is gone forth, and mine arm shall judge the people. **The isles** [*nations of the world*] **shall wait** [*trust, rely*] **upon me**, and on mine arm [*my power*] shall they trust.

Next, Isaiah reminds us that the salvation that comes through the Lord is completely and totally reliable. No matter what else happens, it will always come through.

6 **Lift up your eyes to the heavens, and look upon the earth beneath** [*look everywhere*]; for the heavens shall vanish away like smoke [*D&C 29:23–24*], and the earth shall wax old [*grow old*] like a garment [*like an old piece of clothing*]; and they that dwell therein shall die in like manner. But my salvation [*the salvation I bring*] shall be forever, and my righteousness [*triumph, victory over sin and death*] shall not be abolished [*done away with*].

Next, the Lord tells us not to give in to peer pressure and to ignore those who criticize the Church.

7 **Hearken unto me, ye that know righteousness** [*listen to Me, you who are righteous*], the people in whose heart I have written my law [*you who have taken My gospel to heart*], **fear ye not the reproach** [*insults*] **of men, neither be ye afraid of their revilings** [*stinging criticisms*].

8 **For the moth shall eat them** [*the wicked who revile against the righteous*] **up like a garment** [*they will vanish like moth-eaten clothing*], and the worm shall eat them like wool. **But my righteousness** [*salvation and deliverance*] **shall be forever** [*will last forever*], and my salvation from generation to generation [*throughout eternity*].

Isaiah now depicts Israel as replying to the Lord's assurances in the previous verses. Righteous Israel now invites the Lord to exercise His power in their behalf like he did in ancient times.

9 **Awake, awake! Put on strength, O arm** [*symbolic of power*] **of the Lord**; awake as in the ancient days [*help us like You did in the past*]. Art thou not he that hath cut Rahab [*trimmed Egypt down to size. Rahab is a mythical sea monster and symbolically represents Satan and nations who*

serve him], and wounded the dragon [*Satan; see Revelation 12:7–9*]?

10 Art thou not he who hath dried the sea [*Red Sea*], the waters of the great deep; that hath made the depths of the sea a way [*pathway*] for the ransomed [*redeemed; You saved the children of Israel from Egypt; symbolic of the Atonement's redeeming us from our sins*] to pass over [*parting of the Red Sea*]?

Next, Isaiah prophesies that sometime in the future, the gathering of Israel will take place. We live in that day when this prophecy is literally being fulfilled.

11 Therefore [*because of your power*], **the redeemed of the Lord shall return** [*the gathering of Israel*], and come with singing unto Zion; and **everlasting joy and holiness shall be upon their heads; and they shall obtain gladness and joy; sorrow and mourning shall flee away** [*ultimate results of righteousness*].

The Lord now replies to righteous Israel's request in verse 9, above.

12 **I am he; yea, I am he that comforteth you. Behold, who art thou, that thou shouldst be afraid of man** [*why should you fear mortal men*], who shall die [*in other words, trust in God, not man*], and of the son of man [*mortal men*], who shall be made like unto grass [*in other words, the influence of God is permanent, but the influence of people is temporary*]?

13 **And forgettest the Lord thy maker, that hath stretched forth the heavens, and laid the foundations of the earth** [*created the heavens and the earth; how could you forget Me, your Creator, after all I've done for you?*], and hast feared continually every day, because of the fury of the oppressor [*Israel's captors who have oppressed them; see 2 Nephi 8, footnote 13c*], as if he were ready to destroy [*German Bible: whose intent is to destroy; why should you live in fear of mortal men*]? And where is the fury of the oppressor? [*If you live righteously, the day will come when enemies won't be able to hurt you anymore.*]

14 **The captive exile hasteneth, that he may be loosed** [*Israel wants to be free; the day will come when Israel will be set free; see Isaiah 52:1–2*], and that he should not die in the pit [*not die in captivity*], nor that his bread should fail [*run out; famine, etc.*].

Next, the Lord reminds Israel that He has not lost His power. He can still save them, as he has done in the past.

15 **But I am the Lord thy God, whose waves roared** [*as they drowned Pharaoh's armies in the Red Sea; see 1 Nephi 4:2*]; the Lord of Hosts is my name.

16 And I have put my words in thy mouth [*have given you My gospel*], and have covered [*protected*] thee in the shadow of mine hand, that I may plant the heavens and lay the foundations of the earth [*I created the heavens and the earth*], and say unto Zion: **Behold, thou art my people** [*I haven't deserted you*].

17 **Awake, awake, stand up, O Jerusalem** [*cheer up*], which hast drunk at the hand of the Lord the cup of his fury [*you have been punished a lot*]—thou hast drunken the dregs [*bitter residue at the bottom of a cup*] of the cup of trembling wrung out [*you have paid a terrible price for your wickedness*]—

18 And none to guide her [*Israel*] among all the sons she hath brought forth [*you have spent many years without prophets*]; neither that taketh her by the hand, of all the sons she hath brought up.

19 These two sons [*two prophets in the last days who will help keep enemies of the Jews from totally destroying them; see Revelation 11*] are come unto thee, who shall be sorry for thee [*who will care about you*]—thy desolation and destruction, and the famine and the sword—and by whom shall I comfort thee?

20 Thy sons [*your people*] have fainted, save [*except*] these two [*the two prophets in Revelation 11*]; they [*your people*] lie at the head of all the streets [*German Bible: are being destroyed right and left*]; as a wild bull in a net [*implies that they are trapped in a net woven by their own wickedness*], they are full of the fury of the Lord [*they are catching the full anger of the Lord*], the rebuke of thy God [*the punishments of God*].

Next, the Lord tells Israel, who has been beaten and badly treated for centuries because of their own wickedness, that in the last days He will exercise His power and save them from their enemies.

21 **Therefore hear now this**, thou [*Israel*] afflicted, and drunken [*out of control*], and not with wine [*rather, with wickedness*]:

22 Thus saith thy Lord, **the Lord and thy God pleadeth the cause of his people** [*I have not deserted you*]; behold, I have taken out of thine hand the cup of trembling [*the terrible troubles and conditions you have been through*], the dregs of the cup of my fury; **thou shalt no more drink it again** [*Christ will save the Jews in the last days; see 2 Nephi 9:1–2*].

23 **But I will put it** [*the cup in verse 22*] **into the hand of them that afflict thee** [*your enemies will get what they gave you*]; who have said to thy soul: Bow down, that we may go over [*lie down while we walk all over you!*]—and thou hast laid thy body

as the ground and as the street to them that went over [*you have been walked on by your enemies*].

24 **Awake, awake, put on thy strength, O Zion** [*return to righteousness and the proper use of the priesthood; see D&C 113:7, 8*]; **put on thy beautiful garments** [*dress in your finest, including your finest righteous living, and prepare to be with the Savior; see Revelation 21:2–3*], O Jerusalem, the holy city; for henceforth [*from now on*] there shall no more come into thee the uncircumcised and the unclean [*the wicked*].

25 **Shake thyself from the dust** [*stop being wicked and being walked on by your enemies, verse 23; see also 2 Nephi 13:26*]; **arise** [*from being walked on, verse 23*], **sit down** [*in dignity, redeemed at last*], O Jerusalem; **loose thyself** [*free yourself*] **from the bands of thy neck** [*from captivity, bondage, wickedness*], O captive daughter of Zion.

2 NEPHI 9

Jacob has just finished quoting several of the teachings of Isaiah, a great Old Testament prophet who lived about 100 to 150 years before Lehi and his family left Jerusalem in 600 BC. Isaiah's writings and teachings were included on the brass plates of Laban, and that's why Jacob could read them to his people. Having read about the Atonement of Christ from the words of Isaiah, Jacob will now proceed to explain the Atonement to his people.

In case you don't exactly know what the Atonement of Christ is, let's give you a brief definition. The "Atonement of Christ" means everything the Savior did to suffer and pay for our sins, including in the Garden of Gethsemane and on the cross, so that, if we repent of our sins, we can be forgiven and return to live with Heavenly Father in heaven, after we die. This is called "eternal life."

The Atonement also includes the Savior's Crucifixion and death on the cross plus His Resurrection with which He overcame physical death. This makes it so that everyone, whether or not they repent from their sins, will be resurrected and live forever. This is called "immortality." By the way, "resurrection" is when our spirit and our body come back together after we have died. For righteous, faithful members of the Church living now, that will be at the Second Coming of Christ.

Watch now, as Jacob explains the Atonement to his people, using the teachings of Isaiah as a background. This chapter is loaded with specific doctrines of the gospel, meaning facts about the plan of salvation.

1 AND now, my beloved brethren, I [*Jacob*] have read these things [*Isaiah's writings*] **that ye might know concerning the covenants** [*promises*] **of the Lord** that he has

covenanted with all the house of Israel [*in other words, with all of us*]—

2 **That he has spoken unto the Jews**, by the mouth of his holy prophets, even from the beginning down, from generation to generation, until the time comes **that they shall be restored to the true church and fold of God** [*this hasn't happened yet, to any significant degree as far as numbers are concerned*]; when they shall be gathered home to the lands of their inheritance, and shall be established in all their lands of promise.

Next, Jacob reminds us that the Atonement is designed to make us happy.

3 Behold, my beloved brethren, **I speak unto you these things that ye may rejoice**, and lift up your heads forever [*to encourage you*], because of the blessings which the Lord God shall bestow upon your children.

4 For I know that ye have searched much, many of you, to know of things to come; wherefore I know that **ye know that our flesh** [*bodies*] **must** [*will*] **waste away and die**; **nevertheless, in our bodies we shall see God** [*we will all be resurrected; see verse 22*].

5 Yea, I know that **ye know that in the body** [*in a physical, mortal body*] **he** [*Christ*] **shall show himself unto those at Jerusalem**, from whence [*where*] we came; for it is expedient [*necessary*] that it should be among them [*it has to be that Christ is born and lives among the Jews*]; for it behooveth [*is required of*] the great Creator [*Christ*] that **he suffereth** [*allows*] **himself to become subject unto man in the flesh, and die for all men**, that all men might become subject unto him. [*In other words, Christ had to "buy" us with His life so that we would be in complete debt to Him, in order to be able to offer us the law of mercy and have a chance that we would accept it.*]

Jacob will now build a case for his people as to why they need the Atonement.

6 For **as death hath passed upon all men** [*everyone will eventually die*], to fulfil the merciful plan of the great Creator [*death is a blessing; without it, we couldn't be resurrected*], **there must needs be** [*there has to be*] **a power of resurrection, and the resurrection must needs come unto man by reason of** [*the resurrection is necessary because of*] **the fall** [*the Fall of Adam and Eve*]; and the fall came by reason of **transgression; and because man became fallen they were cut off from the presence of the Lord.**

7 Wherefore, it must needs be [*there has to be*] **an infinite atonement** [*an*

unlimited one]—**save it should be an infinite atonement** [*without the Atonement*] **this corruption** [*mortal body*] **could not put on incorruption** [*we could not be resurrected*]. Wherefore, **the first judgment** [*the Fall*] which came upon man **must needs have remained to an endless duration** [*without the Atonement, the effects of the Fall would have lasted forever; we could never be resurrected*]. **And if so, this flesh** [*our mortal bodies*] **must have laid down to rot and to crumble to its mother earth, to rise no more** [*we would have died and never been resurrected*].

As you know, the Atonement made it possible for us to overcome two types of death, physical death and spiritual death. At this point, Jacob is emphasizing what would have happened to us if Christ had not overcome physical death for us.

Next, Jacob tells us that if we didn't get resurrected, we would end up with the devil forever.

8 O the wisdom of God, his mercy and grace! For behold, **if the flesh should rise no more** [*if we were not to be resurrected*] **our spirits must** [*would*] **become subject to that angel** [*the devil*] **who fell from before the presence of the Eternal God, and became the devil, to rise no more** [*Satan will never get a physical body; therefore, he will never gain a resurrected body*].

9 And **our spirits must have** [*would have*] **become like unto him, and we become devils, angels to a devil, to be shut out from the presence of our God, and to remain with the father of lies** [*Satan*], in misery, like unto himself; yea, to that being who beguiled [*tempted, deceived*] our first parents [*Adam and Eve*], who transformeth himself nigh unto an angel of light [*who tries to appear as an angel of God in order to deceive people; see D&C 129 for keys to prevent being so deceived by him*], and stirreth up the children of men unto secret combinations [*groups who secretly plot to do evil*] of murder and all manner of secret works of darkness.

In the next verses, Jacob will help us better understand the difference between physical death and spiritual death and will bear his testimony that the Atonement of Christ will help us overcome both types of death.

10 **O how great the goodness of our God, who prepareth a way** [*the Atonement*] **for our escape from the grasp of this awful monster; yea, that monster, death and hell, which I call the death of the body** [*physical death*], **and also the death of the spirit** [*spiritual

death; a spirit can't be killed in the sense of ceasing to exist]. [*Through the Atonement, we can overcome both types of death.*]

11 And **because of the way of deliverance** [*the Atonement*] of our God, the Holy One of Israel [*Christ*], **this death** [*physical death*], of which I have spoken, which is the temporal [*physical*], **shall deliver up its dead; which death is the grave** [*everyone will be resurrected*].

12 And this death of which I have spoken, which is the **spiritual death** [*being cut off from the presence of God forever*], shall deliver up its dead [*through repentance and being forgiven because of Christ's Atonement for sins*]; which **spiritual death is hell; wherefore, death and hell must deliver up their dead, and hell** [*spiritual death*] **must deliver up its captive spirits** [*if they repent*], and **the grave must deliver up its captive bodies** [*physical death is overcome by resurrection*], and **the bodies and the spirits of men will be restored one to the other** [*through the Resurrection*]; and **it is by the power of the resurrection of the Holy One of Israel** [*our resurrection is made possible by Christ's Resurrection*].

13 **O how great the plan** [*the plan of salvation*] **of our God! For on the other hand** [*now we will talk about the righteous*], the paradise of God must deliver up the spirits of the righteous, and the grave deliver up the body of the righteous; and **the spirit and the body is restored to itself again, and all men become incorruptible, and immortal** [*receive permanent, resurrected bodies*], and they are living souls, having a perfect knowledge like unto us in the flesh, save it be that our knowledge shall be perfect [*except we don't have perfect knowledge yet*].

Verse 14, next, is a great doctrinal verse. It clearly teaches that it is possible to have an enjoyable Judgment Day! The first half of the verse shows the misery of the wicked on the day of Final Judgment, but the last half teaches the joy and enjoyment of the righteous on that day.

14 Wherefore, **we** [*Jacob graciously and humbly includes himself in this category, even though we know he belongs with the righteous*] **shall have a perfect knowledge of all our guilt, and our uncleanness, and our nakedness** [*i.e., the wicked will have no "cover up" or no excuses left on Judgment Day*]; and the **righteous shall have a perfect knowledge of their enjoyment, and their righteousness, being clothed with purity, yea, even with the robe of righteousness.**

Jacob emphasizes differences between the wicked and the righteous, like Isaiah does, to encourage us to be righteous and to gain eternal happiness and joy.

Next, he emphasizes accountability—in other words, being responsible for our own lives and what we did on earth. No one fully capable of accountability escapes appearing before Christ to be judged.

15 And it shall come to pass that **when all men shall have passed from this first death unto life** [*when everybody has died and has been resurrected*], insomuch as they have become immortal [*they will now live forever as resurrected beings*], **they must appear before the judgment-seat of the Holy One of Israel** [*Christ*]; and then cometh the judgment, and then must they be judged according to the holy judgment of God.

With respect to verse 15, above, John 5:22 informs us that Christ is the final judge, that the Father has turned this responsibility over to Him.

16 And assuredly, as the Lord liveth, for the Lord God hath spoken it, and it is his eternal word, which cannot pass away, that **they who are righteous shall be righteous still, and they who are filthy shall be filthy still; wherefore, they who are filthy are the devil and his angels** [*and that's how the wicked will end up if they don't repent*]; and they shall go away into everlasting fire [*remorse and punishment*], prepared for them; and their torment is as [*is like*] a lake of fire and brimstone [*fiery, white hot sulphur*], whose flame ascendeth up forever and ever and has no end.

17 O the greatness and the justice of our God! For he executeth all his words, and they have gone forth out of his mouth, and his law must be fulfilled. [*The law of justice will have its full effect on the wicked.*]

Now Jacob emphasizes again the joy and pleasant status the righteous will have eternally.

18 But, behold, **the righteous, the saints of the Holy One of Israel, they who have believed in the Holy One of Israel, they who have endured the crosses** [*the tests and tribulations of remaining righteous*] **of the world, and despised the shame of it, they shall inherit the kingdom of God, which was prepared for them from the foundation of the world** [*which was planned in the premortal councils*], and **their joy shall be full forever.**

19 **O the greatness of the mercy of our God, the Holy One of Israel! For he delivereth his saints from that awful monster the devil, and death, and hell, and that lake of fire and**

brimstone, which is endless torment [*see D&C 19:4–12 for more about endless torment*].

20 O how great the holiness of our **God! For he knoweth all things, and there is not anything save he knows it.**

Sometimes, members of the Church wonder whether Christ paid for the sins of all people or just for those sins that are ultimately repented of. Jacob answers this question in the next verse.

21 And he [*Christ*] cometh into the world that he may save all men if they will hearken unto his voice; for behold, **he suffereth the pains of all men, yea, the pains of every living creature, both men, women, and children, who belong to the family of Adam** [*Christ paid for all sins, whether repented of or not*].

The answer is, Christ paid for all sins, whether repented of or not. However, those who refuse to accept His payment by repenting and becoming righteous will, in effect, be given back the "receipt" for payment of their sins, and will have to be punished for them themselves (see D&C 19:15–19).

22 And **he suffereth this** [*Christ went through His atoning sacrifice*] **that the resurrection might pass upon all men** [*Christ overcame physical death for everyone so that everyone will be resurrected*], **that all might stand before him at the great and judgment day** [*Christ suffered through the Atonement so that it is completely fair for everyone to ultimately be accountable before Him on Judgment Day*].

Next, Jacob again tells us what we must do to overcome spiritual death. "Spiritual death" means dying as far as spirituality is concerned and being refused the privilege of returning to live with God eternally.

23 And he commandeth all men that they must **repent, and be baptized in his name, having perfect faith in the Holy One of Israel** [*having complete faith that Christ can make them clean and fit to be in the presence of God*], or they cannot be saved in the kingdom of God.

24 And **if they will not repent and believe in his name, and be baptized in his name, and endure to the end, they must be damned** [*they will be stopped from eternal progression*]; for the Lord God, the Holy One of Israel, has spoken it.

Eternal progression only applies to those who attain exaltation in the celestial kingdom. In other words, only those who live in the family unit eternally will have eternal progression. Those who go to any other category in the three degrees of glory or into outer darkness will be limited eternally.

25 Wherefore, **he has given a law; and where there is no law given there is no punishment; and where there is no punishment there is no condemnation** [*Final Judgment*]; and **where there is no condemnation the mercies of the Holy One of Israel have claim upon them, because of the atonement; for they are delivered by the power of him.**

Verse 25, above, is context sensitive, meaning that it must be studied along with all the scriptures. Verse 25 teaches that God is completely fair and that a person who has not been properly taught the gospel is not yet accountable for its laws. Taken alone, it sounds like some lucky people (who have passed the age of accountability) will make it simply because they were never taught the gospel. However, we know from D&C 131:6 that we cannot be saved in ignorance of the gospel. And we know from D&C 138 that all who did not get a fair opportunity to learn and accept the gospel in this life will get those opportunities in the spirit world. Therefore, there is no "free" salvation. Verse 26, next, must be studied in the same context.

26 For **the atonement satisfieth the demands of his justice** [*the law of justice*] **upon all those who have not the law given to them, that they are delivered** [*set free*] from that awful monster, death and hell, and the devil, and the lake of **fire and brimstone** [*white hot molten sulphur; not literal, rather, a scary way of saying that suffering for one's own sins is not a small thing; see D&C 19:15–19*], which is **endless torment; and they are restored** [*by way of merciful opportunities provided in the spirit world mission field*] to that God who gave them breath, which is the Holy One of Israel.

27 But **wo unto him that has the law given, yea, that has all the commandments of God, like unto us** [*in other words, those who have a full set of opportunities to understand and live the gospel here on earth*], and **that transgresseth** [*breaks*] **them, and that wasteth the days of his probation** [*who fails the test by not taking the gospel seriously*], for awful is his state!

Jacob now gives his famous sermon on the fate of those who waste their mortal lives in wicked living. He begins with a warning to those who gain much education without having faith in Christ. (Compare with D&C 88:118.)

28 O that cunning plan of the evil one! O the vainness, and the frailties, and the foolishness of men! **When they are learned they think they are wise, and they hearken not unto the counsel of**

God, for they set it aside [*ignore it, neglect it*], **supposing they know of themselves, wherefore, their wisdom is foolishness and it profiteth them not. And they shall perish.**

29 But **to be learned is good if they hearken unto the counsels of God.**

30 **But wo unto the rich, who are rich as to the things of the world. For because they are rich they despise** [*look down at, think they are better than*] **the poor, and they persecute the meek, and their hearts are upon their treasures; wherefore, their treasure is their god. And behold, their treasure shall perish with them also.**

31 **And wo unto the deaf** [*spiritually deaf*] **that will not hear** [*refuse to listen to the gospel*]; **for they shall perish.**

32 **Wo unto the blind** [*spiritually blind*] **that will not see** [*do not want to see spiritual truths*]; **for they shall perish also.**

33 **Wo unto the uncircumcised of heart** [*those who are not loyal to God in their innermost feelings*], **for a knowledge of their iniquities** [*wickedness*] **shall smite them at the last day** [*on Judgment Day*].

34 **Wo unto the liar, for he shall be thrust down to hell.**

35 **Wo unto the murderer** who deliberately killeth [*in other words, first degree murder*], **for he shall die.**

36 **Wo unto them who commit whoredoms** [*those who delight in sexual immorality of any form*], **for they shall be thrust down to hell.**

37 Yea, **wo unto those that worship idols**, for the devil of all devils delighteth in them.

38 And, in fine [*in summary*], **wo unto all those who die in their sins; for they shall return to God, and behold** [*see*] **his face, and remain in their sins.**

39 O, my beloved brethren, **remember the awfulness in transgressing against that Holy God**, and **also the awfulness of yielding to the enticings** [*giving in to sin as an agency choice*] **of that cunning one** [*the devil*]. Remember, **to be carnally-minded** [*to keep your mind focused on worldly things*] **is death** [*brings spiritual death*], and **to be spiritually-minded is life eternal** [*brings exaltation in celestial glory*].

40 **O, my beloved brethren, give ear to my words** [*please listen to me*]. Remember the greatness of the Holy One of Israel [*Christ*]. Do not say that I have spoken hard things

against you [*do not have a bad attitude about what I have taught you*]; for if ye do, ye will revile [*rebel*] against the truth; for **I have spoken the words of your Maker**. I know that the words of truth are hard against all uncleanness; but **the righteous fear them not, for they love the truth and are not shaken**.

Now, having spoken in clear, unmistakable terms, Jacob tenderly invites his people to be loyal to Christ and to remember that the ways of righteousness are simple. By the way, perhaps you've noticed that righteousness is simple and wickedness makes life stressful and complicated.

41 O then, my beloved brethren, **come unto the Lord**, the Holy One. Remember that his paths are righteous. Behold, the way for man is narrow, but it lieth in a straight course before him [*there is nothing complicated about righteousness*], and **the keeper of the gate** [*the One who opens or shuts the gate to heaven for you*] **is the Holy One of Israel** [*Christ*]; and **he employeth no servant there** [*He does not delegate this job*]; and **there is none other way** [*to heaven*] **save it be by the gate** [*there is only one path that leads to salvation*]; for he cannot be deceived, for the Lord God is his name.

42 And **whoso knocketh** [*an agency choice for each of us*], to **him will he open**; and the wise [*in their own minds*], and the learned [*the well-educated, who don't have faith in Christ*], and they that are rich [*whose hearts are set on their wealth*], who are puffed up [*prideful*] because of their learning, and their wisdom, and their riches—yea, they are they whom he despiseth [*whom He will reject*]; and save [*unless*] they shall cast these things away, and consider themselves fools [*not wise in their own eyes; humble*] before God, and come down in the depths of humility, he will not open [*the "door" of heaven*] unto them.

43 But **the things of the wise and the prudent** [*the truly wise and careful*] **shall be hid from them** [*the people who think they are wise and so well-educated that they don't need the gospel*] **forever**—yea, that happiness which is prepared for the saints.

44 **O, my beloved brethren, remember my words**. Behold, I take off my garments, and I shake them before you [*a sign in Jacob's Jewish culture that he has delivered the message God asked him to and that the responsibility for it now lies with them*]; I pray the God of my salvation that he view me with his all-searching eye; wherefore [*therefore*], ye shall know at the last day [*Judgment Day*], when all men shall be judged of

their works, that the God of Israel [*another name for Christ*] did witness that I shook your iniquities from my soul, and that **I stand with brightness before him, and am rid of your blood** [*I am not responsible now in any way for your sins*].

45 O, my beloved brethren, **turn away from your sins; shake off the chains of him** [*the devil*] **that would bind you fast** [*who wants to tie you up tightly in sin*]; **come unto that God who is the rock of your salvation** [*the firm, safe foundation upon which you can build your life*].

Next, Jacob reminds his listeners that they will play a role in their own final judgment. The wicked will have a perfect recollection of all their sins. As far as the righteous are concerned, they can take comfort in the statement of the Lord in D&C 58:42 concerning sins that have been repented of. He said, "Behold, he who has repented of his sins, the same is forgiven, and I, the Lord, remember them no more." Thus, the sins that have been properly repented of will not even be brought up or mentioned on Judgment Day.

46 Prepare your souls for that **glorious day** [*Judgment Day*] when **justice shall be administered unto the righteous**, even the day of judgment, that ye may not shrink with awful fear; **that ye may not remember your awful guilt in perfectness**, and be constrained [*forced*] to exclaim: Holy, holy are thy judgments, O Lord God Almighty—**but I know my guilt; I transgressed thy law, and my transgressions are mine; and the devil hath obtained me, that I am a prey** [*victim*] **to his** [*the devil's*] **awful misery**.

Next, Jacob asks several important questions designed to make his people think seriously about what he has been teaching them.

47 But behold, my brethren, **is it expedient** [*necessary*] **that I should awake you to an awful reality of these things**? Would I harrow up [*tear up*] **your souls if your minds were pure? Would I be plain unto you according to the plainness of the truth if ye were freed from sin?**

48 Behold, **if ye were holy I would speak unto you of holiness**; but as ye are not holy, and ye look upon me as a teacher, it must needs be expedient [*it is necessary*] that I teach you the consequences [*results*] of sin.

49 Behold, **my soul abhorreth sin** [*I am completely not attracted to sin*], and **my heart delighteth in righteousness**; and I will praise the holy name of my God.

50 **Come**, my brethren, **every one that thirsteth, come ye to the waters** [*the "living water" of Christ; see John 4:10*]; and he that hath no money [*you don't have to be wealthy to make it to heaven*], **come buy and eat; yea, come buy wine and milk** [*the very best; in other words, exaltation*] **without money and without price.** [*In other words, the gospel of Christ is available to all, without regard to social status, personal wealth, etc.*]

51 **Wherefore** [*the point is*], **do not spend money for that which is of no worth, nor your labor for that which cannot satisfy** [*eternally*]. Hearken diligently [*faithfully and continually*] unto me, and remember the words which I have spoken; and **come unto the Holy One of Israel** [*Christ*], and **feast upon that which perisheth not** [*which is not temporary*], neither can be corrupted, and let your soul delight in fatness. [*"Fatness," in this context, is a word that means the very best, the finest. Thus, it would be symbolic of exaltation.*]

52 Behold, my beloved brethren, **remember the words of your God; pray unto him continually by day, and give thanks unto his holy name by night. Let your hearts rejoice.**

The phrase "Let your hearts rejoice" in verse 52, above, can be very important for personal joy and satisfaction. In one sense, it can simply mean, "Rejoice." However, in another sense, it can mean, "Allow yourself to be happy and confident that, with the Savior's help, you will make it back to heaven."

53 **And behold** [*pay attention to*] **how great the covenants of the Lord, and how great his condescensions unto the children of men** [*His willingness to work with us who are so far beneath Him*]; and **because of his greatness, and his grace** [*ability to help us*] **and mercy, he has promised unto us that our seed shall not utterly be destroyed, according to the flesh** [*here in mortality*], but that he would preserve them; and **in future generations they shall become a righteous branch unto the house of Israel** [*a prophecy of the Restoration through Joseph Smith and the conversion of the Lamanites in the last days; see D&C 49:24*].

54 And now, my brethren, I would speak unto you more; but on the morrow [*tomorrow*] I will declare unto you the remainder of my words. Amen.

2 NEPHI 10

It is now "tomorrow" and Jacob continues his sermon to his people. He will first teach more about the

Lamanites, then about the descendants of Laman and Lemuel, and then about the Jews and their scattering and last days gathering. He will then teach about the bringing of the gospel to the Lamanites. Finally, he will teach his people about Zion, the work of the Lord in the last days.

1 AND now **I, Jacob, speak unto you again, my beloved brethren, concerning this righteous branch** [*the Lamanites, who will come into the Church in the last days, referred to in 2 Nephi 9:53*] of which I have spoken.

2 For behold, **the promises** [*that the gospel will someday be brought back to the Lamanites*] which we have obtained **are promises unto us according to the flesh** [*that is to say, these promises will be literally fulfilled*]; wherefore, as it has been shown unto me that many of our children [*descendants*] shall perish in the flesh because of unbelief, nevertheless, God will be merciful unto many; and **our children** [*descendants*] **shall be restored** [*compare with D&C 49:24*], **that they may come to that which will give them the true knowledge of their Redeemer.**

Next, Jacob mentions that an angel told him that "Christ" would be the name often used for Jesus when He came to earth, born to Mary, to fulfill His earthly mission. This is another reminder to us that our prophets can receive inspiration that enables them to see into the future and tell us about it.

This prophecy about Christ will be fulfilled in about 550 years from Jacob's lifetime.

3 Wherefore, as I said unto you, it must needs be expedient [*it is necessary*] that **Christ—for in the last night the angel spake unto me that this should be his name—should** [*will*] **come among the Jews**, among those who are the more wicked part of the world; **and they shall crucify him**—for thus it behooveth our God [*Christ has to do this*], and **there is none other nation on earth that would crucify their God**.

Often when members read the last phrase of verse 3, above, they ask, "Is it true that this is the wickedest world?" The answer is "Yes"; see Moses 7:36.

The next question is usually, "What did we do wrong in the premortal life to deserve to be sent to this earth?" The answer is, "You should consider it a great honor to come to this world, where Jesus lived His mortal life and carried out the Atonement for this and all other worlds belonging to Heavenly Father. Your being here is a reminder to you of the trust and confidence the Father has in you."

4 For **should the mighty miracles be wrought** [*if such mighty miracles were done*] **among other nations they would repent**, and know that he be their God.

Next, Jacob tells us how the Jews in the Jerusalem area got to be so wicked that they would crucify Christ.

5 But **because of priestcrafts** [*the Jewish religious leaders exercising religious power and authority for personal prestige and gain; see Alma 1:16*] **and iniquities** [*very serious wickedness*], **they at Jerusalem will stiffen their necks against him** [*Jesus Christ*], **that he be crucified.**

Next, Jacob tells what would happen to the Jews because of crucifying Jesus.

6 Wherefore, because of their iniquities, **destructions, famines, pestilences** [*all kinds of troubles, diseases, etc.*], **and bloodshed shall come upon them** [*the Jews*]; and **they who shall not be destroyed shall be scattered among all nations.**

The gathering of the Jews spoken of next is one of the very visible signs of the times in the last days before the Second Coming of the Savior. We are privileged to live in the time when this great prophecy is being fulfilled.

7 But behold, thus saith the Lord God: **When the day cometh that they** [*the Jews*] **shall believe in me, that I am Christ, then have I covenanted with their fathers** [*promised their ancestors*] that **they shall be restored in the flesh, upon the earth, unto the lands of their inheritance** [*in other words, the restoration of the Jews spoken of is not just symbolic; rather, it is a literal gathering*].

8 And it shall come to pass that **they shall be gathered in** from their long dispersion [*they will remain scattered for a long time*], from the isles of the sea [*from all nations of the earth*], and from the four parts of the earth [*all over the earth*]; and **the nations of the Gentiles shall be great in the eyes of me, saith God, in carrying them forth to the lands of their inheritance**. [*In other words, non-Jewish nations will assist in bringing the Jews back to their homelands.*]

As mentioned previously, Great Britain and other nations voted in the United Nations to restore the Jews to the land of Palestine and to create the nation of Israel in 1948. We understand these to be among the "nations of the Gentiles" spoken of in verse 8, above.

9 Yea, **the kings** [*political leaders*] **of the Gentiles shall be nursing fathers** [*will provide assistance*] unto them [*the Jews*], **and their queens**

shall become nursing mothers; wherefore [*and so you can see*], the promises of the Lord are great unto the Gentiles [*it is a great privilege to help the Lord fulfill prophecies*], for **he hath spoken it, and who can dispute** [*the Lord said it will happen, so who would dare say it won't*]?

10 But behold, this land [*America*], said God, shall be a land of thine inheritance [*Lehi's posterity; the Lamanites*], and the Gentiles [*immigrants from Europe, etc.*] shall be blessed upon the land.

11 And this land [*America; see heading to chapter 10 in your regular Book of Mormon*] shall be a land of liberty unto the Gentiles, and **there shall be no kings upon the land, who shall raise up unto the Gentiles**.

It is a really big promise with a miraculous fulfillment that this land will never have a king in our day (see verse 11, above, as well as the following verses). In that alone we can see the hand of the Lord, especially when we look at the fact that nearly all other nations and peoples on earth have generally had kings as their political leaders.

12 And **I will fortify this land against all other nations**.

13 And **he that fighteth against Zion** [*this land—see verse 12, above—and the work of the Lord, in general*] **shall perish**, saith God.

14 For **he that raiseth up a king against me shall perish**, for **I, the Lord, the king of heaven, will be their king**, and **I will be a light unto them forever, that hear my words**.

15 Wherefore, **for this cause** [*this is why*], **that my covenants** [*promises*] **may be fulfilled** which I have made unto the children of men [*all people*], that I will do unto them while they are in the flesh [*during their mortal lives*], **I must needs destroy the secret works of darkness, and of murders, and of abominations**.

The next verse is fair warning to all people that no one will ultimately, successfully, fight against Zion (the Lord's work; the Restoration of the gospel in the last days).

16 Wherefore, **he that fighteth against Zion, both Jew and Gentile, both bond** [*including slaves and servants*] **and free, both male and female** [*in other words, anyone, no matter who*], **shall perish**; for **they are they who are the whore of all the earth** [*they are all on Satan's team*]; for **they who are not for me are against me, saith our God**.

The phrase "they are they who are the whore of all the earth" in verse 16, above, is unmistakably strong. You may recall that the "whore of all the earth" is the "church of the devil" (see 1 Nephi 14:10). The message is clear: if we are not helping the Lord build up His kingdom here on earth, we are helping the devil. There is no neutral ground.

17 For **I will fulfil my promises** which I have made unto the children of men, that I will do unto them while they are in the flesh—

18 Wherefore, my beloved brethren, **thus saith our God: I will afflict** [*cause trouble for*] **thy seed** [*the Lamanites*] **by the hand of the Gentiles** [*the Lamanites will be badly treated by those who settle America*]; nevertheless [*however*], I will soften the hearts of the Gentiles, that they shall be like unto a father to them; wherefore, **the Gentiles shall be blessed and numbered among the house of Israel** [*will become part of covenant Israel*].

19 Wherefore, **I will consecrate** [*bless and give*] this land [*America; North and South America*] **unto thy seed**, and them who shall be numbered among thy seed, forever, for the land of their inheritance; for **it is a choice land**, saith God unto me, **above all other lands**, wherefore **I will have all men that dwell thereon that they shall worship me, saith God**.

The last phrase of verse 19, above, is very serious. It reminds us that to have the Lord's promises fulfilled concerning America, the inhabitants of America must live the gospel.

20 And **now, my beloved brethren, seeing that our merciful God has given us so great knowledge concerning these things, let us remember him, and lay aside our sins, and not hang down our heads** [*not get discouraged*], for we are not cast off; nevertheless, we have been driven out of the land of our inheritance [*Jerusalem area*]; but we have been led to a better land, for the Lord has made the sea our path, and **we are upon an isle of the sea**.

As mentioned in previous notes, the phrase "we are upon an isle of the sea" in verse 20, above, means the Americas. In Jewish culture and language at the time of Lehi, the phrase "isles of the sea" means all lands and continents other than Asia and Africa.

21 But great are the promises of the Lord unto them who are upon the isles of the sea; wherefore as it says isles [*plural*], there must needs be more than this [*there must be other continents besides this one on which we live*], and they are inhabited also by our

brethren. [*In other words, all people are our brothers and sisters.*]

Next, Jacob teaches us that there are many peoples who have been led away by the Lord. In other words, there have been many "scatterings" throughout history. It will be fascinating someday to meet them and learn of their history.

22 For behold, **the Lord God has led away from time to time from the house of Israel, according to his will and pleasure**. And now behold, the Lord remembereth all them who have been broken off [*all people will eventually be "gathered in" as part of the gathering of Israel*], wherefore he remembereth us also [*keeps his covenants to restore us and our people also*].

Next, in verse 23, we find one of Jacob's most famous teachings.

23 Therefore, cheer up your hearts, and remember that **ye are free to act for yourselves—to choose the way of everlasting death or the way of eternal life**.

Just a reminder, with respect to verse 23, above. There is no such thing as the actual destruction of a person's spirit. Therefore, the term "everlasting death" means "spiritual death," or what is often referred to as the "second death." In other words, being cut off from being in the presence of God forever. Another way to put it might be to say "never having the personal spirituality needed to be comfortable in the presence of God and other celestial beings forever."

"Eternal life" is also used in verse 23. As you might already know, the celestial kingdom has three degrees in it (see D&C 131:1–3) and "eternal life" always means "exaltation" in the highest degree of the celestial kingdom. D&C 14:7 teaches this by telling us that "eternal life . . . is the greatest of all the gifts of God." Exaltation means living in the family unit forever, becoming gods, having spirit children, creating worlds for them to live on, and using the same plan of salvation for them as our Heavenly Father used for us. The First Presidency made this clear in 1916 in the following statement:

"Only resurrected and glorified beings can become parents of spirit offspring. Only such **exalted souls** have reached maturity in the appointed course of eternal life; and **the spirits born to them in the eternal worlds will pass in due sequence through the several stages or estates by which the glorified parents have attained exaltation**" (Smith, Lund, and Smith, 1916 First Presidency Statement, p. 942).

24 Wherefore, my beloved brethren, **reconcile yourselves to the will of God, and not to the will**

of the devil and the flesh; and remember, after ye are reconciled unto God, that it is only in and through the grace of God that ye are saved.

The word "reconcile" as used in verse 24, above, comes from Latin and means "to sit with again." The word breakdown is as follows:

"re" means "again"

"con" means "with"

"cile" means "sit"

Therefore, in this context, "reconcile" basically means to make agency choices that will allow you to return to God and sit down with Him again in His kingdom.

25 Wherefore, may God raise you from death [*physical death*] **by the power of the resurrection**, and also from everlasting death [*spiritual death; dying as to things that are spiritual*] **by the power of the atonement, that ye may be received into the eternal kingdom of God** [*celestial glory*], that ye may praise him **through grace** [*God's power and willingness to help us*] divine. Amen.

2 NEPHI 11

Nephi's younger brother, Jacob, has been teaching us, in 2 Nephi chapters 6 through 10. Now Nephi will take over again. Because of his great love and appreciation for Isaiah's teachings, Nephi will quote Isaiah in chapters 12–24 and 27. As he introduces these next 13 chapters quoting Isaiah (plus one more when we get to 2 Nephi 27), he will explain why he is going to quote so many chapters of Isaiah to us. You will see some of his reasons for reading Isaiah to us, especially in verses 2, 4, 5, 6, and 8.

Many members of the Church find these chapters of Isaiah very difficult to understand. Some skip them in their reading of the Book of Mormon, while others read every word without getting much out of them. Yet others see some beautiful teachings and gain some understanding but still miss much.

If you will study these Isaiah chapters of the Book of Mormon along with the notes provided, praying for help each time you read, it is quite likely that you will be ahead of many members of the Church in understanding and appreciating the important messages in the writings of Isaiah.

Also, be patient with yourself if you don't understand it all. As you read and study the Book of Mormon throughout your life, remember that the Holy Ghost is your main teacher, and He often teaches us more each time we read it.

1 AND now, **Jacob spake** [*spoke*] **many more things to my people at that time**; nevertheless only these things have I caused to be written, for the things which I

have written sufficeth me [*are suficient as far as my purposes are concerned*].

2 **And now I, Nephi, write more of the words of Isaiah, for my soul delighteth in his words** [*I love the teachings of Isaiah*]. For **I will liken his words unto my people** [*the words of Isaiah apply to my people*], and I will send them forth unto all my children, for **he** [*Isaiah*] verily [*absolutely, truly*] **saw my Redeemer** [*the Savior*], **even as I have seen him** [*Nephi has seen the Savior also*].

3 **And my brother, Jacob, also has seen him** as I have seen him; **wherefore** [*this is why*], **I will send their words** [*the words of Isaiah and Jacob*] **forth unto my children to prove unto them that my words are true**. Wherefore, by the words of three [*the law of witnesses*], God hath said, I will establish my word. Nevertheless, God sendeth more witnesses, and he proveth all his words.

Next, we see some reasons Nephi wants his people to study Isaiah.

4 Behold, **my soul delighteth in proving unto my people the truth of the coming of Christ**; for, for this end [*purpose*] hath the law of Moses been given [*this is the reason the Lord gave the law of Moses to the children of Israel was to teach them about Christ*]; and **all things which have been given of God from the beginning of the world, unto man, are the typifying of him** [*"typifying of" means "symbolic of," in other words, everything God has told us, from Adam and Eve to now, teaches us about Christ*].

5 And also **my soul delighteth in the covenants** [*promises, including things we agree to do, like at baptism*] **of the Lord which he hath made to our fathers** [*ancestors*]; yea, **my soul delighteth in his grace** [*his kindness in using His power to help us*]**, and in his justice** [*the law of justice*]**, and power, and mercy** [*the law of mercy*] **in the great and eternal plan of deliverance from death.**

6 And **my soul delighteth in proving unto my people that save Christ should come all men must perish** [*if it were not for Christ, we would all be destroyed*].

Sometimes we shy away from logic in gospel discussions and gospel teaching because shallow logic, based on falsehoods or half truths, has been used by so many people to try to prove that there is no God, etc. However, when logic is based on truth, it has tremendous power. Watch Nephi's powerful "true logic" in verse 7, next.

7 For **if there be no Christ there be no God**; and **if there be no God we are not** [*we do not exist*], for

there could have been no creation. But there is a God, and **he is Christ**, and **he** cometh in the fulness of his own time [*He will come to live on earth when the time is right*].

8 And now I write some of the words of Isaiah, that **whoso of my people shall see these words may lift up their hearts and rejoice for all men.** Now these are the words, and ye may liken them unto you and unto all men [*they apply to you and to everyone*].

> No wonder Nephi invites us to "lift up [our] hearts and rejoice for all men." And no wonder he wants us to read and understand Isaiah's great message, because it shows how effective and far-reaching Christ's Atonement is.

2 NEPHI 12

For those of you who want to know a little more about how the Book of Mormon helps us better understand the Bible, be aware that of the 433 verses of Isaiah in the Bible that are quoted in the Book of Mormon, over half of them are given differently than in the Bible, while about two hundred of them are the same (see 2 Nephi 12, footnote 2a). Thus, the Book of Mormon is a major source of clarification and help for understanding Isaiah in the Bible.

This chapter, 2 Nephi 12, is similar to Isaiah, chapter 2, in the Bible. It deals with the gathering of Israel to the true Church in the last days, the Millennium (the 1,000 years of peace after Christ comes to earth again for His Second Coming), and the destruction of the proud and the wicked at the Second Coming.

Many of you have, no doubt, heard our current prophets say a lot about the gathering of Israel now in preparation for the Second Coming of the Savior.

1 **The word that Isaiah, the son of Amoz, saw** concerning Judah [*the Jews as a political kingdom as well as the Jews as Israelites*] and Jerusalem:

> Isaiah uses a lot of symbolism. Sometimes, this can make it difficult to understand his writings. And because he uses so much symbolism, his writings can have many different meanings and applications. Next, in verse 2 for instance, the phrase "mountain of the Lord's house" can mean the headquarters of the Church in Salt Lake City, Utah, in the Rocky Mountains in the last days. Also, since "mountains" are often symbolic of temples ("high places" where we can draw closer to God), "mountain of the Lord's house" can also mean temples.

2 And it shall come to pass in the last days, when **the mountain of the Lord's house** [*Church headquarters in the last days; also temples will be established*] shall be established **in the top of the mountains**, and shall

be exalted above the hills [*you can get "higher," or closer to God in the temples through covenant-making than on the highest mountains*], and **all nations** [*the gathering of Israel involves people from every nation*] **shall flow unto it** [*the true Church in the last days*].

3 And **many people shall** go and **say**, Come ye, and **let us go up to the mountain of the Lord** [*to the true Church; temples*], **to the house of the God of Jacob** [*to the temples of the God of covenant Israel*]; and **he will teach us of his ways, and we will walk in his paths** [*we will live the gospel*]; **for out of Zion shall go forth the law, and the word of the Lord from Jerusalem** [*"law" and "word" mean the same thing here*].

There will be two headquarters of the Church during the Millennium, one in Zion (Jackson County, Missouri) and one in Old Jerusalem.

4 **And he** [*Christ*] **shall judge** [*rule*] **among the nations, and shall rebuke** [*teach correct principles to*] **many people**: and they shall beat their swords into plow-shares [*will turn their swords into the leading edge of plows for farming; the promised millennial peace will come*], and their spears into pruning-hooks [*there will be peace*]—nation shall not lift up sword against nation, neither shall they learn war any more [*there will be peace during the Millennium*].

Did you notice that Isaiah repeated the same thing with different words in verse 4, above? He does this to emphasize certain points. It is part of his teaching style. But it can be confusing to some people who think, "He can't be saying the same thing that many times. I must be missing something!" They are not missing something. He is repeating the same thing. In this case, he is emphasizing that there will be peace during the Millennium.

Isaiah now switches from way in the future back to his own time and people who have become very wicked, inviting them to repent and return to the Lord.

5 **O house of Jacob** [*Israel*], **come ye and let us walk in the light of the Lord** [*repent and live the gospel*]; yea, come, for **ye have all gone astray, every one to his wicked ways.**

Next, Isaiah explains why the blessings of the Lord are not coming upon the Israelites of his day.

Remember that the phrase "house of Jacob," at the beginning of verse 5, above, means "family of Jacob," or in other words, "descendants of Abraham, Isaac, and Jacob," who are the covenant people of the Lord. Remember also that Jacob's name was changed to "Israel" (Genesis 32:28), so "House of Jacob" is often written "House of Israel" in the scriptures. The "children of Israel" are descendants of Jacob. And the descendants of Jacob are the covenant people of the Lord, often referred to as "Israel," "covenant Israel," or "Israelites."

And the reason they are called "covenant Israel" is that the Lord made a covenant (a very serious promise and agreement) with Abraham (Abraham 2:9–11) that God would take the gospel to all the world through his posterity. His covenant posterity comes through his son Isaac, and on down through Isaac's son Jacob.

In your patriarchal blessing, you will likely have something to the effect that, through your faithfulness in the gospel, you will eventually receive all the blessings of Abraham, Isaac, and Jacob, which include the blessings of exaltation and the responsibility to help take the gospel to all the world.

Remember also that all people are invited by the gospel of Jesus Christ to join with the "covenant people of the Lord" through baptism, whether or not they are bloodline descendants of Jacob. Thus, all can become covenant people and ultimately enter into celestial exaltation.

Now, back to the reason the Lord has quit blessing the Israelites in Isaiah's day.

6 **Therefore** [*this is the reason why*], **O Lord, thou hast forsaken** [*quit blessing and helping*] **thy people, the house of Jacob** [*the Israelites*], **because they be replenished from the east** [*they are leaving the true gospel and adopting false eastern religions*], **and hearken unto soothsayers** like the Philistines [*are into witchcraft, sorcery etc.; see 3 Nephi 21:16*], and **they please themselves in the children of strangers** [*they are mixing and marrying with foreigners, nonmembers, people not of covenant Israel; they are "marrying" themselves right out of the Church, so to speak*].

The word "strangers," as used in Isaiah's writings (see verse 6, above), almost always means "foreigners" or in other words, non-Israelites.

7 **Their land also is full of silver and gold, neither is there any end of their treasures** [*they have become materialistic; in other words, they are mainly interested in money and wealth, etc., rather than God and religion*]; **their land is also full of horses, neither is there any end of their chariots.**

Horses and chariots are symbolic of military equipment and preparations for war in Isaiah's writings. They can also represent military might and ability to conquer.

8 **Their land is also full of idols** [*they are in a condition of deep apostasy; in other words, they have left God and are worshiping idols instead*]; **they worship the work of their own hands** [*they use idols to worship, that they made themselves, instead of worshiping God*], **that which their own fingers have made** [*which is pretty stupid*].

9 And **the mean man** [*poor, low in social status*] **boweth not down** [*is not humble*], **and the great man** [*wealthy, powerful, high in social status*] **humbleth himself not, therefore, forgive him not** [*nobody is humble, therefore, no forgiveness!*].

If you want to be a bit more of a scholar in the scriptures, read the note here, which follows:

Verse 9, above, is a great example of the value of the Book of Mormon Isaiah verses. In the Bible, the equivalent of verse 9 reads as follows:

Isaiah 2:9

9 And the mean man boweth down, and the great man humbleth himself: therefore forgive them not.

When you compare 2 Nephi 12:9 with Isaiah 2:9, you see that the word "not" is left out twice in the Bible version and makes all the difference! If you were reading Isaiah in the Bible and trying to understand God's mercy and His dealings with people based on Isaiah 2:9, you would be in trouble. This is an example of the meaning of the eighth article of faith, which says: "We believe the Bible to be the word of God as far as it is translated correctly; we also believe the Book of Mormon to be the word of God" (Pearl of Great Price, Article of Faith 1:8).

Next, Isaiah warns the wicked that they will not be able to hide from the destruction of the wicked at the Second Coming of Christ.

10 O ye wicked ones, enter into the rock [*caves; see verse 19*], and hide thee in the dust, for the fear of the Lord and **the glory of his majesty shall smite thee.**

Many people wonder how the wicked will be burned at the time of the actual Second Coming. We learned the answer in verse 10, above. As stated, they will be burned by His glory. This is stated again in verses 19 and 21.

Some years ago, a student asked me how the temples would survive the burning at the Second Coming. Verses 10, 19, 21, plus D&C 5:19 provide a simple answer. Temples can stand the glory of the Lord. Therefore, they will not be burned.

11 And it shall come to pass that the lofty looks [*pride*] of man shall be humbled, and the haughtiness

[*pride*] of men shall be bowed down [put down], and the Lord alone shall be exalted in that day [*the Lord will demonstrate that He has power over all things at the Second Coming*].

Verse 11, above, is a good example of the fact that Isaiah repeats important concepts as he writes and teaches. The phrases "lofty looks" and "haughtiness of men" both mean pride. If people do not understand that Isaiah uses repetition as a technique for emphasizing important points, they could spend a lot of time and fruitless effort in trying to figure out the difference in message between these two phrases. In fact, in verse 12, next, Isaiah says "pride" three different ways. They are in **bold**. This emphasis against pride continues in following verses.

12 For the day of the Lord of Hosts [*the Second Coming*] soon cometh upon [*against*] all nations, yea, upon every one [*who is wicked*]; yea, upon the **proud** and **lofty**, and upon every one who is **lifted up** [*prideful*], and he shall be brought low [*humbled*].

13 Yea, and **the day of the Lord shall come upon all the cedars of Lebanon** [*symbolic of wicked, high and mighty, prideful people*], for they are **high and lifted up** [*full of pride*]; and upon all the **oaks** [*people*] **of Bashan**;

14 And upon all the high mountains [*where people worship idols*], and upon all the hills [*where they worship idols*], and upon all the nations which are **lifted up** [*in pride, etc.*], and upon every people;

15 And upon every high tower, and upon every fenced wall [*symbolic of the pride and "trusting in the arm of flesh," which can go along with man-made defenses*];

16 And upon all the ships of the sea, and upon all the ships of Tarshish [*noted for ability to travel long distances, carry large cargos, and have the strength of a warship; apparently symbolic of pride and materialism*], and upon all pleasant pictures [*pleasure ships upon which the wealthy traveled*].

17 And the **loftiness** [*pride*] of man shall be bowed down [*shall be brought down*], and the **haughtiness of men shall be made low** [*brought down*]; and the Lord alone shall be exalted in that day.

You can tell from how many times Isaiah warns us against pride, in the verses we've just read, that pride is one of the major sins that leads to spiritual destruction. We definitely need to stay humble and avoid pride, whatever it takes to do so.

18 And **the idols he** [*Christ*] **shall utterly abolish** [*completely destroy, at the Second Coming*].

In verse 19, next, Isaiah describes the terror of the wicked as they try to hide from the Savior at the time of His Second Coming.

19 And **they** [*the wicked*] **shall go into the holes of the rocks** [*caves*], **and into the caves of the earth, for the fear of the Lord shall come upon them and the glory of his majesty shall smite them** [*as mentioned in D&C 5:19*], **when he ariseth to shake terribly the earth** [*when He comes*].

Next, Isaiah prophesies that, at the time of the Second Coming of the Savior, wicked people will try to get rid of the wicked idols they have made for themselves. This could include anything they have, such as dirty videos, pornography, drugs, boats they use on Sunday instead of going to Church, and so forth.

20 **In that day** [*the Second Coming*] **a man shall cast his idols of silver, and his idols of gold, which he hath made for himself to worship, to the moles and to the bats** [*creatures who live in darkness; symbolic of wicked people who live in spiritual darkness*];

21 To go into the clefts of the rocks, and into the tops of the ragged rocks [*to try to hide from God*], for the fear of the Lord shall come upon them and **the majesty of his glory shall smite them**, when he ariseth to shake terribly the earth [*when He comes at the time of the Second Coming*].

22 **Cease ye from man**, whose breath is in his nostrils; for wherein is he to be accounted of [*why trust in man, why trust in the arm of flesh when God is truly powerful and can save you*]?

2 NEPHI 13

This chapter is to be compared with Isaiah 3 in the Bible. In it, Isaiah prophesies (predicts the future) that the people in Jerusalem and the Jerusalem area are going to be punished because of their wickedness.

Starting with verse 16, he will especially point out that when women get as bad as men, as far as wickedness is concerned, the nation is heading for deep trouble and destruction.

Beginning with verse 1, the main point is that when people get wicked enough, God stops blessing them and things start going very badly for them.

1 **For behold** [*watch this*], **the Lord, the Lord of Hosts** [*another name for Christ*], **doth take away from Jerusalem, and from Judah, the stay** [*supply*] **and the staff** [*support*],

the whole staff **of bread, and the whole stay of water** [*the Lord is going to stop blessing them, and the whole kingdom of the Jews will collapse*]—

2 **The mighty man** [*powerful leaders*], and **the man of war** [*capable military leaders*], **the judge** [*good judges*], and **the prophet** [*true prophets*], and **the prudent** [*wise citizens*], and **the ancient** [*older people with wisdom*]; [*In other words, all the stable, capable leaders will be gone.*]

3 **The captain of fifty**, and **the honorable man** [*leaders who are honest and have integrity*], and **the counselor**, and **the cunning artificer** [*skilled craftsman*], and **the eloquent orator** [*the skilled speaker who can explain things well; in other words, all capable leaders and craftsman will be gone*].

4 And **I will give children unto them to be their princes** [*leaders*], and **babes shall rule over them** [*immature, irresponsible political leaders will take over*].

5 And **the people shall be oppressed, every one by another and every one by his neighbor** [*anarchy, gangs, citizens against citizens, etc.*]; **the child shall behave himself proudly against the ancient, and the base** [*crude, rude*] **against the honorable** [*no respect for authority*].

Next, Isaiah describes how bad things will get when society—in other words, the nation—crumbles. People will get desperate for anyone to lead them.

6 When **a man shall take hold of his brother of the house of his father, and shall say: Thou hast clothing, be thou our ruler**, and let not this ruin come under thy hand [*don't let this happen to us; you've got half-decent clothing—you be our leader*]—

The brother, in verse 6, above, will say, "I don't want to be your leader. In fact, I can't lead you! I'm starving myself!"

7 In that day shall he swear [*protest*], saying: **I will not be a healer** [*I can't lead you nor defend and protect you!*]; for in my house there is neither bread nor clothing [*I've got my own problems*]; **make me not a ruler of the people.**

Next, Isaiah describes the end result of a society that allows wide open evil and wickedness.

8 For **Jerusalem is ruined**, and Judah is **fallen, because their tongues and their doings have been against the Lord, to provoke the eyes of his glory** [*in word and actions, the people are completely wicked and are against the Lord*].

9 **The show of their countenance doth witness against them** [*they*

even look wicked], and doth declare their sin to be even as Sodom [*wicked through and through, including accepting homosexuality; see Gen. 19, footnote 5a*], **and they cannot hide it** [*blatant sin; can't be rationalized away or hidden from God*]. Wo unto their souls, for they have rewarded evil unto themselves [*they are getting what they deserve*]!

So far, this chapter is pretty depressing. Next, in order to make sure that the righteous do not give up, who are trying to survive spiritually and otherwise in such a society, the Lord assures them that they will ultimately be rewarded for their righteousness.

10 **Say unto the righteous that it is well with them; for they shall eat the fruit of their doings** [*they will be blessed and rewarded for their righteousness*].

Now, back to the wicked.

11 **Wo unto the wicked, for they shall perish; for the reward of their hands shall be upon them!** [*As ye sow, so shall ye reap; in other words, whatever you plant, you will harvest.*]

Isaiah continues to describe the end results of such uncontrolled wickedness among the Jews. This of course applies to any nation or individual, any time in history, anywhere.

12 And my people, **children** [*immature leaders*] **are their oppressors, and women rule over them** [*breakdown of traditional family; men are weak leaders, so women have to take over*]. **O my people, they who lead thee cause thee to err and destroy the way of thy paths** [*leadership without basic gospel values causes terrible damage*].

Next, Isaiah will challenge the wicked leaders of the Jews for selfishly taking all they possibly can from the very people they are supposed to protect as leaders.

13 **The Lord standeth up to plead** [*God will catch up with you; you are in big trouble*], and standeth to judge the people.

14 **The Lord will enter into judgment with the ancients** [*the wicked elders and leaders*] of his people and the princes [*leaders*] thereof; for **ye have eaten up the vineyard** [*you have destroyed the country*] **and the spoil of the poor in your houses** [*you have all kinds of loot in your houses that you have taken from the poor; you were supposed to protect them, but, instead, you ruin them*].

15 **What mean ye** [*what have you got to say for yourselves*]? Ye beat my people to pieces, and grind the faces of the poor [*push the poor farther into poverty*], saith the Lord God of Hosts.

Isaiah now shows what happens when women get as wicked as men, and he points out that when this happens, society is doomed, as pointed out in verses 25 and 26.

16 **Moreover** [*in addition to all the problems mentioned above*], the Lord saith: **Because the daughters of Zion** [*the Israelite women; members of the Church*] **are haughty** [*full of wicked pride*], **and walk with stretched-forth necks** [*pride*] **and wanton** [*lustful*] **eyes, walking and mincing** [*short, rapid steps; see Isaiah 3, footnote 16e*] as they go, and **making a tinkling with their feet** [*wearing expensive shoes so people will notice them*]—

17 **Therefore** [*for these reasons*] **the Lord will smite with a scab the crown of the head** [*make them bald; perhaps the "scab" is a result of being shaved as slaves*] of **the daughters of Zion, and the Lord will discover their secret parts** [*expose their evil deeds*].

In verse 17, above, Isaiah prophesied that the Lord's covenant people would go into captivity because of their wickedness. Below, he describes the taking away of all that has been precious in the hearts and minds of the women who have become wicked in Isaiah's day. This same scene is typical of any society whose morals and values decay.

18 **In that day** [*when Jerusalem is captured and destroyed by enemy nations because of their wickedness*] **the Lord will take away the bravery** [*decoration, beauty*] of **their tinkling ornaments** [*expensive shoes*], and **cauls, and round tires like the moon** [*female ornamentations, such as jewelry, expensive necklaces, clothing, etc., representing high status in materialistic society*];

19 **The chains** [*necklaces*] and the **bracelets, and the mufflers** [*veils*];

20 The **bonnets, and the ornaments of the legs, and the headbands, and the tablets** [*musk boxes, perfume boxes*], and the **ear-rings;**

21 The **rings, and nose jewels;**

22 **The changeable suits of apparel** [*party clothes*], and the **mantles** [*gowns, robes*], and the **wimples** [*medieval women's head coverings*], and the **crisping-pins** [*money purses*];

23 The **glasses** [*mirrors; Hebrew: "see-through clothing"; see Isaiah 3, footnote 23a*], and the **fine linen, and hoods** [*turbans*], and the **veils.**

As indicated above, Isaiah has described female high-society fashions, arrogance, sexual immorality, and materialism in terms of such things in his day. Next, he prophetically describes the end results of such wickedness for these women, and literally and symbolically for Jerusalem and the kingdom of Judah.

The same thing happens, basically, to any of us who get caught up in wealth, peer pressure, and the ways of the world, breaking our covenants and leaving God out of our lives.

24 **And it shall come to pass, instead of sweet smell** [*perfume*] **there shall be stink** [*including from corpses of people killed by invading armies; also the stench associated with miserable slavery conditions*]; and **instead of a girdle** [*nice, fashionable waistband*], a rent [*rags*]; and **instead of well set hair, baldness** [*slaves, in Isaiah's day, had shaved heads*]; **and instead of a stomacher** [*a nice robe*], **a girding of sackcloth** [*being dressed in burlap*]; **burning instead of beauty** [*being branded, a mark of slavery; see Isaiah 3, footnote 24d*].

In the above verses, Isaiah spoke of "shaved" heads. Symbolically, this represents slavery or bondage. Literally, conquering armies often kept the best captives who would bring a good price in the slave markets back home. They shaved the hair off of these slaves for three basic reasons:

- Humiliation
- Identification (makes it easier to spot a runaway slave)
- Sanitation

25 **Thy men shall fall by the sword and thy mighty in the war** [*wars will deplete your male population*].

26 **And her gates** [*Jerusalem's; see verse 8*] **shall lament and mourn** [*be very sad*]; and **she** [*Jerusalem*] **shall be desolate** [*empty, cleaned out; see Isaiah 3, footnote 26d*], **and shall sit upon the ground** [*Jerusalem, symbolic of the wicked, will be brought down completely and conquered—one fulfillment of this prophecy was the Babylonian captivity, which ended about 587 BC*].

2 NEPHI 14

As you can see, this is a very short chapter of Isaiah. The first verse fits with the end of chapter 13, which we just read, and tells what will happen as a result of the loss of so many men in war as prophesied in verse 25 of that chapter. With hardly any men left, the remaining women will plead with the few men available to let several women marry just one of them.

1 **And in that day** [*when Jerusalem has been badly beaten down by famine and war, referred to in chapter 13:25–26*], **seven women shall take hold of one man, saying: We will eat our own bread, and wear our own apparel** [*we will pay our own way*]; **only let us be called by thy name** [*please marry us*] to take away our reproach [*the stigma of being unmarried and childless*].

Verse 2, next, starts a new topic, way in the future, namely conditions during the Millennium when Christ will rule on earth for 1,000 years of peace.

2 **In that day** [*the Millennium*] **shall the branch of the Lord be beautiful and glorious** [*things will be wonderful for Christ and the righteous people during the Millennium*]; **the fruit of the earth excellent** [*the earth will be like a paradise*] **and comely** [*pleasant to look at*] **to them that are escaped of Israel** [*to the righteous who have escaped the destruction of the wicked at the Second Coming*].

3 And it shall come to pass, **they** [*the righteous*] **that are left in Zion and remain in Jerusalem shall be called holy** [*will be righteous*], every one that is written among the living [*those saved by approval of the Messiah*] in Jerusalem—

4 **When the Lord shall have washed away the filth of the daughters of Zion** [*when the Lord has cleansed the earth and destroyed the wicked*], **and shall have purged the blood of Jerusalem from the midst thereof by the spirit of judgment and by the spirit of burning** [*the law of justice will be in action as the earth is cleansed by fire*].

The Angel Moroni quoted verses 5 and 6 to Joseph Smith in reference to the last days before the Second Coming of Christ (see *Messenger and Advocate*, Apr., 1835, p. 110).

Next, Isaiah depicts the peace and security that will be everywhere for the righteous during the Millennium as a result of having the presence of the Savior here on earth.

5 **And the Lord will create upon every dwelling-place of mount Zion** [*every home in Jerusalem and every place on the whole earth during the Millennium*], and upon her assemblies, **a cloud and smoke by day and the shining of a flaming fire by night; for upon all** [*everyone*] the glory of Zion shall be a defence [*the presence of the Savior and His glory and protection will be everywhere on earth*].

In verse 6, next, Isaiah will emphasize that the righteous will live under the wonderful protection of the Savior during the Millennium. You will see that He repeats it several times with different words.

6 **And there shall be a tabernacle** [*shelter; can symbolize Hebrew marriage canopy, thus symbolically representing the remarriage of Christ and his people who were worthy to meet Him when He came at the time of the Second Coming; see Jeremiah 3:1*] **for a shadow** [*protection*] in the daytime from the heat, and for a place of refuge, **and a covert** [*protection*]

from storm and from rain [*millennial peace and protection*].

2 NEPHI 15

In this chapter, the Lord starts out by telling us a story or parable about His covenant people, Israel, and how He did everthing He could to bless and protect them so that they could have every chance to live the gospel and have a good life. He involves us by letting us see how they have become so wicked that He has had to stop blessing and protecting them.

Then, He invites us to be the judge between Him and His people. It is really quite fascinating, and you will get so involved that you will want to see how the parable turns out.

First, He gives them every chance to be good.

1 **And then will I sing to my well-beloved a song** [*I will tell you a story*] **of my beloved** [*Christ*], **touching his vineyard** [*concerning Israel*]. **My well-beloved** [*Christ*] **hath a vineyard** [*Israel; see verse 7*] **in a very fruitful hill** [*on a very good piece of ground; Israel*].

2 **And he fenced it** [*protected it*], **and gathered out the stones thereof** [*removed stumbling blocks or gave it every chance to succeed*], **and planted it with the choicest vine** [*the best plants, symbolic of the men of Judah, in other words, covenant Israel; see verse 7*], **and built a tower in the midst of it** [*put prophets among the people to watch out for enemies*], **and also made a winepress therein** [*planned on getting a good harvest*]; **and he looked** [*He planned*] **that it should bring forth grapes** [*the desired product, such as faithful people*], **and it brought forth wild grapes** [*instead, it produced bad fruit, symbolic of apostasy, wicked people*].

3 **And now, O inhabitants of Jerusalem, and men of Judah, judge, I pray you, betwixt me** [*Christ*] **and my vineyard** [*apostate Israel; in other words, I'll give you the facts, and you be the judge*].

> Next, He asks, "Why did My people go bad? Didn't I do My job right?

4 **What could have been done more to my vineyard that I have not done in it** [*The main question: Have I not done My job? Is that why you are wicked*]? **Wherefore** [*the fact is*], **when I looked** [*planned*] **that it should bring forth grapes** [*righteous people*] **it brought forth wild grapes** [*apostasy, wicked people who left the gospel*].

> Next, the Lord says what He is going to do to Israel, since they have become wicked and have quit following His teachings.

5 **And now go to** [*All right. That's settled*]; **I will tell you what I will**

do to my vineyard [*Israel*]—**I will take away the hedge thereof** [*I will take away My protection*], **and it** [*Israel*] **shall be eaten up** [*destroyed*]; **and I will break down the wall** [*withdraw my protection*] **thereof, and it shall be trodden down** [*walked on and smashed down by enemies*];

6 **And I will lay it waste; it shall not be pruned nor digged** [*the Spirit will withdraw; no prophets will be left to "prune" out false doctrines and warn against evil*]; **but there shall come up briers and thorns** [*apostate doctrines and wicked behaviors will grow and take over*]; **I will also command the clouds that they rain no rain upon it** [*drought, famine will come*].

Isaiah now explains what the various things in his parable represent.

7 For **the vineyard of the Lord of Hosts** [*Christ*] **is the house of Israel**, and **the men of Judah his pleasant plant**; and **he looked for judgment** [*expected justice, fairness, kindness, honesty, etc., from them*], **and behold, oppression** [*and look what He got instead; He found them oppressing one another*]; **for righteousness, but behold, a cry** [*in place of righteousness, He found riotous living*].

On occasions, people have been known to use the phrase "join house to house" in verse 8, next, to criticize builders and contractors who construct and sell apartment buildings and condominiums. While this is perhaps amusing, it also shows how badly Isaiah can be misinterpreted.

What Isaiah is really saying is that the wealthy wicked who keep cheating the poor out of their houses and land in order to add those houses and properties to what they already own will be in big trouble with God!

8 **Wo unto them** [*the powerful, wealthy*] **that join house to house** [*who grab up house after house*], **till there can be no place, that they** [*the poor*] **may be placed** [*can live*] alone in the midst of the earth [*those in power cheat and push the poor farmers off their land, taking their houses from them in the process*]!

9 In mine ears [*Isaiah's ears*], said the Lord of Hosts, of a truth **many houses shall be desolate, and great and fair cities without inhabitant** [*great troubles are coming because of your wickedness; many of you will be captured and taken far away, and your cities will be deserted*].

As we have said many times, Isaiah is a master at painting mental images with words. Watch now as he describes the deep poverty that awaits rebellious Israel when He withdraws His help and protection from them.

10 Yea, **ten acres of vineyard** [*fields where grapes are grown*] **shall yield one bath** [*will produce about 8¼ US gallons of grape juice*], and **the seed of a homer** [*6½ bushels of seed*] **shall yield an ephah** [*only one-half bushel of seed at harvest time; in other words, a terrible famine is coming!*].

Next, Isaiah condemns the riotous partying lifestyle of the wicked, which includes drunkenness.

11 **Wo unto them** [*trouble is coming to them*] that rise up early in the morning, **that they may follow strong drink** [*who keep drinking alcohol all day*], **that continue until night, and wine inflame them** [*makes them drunk*]!

Isaiah now describes the hypocritical (wanting to look good to others but secretly wanting to commit sin and be wicked) religious worship services among the apostate Israelites. They go through the motions of true religious worship, having all the elements of that proper worship as prescribed by past prophets, but their lives make a mockery of it.

As he "paints" this picture with words, he will describe musical instruments that were properly a part of their religious services in his day. It would be like describing the proper components of our worship services today by saying:

"You have your music, your prayers, your meetings, and your sacrament. You pay your tithing and fast offering, hold temple recommends, attend the temple, etc., but then you cheat, lie, steal at school and work, take unfair advantage of your neighbors, view pornography, break the Sabbath, get involved in sexual immorality, gossip, etc."

In other words, "Your worship and rituals are hollow and empty. You are hypocrites."

12 And **the harp, and the viol** [*Hebrew: lyre; a small stringed instrument of the harp family*], the **tabret** [*drum or tambourine*], **and pipe** [*flute, or musical instruments associated with worship of the Lord in Isaiah's culture*], **and wine are in their feasts; but they regard not** [*don't pay attention to*] **the work of the Lord, neither consider the operation of his hands** [*their worship is empty, hypocritical; they do not actually acknowledge God, nor do they hardly even think about Him in their daily lives*].

13 **Therefore** [*this is why*], **my people are gone into captivity** [*prophecy about Israel's future captivity*], **because they have no knowledge** [*they don't know the gospel any more*]; **and their honorable men are famished** [*they have lost their true prophets and righteous leaders*], and their multitude dried up with thirst [*dual: fits with Amos 8:11–12 about a famine of hearing the words of the Lord; also, literal results of famine*].

Next, Isaiah uses very interesting language and imagery to describe where Israel is going because of her wickedness.

14 **Therefore** [*this is why*], **hell hath enlarged herself** [*they've had to add on to hell to make room for you!*], **and opened her mouth without measure** [*seemingly without limit because there are so many of you heading for it*]; and **their glory** [*the popularity of the wicked*], and their multitude, and **their pomp, and he that rejoiceth** [*in wicked, riotous living*], **shall descend into it** [*will end up in hell*].

Next, Isaiah explains that the whole society is riddled with pride. In other words, no one is humble. Isaiah's writing here demonstrates his use of repetition for emphasis.

15 And **the mean** [*poor*] **man shall be brought down** [*humbled*], and **the mighty** [*wicked wealthy, powerful*] **man shall be humbled, and the eyes of the lofty** [*proud*] **shall be humbled** [*everyone needs humbling and will be humbled*].

16 **But the Lord of Hosts** [*Christ*] **shall be exalted in judgment** [*will be proven to be right on Judgment Day*], and **God that is holy shall be sanctified in righteousness** [*the Lord will triumph*].

Next, Isaiah describes the completeness of the destruction and devastation that will come upon wicked Israel unless they repent.

17 **Then shall the lambs feed** [*graze where the Lord's vineyard, Israel, once stood; the destruction will be so complete that animals will graze where wicked Israelites once lived*] after their manner [*where the city once stood*], **and the waste places of the fat ones** [*of the former wealthy, wicked*] **shall strangers** [*foreigners*] **eat.**

18 **Wo unto them that draw** [*pull*] **iniquity** [*wickedness*] **with cords of vanity** [*pride*], **and sin as it were with a cart rope** [*you are tied to your sins; they follow you around like a cart follows the animal pulling it!*];

In verse 19, next, we see the arrogance and pride that wickedness can bring upon individuals and societies. We see the wicked challenging God to be more obvious about His existence if He actually expects people to pay any attention to Him. This reminds us of some of the antichrists in the Book of Mormon, such as Sherem, Nehor, and Korihor, who demanded a sign from God to prove His existence.

19 **That say: Let him** [*the Lord*] make speed, hasten his work, that we may see it [*it is up to God to prove to us that he exists*]; and **let the counsel** [*plans*] **of the Holy One of Israel draw nigh and come** [*tell God to be more obvious about His existence*], **that**

we may know it [*we are "calling His bluff"; tell Him to follow through with His threats so we can know He really exists!*].

Next comes one of the most famous of all the writings and teachings of Isaiah. We are witnessing this problem on every side today in our world. It seems that one of Satan's most effective tools is getting people to think and act just the opposite of what God says.

20 **Wo unto them that call evil good, and good evil, that put** [*substitute*] **darkness for light, and light for darkness, that put bitter for sweet, and sweet for bitter!**

In other words, Isaiah is saying that people will be in big trouble who say evil is good and good is evil and who turn things around to say just the opposite of what God says. For example, many people say that abortion is good and having babies is bad, because it is overcrowding the earth. Some say that drinking coffee is good and not drinking some coffee is bad for the body. Some say that going to church is foolish and not going to church is good because it gives you more time for recreation. As you can see, this list goes on and on.

21 **Wo unto the wise in their own eyes** [*full of evil pride*] **and prudent in their own sight** [*the wicked who think they are wiser than God, who make their own rules*]!

22 **Wo unto the mighty to drink wine, and men of strength to mingle strong drink** [*drunkenness and riotous living*];

Next, Isaiah reminds us that dishonest judges, lawyers, and other parts of judicial systems and processes go along with the downfall of a society.

23 **Who justify the wicked for reward** [*take bribes, corrupt the judicial system, etc.*], **and take away the righteousness of the righteous from him** [*deprive the innocent of his rights*]!

Next, Isaiah describes the downfall and destruction of the wicked. Watch as he masterfully says the same thing in many different ways for teaching emphasis.

24 **Therefore** [*because of such wickedness*], **as the fire devoureth the stubble** [*just as fire easily burns dry grain stocks such as straw*], **and the flame consumeth the chaff** [*highly flammable byproduct of harvesting grain*], **their root shall be rottenness** [*the wicked lose their roots, anchor, stability; family ties*], **and their blossoms** [*potential to bear fruit; families*] **shall go up as dust** [*in summary: the wicked will not bear fruit; no posterity in the next life and destruction of many in this life*]; **because they have cast away the law of the Lord of**

Hosts, and despised the word of the Holy One of Israel.

You've noticed by now that Isaiah always explains the "why" of what is going to happen, like he did in the last lines of verse 24, above. This reminds us that the Lord wants us to have understanding so we can make wise and advantageous agency choices.

25 **Therefore** [*for the above reasons*], **is the anger of the Lord kindled against his people, and he hath stretched forth his hand** [*exercised His power*] **against them, and hath smitten** [*punished*] them; and the hills did tremble, and their carcasses [*dead bodies*] were torn in the midst of the streets [*terrible destruction resulting from Israel's wickedness*]. **For** [*because of*] **all this his anger is not turned away, but his hand is stretched out still** [*inviting you to repent; in other words, despite all this, you can still repent; compare with 2 Nephi 28:32 and Jacob 6:4 and 5*].

The end of verse 25, above, is a strong and very comforting reminder that the Lord wants us to use His Atonement and be freed from the burden of sin, even if we have a long history of not living the gospel.

It appears that Isaiah was shown our day in a vision and that he saw modern forms of transportation involved in the process of gathering Israel. It is interesting to consider his dilemma as far as how to describe trains, airplanes, etc. when such things did not exist in his day. Watch as he uses terminology and objects of his time and day to describe objects of our time and day.

26 And **he will lift up an ensign** [*flag, rallying point; the true gospel*] **to the nations from far, and will hiss** [*whistle; a signal to gather*] unto them from the end of the earth; and behold, **they** [*the righteous*] **shall come with speed swiftly** [*because of modern transportation?*]; none shall be weary nor stumble among them. [*They will travel so fast and arrive so soon, compared to wagon trains, handcarts, ships, etc., that they won't even get tired.*]

27 None shall slumber nor sleep; neither shall the girdle of their loins be loosed, nor the latchet of their shoes be broken [*perhaps meaning that they will travel so fast via modern transportation that they won't need to change clothes; get pajamas on, or even take their shoes off*];

28 Whose arrows shall be sharp [*airplane fuselages perhaps looked to Isaiah like arrows poised in a bow?*], and all their bows bent [*like airplane wings?*], and their horses' hoofs shall be counted like flint [*making sparks like train wheels do?*], and their wheels like a whirlwind [*going around extremely*

fast?], their roaring like a lion [*the deafening roar of trains, airplanes?*].

29 They shall roar [*airplanes, etc.?*] like young lions; yea, they shall roar, and lay hold of the prey [*passengers, converts will board them?*], and shall carry away safe [*will transport them safely, securely*], and none shall deliver [*no enemies can stop them or prevent the gathering*].

Elder LeGrand Richards of the Quorum of Twelve Apostles commented on verses 26–29, above, as follows:

"In fixing the time of the great gathering, Isaiah seemed to indicate that it would take place in the day of the railroad train and the airplane (Isaiah 5:26–29):

"Since there were neither trains nor airplanes in that day, Isaiah could hardly have mentioned them by name. However, he seems to have described them in unmistakable words. How better could 'their horses' hoofs be counted like flint, and their wheels like 'a whirlwind' than in the modern train? How better could 'their roaring be like a lion' than in the roar of the airplane? Trains and airplanes do not stop for night. Therefore, was not Isaiah justified in saying: 'none shall slumber nor sleep; neither shall the girdle of their loins be loosed, nor the latchet of their shoes be broken'? With this manner of transportation the Lord can really 'hiss unto them from the end of the earth,' that 'they shall come with speed swiftly.' Indicating that Isaiah must have foreseen the airplane, he stated: 'Who are these that fly as a cloud, and as the doves to their windows?' (Isaiah 60:8)" (Richards, *Israel! Do You Know?*, p. 182).

30 And **in that day** [*the last days*] they shall roar against them like the roaring of the sea; and **if they look unto the land, behold, darkness and sorrow, and the light is darkened in the heavens thereof** [*perhaps referring to conditions in the last days, war, smoke, pollutions, etc., while the righteous are gathering to Zion and to the gospel in various locations throughout the world*].

2 NEPHI 16

This chapter is a short one and will give you a good opportunity to see how important it is to get a basic understanding of symbolism used by Isaiah in his writings. If you don't understand symbolism, this chapter will hardly make any sense at all to you.

We all use symbolism in our daily talk. For example, we say, "My heart is warm." What we are actually saying is that we have a warm feeling about something. In other words, we are feeling warm and pleasant about someone or something. It has nothing to do with what temperature our heart really is.

Another example of symbolism is "Tears flowed down her face like a river." But we might just say, "A river was flowing from her eyes." We know what it means. She was crying really hard. This is using symbolism to communicate. Isaiah does the same thing, but, since we don't understand a lot of things from his culture, we often don't get it.

Another problem for us is that Isaiah uses a lot of idioms in his writings. We do the same thing. We say, "He is on the ball." What we are saying is that he is doing a good job. We are not saying that he is trying to balance on top of a ball. It is an idiom, meaning that the words don't make sense if we take them literally.

This chapter has beautiful Atonement symbolism and is perhaps one of the very best chapters of Isaiah to study to get a feel for the power and majesty of Isaiah's inspired writings. This chapter deals with Isaiah's call, either his initial call or a subsequent call to major responsibility, and how the Atonement of Christ made it possible for him to accept the call.

First, Isaiah tells us when he saw this vision and that he saw the Savior during the vision.

1 **In the year that king Uzziah** [*king of Judah*] **died** [*about 750–740 BC*], **I** [*Isaiah*] **saw also the Lord** [*Jesus; see verse 5*] **sitting upon a throne, high and lifted up** [*high in authority*], and **his train** [*skirts of His robe; wake, light; can also mean His power and authority*] **filled the temple.**

2 Above it [*the Savior's throne*] **stood the seraphim** [*angelic beings*]; **each one had six wings** [*wings are symbolic of power to move, act, etc., in God's work; see D&C 77:4*]; with twain [*two*] he covered his face, and with twain he covered his feet, and with twain he did fly.

To cover one's face (verse 2, above) is a way of showing respect and humility before God in many cultures.

3 And one cried unto another, and said: **Holy, holy, holy** [*repeated three times means the very best*], **is the Lord of Hosts** [*Christ*]; the whole earth is full of his glory.

Next, he uses symbolism to describe the power and glory of the presence of the Lord.

4 And **the posts of the door moved** [*shook*] **at the voice of him that cried, and the house was filled with smoke** [*symbolic of God's presence, as with the shaking of the mountain on Mt. Sinai, Exodus 19:18, when the Lord was there*].

Next, Isaiah expresses deep feelings of inadequacy and unworthiness to be in the presence of the Lord. Watch as the Atonement takes away his shortcomings and feelings of falling short and gives him confidence to do the work to which the Lord is calling him. The same principle applies to each of us as we realize our dependence on the Lord and try to do His work.

5 **Then said I** [*Isaiah*]: **Wo is unto me! for I am undone** [*I feel completely overwhelmed*]; because I am a man of unclean lips [*I am so imperfect, inadequate!*]; and I dwell in the midst of a people of unclean lips [*none of us mortals is worthy to be in the presence of God*]; **for mine eyes have seen the King, the Lord of Hosts** [*I am feeling completely overwhelmed because I have just seen the Savior*].

Watch the beautiful Atonement symbolism now, in verses 6 and 7, as Isaiah describes how the Atonement made him clean and worthy to accept the call from the Lord.

6 **Then flew one of the seraphim** [*one of the angelic beings mentioned in verse two, symbolic of a being with authority*] **unto me, having a live coal** [*symbolic of the Holy Ghost's power to cleanse "by fire"*] in his hand, **which he had taken** with the tongs from **off the altar** [*symbolic of the Atonement; Christ was sacrificed for us on the "altar" cross*];

7 **And he laid it upon my mouth** [*applied the Atonement to me*], **and said: Lo, this** [*the Atonement of Christ*] **has touched thy lips** [*symbolic of Isaiah's sins, shortcomings, imperfections, and feelings of inadequacy*]; **and thine iniquity is taken away, and thy sin purged** [*his sins and shortcomings are cleansed; the results of the Atonement; compare with Isaiah 1:18*].

Next, watch what the application of the Atonement did to Isaiah's confidence to go out in the service of the Lord.

8 Also **I heard the voice of the Lord, saying: Whom shall I send, and who will go for us**? Then I [*Isaiah*] said: **Here am I; send me** [*the cleansing power of the Atonement gave Isaiah the needed confidence to accept the call*].

Next, the Lord will give Isaiah a brief description of the people to whom he will be preaching as a prophet. You will notice that the people are going to be extremely difficult to reach. Perhaps this is a bit of an "MTC" experience for Isaiah to help him get ready for the difficulties ahead.

9 **And he** [*the Lord*] **said: Go and tell this people—Hear ye** indeed, **but they understood not**; and **see ye** indeed, **but they perceived not** [*didn't understand his message; Isaiah's task is not going to be easy with these kinds of people*].

10 **Make the heart of this people fat** [*picture in your mind that the people's hearts are insulated against your message; in other words, they are hard-hearted*

against truth], **and make their ears heavy** [*picture them as being spiritually deaf*], and **shut their eyes** [*picture them as being spiritually blind*]—**lest they** [*for fear that they will*] **see with their eyes, and hear with their ears, and understand with their heart, and be converted and be healed.**

It may be that verse 11, next, can be viewed as a reminder that the Lord has a sense of humor.

11 **Then said I** [*Isaiah*]**: Lord, how long** [*how long will people be like this*]? **And he said: Until the cities be wasted without inhabitant, and the houses without man, and the land be utterly desolate** [*empty; in other words, when you go to preach some morning and no one is left in the city, you will not have this problem with such people; as long as people are around, you will run into such people*];

12 **And the Lord have removed men far away, for there shall be a great forsaking** [*many deserted cities*] in the midst of the land.

Verse 13, next, is a great example of Isaiah's use of symbolism understood by people in his time and culture. It is also an example of a verse that is pretty much impossible for us in our time and culture to understand without help.

13 **But yet there shall be a tenth** [*a remnant of Israel; in other words, a small part of the people of Israel will remain alive*], **and they** [*Israel*] **shall return, and shall be eaten** [*pruned, as by animals eating the lower limbs, leaves, and branches in an orchard; the Lord "prunes" his vineyard, cuts out old false doctrines and apostates, etc., destroys old unrighteous generations so new ones may have a chance to live the gospel and stay active in the Church*], **as a teil-tree** [*like pruning a lime tree. See Bible Dictionary, under Teil tree*], **and as an oak whose substance** [*sap*] is in them when they cast their leaves [*they still have sap in them when they shed the old, non-functioning leaves and look dead in winter*]; **so the holy seed** [*Israel, the Lord's covenant people*] **shall be the substance thereof** [*Israel may look dead, but there is still life in it*].

In summary, verse 13, above, explains that although various Israelites will be carried away into captivity and thus be scattered and seemingly die out as a people, yet the Lord will eventually "prune" them—shape them and guide them—to become a righteous covenant people again. They will look dead, as a people, like a fruit tree does in winter, but Israel will be gathered again and become powerful in the last days. We are watching the fulfillment of this prophecy as we see the great gathering of Israel now taking place under the direction of our modern prophets.

2 NEPHI 17

This next chapter is similar to Isaiah chapter 7 in the Bible. It deals with actual historical events, including the virgin birth of the Savior.

King Ahaz is a wicked, idol-worshipping king of Judah. Judah is made up of the Jews and part of the tribe of Benjamin. They live in the southern part of the Holy Land at this time. King Ahaz's nation is being threatened from the north by both Israel (the ten tribes of Israel, who have their own nation called "Israel") and by the nation of Syria. Israel and Syria are plotting to take over Judah and Jerusalem and to set up a puppet government in Jerusalem, controlled by themselves.

Watch Ahaz's reaction as the Lord tells Isaiah to bring him the news that if he will trust in the Lord, he has no need to fear these two enemy nations. It is a reminder, among other things, that the wicked live in fear, despite the availability of help and safety with the Lord.

1 **And it came to pass in the days of Ahaz** [*a wicked, idol-worshipping king of Judah about 734 BC*] the son of Jotham, the son of Uzziah, king of Judah [*the Jews*], **that Rezin, king of Syria, and Pekah the son of Remaliah, king of Israel** [*the ten tribes or northern Israel*], **went up toward Jerusalem to war against it, but could not prevail against it** [*didn't win*].

Next, Isaiah tells us that King Ahaz was terrified that these two enemy nations would attack his nation and win.

2 **And it was told the house of David** [*King Ahaz and his people, the Jews, who were descendants of King David*] **Syria is confederate** [*has joined*] **with Ephraim** [*the ten tribes; northern Israel*]. **And his heart was moved** [*was shaken, he was terrified*], **and the heart of his people, as the trees of the wood are moved with the wind** [*the people of Judah were trembling with fear, shaking like tree limbs in a strong wind*].

Next, the Lord tells Isaiah to take his son and go meet King Ahaz. He also tells him where Ahaz is hiding.

3 **Then said the Lord unto Isaiah: Go forth now to meet Ahaz, thou and Shear-jashub thy son, at the end of the conduit of the upper pool in the highway of the fuller's field** [*Ahaz is hiding where the women do their laundry; in other words, he is hiding behind the women's skirts; he is a coward*];

4 **And say unto him** [*King Ahaz*]: **Take heed, and be quiet** [*Relax!*]; **fear not**, neither be faint-hearted for [*because of*] the two tails of these smoking firebrands [*don't worry because of the threats from Syria and Israel*], **for** [*because of*] **the fierce anger of**

Rezin with Syria, and of the son of Remaliah [*don't worry about continued threats from Syria and Israel; they think they are powerful but are nothing but smoldering stubs of firewood*].

5 **Because Syria, Ephraim** [*the nations of Syria and northern Israel*], **and the son of Remaliah** [*northern Israel's king*], **have taken evil counsel** [*are plotting*] **against thee, saying:**

Next, Isaiah tells King Ahaz what the two enemy nations are plotting to do.

6 **Let us go up against Judah and vex it** [*cause trouble for Judah*], **and let us make a breach** [*an opening*] **therein for us, and set a king in the midst of it** [*let's set up our own king in Jerusalem*], yea, the son of Tabeal.

7 **Thus saith the Lord God: It shall not stand, neither shall it come to pass** [*The plot will fail, so don't worry about it, Ahaz*].

8 **For the head** [*capital city*] **of Syria is Damascus, and the head** [*leader*] **of Damascus, Rezin**; and **within three score and five years** [*sixty-five years*] **shall Ephraim** [*the ten tribes*] **be broken that it be not a people** [*within sixty-five years the ten tribes will be lost*].

9 **And the head** [*capital city*] **of Ephraim** [*the ten tribes, who at this time are enemies of Judah*] **is Samaria** [*about 35 miles north of Jerusalem*], **and the head** [*leader*] **of Samaria is Remaliah's son. If ye** [*Ahaz and his people, the tribe of Judah, plus some of Benjamin*] **will not believe surely ye shall not be established** [*will not be saved by the Lord's power; see Isaiah 7, footnote 9b*].

Next, in a very unusual move, the Lord invites wicked King Ahaz to ask for any sign from the Lord he wants to, in order to convince him that the Lord is indeed speaking to him through Isaiah, the prophet.

10 **Moreover, the Lord spake again unto Ahaz, saying:**

11 **Ask thee a sign** [*to assure you that the Lord is speaking to you*] of the Lord thy God; ask it either in the depths, or in the heights above [*ask anything you want*].

12 **But Ahaz said: I will not ask, neither will I tempt** [*test*] **the Lord** [*he refuses to follow the prophet's counsel; he is deliberately avoiding the issue because he is already secretly depending on the nation of Assyria for help*].

13 **And he** [*Isaiah*] **said: Hear ye now, O house of David** [*Ahaz and his people of the tribe of Judah*]; is it a small thing for you to weary men,

but **will ye weary my God also** [*do you realize how serious it is to test the patience of God*]?

Next, Isaiah prophesies that one of the most important signs of all will be a wonderful sign, given in the future; namely, that the Son of God will be born to a virgin.

14 **Therefore** [*because of your disobedience*], the Lord himself shall give you a sign—**Behold, a virgin** [*Mary*] **shall conceive, and shall bear a son**, and shall call his name **Immanuel** [*meaning "God is with us;" in other words, the day will come when the Savior will be born and live among men*].

Next, Isaiah prophesies that Jesus will be considered poor and lowly in social status.

15 **Butter and honey** [*curd and honey, the only foods available to the poor at times; see Isaiah 7, footnote 15a*] **shall he eat** [*Jesus will eat what the poor people eat; in other words, He will not be considered high in social status*], that he may know to refuse the evil and to choose the good.

Next, Isaiah prophesies that in just a few years, the two enemy nations (Syria and Israel—the northern ten tribes) that are threatening King Ahaz and the people of Judah will be conquered themselves, so don't worry about them.

16 **For before the child shall know to refuse the evil and choose the good** [*in as many years as it takes for the child to be old enough to know good from evil, or in just a few years*], **the land** [*northern Israel*] **that thou** [*Judah*] **abhorrest** [*are afraid of*] **shall be forsaken of both her kings** [*both Syria and the northern ten tribes will be taken by Assyria; see Isaiah 8:4, 2 Nephi 17:17*].

17 **The Lord shall bring upon thee** [*Ahaz*], **and upon thy people** [*Judah*], and upon thy father's house, days that have not come from the day that Ephraim departed from Judah [*when the northern ten tribes split from you*], **the king of Assyria** [*the king of Assyria will bring troubles like you have not seen since the twelve tribes of Israel split apart, about 975 BC, into the northern kingdom under Jeroboam I, and the tribe of Judah under Rehoboam*].

In verses 18–20, next, Isaiah compares Assyria, the enemy nation spoken of in verse 17, to flies and bees that will get into everything and cause much misery as they invade Israel.

18 **And it shall come to pass in that day** [*when Assyria attacks you*] that **the Lord shall hiss** [*signal, call for*] **for the fly** [*associated with plagues, troubles; this will remind you of the plagues in Egypt*] that is in the uttermost part of Egypt, **and for the bee** [*sting*]

that is in the land of Assyria [*the Assyrians will come like flies and bees*].

19 And they shall come, and shall rest all of them in the desolate valleys, and in the holes of the rocks, and upon all thorns, and upon all bushes [*your enemies will be everywhere, will overrun your land*].

In verse 20, next, Isaiah describes how wicked King Ahaz and his people will become slaves to the Assyrians. One of the things conquering armies did was to shave the people completely to show that they were conquered and were now their slaves.

20 **In the same day** [*when this terrible day comes upon you because you refuse to return to the Lord*] **shall the Lord shave with a razor** [*fate of captives, slaves—for humiliation, sanitation, identification*] that is hired [*Assyria will be "hired" to do this to Judah*], by them beyond the river, **by the king of Assyria, the head, and the hair of the feet; and it shall also consume the beard** [*they will shave you completely; will conquer you completely*].

Next, Isaiah uses an interesting way to say that there will not be many people left at home in Israel after the Assyrians have conquered them.

21 And it shall come to pass **in that day** [*after the above-mentioned devastation*], **a man shall nourish a young cow and two sheep**;

22 And it shall come to pass, for the **abundance of milk** they [*the few remaining domestic animals*] shall give he shall eat butter; for **butter and honey** shall every one eat that is left in the land [*there won't be many people left, so a few animals can supply them well and there will be plenty of weed blossoms and flowers for bees to make honey*].

Next, Isaiah says with his interesting writing style that the farms and fields and gardens, etc., that Ahaz and his people had before the Assyrian invasion (and the Babylonian invasion later) will be taken over by weeds. It is another way of saying that most of the wicked people of Israel will be gone.

23 And it shall come to pass **in that day**, every place shall be, **where there were** [*used to be*] **a thousand vines** at a thousand silverlings [*worth a thousand pieces of silver*], which shall be for **briers and thorns** [*formerly valuable, cultivated land will become overgrown with weeds; this can be symbolic of apostasy*].

Isaiah continues, emphasizing that Judah will be conquered and her inhabitants scattered to the point that relatively few of them will remain. The Babylonian captivity in about 587 BC was one fulfillment of this prophecy. Other devastations and scatterings of the Jews have also occurred.

24 **With arrows and with bows shall men come thither**, because all the land shall become briers and thorns [*previously cultivated land will become wild and overgrown such that hunters will hunt wild beasts there where you used to live*].

25 And all hills that shall be digged with the mattock [*that were once cultivated with the hoe*], there [*you*] shall not come thither [*because of*] the fear of briers and thorns; **but it shall be for the sending forth** [*pasturing*] **of oxen, and** the treading of **lesser cattle** [*sheep or goats; your once-cultivated lands will revert to wilds; symbolic of apostasy*].

2 NEPHI 18

The Lord has Isaiah continue spreading the unpopular word that an attack by the Assyrians (a large, wicked, powerful nation in approximately the region occupied by Iraq today) is coming unless the people and their political leaders repent and return to their God.

This time, the prophecy of coming destruction includes Syria and Israel (Samaria, where the Ten Tribes to the north set up their nation) as well as Ahaz and his people. Remember that Syria and Israel were the nations who threatened to attack and conquer Ahaz and his people in chapter 17.

Isaiah will be asked by the Lord to use a large scroll on which he can write a warning in large letters for all the people to see. He is also asked to give his son a name, the meaning of which is that the Assyrians will be quick to ruin the country.

In contrast to the cruel devastation coming at the hands of the Assyrians, Isaiah invites the people to enjoy the gentle "waters of Shiloah" (verse 6), symbolic of the mercy and kindness of the Savior. If they turn to Christ, He will protect them. The choice is theirs. There is much symbolism in this for us.

1 Moreover [*in addition*], the word of the Lord said unto me [*Isaiah*]: **Take thee a great roll** [*a large scroll*], **and write in it** with a man's pen, concerning Maher-shalal-hashbaz [*a Hebrew saying, meaning "destruction is imminent" or "to speed to the spoil, he hasteneth the prey"; in other words, Assyria will be here soon and destruction will overtake you soon*].

Next, Isaiah asks two good men to serve as witnesses to the prophecy he is giving.

2 And I [*Isaiah*] took unto me faithful witnesses to record, Uriah the priest, and Zechariah the son of Jeberechiah [*these were required witnesses and legal authorities for a proper Hebrew wedding*].

Verse 3 tells us that Brother and Sister Isaiah had a baby boy.

3 And I went unto **the prophetess** [*Isaiah's wife*]; and she **conceived and bare a son**. Then said the Lord to me: Call his name, Maher-shalal-hash-baz [*meaning "destruction is imminent"*].

Next, Isaiah indicates that the Assyrians will be upon Syria and the northern ten tribes in about as much time as it takes his baby boy to learn to say "Daddy" or "Mommy."

4 For behold, the child shall not have knowledge to cry, My father, and my mother, before **the riches of Damascus** [*Syria*] **and the spoil** [*wealth*] **of Samaria** [*northern Israel*] **shall be taken away** before [*by*] the king of Assyria [*before my son is old enough to say "Daddy" or "Mommy," Assyria will attack northern Israel and Syria*].

5 The Lord spake also unto me [*Isaiah*] again, saying:

6 **Forasmuch as** [*because*] **this people** [*Judah, Jerusalem*] **refuseth the waters of Shiloah** [*the gentle help of Christ, John 4:14*] that go softly [*mercifully*], and rejoice in Rezin and Remaliah's son [*place more trust in Syria and northern Israel instead of the Lord*];

7 **Now therefore, behold, the Lord bringeth up upon them** [*Judah*] the waters of the river [*you'll be flooded with Assyrians*], strong and many, even **the king of Assyria** and all his glory [*his pomp and armies*]; and he shall come up over all his channels, and go over all his banks [*you will have a flood of Assyrians*].

8 And he [*Assyria*] shall pass through Judah; he shall overflow and go over, he shall reach even to the neck [*you will be up to your neck in Assyrians; can also mean "will reach clear to Jerusalem, the head or capital city," which Assyria did before being stopped via the death by plague of 185,000 soldiers; see 2 Kings 19:32–36*]; and the stretching out of his wings [*Assyria*] shall fill the breadth of thy land [*Judah*], O Immanuel [*the land of the future birth and ministry of Christ*].

9 **Associate yourselves** O ye people [*of Judah; in other words, if you form political alliances with other nations for protection rather than turning to God*], **and ye shall be broken in pieces**; and give ear all ye of far countries [*foreign nations who might rise against Judah*]; gird yourselves [*prepare for war*], and ye [*foreign nations who attack Judah*] shall be broken in pieces; gird yourselves, and ye shall be broken in pieces [*note that "broken in pieces" is repeated three times for emphasis; three times in Hebrew is a form of superlative, the most or the best*].

10 Take counsel together [*go ahead, plot against Judah, you foreign nations*],

and it shall come to naught [*won't succeed*]; speak the word, and it shall not stand [*and it will still not happen*]; for God is with us [*Judah won't be destroyed completely*].

The Lord has asked Isaiah, His prophet, to give some very unpopular messages to the citizens and political leaders of wicked Judah. This must have been extremely hard on Brother and Sister Isaiah and their little family. Next, the Lord gives Isaiah strong instructions not to give in to peer pressure and tell the Jews what they want to hear concerning making treaties with other nations for protection from their enemies, rather than turning to righteousness for God's protection. He then counsels Isaiah to stick with the Lord no matter what.

11 For **the Lord spake thus to me** [*Isaiah*] with a strong hand [*firmly*], and instructed me **that I should not walk in the way of this people** [*do not say things that the people of Judah would like you to say to them*], saying:

12 **Say ye not, A confederacy** [*don't tell them to go ahead and make a treaty*], to all to whom this people shall say, A confederacy; neither fear ye their fear, nor be afraid [*"Isaiah, don't endorse Judah's plan to make a treaty with Assyria. Don't tell them what they want to hear."*].

13 **Sanctify the Lord of Hosts himself, and let him be your fear**, and let him be your dread [*"Isaiah, you rely on the Lord, not public approval."*].

14 **And he** [*the Lord*] **shall be for a sanctuary** [*for you, Isaiah*]; **but for a stone of stumbling**, and for a rock of offense [*a rock that makes them fall rather than the Rock of their salvation*] **to both the houses of** [*wicked*] **Israel** [*Judah and Ephraim—the ten tribes*], for a gin [*a trap*] and a snare to the inhabitants of Jerusalem.

Notice how simple but powerful Isaiah's wording is in the next verse as he says is several ways that they will be in big trouble if they don't repent and return to God.

15 And many among them shall **stumble** and **fall**, and be **broken**, and be **snared**, and be **taken**.

16 **Bind up the testimony** [*record your testimony, Isaiah*], seal the law among my disciples [*righteous followers*].

We discover from verse 16, above, that there were other faithful Saints among the people of Judah, in addition to Isaiah and his family.

Next, Isaiah responds to the Lord's counsel to him to remain faithful at all costs. He is a very good man!

17 **And I** [*Isaiah*] **will wait upon** [*trust*] **the Lord**, that hideth his face [*is holding His blessings back*] from the house of Jacob [*Israel*], and I will look for him.

18 **Behold, I and the children whom the Lord hath given me are for signs and for wonders in Israel from the Lord of Hosts** [*Christ*], which dwelleth in Mount Zion. [*My family and I are a reminder to Israel that the Lord lives.*]

It seems that too often the wicked just can't get the obvious! They are so blind that they can't see that the only way to preserve their freedom is to follow the commandments and guidelines of the gospel of Christ. In this case, rather than repenting and returning to the God of Israel, which would restore civil peace and security to them, they turn to witchcraft and sorcery, which are controlled by forces of evil and of Satan. Wickedness certainly keeps these people from thinking straight!

19 **And when they** [*the wicked*] **shall say unto you: Seek unto them** [*spiritualists, witches, mediums, fortune tellers, and so forth*] **that have familiar spirits** [*who contact dead relatives and friends*], **and unto wizards that peep and mutter** [*into their "crystal balls"*]— **should not a people seek unto their God** for the living to hear from the dead? [*In other words, wouldn't it be wise for them to turn to God for help?*]

Next, Isaiah wisely counsels his people to compare any advice, counsel, etc. they receive from any source, to the scriptures. We often refer to our scriptures as the "standard works," which means "the standard by which all things should be measured."

20 **To the law and to the testimony** [*to the scriptures*]; **and if they** [*the spiritualists and their media*] **speak not according to this word** [*the scriptures*], **it is because there is no light in them** [*the fortunetellers, mediums, and so forth*].

21 **And they** [*the wicked of Judah*] **shall pass through it** [*the land; the trouble described in verses 7 and 8*] **hardly bestead** [*severely distressed*] **and hungry**; and it shall come to pass that when they shall be hungry, they shall fret themselves [*become enraged*], and curse their king and their God, and look upward [*proud, defiant*].

22 And **they shall look unto the earth** [*will look around them*] **and behold** [*see only*] **trouble, and darkness, dimness of anguish** [*gloom; Hebrew: dark affliction*], **and shall be driven to darkness** [*thrust into utter despair; results of wickedness*].

2 NEPHI 19

This is a continuation of the topic in chapter 18. King Ahaz of Judah ignored the Lord's counsel and made a treaty with Assyria anyway. Remember, as mentioned before, that Isaiah uses much symbolism. Symbolism here can include that Assyria would represent the devil and his evil, prideful ways. King Ahaz could symbolize foolish and wicked people who make alliances with the devil or his evil ways and with wicked people, and foolishly think that they are thus protected from destruction spiritually and often physically.

In this next chapter, which can be compared to Isaiah 9 in the Bible, Isaiah gives one of the most famous and beautiful of all his prophecies about Christ. He prophesies that Christ will come. Handel's *Messiah* puts some of this chapter to magnificent music.

Verse one is the last verse of chapter 8 in the Hebrew Bible and in the German Bible. It serves as a natural transition from chapter 18 to verse 2 in chapter 19.

In verses 1–7, Isaiah invites us to see the difference between the troubles and punishments from God that the wicked have and the beautiful blessings that come to the righteous as they try to faithfully live the gospel and take advantage of the Savior's mission and Atonement.

1 **Nevertheless, the dimness** [*darkness; troubles referred to in 18:22*] **shall not be such as was** in her vexation, **when at first** [*the first Assyrian attacks in Isaiah's day*] **he lightly** [*strictly*] **afflicted the land of Zebulun** [*the Nazareth area, part of northern Israel; see maps 5 & 14 in the first editions of the LDS Bible*], **and the land of Naphtali** [*in northern Israel*], **and afterwards did more grievously afflict** [*Hebrew: gloriously bless, brought honor to*] by the way of the Red Sea beyond Jordan in Galilee of **the nations** [*Jesus grew up in Galilee and righteous Israel has been gloriously blessed through Him, whereas wicked Israel has been grievously afflicted as a result of rejecting Him*].

2 **The people that walked in darkness** [*spiritual darkness; apostasy and captivity*] **have seen a great light** [*the Savior and His teachings*]; they that dwell in the land of the shadow of death, upon them hath the light shined [*the gospel of Christ is made available to them*].

3 **Thou** [*the Savior*] **hast** multiplied the nation, and **increased the joy**—they joy before thee according to the joy in harvest, and as men rejoice when they divide the spoil [*Christ and His faithful followers will ultimately triumph and share the benefits; reap the rewards of righteous living as they enjoy celestial exaltation*].

Next, Isaiah continues prophesying about the future and the

redemption made available by the Savior.

4 **For thou** [*Christ*] **hast broken the yoke of his burden** [*Israel's captivity, bondage*], **and the staff of his shoulder, the rod of his oppressor** [*the power of Israel's enemy*].

In verse 5, next, Isaiah says that most battles involve a lot of noise and bloodshed, but that the final destruction of the wicked will be different because they will be destroyed by fire at the time of the Second Coming.

5 For **every battle of the warrior is with confused noise, and garments rolled in blood; but this shall be with burning** [*the burning at the Second Coming, according to Joseph Smith; see Isaiah 9, footnote 5b*] **and fuel of fire.**

6 **For unto us a child** [*Christ*] **is born, unto us a son is given; and the government shall be upon his shoulder; and his name shall be called, Wonderful, Counselor, The Mighty God, The Everlasting Father, The Prince of Peace.**

7 **Of the increase of government and peace there is no end** [*for the righteous*], upon the throne of David, and upon his kingdom to order it, and to establish it with judgment [*fairness*] and with justice from henceforth, even forever. **The zeal of the Lord of Hosts will perform this** [*God will do this*].

The Lord now continues His message of warning to the northern ten tribes (known at this point in history as Israel). He addresses their prideful claims that they can get along well without Him or His help.

8 **The Lord sent his word unto Jacob** [*Israel*] and it [*the message from the Lord*] hath lighted upon Israel.

9 **And all the people shall know**, even Ephraim [*the northern ten tribes, Israel*] and the inhabitants of Samaria [*the northern ten tribes, Israel*], **that say** [*boast*] **in the pride and stoutness of heart:**

10 **The bricks are fallen down, but we will build with hewn stones** [*boastful Israel claims they can't be destroyed successfully, but would simply rebuild with better materials than before*]; the sycamores [*trees*] are cut down, but we will change them into cedars [*more valuable trees*].

11 **Therefore** [*this is why, in other words, because of wicked pride*] **the Lord shall set up the adversaries of Rezin** [*Syria*] **against him** [*Israel*], **and join his enemies together;**

A very important theme is repeated over and over in Isaiah's writings. It is, "but his hand is stretched out still." We will see it in verse 12 and again in verses 17 and 21. The message is that no matter what mistakes you have made in the past, the mercy of the Atonement is still being offered to you by the outstretched hand of the Savior.

Remember too that when something is repeated three times in the Bible culture, it means it is the very best, the very most important, etc. As mentioned above, the message, "but his hand is stretched out still" is repeated three times in this chapter!

In verse 12, next, Isaiah says that Israel is surrounded with enemies.

12 The Syrians before [*on the East*] and the Philistines behind [*on the West*]; and they shall devour Israel with open mouth. For all this his anger is not turned away, **but his hand is stretched out still** [*the Lord will still let you repent if you will turn to him; see also Jacob 6:4 and 5; see also Isaiah 9, footnote 12d. Laman and Lemuel need to hear this message of mercy, as do we in our day*].

13 For the [*wicked*] people turneth not unto him [*the Lord*] that smiteth [*punishes*] them, neither do they seek the Lord of Hosts [*the people won't repent; they are going through the pain without learning the lesson*].

14 Therefore [*for this reason*] will the Lord cut off from Israel head [*leaders*] and tail [*false prophets*], branch [*Hebrew: palm branch, triumph and victory; see John 12:13*] and rush [*reed; people low in social status*] in one day.

Isaiah now explains some of the symbolism above.

15 The ancient [*elders, leaders*], he is the head; and the prophet that teacheth lies, he is the tail.

16 For the leaders of this people cause them to err [*wicked leaders are causing the people to become wicked themselves*]; and they that are led of them are destroyed.

17 Therefore the Lord shall have no joy in their young men, neither shall have mercy on their fatherless and widows [*all levels of society have gone bad and become wicked; no one qualifies for mercy*]; for every one of them is a hypocrite and an evildoer, and every mouth speaketh folly [*foolishness*]. For all this [*in spite of all this*] his anger is not turned away, **but his hand is stretched out still** [*you can still repent; please do*].

18 For wickedness burneth as the fire [*wickedness destroys like wildfire*]; it shall devour the briers and thorns [*symbolic of wicked people and apostate philosophies and doctrines*], and shall kindle [*burn*] in the thickets of the forests, and they shall mount up like the lifting up of smoke [*when*

destruction comes it will come rapidly like wildfire].

19 Through the wrath of the Lord of Hosts [*Christ*] is the land darkened [*bad conditions prevail*], and the [*wicked*] people shall be as the fuel of the fire; no man shall spare his brother [*when people turn so wicked, they are no longer loyal, even to family members*].

20 And he shall snatch on the right hand and be hungry; and he shall eat on the left hand and they shall not be satisfied; they shall eat every man the flesh of his own arm [*the wicked will turn against each other*]—

21 Manasseh, Ephraim; and Ephraim, Manasseh [*the ten tribes to the north*]; they together shall be against Judah. For all this his anger is not turned away, **but his hand is stretched out still** [*you can still repent; please do!*].

2 NEPHI 20

In the heading to chapter 20 in your Book of Mormon you will find the phrase, "Destruction of Assyria is a type of destruction of wicked at the Second Coming." The word type means something that is symbolic of something else. For example, both Joseph who was sold into Egypt and Isaac, son of Abraham and Sarah, were types of Christ—that is to say, many of the things that happened to them were symbolic of the Savior. The following charts show some of the ways in which these great prophets were types of Christ.

"TYPES" OF CHRIST

JOSEPH IN EGYPT	CHRIST
Was sold for the price of a common slave	Was sold for the price of a common slave
Was thirty years old when he began his mission as prime minister to save his people	Was thirty years old when He began His formal mission to save His people
Gathered food for seven years to save his people	Used seven "days" to create the earth in which to offer salvation to us
Forgave his persecutors	Forgave His persecutors
ISAAC	**CHRIST**
Was the only begotten of Abraham and Sarah	Is the Only Begotten of the Father

Was to be sacrificed by his father	Was allowed to be sacrificed by His Father
Carried the wood for his sacrifice	Carried the cross for His sacrifice
Volunteered to give his life (Abraham was too old to restrain him.)	Gave His life voluntarily

Having considered the use of "types" [*sometimes called "types and shadows"*] in the scriptures, we will now continue with Isaiah's teachings and watch as Assyria is used as a "type" of the destruction of the wicked at the Second Coming.

As mentioned above, the heading tof chapter 20 in your Book of Mormon says "Destruction of Assyria is a type of destruction of wicked at the Second Coming." The Assyrian armies did come and attack Syria and Israel, as prophesied in chapter 18, verse 4, and elsewhere. And their armies also came into Judah and got as far as the city gates of Jerusalem, as mentioned in verse 32 of this chapter, chapter 20. But there, the Lord stopped the Assyrian army cold, as stated symbolically in verses 33–34. 185,000 Assyrian soldiers died overnight, as mentioned in 2 Kings 19:35, and the few that were left went back home.

Similarly, as stated in the heading, "Few people shall be left after the Lord comes again," because the wicked will be destroyed at the Second Coming. In that way, the death of the Assyrian soldiers is a "type" of the destruction of the wicked at the Second Coming.

This chapter starts out describing dishonest and corrupt political leaders who do much to ruin their country.

1 **Wo unto them** [*political leaders; kings*] **that decree unrighteous decrees** [*who make unrighteous laws*], **and that write grievousness** [*laws designed to oppress their people*] which they have prescribed;

2 **To turn away the needy from judgment** [*designed to keep the needy from fair treatment*], **and to take away the right from the poor of my people**, that widows may be their prey [*victims*], and that they may rob the fatherless [*they are greedy and brutal even to orphans*]!

Next, the Lord, through Isaiah, asks what these corrupt political leaders will do when they, themselves are badly treated by the Assyrian armies.

3 **And what will ye** [*the wicked*] **do in the day of visitation** [*punishment*], and in the desolation which shall come from far [*from Assyria; in other words, what will you wicked, greedy leaders do when the Assyrians attack you*]? **to whom will ye flee for help?**

and where will ye leave your glory [*wealth, etc.*]?

4 **Without me** [*the Lord; without the help of the Lord*] **they shall bow down under the prisoners** [*huddle among the prisoners*], **and they shall fall under the slain** [*be killed*]. For all this his anger is not turned away, **but his hand is stretched out still** [*you can still repent*].

Now Isaiah gives a message from the Lord to the Assyrian king, Sargon. Sargon thinks that he is terrific in and of himself. He isn't.

5 **O Assyrian, the rod of mine anger** [*tool of destruction used by the Lord to punish Israel*], and the staff in their hand is their indignation.

6 **I will send him** [*Assyria*] **against a hypocritical nation** [*Israel*], and against the people of my wrath [*Israel*] will I give him [*Assyria*] a charge [*an assignment*] to take the spoil [*Israel's wealth*], and to take the prey [*Israel*], and to tread them [*Israel*] down like the mire [*mud*] of the streets [*see 2 Nephi 8:23*].

7 **Howbeit he meaneth not so** [*doesn't think so*], neither doth his heart think so [*the king of Assyria doesn't realize he is a tool in God's hand; thinks he doing it on his own*]; but in his heart it is to destroy and cut off nations not a few [*he is a wicked man, takes pleasure in destroying others*].

8 **For he** [*the Assyrian king*] **saith** [*boasts*]: **Are not my princes** [*military commanders*] **altogether kings** [*just like kings in other countries*]?

Isaiah describes the Assyrian king, who is a "type" of Satan, naming off the cities he has easily conquered on his way toward Jerusalem.

9 Is not **Calno** as **Carchemish**? Is not **Hamath** as **Arpad**? Is not **Samaria** as **Damascus** [*cities and areas conquered by Assyria; see Map 10 in LDS Bible, first editions; see also 2 Kings 19:8–13 for Sennacherib's boastful letter to Hezekiah, King of Judah*]?

Next, the Assyrian king boasts that he and his armies are more powerful than the idols or gods worshiped by the countries and cities he has conquered. And he claims that those idols are obviously more powerful than the God of Jerusalem. He is wrong!

10 **As my hand** [*Assyria's hand*] **hath founded** [*acquired, conquered*] **the kingdoms of the idols**, and **whose graven images did excel them of Jerusalem and of Samaria** [*I've taken many cities whose idols are more powerful than those of Jerusalem and Samaria*];

11 **Shall I not, as I have done unto Samaria and her idols, so do to Jerusalem and to her idols** [*Assyria's king boasts that other nations'*

idols, gods, did not stop him and neither will Jerusalem's God stop him]?

12 Wherefore it shall come to pass that **when the Lord hath performed his whole work upon Mount Zion and upon Jerusalem** [*when the Lord is through using Assyria to punish Israel*], **I** [*the Lord*] **will punish** the fruit of the stout heart of **the king of Assyria**, and the glory [*pompousness*] of his high looks [*when I'm through using Assyria against Israel, then proud, haughty Assyria will get its deserved punishment*].

13 **For he** [*the Assyrian king*] **saith** [*brags*]: By the strength of my hand and by my wisdom I have done these things; for I am prudent; and I have moved the borders of the people, and have robbed their treasures, and I have put down the inhabitants like a valiant [*mighty*] man [*he is bragging*];

14 And my hand hath found as a nest the riches of the people; and as one gathereth eggs that are left have I gathered all the earth [*I'm mighty powerful!*]; and there was none that moved the wing, or opened the mouth, or peeped [*everybody is afraid of me, just like an old hen when a person takes the eggs from her nest!*].

Isaiah next uses some very fascinating imagery in describing how ridiculous it is for the king of Assyria to take credit to himself for his "amazing" accomplishments. There is an important message in this for all of us who might at times take or accept credit for accomplishments in the work of the Lord.

As you read verse 15, you might even find it a bit humorous.

15 **Shall the ax** [*king of Assyria*] **boast itself against him** [*the Lord*] **that heweth** [*chops*] **therewith** [*shall the ax brag that it is doing all the work by itself and doesn't need the man to swing it*]? **Shall the saw magnify itself against** [*defy*] **him that shaketh it** [*uses it*]? **As if the rod** [*wooden club*] **should shake itself against them that lift it up** [*as if a wooden club should suddenly turn to the man who is swinging it and say, "Let go of me. I can do it myself!"*], **or as if the staff should lift up itself as if it were no wood** [*as if the staff were not simply a piece of wood*]!

16 **Therefore** [*because of the King of Assyria's wicked deeds and cocky attitude*] **shall the Lord, the Lord of Hosts, send among his fat** [*powerful*] **ones, leanness** [*disease, or trouble, is coming to Assyria*]; **and under his** [*Assyria's*] **glory he shall kindle a burning like the burning of a fire** [*the Lord will trim Assyria down to size*].

17 **And the light of Israel** [*Christ*] **shall be for a fire, and his** [*Israel's*] **Holy One** [*Christ*] **for a flame,**

and shall burn and shall devour his [*Assyria's*] **thorns and his briers in one day**;

The prophecy of destruction upon Assyria, given in verse 17, above, happened suddenly, as mentioned previously. 185,000 Assyrians died of devastating sickness in one night as they prepared to attack Jerusalem; see 2 Kings 19:35–37. The prophecy is continued with additional repetition in verses 18 and 19.

18 And **shall consume** the glory of **his forest** [*Assyria's armies*], and of **his fruitful field** [*his very productive military*], both **soul and body**; and they shall be **as when a standard-bearer fainteth** [*as when the last flag bearer falls, and the flag with him; your armies will be destroyed*].

19 And **the rest of the trees of his forest** [*the remnants of Assyria's army*] **shall be few**, that a child may write them [*so few Assyrians will remain that a small child could count them with his limited counting ability*].

20 **And it shall come to pass in that day** [*the last days*], **that the remnant of Israel**, and such as are escaped [*survive*] of the house of Jacob [*Israel*], **shall no more again stay** [*be dependent*] **upon him** [*Israel's enemies*] that smote them [*Israel*], **but shall stay** [*depend*] **upon the Lord**, the Holy One of Israel, in truth. [*In other words, the day will come in which Israel will become a righteous people who depend on and trust in the Lord.*]

Next, Isaiah again emphasizes the future return of Israel to their God. This is happen now, in our day, with the gathering of Israel that is taking place under the direction of our current prophets.

21 **The remnant shall return**, yea, even the remnant of Jacob, unto the mighty God [*Dual: 1. A remnant remains in the land after Assyrian destruction. 2. In the future, a righteous remnant of Israel will be gathered in; see 2 Nephi 21:11–12*].

22 For though [*although*] thy people Israel be as the sand of the sea, yet **a remnant of them shall return** [*only a remnant will be converted; gathering*]; the consumption decreed [*destruction at the end of the world*] shall overflow [*will overcome the wicked*] with righteousness [*because of God's power or under God's direction; see the following verse*].

23 **For the Lord God of Hosts shall make a consumption, even determined** [*the decreed or prophesied destruction; see Isaiah 10, footnote 23a*] in all the land.

Next, Isaiah emphasizes and repeats again the prophecy that the Lord will stop the Assyrians in their tracks. He adds that they will be stopped at the very last moment, just as they position themselves to enter Jerusalem.

24 **Therefore, thus saith the Lord God** of Hosts: O my people that dwellest in Zion, **be not afraid of the Assyrian**; he [*the Assyrian armies*] shall smite thee with a rod, and shall lift up his staff against thee, after the manner of Egypt [*like Egypt did in earlier times*].

25 For yet a very little while, and the indignation [*the anger of the Lord against Israel*] shall cease, and mine anger in their destruction [*my anger will be directed toward the destruction of the Assyrians*].

26 **And the Lord of Hosts shall stir up a scourge for him** [*the Assyrians*] according to [*like*] the slaughter of Midian at the rock of Oreb [*Judges 7:23–25, where Gideon and his three hundred miraculously defeated the overwhelming armies of the Midianites*]; and as his rod was upon the sea [*His power came upon the Red Sea to drown the Egyptian armies*] so shall he lift it up after the manner of Egypt [*God will stop the Assyrian armies like He did the Egyptians when they pursued the children of Israel into the parted waters of the Red Sea*].

27 And it shall come to pass in that day that his [*Israel's enemies, such as Assyria and others*] burden shall be taken away from off thy [*Israel's*] shoulder, and his yoke [*bondage*] from off thy neck, and **the yoke shall be destroyed because of the anointing** [*because of Christ, the "Anointed One"*].

As previously stated, Isaiah is a master of drama. Next, he will create a high degree of tension as he prophesies the advance of the Assyrian armies upon Jerusalem. It will look like Assyria will not be stopped; Assyrians will easily take several cities leading right up to the outskirts of Jerusalem, and it will look like Jerusalem is doomed despite Isaiah's prophecies to the contrary in verse 26. We will **bold** the names of the cities that the Assyrian king conquers as he heads toward Jerusalem.

28 He [*the Assyrian king with his powerful armies*] is come to **Aiath**, he is passed to **Migron**; at **Michmash** he hath laid up his carriages [*horses and carriages are symbolic of military might*].

29 They [*Assyria*] are gone over the passage [*they have come over the pass*]; they have taken up their lodging at **Geba**; **Ramath** is afraid; **Gibeah** of Saul is fled.

30 Lift up the voice [*weep!*], O daughter of **Gallim**; cause it to be heard unto **Laish**, O poor **Anathoth**.

31 **Madmenah** is removed; the inhabitants of **Gebim** gather themselves to flee.

32 As yet shall he [*Assyria*] remain at **Nob** [*just outside of Jerusalem*] that day; he shall shake his hand against the mount of the daughter of Zion [*Jerusalem*], the hill of Jerusalem.

33 **Behold, the Lord, the Lord of Hosts shall lop the bough with terror** [*when Assyrian armies get right to Jerusalem, the Lord will "trim them down to size," "clip their wings," stop them in their tracks*]; and the high ones [*leaders of Assyrian armies*] of stature shall be hewn down; and the haughty shall be humbled.

34 **And he shall cut down the thickets of the forests** [*the Assyrian armies*] with iron [*an axe*], and Lebanon shall fall by a mighty one [*the Lord did stop Assyria by sending a sudden plague, which killed 185,000 of them in one night as they camped outside Jerusalem; see 2 Kings 19:32–35*].

The Assyrian armies came up to Jerusalem, as prophesied, and were stopped suddenly by the Lord, as promised. This was one fulfillment of this prophecy.

However, this may be a dual prophecy—that is, one with more than one fulfillment. It also could refer to the attacks on Jerusalem and Israel in the last days, as powerful nations gather together to attempt to destroy them. In this case also, the Jews and Jerusalem will be spared also because of the Savior. He will appear on the Mount of Olives, which will split in two. The Jews will flee into the valley caused by the split and will see their Savior there. They will ask questions and He will answer. We will use prophecies recorded in Zechariah to review these future events and will use **bold** for teaching purposes.

Zechariah 12:8–9

8 In that day shall the LORD defend the inhabitants of Jerusalem; and he that is feeble among them at that day shall be as David; and the house of David shall be as God, as the angel of the LORD before them.

9 And it shall come to pass in that day, that I will seek to destroy all the nations that come against Jerusalem.

Zechariah 14:4–5

4 And his [Christ's] *feet shall stand in that day upon the mount of Olives, which is before* [across the valley from] *Jerusalem on the east, and the mount of Olives shall cleave in the midst thereof toward the east and toward the west, and there shall be a very great valley; and half of the mountain shall remove toward the north, and half of it toward the south.*

5 And ye [the Jews] *shall flee to the valley of the mountains; for the valley of the mountains shall reach unto Azal: yea, ye shall flee, like as ye fled from before the earthquake in the days of Uzziah king of Judah: and the LORD my God shall come, and all the saints with thee.*

Zechariah 13:6

6 And one shall say unto him, What are these wounds in thine hands? Then he shall answer, Those with which I was wounded in the house of my friends.

2 NEPHI 21

This chapter is similar to Isaiah, chapter 11 in the Bible. In Joseph Smith—History, in the Pearl of Great Price, chapter 1, verse 40, Joseph Smith said that the angel Moroni quoted this chapter to him when he appeared to him on September 23, 1823, and said that it was about to be fulfilled.

In this chapter, we are taught that powerful leaders will come forth in the last days to lead the gathering of Israel. We are instructed in Christlike qualities of leadership. We will be shown the peace that will be here during the Millennium, and Isaiah will also teach us some things about the last days gathering of Israel. As you know, our prophets are strongly emphasizing the gathering of Israel today.

1 **And there shall come forth a rod** [*D&C 113:3–4 defines this "rod" as "a servant in the hands of Christ, who is partly a descendant of Jesse as well as of Ephraim . . . on whom there is laid much power."*] **out of the stem of Jesse** [*Christ; see D&C 113:1–2*], and a branch shall grow out of his roots.

Perhaps the imagery here in verse one grows out of the last two verses of chapter 20, where the wicked leaders end up as "stumps" and have been destroyed. In the last days, new, righteous, powerful leaders will be brought forth to replace the "stumps" of the past and will have their origins from the "roots" of Christ. Roots can symbolically represent being solid and firmly rooted in God.

Christlike qualities of leadership are described next. These are the leadership qualities that you will need to have and learn to have as you are called to various assignments in the Church throughout your life. These next verses also show us the qualities of righteous leadership Christ Himself will have.

2 And **the Spirit of the Lord shall rest upon him**, the spirit of **wisdom** and **understanding**, the spirit of **counsel** and **might**, the spirit of **knowledge** and of the **fear of the Lord** [*respect for the Lord*];

3 And shall make him **of quick understanding** in the fear of the Lord; and he shall not judge after the sight of his eyes, neither reprove after the hearing of his ears.

These next two verses refer directly to the Savior.

4 But **with righteousness shall he judge** the poor, and **reprove with equity for the meek** of the earth; and **he shall smite the earth with the rod** [*power and authority*] **of his mouth**, and **with the breath of his lips shall he slay the wicked**.

5 And **righteousness** shall be the girdle of his loins, and **faithfulness** the girdle of his reins [*Christ will be clothed with righteousness and faithfulness; in other words, He will demonstrate these personal qualities*].

Isaiah now makes the transition directly into the Millennium. He shows, in several ways, that there will be peace during the 1,000 years when Christ is here on earth after His Second Coming.

6 **The wolf also shall dwell with the lamb**, and **the leopard shall lie down with the kid** [*young goat*], and **the calf and the young lion and fatling together**; and a little child shall lead [*herd*] them [*Millennial conditions*].

7 And **the cow and the bear shall feed** [*graze*]; **their young ones shall lie down together**; and **the lion shall eat straw like the ox** [*rather than eating other animals*].

8 And **the suckling child** [*nursing child*] **shall play on the hole of the asp** [*viper, a poisonous snake*], and **the weaned child** [*toddler*] **shall put his hand on the cockatrice's** [*venomous serpent's*] **den**.

9 **They shall not hurt nor destroy in all my holy mountain**, for **the earth shall be full of the knowledge of** [*devotion to*] **the Lord**, as the waters cover the sea. [*There will be great and wonderful peace on earth during the Millennium, and, eventually, almost everybody on earth will know and live the gospel.*]

10 And **in that day there shall be a root of Jesse** [*probably Joseph Smith, but we don't know for sure*], which shall stand for an ensign of the people [*will signal that the gathering of Israel in the last days is about to begin*]; to it [*the "ensign" or flag signaling the beginning of an event*] shall the Gentiles seek; and his rest shall be glorious.

11 **And it shall come to pass in that day that the Lord shall set his hand again the second time** [*dual: a remnant returned after the Babylonian captivity / last days gathering of Israel*] **to recover the remnant of his people** which shall be left, from Assyria, and from Egypt, and from Pathros, and from Cush, and from Elam, and from Shinar, and from Hamath, and from the

islands of the sea. [*In other words, in the last days, Israel will be gathered from every nation in the world.*]

12 And he [*the Lord*] shall set up an ensign [*the Church in the last days*] for the nations, and shall assemble the outcasts of Israel, and gather together the dispersed of Judah [*the Jews*] from the four corners of the earth.

As you will recall from your study of Isaiah so far, and from the history of the Holy Land, the twelve tribes split into two nations in a bitter dispute over high taxes, etc., after the death of Solomon. Over the years, Ephraim (the ten tribes whose nation was in the northern portion of the Holy Land) and Judah (the southern kingdom with Jerusalem as their capital city) became bitter enemies. Therefore, the prophecy that follows is marvelous! It is a prophecy that the day will come when the Jews and the descendants of Ephraim will get along well. We are seeing this today.

13 The envy of Ephraim also shall depart, and the adversaries of Judah shall be cut off; **Ephraim shall not envy Judah, and Judah shall not vex Ephraim** [*the United States and others will be on good terms with the Jews*].

Next, Isaiah prophesies about conditions in the Middle East in the last days before the Second Coming of the Savior.

14 **But they** [*the Jews, with Ephraim's help*] **shall fly upon the shoulders of the Philistines towards the west** [*attack the western slopes that were once Philistine territory*]; **they shall spoil them of the east** together; **they shall lay their hand upon Edom and Moab; and the children of Ammon shall obey them** [*the Jews will be powerful against the enemy nations that surround them in the last days rather than being easy prey for their enemies as they have been throughout history*].

15 And **the Lord shall utterly destroy the tongue of the Egyptian sea** [*productivity of Nile River ruined?—see Isaiah 19:5–10*]; and with his mighty wind he shall shake his hand over the river, and shall smite it in the seven streams, and make men go over dry shod.

16 And there shall be a highway for the remnant of his people which shall be left, from Assyria, like as it was to Israel in the day that he came up out of the land of Egypt [*the Lord will establish His gospel, which will serve as a "highway" for Israel to return to Him*].

2 NEPHI 22

This chapter compares to Isaiah, chapter 12 in the Bible. It is a short but beautiful chapter describing how it will be to live on earth during the Millennium. It describes the faithful who survive the destruction at the Second Coming of Christ as praising the Lord and rejoicing at the salvation that has come to them.

1 **And in that day** [*the Millennium*] **thou** [*Israel*] **shalt say: O Lord, I will praise thee; though thou wast angry with me** [*in the past because I was rebellious and didn't live the gospel*] **thine anger is turned away** [*because I have repented and turned back to Thee*], **and thou comfortedst me.**

2 Behold, God is my salvation; I will trust, and not be afraid; for **the Lord JEHOVAH** [*Jesus*] **is my strength and my song; he also has become my salvation.**

3 Therefore, **with joy shall ye draw water out of the wells of salvation** [*"living water," John 4:10; 7:38–39, in other words, during the Millennium, we will have the pure gospel of Jesus Christ, which will bring salvation to us*].

4 And **in that day shall ye say**: Praise the Lord, call upon his name, declare his doings among the people, make mention that his name is exalted.

5 **Sing unto the Lord**; for he hath done excellent things; this is known in all the earth [*knowledge of the Lord will cover the earth*].

6 **Cry out and shout, thou inhabitant of Zion; for great is the Holy One of Israel** [*Christ*] **in the midst of thee.**

2 NEPHI 23

In chapter 20, the destruction of Assyria was a type of (or symbolic of) the destruction of the wicked at the Second Coming of Christ. We discussed the definition of "type" in the notes at the beginning of that chapter. In this chapter, the destruction of Babylon is likewise a type of the destruction of Satan's kingdom at the time of the Second Coming.

It will be helpful for you to understand that the ancient city of Babylon was a huge city full of wickedness, about 1,000 miles east of Jerusalem. In fact, Babylon was so big, its walls were 56 miles around it, 335 feet high, and 85 feet wide. It was so big and powerful that people didn't think it could ever be conquered. Over time, Babylon has come to symbolize the wickedness of the world and Satan's kingdom. So big that it seems like it could not possibly be destroyed. Yet, you will see in this chapter that Isaiah prophesies that Babylon, the actual city, and Satan's kingdom, symbolically, will indeed be destroyed.

1 **The burden of** [*message of doom and destruction to*] **Babylon, which Isaiah the son of Amoz did see.**

Verses 2–5, next, describe how the Lord will gather his righteous forces together to fight against sin and evil. We are watching His righteous people being gathered from throughout the world now, in the last days before the Second Coming of Christ, as the gathering of Israel takes place.

2 **Lift ye up a banner** upon the high mountain, **exalt the voice** [*call*] **unto them** [*the righteous*], **shake the hand** [*wave the hand, signal*], **that they may go into the gates of the nobles** [*so that they can gather with the righteous*].

Next, Isaiah says, in effect, that the Savior is leading the gathering of Israel.

3 **I have commanded my sanctified ones** [*my Saints*], **I have also called my mighty ones**, for mine anger is not upon them that rejoice in my highness.

4 **The noise of the multitude in the mountains like as of a great people** [*the gathering of Israel in the last days will be very large*], a tumultuous noise of the kingdoms of nations **gathered together**, **the Lord of Hosts** [*Christ*] **mustereth** [*gathers*] **the hosts of the battle**.

5 **They come from a far country, from the end of heaven** [*the righteous will be gathered from all over the world*], yea, the Lord, and the weapons of his indignation, **to destroy the whole land** [*the wicked*].

Next, Isaiah switches topics from the gathering of the righteous to fight together against wickedness to a strong warning to the wicked, who will soon be facing the consequences of their evil ways.

6 **Howl ye** [*the wicked*], for the day of the Lord [*Second Coming*] is at hand; it shall come as a destruction from the Almighty.

7 **Therefore** [*because the wicked will get caught*] **shall all hands be faint** [*hang limp*], **every man's** [*wicked men*] **heart** [*courage*] **shall melt**;

8 And **they shall be afraid**; pangs and sorrows shall take hold of them; they shall be amazed [*will look in fear*] one at another; their faces shall be as flames [*burn with shame*].

9 **Behold, the day of the Lord** [*Second Coming*] **cometh**, cruel [*it will appear cruel to the wicked*] both with wrath and fierce anger, to lay the land desolate; and he [*the Lord*] shall destroy the sinners thereof out of it [*a purpose of the Second Coming*].

10 For **the stars of heaven and the constellations thereof shall not give their light; the sun shall be darkened in his going forth, and the moon shall not cause**

her light to shine [*signs of the times preceding the Second Coming of Christ*].

11 And **I will punish the world for evil, and the wicked for their iniquity** [*sins and wickedness*]; **I will cause the arrogancy** [*pride*] **of the proud to cease**, and will lay down the haughtiness [*pride*] of the terrible [*tyrants; typical Isaiah repetition to drive home a point*].

12 **I will make a man** [*a righteous man, meaning righteous people*] **more precious** [*scarce*] **than fine gold**; even a man than the golden wedge of Ophir [*a land rich in gold, possibly in southern Arabia; in other words, there will be relatively few survivors of the Second Coming compared to the large numbers of wicked prior to Christ's coming*].

13 **Therefore** [*because of the wickedness on earth prior to the Second Coming*], **I will shake the heavens, and the earth shall remove out of her place**, in the wrath of the Lord of Hosts, and in the day of his fierce anger.

14 **And it** [*dual: Babylon literally as a city; also the wicked in general*] **shall be as the chased roe** [*hunted deer*], **and as a sheep that no man taketh up** [*no shepherd, no one to defend it*]; and they shall every man turn to his own people, and flee every one into his own land [*foreigners who have had safety in Babylon, because of Babylon's great power, will return to their homelands because Babylon is no longer powerful and safe*].

15 **Every one that is proud shall be thrust through** [*stabbed; destroyed*]; yea, **and every one that is joined to the wicked shall fall by the sword**.

16 **Their children, also shall be dashed to pieces before their eyes; their houses shall be spoiled and their wives ravished** [*fate of Babylon; innocent people suffer because of the wicked*].

Next, Isaiah gives a very specific prophecy regarding how the ancient city of Babylon was to be conquered.

17 Behold, **I will stir up the Medes against them** [*the Medes, from Persia, conquered Babylon easily in 538 BC*], which shall not regard silver and gold, nor shall they delight in it [*you Babylonians will not be able to bribe the Medes not to destroy you*].

18 Their bows shall also dash the young men to pieces, and they shall have no pity on the fruit of the womb [*babies*]; their eyes shall not spare children.

19 **And Babylon, the glory of kingdoms, the beauty of the Chaldees' excellency, shall be**

as when God overthrew Sodom and Gomorrah.

> Isaiah prophesied that Babylon would be completely destroyed and never inhabited again. And that is exactly what happened. It remains in ruins even today. The symbolism is clear. Satan's kingdom will be destroyed by the Savior at the time of His Second Coming, and again after the "little season" at the end of the Millennium, never again to be rebuilt. (See D&C 88:111–14.)

20 **It shall never be inhabited, neither shall it be dwelt in from generation to generation**: neither shall the Arabian pitch tent there; neither shall the shepherds make their fold there.

21 **But wild beasts of the desert shall lie there**; and their houses [*the ruins*] shall be full of doleful creatures [*such as owls*]; and owls shall dwell there, and satyrs [*male goats*] shall dance there.

22 **And the wild beasts of the islands shall cry** [*howl and yowl*] **in their desolate houses**, and dragons [*hyenas, wild dogs, jackals*] in their pleasant palaces; and her time is near to come, and her day shall not be prolonged [*Babylon's time is up, her days are almost over*]. **For I will destroy her speedily**; yea, for **I will be merciful unto my people** [*the righteous*], **but the wicked shall perish**.

2 NEPHI 24

In this next chapter, you will see again that Isaiah is a master teacher. He is an expert at helping us see things because of the words he choses to use in his writing. He will use very colorful style and imagery as he prophesies concerning the future downfall of the king of Babylon and, symbolically, the downfall of Satan's kingdom, starting with verse 4.

But first, he assures us that Israel will indeed be gathered in the last days, in preparation for the Second Coming. And then he assures the righteous that they will enjoy long-awaited peace during the Millennium.

1 **For the Lord will have mercy on Jacob** [*the house of Israel*], and will yet choose Israel, and set them in their own land [*One historical fulfillment of this was when Cyrus the Great of Persia allowed Jewish captives in Babylon to return, 538 BC; another group returned in 520 BC. This is also being fulfilled in our day with the modern-day gathering of Israel.*]; and the strangers shall be joined with them [*foreigners will live with them*], and they shall cleave to the house of Jacob.

2 **And the people** [*many nations who will help Israel return*] **shall take them** [*Israel*] **and bring them to their**

place; yea, from far unto the ends of the earth; **and they** [*Israel*] **shall return to their lands of promise**. And the house of Israel shall possess them and the land of the Lord shall be for servants and handmaids; **and they** [*Israel*] **shall take them** [*nations who used to dominate Israel*] **captives unto whom they** [*Israel*] **were captives; and they** [*Israel*] **shall rule over their oppressors** [*the tables will be turned in the last days*].

Notice that "lands" in verse 2, above, is plural. Among other things, this reminds us that in the last days there are to be several gathering places for Israel. In our day, members are being gathered into stakes of Zion throughout the world.

Now Isaiah switches to prophesying about the Millennium.

3 **And it shall come to pass in that day** [*Millennium*] **that the Lord shall give thee** [*Israel; the Lord's covenant people; the members of the Church*] **rest**, from thy sorrow, and from thy fear, and from the hard bondage wherein thou wast made to serve [*Israel will finally be free from subjection by foreigners*].

Next, Isaiah paints a future scene with words in which he depicts two things: namely, the literal fall of Babylon and her wicked king, and also, symbolically, the future fall of Satan and his wicked kingdom. Such prophecies of Isaiah are known as "dual meaning" prophecies.

As he sets things up for his students, Isaiah creates interest and intrigue by telling them that downtrodden Israel will someday come to the point when they will see the king of Babylon (symbolic of all wicked earthly leaders) as well as Satan himself trimmed down to size, with no more power to afflict and distress them. Isaiah then creates fascinating imagery to drive home his point that the faithful righteous will eventually triumph over all evil by staying close to God.

4 **And it shall come to pass in that day, that thou** [*Israel; the faithful people of the Lord*] **shalt take up this proverb** [*taunting, a saying making fun of*] **against the king of Babylon** [*dual: literally king of Babylon; refers also to Satan plus any wicked leader*], **and say: How hath the oppressor ceased** [*what happened to you!*], the golden city ceased [*your "unconquerable city," kingdom, is gone*]!

In verse 5, below, Isaiah confirms that it is the power of the Lord that will ultimately break the power of the wicked to afflict the righteous.

5 **The Lord hath broken the staff of** [*power of*] **the wicked**, the scepters [*power*] of the [*wicked*] rulers.

6 **He** [*dual: king of Babylon; Satan*] **who smote the people in wrath with a continual stroke** [*never ceasing*], **he that ruled the nations in anger, is persecuted** [*is now being punished*], **and none hindereth** [*nobody can stop it*].

7 **The whole earth is at rest, and is quiet** [*Millennium with wonderful peace*]; they break forth into singing [*during the Millennium*].

The imagery in verse 8, next, is that of a great big tree being cut down by a lumberjack. The symbolism, as you will see, is that of the Lord cutting down Satan and his wicked followers so they have no more power over the righteous.

8 **Yea, the fir-trees** [*people*] **rejoice at thee** [*at what has happened to Satan*], and also the cedars [*people*] of Lebanon, saying: **Since thou art laid down** [*since you got chopped down*] **no feller** [*tree cutter, lumberjack*] **is come up against us**.

9 **Hell** [*spirit prison*] from beneath **is moved for thee** [*is getting ready to receive you*] **to meet thee at thy coming**; it stirreth up the dead for thee, even all the chief ones [*dead wicked leaders*] of the earth; it hath raised up from their thrones all the [*wicked*] kings of the nations.

The "picture" that Isaiah paints for us next, in verses 10–11, is somewhat humorous in a way. It is that the wicked residents of hell will mock Satan (dual, the king of Babylon) when he is cut down to size and his kingdom is finally destroyed by the Lord.

10 **All they shall speak and say unto thee** [*dual: Satan; king of Babylon*]: **Art thou also become weak as we** [*what happened to your power*]? **Art thou become like unto us** [*did you get your power taken away too, like we did*]?

11 Thy pomp is brought down to the grave [*was destroyed with you*]; the noise of thy viols [*royal harp music*] is not heard; the worm is spread under thee, and the worms cover thee. [*Maggots are destroying your dead body just like they destroyed ours. You're no better off here in hell than we are, so hah, hah, hah! Refers only to the king of Babylon since Satan has no mortal body.*]

Next comes one of the most famous quotes from Isaiah regarding Lucifer. It deals with his fall from heaven, after his rebellion in the premortal life plus his complete fall and the destruction of his evil kingdom after the final battle after the end of the Millennium.

12 **How art thou fallen from heaven** [*What happened to you?*], **O Lucifer, son of the morning**! Art thou cut down to the ground, which did weaken the nations [*you used to destroy nations; now your power is destroyed*]!

Next, Isaiah tells us what Lucifer's real thoughts and motives were when he rebelled against God in the premortal war in heaven.

13 **For thou hast said in thy heart** [*these were your motives*]: **I will ascend into heaven, I will exalt my throne above the stars of God** [*I want to take over Heavenly Father's position and be the highest*]; I will sit also upon the mount of the congregation, in the sides of the north [*mythical mountain in the north where gods assemble*];

14 I will ascend above the heights of the clouds; **I will be like the Most High** [*Moses 4:1 indicates he wanted to be the Most High!*].

15 **Yet thou** [*Lucifer; Satan's name before he rebelled and started the war in heaven*] **shalt be brought down to hell, to the sides of the pit** [*to the lowest part of the world of the dead—in other words, outer darkness*].

16 **They** [*the residents of hell*] **that see thee** [*Lucifer; king of Babylon*] **shall narrowly look upon thee** [*scorn you, mock you*], and shall consider [*look at*] thee, **and shall say: Is this the man that made the earth to tremble, that did shake kingdoms**?

17 **And made the world as a wilderness, and destroyed the cities thereof, and opened not the house of his prisoners** [*refused to free his prisoners*]?

18 **All the kings of the nations, yea, all of them, lie in glory, every one of them in his own house** [*all other kings have magnificent tombs*].

19 **But thou** [*dual: king of Babylon literally; Satan figuratively because he doesn't even have a physical body*] **art cast out of thy grave like an abominable branch** [*pruned off and thus worthless*], and the remnant of those that are slain [*you are just like any other dead wicked person*], thrust through with a sword, that go down to the stones of the pit [*to the very bottom*]; **as a carcass trodden under feet**.

20 **Thou** [*king of Babylon; Satan*] **shalt not be joined with them** [*other powerful, wicked rulers*] **in burial, because thou hast destroyed thy land and slain thy people**; the seed of evil-doers shall never be renowned [*none of your evil family will survive, king of Babylon*].

21 **Prepare slaughter for his** [*king of Babylon*] **children for the iniquities of their fathers, that they do not rise, nor possess the land, nor fill the face of the world with cities** [*none of your children will rule the earth like you have*].

Next, Isaiah repeats that it is ultimately the Lord who will stop

Lucifer and all powerful wicked leaders and rulers like the king of Babylon. Note how thoroughly Isaiah defines their destruction.

22 **For I will rise up against them** [*the Lord will stop Lucifer; king of Babylon*], saith the Lord of Hosts, **and cut off** from Babylon the **name**, and **remnant**, and **son**, and **nephew** [*I will destroy Babylon completely*], saith the Lord.

One of Isaiah's favorite methods of driving home the point that a wicked kingdom will be destroyed completely is to picture it after the destruction as being desolate and deserted, where only birds and animals live, avoiding humans. We see this technique in the next verse.

23 **I will also make it** [*Babylon*] **a possession for the bittern** [*owls*], **and pools of water**; and **I will sweep it with the besom** [*broom*] **of destruction** [*a "clean sweep"*], **saith the Lord of Hosts.**

Isaiah has finished with Babylon, and starts a new topic now—namely, the fate of Assyria, another powerful nation that caused a lot of trouble and pain for the Lord's covenant people.

24 **The Lord of Hosts** [*Christ*] **hath sworn** [*covenanted, promised*], saying: **Surely as I have thought** [*planned*], **so shall it come to pass** [*here is something else I will do*]; and as I have purposed [*planned*], so shall it stand [*it will happen*]—

25 That **I will bring the Assyrian in my land** [*the land of Judah; the Jerusalem area*], **and upon my mountains** [*the mountains of Judah*] **tread him** [*Assyria*] **under foot** [*destroy his armies*]; **then shall his yoke** [*Assyrian bondage*] **depart from off them** [*my people*], and his burden depart from off their shoulders [*dual: the Assyrian downfall in Judah, 701 BC; also, the forces of the wicked will be destroyed at the Second Coming and again at the end of the earth*].

26 **This is the purpose** [*the plan; the pattern*] **that is purposed upon the whole earth**; **and this is the hand** [*the power of the Lord*] **that is stretched out upon all nations** [*the eventual fate of all wicked*].

27 **For the Lord of Hosts hath purposed** [*planned*], **and who shall disannul** [*prevent it*]? And his [*the Lord's*] hand is stretched out, and **who shall turn it back** [*who can stop the Lord*]?

Isaiah has finished with the Assyrians and now switches to the Philistines, an enemy nation to the south and west of Jerusalem.

28 **In the year that king Ahaz died** [*about 720 BC*] **was this burden** [*message of doom to the Philistines*].

29 **Rejoice not** [*don't get happy and start celebrating*] thou, whole Palestina [*Philistia; in other words, the nation of the Philistines*], **because the rod** [*power*] **of him** [*Shalmaneser, King of Assyria from 727–22 BC*] **that smote thee is broken** [*in other words, don't rejoice because a powerful enemy's king has died*]**; for out of the serpent's root** [*"snakes lay eggs," or, from the same source, Assyria*]; **shall come forth a cockatrice** [*One "snake" is dead—Shalmaneser—and a worse one will yet come—Sennacherib, King of Assyria, 705–687 BC. The Philistines rejoiced when Sargon, King of Assyria from 722 to 705 BC, took over at Shalmaneser's death. Sargon was not as hard on them as his predecessor was.*], **and his fruit** [*but his son, Senacherib*] **shall be a fiery flying serpent**.

Verse 30, next, is Isaiah's prophetic warning that if the Philistines repent and accept the Lord and live His gospel, they can have peace. But if they refuse to, they will be destroyed.

30 **And the first-born of the poor shall feed, and the needy shall lie down in safety** [*if you Philistines will join with the Lord, repent, etc., you too can enjoy peace and safety, otherwise . . .*]; **and I will kill thy** [*Philistines*] **root with famine, and he shall slay thy remnant** [*you will be utterly destroyed*].

31 **Howl, O gate; cry, O city; thou, whole Palestina** [*Philistia*], art dissolved [*reduced to nothing*]; for there shall come from the north a smoke [*cloud of dust made by an approaching enemy army*], and none shall be alone in his appointed times [*the enemy army will have no cowards in it*].

32 **What shall then answer the messengers of the nations?** [*What will one say when people ask, "What happened to the Philistines?" Answer:*] **That the Lord hath founded Zion, and the poor of his people shall trust in it** [*that the Lord is the one who caused the destruction of the wicked and established Zion*].

2 NEPHI 25

One of the great advantages that we enjoy as far as understanding Isaiah is concerned is that Nephi explains what we have just read in the previous Isaiah chapters. As of verse 9, he will begin giving specific explanations. In verses 1–8, he will explain that his own people had difficulty understanding Isaiah also. This can perhaps make us feel a bit better about having difficulty understanding Isaiah's writings ourselves.

1 NOW I, Nephi, do speak somewhat concerning the words which I have written, which have been spoken by the mouth of Isaiah. For behold, **Isaiah spake many**

things which were hard for many of my people to understand; for they know not concerning the manner of prophesying among the Jews.

2 For **I, Nephi, have not taught them many things concerning the manner of the Jews**; for their works [*what they were doing in their daily lives*] were works of darkness [*evil and wickedness*], and their doings were doings of abominations [*the Jews were deeply involved in sin and wickedness*].

3 **Wherefore** [*this is why*], **I write** unto my people, **unto all those that shall receive hereafter these things which I write** [*in other words, this is written to all who get the Book of Mormon*], **that they may know the judgments** [*punishments*] **of God, that they come upon all nations**, according to the word which he hath spoken [*in other words, all people will ultimately be accountable to God*].

4 Wherefore, **hearken, O my people, which are of the house of Israel** [*the Lord's covenant people, coming from Abraham, Isaac, and Jacob, which ultimately includes everyone who is baptized*], **and give ear unto my words** [*listen carefully*]; for because the words of Isaiah are not plain unto you, nevertheless they are plain unto all those that are filled with the spirit of prophecy [*the Holy Ghost*]. But **I give unto you a prophecy, according to the spirit which is in me**; wherefore **I shall prophesy** according to the plainness which hath been with me from the time that I came out from Jerusalem with my father; for behold, **my soul delighteth in plainness unto my people, that they may learn**.

As mentioned in verses 1 and 2, above, Nephi's own people have difficulty understanding Isaiah because they have not grown up among the Jews. However, people often ask whether the Jews themselves understood the words of Isaiah. Next, in verse 5, Nephi answers this question. The answer is "Yes."

5 Yea, and **my soul delighteth in the words of Isaiah, for I came out from Jerusalem**, and mine eyes hath beheld the things of the Jews, and **I know that the Jews do understand the things of the prophets**, and there is **none other people** that **understand the things which were spoken unto the Jews like unto them**, save it be that they are taught after the manner of the things of the Jews.

Again, as stated in verse 2, above, Nephi has avoided teaching his people many things about life among the Jews in the Jerusalem area because of the wicked lifestyle of that culture. Therefore, his people are a lot like us in the sense that they don't understand the background, setting, and symbolism used by Isaiah. In the next verses, Nephi tells us that he will help us by teaching us in plain words what Isaiah was teaching. This gives us a huge advantage in understanding Isaiah over people who only have the Bible.

6 But behold, I, Nephi, have not taught my children after the manner of the Jews; but **behold, I, of myself, have dwelt at Jerusalem, wherefore** [*this is why*] **I know concerning the regions round about**; and I have made mention unto my children concerning the judgments [*punishments*] of God, which hath come to pass among the Jews, unto my children, according to all that which Isaiah hath spoken, **and I do not write them**.

7 **But behold, I proceed with mine own prophecy** [*I will teach Isaiah in my own words*], according to my plainness; in the which I know that no man can err; nevertheless, **in the days that the prophecies of Isaiah shall be fulfilled** [*this is happening a lot now in our day*] **men shall know of a surety, at the times when they shall come to pass**.

One of the prophecies of Isaiah that fulfills the prophecy of Nephi in verse 7, above, is Isaiah 2:2–3, where it says that the headquarters of the Church in the last days will be in the tops of the mountains, meaning Salt Lake City, Utah.

In verse 8, below, Nephi prophesies that in the last days, people will understand the writings of Isaiah. You are part of the fulfillment of this prophecy as you grow in ability to understand them because of the Book of Mormon and Nephi's explanations.

8 **Wherefore, they** [*the words of Isaiah*] **are of worth unto the children of men**, and he that supposeth that they are not, unto them will I speak particularly, and confine the words unto mine own people; for I know that they shall be of great worth unto them **in the last days**; for in that day **shall they understand them**; wherefore, for their good have I written them.

Next, Nephi begins his explanation of the Isaiah chapters that he included in his small plates, which we are reading now at this point in the Book of Mormon. He will make Isaiah's writings much clearer for us, starting with verse 9, next, where he explains one major message of Isaiah to us.

9 And **as one generation hath been destroyed among the Jews because of iniquity, even so have they been destroyed from generation to generation according to their iniquities** [*the scattering of Israel because of their wickedness; see 2 Nephi 13:11*]; **and never hath any of them been destroyed save it were foretold them by the prophets of the Lord** [*they always had fair warning from their prophets before the destruction came*].

As you saw in verse 9, above, near the end, we find an important doctrine; namely, that the Lord always gives fair warning of coming destruction or scattering because of wickedness. This way, people have a chance to use their moral agency wisely and are accountable for what happens to them.

Nephi gives us an example of this next.

10 **Wherefore, it hath been told them** [*the Jews*] **concerning the destruction** [*the Babylonian captivity*] **which should come upon them, immediately after my father left Jerusalem**; nevertheless, they hardened their hearts [*refused to repent*]; and according to my prophecy they have been destroyed [*Jerusalem has been destroyed*], save [*except*] it be those which are carried away captive into Babylon.

Next, Nephi explains that one of Isaiah's most dominant teachings is the "gathering" of Israel. On a personal note, each of us is invited constantly by the Lord to be "gathered" to Him.

11 **And now this I speak because of the spirit which is in me** [*Nephi is bearing his testimony to us that what he is saying is true*]. **And notwithstanding** [*even though*] **they** [*the Jews*] **have been carried away they shall return again** [*the gathering*], **and possess the land of Jerusalem** [*this became a fact when the nation of Israel was formed by the United Nations in 1948*]; wherefore, **they shall be restored again to the land of their inheritance** [*the Holy Land*].

Next, Nephi explains that Isaiah prophesied that the Son of God would actually come to earth and live among the Jews.

12 But, behold, they [*the Jews*] shall have wars, and rumors of wars; and when the day cometh that **the Only Begotten of the Father** [*Jesus*], yea, even the Father of heaven and of earth [*yes, I mean Heavenly Father*], **shall manifest himself unto them in the flesh**, behold, **they** [*the Jews*] **will reject him**, because of their iniquities [*because of their wickedness*], and the hardness of their hearts, and the stiffness of their necks [*their pride and lack of humility*].

13 Behold, **they will crucify him; and after he is laid in a sepulchre** [*a tomb*] **for the space of three days he shall rise from the dead** [*He will be resurrected*], **with healing in his wings** [*with full power to heal all of us from our sins*]; **and all those who shall believe on his name shall be saved in the kingdom of God**. Wherefore, my soul delighteth to prophesy concerning him [*this is why I love to teach about Christ*], for **I have seen his day**, and my heart doth magnify his holy name [*I have indescribable feelings of appreciation for Him in my heart*].

The phrase "healing in his wings" in verse 13, above, has beautiful symbolism. "Healing" is, of course, the Savior's ability and power to heal all of us of the effects of sins and inadequacies. "Wings" symbolize the power to be wherever He is needed instantly, in order to minister to us. See D&C 77:4 for a brief explanation of "wings" given by the Prophet Joseph Smith.

14 And behold it shall come to pass that **after the Messiah hath risen from the dead, and hath manifested** [*shown*] **himself unto his people**, unto as many as will believe on his name, behold, **Jerusalem shall be destroyed again** [*by the Romans, about AD 70–73*]; for wo unto them that fight against God and the people of his church.

Nephi now continues teaching what Isaiah taught; namely, that the Jews would be scattered and badly treated for centuries after they crucify Christ. And then, a wonderful thing begins to happen as the Jews begin to believe in Christ and His Atonement. A great gathering begins among them.

15 Wherefore, **the Jews shall be scattered among all nations**; yea, and **also Babylon shall be destroyed** [*it was, in 538 BC by the Persians*]; wherefore, the Jews shall be scattered by other nations [*this would include Rome as well as Hitler and other tyrants*].

16 And **after they have been scattered, and** the Lord God hath **scourged** [*punished*] them by other nations for the space of many generations, yea, even down from generation to generation **until they shall be persuaded to believe in Christ, the Son of God, and the atonement**, which is infinite for all mankind—and **when that day shall come that they shall believe in Christ, and worship the Father in his name, with pure hearts and clean hands, and look not forward any more for another Messiah** [*this time is just beginning to happen among the Jews*], **then**, at that time, **the day will come** [*is still future*] that it must needs be expedient [*it is*

necessary] **that they should** [*will*] **believe these things**.

For several verses, Nephi has been speaking very specifically about the Jews. You will notice that his prophecy now begins to broaden in scope to include the gathering of all of Israel in the last days. This is typical of Isaiah and other Bible prophets. They will be talking about one thing and even in the middle of a verse, they will make the transition to other related topics.

17 **And the Lord will set his hand again the second time** [*in the last days; see Jacob 6:2 and the heading to Jacob 6*] **to restore his people from their lost and fallen state**. Wherefore, he will proceed to do **a marvelous work and a wonder** [*the Restoration of the gospel through Joseph Smith*] among the children of men [*in all the earth*].

18 **Wherefore** [*in this whole process of restoring the gospel*], **he shall bring forth his words unto them** [*the Jews*], which words shall judge them at the last day, for they shall be given them for the purpose of convincing them of the true Messiah, who was rejected by them; and unto the convincing of them that they need not look forward any more for a Messiah to come, for there should not any come, save it should be a false Messiah which should deceive the people; for **there is save** [*only*] **one Messiah** spoken of by the prophets, **and that Messiah is he** [*Jesus Christ*] **who should be rejected of the Jews**.

19 For according to the words of the prophets, **the Messiah cometh in six hundred years from the time that my father left Jerusalem** [*600 BC*]; and according to the words of the prophets, and also the word of the angel of God, **his name shall be Jesus Christ, the Son of God.**

Nephi certainly does teach clearly! He emphasizes the simplicity of the gospel next by calling to his readers' minds the brass serpent set up by Moses, so his people, who had been bitten by poisonous snakes, could be healed if they would simply look at it. But it was too simple for many of them! He reminds us that Isaiah's message, too, is beautifully simple: "Turn to Christ and live."

20 And now, my brethren, **I have spoken plainly** that ye cannot err [*you cannot misunderstand what I have taught*]. **And as the Lord God liveth that brought Israel up out of the land of Egypt, and gave unto Moses power that he should heal the nations** [*the twelve tribes of Israel*] **after they had been bitten by the poisonous**

serpents, if they would cast their eyes unto the serpent [*the brass serpent Moses made and put up on a pole for his people to see*] **which he did raise up before them**, and also gave him power that he should smite the rock and the water should come forth [*symbolic of the "living waters" from Christ; see John 10:4*]; yea, behold I say unto you, that **as these things are true**, and as the Lord God liveth, **there is none other name given under heaven save it be this Jesus Christ, of which I have spoken, whereby man can be saved.** [*In other words, it is just that simple. You can be saved by Christ. No one else can save you.*]

21 **Wherefore, for this cause hath** [*this is why*] **the Lord God promised unto me that these things** [*Nephi's part of the Book of Mormon*] **which I write shall be kept and preserved, and handed down unto my seed** [*posterity; the Lamanites*], from generation to generation, **that the promise may be fulfilled unto Joseph** [*who was sold into Egypt*], **that his seed** [*his posterity, the tribes of Ephraim and Manasseh*] **should never perish as long as the earth should stand.**

22 **Wherefore, these things** [*Nephi's writings on the small plates, which have become part of our Book of Mormon*] **shall go from generation to generation as long as the earth shall stand**; and they shall go according to the will and pleasure of God [*according to His timetable*]; **and the nations who shall possess them shall be judged of them** [*will be held accountable for their knowledge of them*] according to the words which are written.

23 For **we labor diligently to write** [*it is very difficult to make metal plates and write on them*], **to persuade our children, and also our brethren, to believe in Christ**, and to be reconciled to God [*to be at peace with God*]; for we know that **it is by grace that we are saved, after all we can do.**

The last phrase of verse 23, above, is a very important doctrinal statement. Many Christians today are taught that it is by grace that they are saved, and that works are not a part of the requirements for salvation. They misquote Paul and ignore James, chapter 2:17–24. Nephi leaves no doubt as to the need for both faith and works in order to have the grace of Christ save us. "Grace" in the simplest terms means "help of Christ."

24 And, notwithstanding [*even though*] we believe in Christ, **we keep the law of Moses, and look forward with steadfastness unto**

Christ, until the law [*of Moses*] **shall be fulfilled.**

The law of Moses was designed to point the people's minds toward Christ and the great sacrifice for their sins, which He would offer through the Atonement.

25 **For, for this end** [*purpose*] **was the law** [*the law of Moses*] **given**; wherefore [*this is why*] the law hath become dead unto us [*is no longer uppermost in our minds, even though we keep it*], and **we are made alive in Christ** [*we are being saved through the Atonement of Christ*] **because of our faith**; yet we keep the law [*of Moses*] because of the commandments [*because we are told to do so by God for the time being until Christ comes to begin His mortal ministry*].

The next verse is an excellent one to quote to anyone who claims that we do not believe in Christ.

26 And **we talk of Christ, we rejoice in Christ, we preach of Christ, we prophesy of Christ**, and we write according to our prophecies, that our children may know to what source they may look for a remission of their sins.

Verse 27, next, is perhaps one of the best and simplest summaries anywhere in scripture of the purpose of the law of Moses in relationship to the gospel of Jesus Christ. If the Jews at the time of Christ had allowed themselves to understand this, which was clearly taught by Old Testament prophets according to Nephi, they would have welcomed Jesus.

27 **Wherefore** [*this is why*], **we speak concerning the law** [*the law of Moses*] **that our children may know the deadness of the law** [*that it does not have the power to save us*]; **and they, by knowing the deadness of the law, may look forward unto that life** [*eternal life; exaltation*] **which is in Christ**, and know for what end [*purpose*] the law was given [*so that our children will understand why the law of Moses was given*]. And after the law [*of Moses*] is fulfilled in Christ, that they need not harden their hearts against him [*like the Jews will when He comes among them*] when the law ought to be done away [*it was intended that the law of Moses be done away with by Christ*].

It appears that Nephi's people are becoming less committed to God and more hardened against spiritual things, and that some apostasy is settling in among them. We conclude this because of what Nephi says next.

28 And **now behold, my people, ye are a stiffnecked people**; wherefore [*this is why*], **I have spoken plainly unto you, that ye cannot misunderstand**. And the words which I have spoken

shall stand as a testimony against you; for they are sufficient to teach any man the right way; for **the right way is to believe in Christ and deny him not**; for by denying him ye also deny the prophets and the law [*the Old Testament teachings about Christ*].

> The "prophets," at the end of verse 28, above, are the Old Testament prophets such as Abraham, Enoch, Isaiah, Jeremiah, and so forth. The "law" consists of the writings of Moses: namely, Genesis, Exodus, Leviticus, Numbers, and Deuteronomy.

29 And now behold, I say unto you that **the right way is to believe in Christ**, and deny him not; and **Christ is the Holy One of Israel**; wherefore **ye must bow down before him, and worship him with all your might, mind, and strength, and your whole soul**; and if ye do this ye shall in nowise be cast out [*you will by no means lose your exaltation in celestial glory*].

> Nephi is speaking to his own people next as he tells them that they are obligated to keep the law of Moses until Christ comes to earth to fulfill it.

30 And, inasmuch as it shall be expedient [*necessary*], **ye must keep the performances and ordinances of God** [*the sacrifices and detailed rules of the law of Moses*] **until the law shall be fulfilled which was given unto Moses**.

2 NEPHI 26

Having explained the simple, basic messages of Isaiah to his people, in chapter 25, Nephi now continues, prophesying about the ministry of the Savior to the people in America, after He has been crucified by the Jews. He will continue, even prophesying about the last days in which we now live.

Nephi is a great teacher and we are very fortunate to have him teaching us now, in this part of the Book of Mormon. You may wish to pay special attention to the parts of Nephi's prophecies and teachings that apply especially to you as one who is living in the last days before the Second Coming of Christ.

1 **AND after Christ shall have risen from the dead he shall show himself unto you, my children, and my beloved brethren** [*Nephi's righteous descendants, the Nephites, who are around when Christ comes to America*]; **and the words which he shall speak unto you shall be the law which ye shall do**. [*In other words, you will no longer be required to live the law of Moses. Rather, you will live according to the gospel as taught by Christ.*]

2 For behold, I say unto you that **I have beheld** [*I have seen in vision*] **that many generations shall**

pass away, and there shall be great wars and contentions among my people [*including those recorded in Alma and Helaman*].

Next, after prophesying about the signs that will be given among the Nephites and Lamanites in America concerning the Savior's mortal mission, Nephi will explain why some people will be killed in the destructions which precede the coming of Christ to America.

Many of my students over the years have asked, "How good do you have to be to not be destroyed by the fire at the Second Coming of the Savior?" We understand from verse 3, below, that those who live telestial lifestyles or below will be destroyed by fire at the Second Coming. Therefore, anyone who is living a terrestrial (D&C 76:71–79) lifestyle or a celestial (D&C 76:50–53) lifestyle will be spared.

3 And **after the Messiah shall come** [*is born in Bethlehem*] **there shall be signs given unto my people of his birth** [*see Helaman 14:3–6*], and also of his death and resurrection [*see Helaman 14:20–28*]; and **great and terrible shall that day be unto the wicked** [*when the resurrected Christ comes to visit the Nephites*], for they shall perish; and **they perish because they cast out the prophets, and the saints, and stone them, and slay them**; wherefore the cry of the blood of the saints shall ascend up to God from the ground against them.

Nephi's prophecy of burning in verse 4, next, can apply to those of his descendants who were destroyed by fire (3 Nephi 9:9) as well as to the burning of the wicked at the time of the Second Coming.

4 Wherefore, **all those who are proud, and that do wickedly, the day that cometh shall burn them up**, saith the Lord of Hosts, for they shall be as stubble [*dry grain stalks, straw*].

5 And **they that kill the prophets, and the saints, the depths of the earth shall swallow them up**, saith the Lord of Hosts; and **mountains shall cover them**, and **whirlwinds shall carry them away**, and **buildings shall fall upon them** and crush them to pieces and grind them to powder.

6 And they shall be visited [*punished*] with **thunderings**, and **lightnings**, and **earthquakes**, and **all manner of destructions**, for the fire of the anger of the Lord shall be kindled against them, **and they shall be as stubble** [*they will be like dry straw in a wildfire*], **and the day that cometh** [*the coming of the Lord*] **shall consume them, saith the Lord of Hosts.**

As we read the previous verses about the destruction of the wicked at the coming of Christ to the Nephites, we see many parallels between that and the Second Coming.

This vision was very hard on Nephi because of his kindness and tenderness, as we see in verse 7, next. While he wishes that such destructions might not take place, he realizes that the law of justice must not be robbed (see Alma 42:25).

7 **O the pain, and the anguish of my soul for the loss of the slain of my people!** For I, Nephi, have seen it, and it well nigh consumeth me before the presence of the Lord; but I must cry unto my God: Thy ways are just.

Next, Nephi reminds us of the attitudes and behaviors of the righteous who will not be destroyed.

8 But behold, **the righteous** that **hearken unto the words of the prophets**, and destroy them not [*literally, don't destroy the prophets; symbolically, don't destroy the words of the prophets by ignoring them*], but **look forward unto Christ with steadfastness** [*steadiness*] for the signs which are given, notwithstanding [*in spite of*] all persecution—behold, **they are they which shall not perish.**

Looking back at verse 8, above, one way for us in our day of ignoring the prophets might be if you decided not to watch general conference when you otherwise could.

9 But **the Son of righteousness** [*Christ*] **shall appear unto them** [*in America, as recorded in Third Nephi, starting with chapter 11*]; **and he shall heal them**, and **they shall have peace with him**, until three generations shall have passed away, and many of the fourth generation shall have passed away in righteousness [*200 years of peace among the Nephites, after the Savior's visit to them; see 4 Nephi 1:1–22*].

10 **And when these things** [*the two hundred years of peace*] **have passed away a speedy destruction cometh unto my people**; for, notwithstanding the pains of my soul, **I have seen it**; wherefore, I know that it shall come to pass; and **they sell themselves for naught** [*things of no value*]; for, for the reward of their **pride** and their **foolishness** they shall reap destruction; for because **they yield unto the devil and choose works of darkness** [*wickedness*] **rather than light**, therefore they must go down to hell.

A very sobering warning is given to all of us in verse 11, next. There are eternal laws by which the Lord is bound, such that He will never overule our agency. Therefore, if we choose to sin and live wickedly, and demonstrate our choices by our actions, His Spirit must withdraw from us.

11 For **the Spirit of the Lord will not always strive** [*work*] **with man.** And **when the Spirit ceaseth to strive with man then cometh speedy destruction,** and this grieveth my soul.

Verse 12, next, uses the word "Gentile." As I mentioned to you a while back, the word "Gentile" has many different meanings depending on the situation in which it is used. This is what is called "context." In other words, the meaning of "Gentiles" is always "context sensitive." Verse 12, next, is an example of this. In this case it means everyone who is not a Jew.

Nephi's message here is that not only must the Jews be convinced that Jesus is the Christ, but also the Gentiles.

12 And as I spake concerning the convincing of the Jews, that Jesus is the very Christ, **it must needs be** [*it is necessary that*] **that the Gentiles be convinced also that Jesus is the Christ, the Eternal God;**

The term "Eternal God" is context sensitive. In this case, it means Christ. In other contexts, it can mean the Father.

Next, Nephi teaches the necessary role of the Holy Ghost in bearing witness of Christ and teaching us about the Savior.

13 And that **he** [*Christ*] **manifesteth himself unto all those who believe in him, by the power of the Holy Ghost;** yea, unto every nation, kindred, tongue, and people, working mighty miracles, signs, and wonders, among the children of men according to their faith.

Next, Nephi teaches things of extra interest to us, since we live in the last days and are watching the fulfillment of many of these prophecies.

14 But behold, **I prophesy unto you concerning the last days** [*the final days leading up to the Second Coming of the Savior*]; concerning the days when the Lord God shall bring these things [*the Book of Mormon*] forth unto the children of men.

Nephi uses military imagery next as he describes the Lord's efforts to humble His people sufficiently that they will return to Him.

15 **After my seed** [*the Nephites*] **and the seed of my brethren** [*the Lamanites*] **shall have dwindled in unbelief** [*have gradually left God and the gospel*], **and shall have been smitten** [*very badly treated*] **by the Gentiles** [*the early immigrants and settlers who came to America*]; yea, **after the Lord God shall have camped**

against them round about [*surrounded them with punishments because of their wickedness*], **and shall have laid siege against them with a mount, and raised forts against them** [*symbolism for being attacked by punishments from God*]; **and after they shall have been brought down low in the dust** [*after they have been humbled*], even that they are not [*even to the point that they are virtually destroyed as a people*], **yet the words of the righteous** [*the Book of Mormon prophets*] **shall be written, and the prayers of the faithful shall be heard, and all those who have dwindled in unbelief shall not be forgotten** [*the gospel will be restored to them*].

16 For **those who shall be destroyed** [*the Book of Mormon peoples*] **shall speak unto them** [*all people in the last days*] **out of the ground** [*out of the Hill Cumorah where Joseph Smith got the gold plates*], and their speech shall be low out of the dust, and their voice shall be as one that hath a familiar spirit; for the Lord God will give unto him power, that he may whisper concerning them, even as it were out of the ground; and their speech shall whisper out of the dust.

The people speaking "out of the dust" and the term "familiar spirit" as used in verse 16, above, would be familiar phrases to those in Isaiah's and Nephi's day. We will give a quote from Daniel H. Ludlow in the 1996 *Book of Mormon Student Manual* used in the Institutes of Religion of the Church for explanation of these terms. It is as follows:

"Nephi is evidently quoting from a statement found in **Isaiah 29:4** when he refers to a destroyed people whose record shall come '**out of the ground, and their speech shall be low out of the dust, and their voice shall be as one that hath a familiar spirit**' (2 Nephi 26:16).

"A careful reading of this scripture, particularly when read together with Nephi's explanation, would indicate that the term it **'hath a familiar spirit'** means that this record (the Book of Mormon) would **speak with a 'familiar voice' to those who already have the Bible**. In other words, Nephi is evidently saying here that **the doctrinal teachings of the Book of Mormon would seem familiar to people who had already read and accepted the Bible"** (Ludlow, *A Companion to Your Study of the Book of Mormon*, pp. 37 and 146; *Book of Mormon Student Manual*, p. 36).

17 For thus saith the Lord God: **They** [*Book of Mormon prophets*] **shall write the things which shall be done among them, and they**

shall be written and sealed up in a book [*the gold plates*], and those who have dwindled in unbelief shall not have them, for they seek to destroy the things of God. [*In other words, the gold plates will be protected from those wicked who would destroy them, perhaps by melting them down and selling the gold for profit.*]

18 Wherefore, as **those who have been destroyed have been destroyed speedily**; and the multitude of **their terrible ones** [*tyrants, powerful wicked leaders*] **shall be as chaff** [*the very lightweight husks of wheat that are removed in the threshing process*] **that passeth away** [*that blows away in the wind*]—yea, thus saith the Lord God: **It** [*the prophesied destruction*] **shall be at an instant, suddenly**—

19 And it shall come to pass, that those [*Lamanites*] who have dwindled in unbelief shall be smitten by the hand of the Gentiles [*the early explorers and people such as Cortez, who came to the Americas*].

Nephi is reviewing for us many of the prophecies he saw in vision in 1 Nephi 13. Next, he reviews the building up of many churches during the dark ages and beyond, which led up to the time of Joseph Smith and the Restoration. He points out the motives adopted by many of these churches. Remember that "Gentiles" here means everyone except the Jews.

20 And **the Gentiles are lifted up in** the **pride** of their eyes, and have stumbled, because of the greatness of their stumbling block, that **they have built up many churches**; nevertheless, **they put down the power and miracles of God, and preach** up unto themselves **their own wisdom and their own learning**, **that they may get gain** [*to get money and wealth*] and grind upon the face of the poor [*they don't really care about the poor*].

21 And there are **many churches** built up which **cause envyings**, and **strifes**, and **malice** [*hatred; evil feelings toward one another*].

As Nephi continues, we see our day and age in his prophetic description of the future.

22 And **there are also secret combinations** [*secret groups inspired by the devil, organized to tear down that which is righteous and to get power and to rob and murder; compare with Helaman 6:17–39*], even as in times of old, according to the combinations of **the devil**, for he **is the founder of all these things**; yea, the founder of **murder**, and **works of darkness**; yea, and he leadeth them by the neck with a flaxen cord [*a light, thin string; symbolic of temptations and sins that*

could be relatively easily overcome at first but combined together over time bind you tightly; compare with 2 Nephi 28:8], **until he bindeth them with his strong cords** [*the chains of hell*] **forever**.

Nephi is a powerful teacher and has a great desire to alert us and warn us about Satan's methods for pulling people down. We would do well to listen carefully to what he is teaching us here.

23 For behold, my beloved brethren, I say unto you that **the Lord God worketh not in darkness** [*like the devil does*].

24 **He** [*the Lord*] **doeth not anything save it be for the benefit of the world**; for he loveth the world, even that **he layeth down his own life that he may draw all men unto him** [*giving His own life gave Christ the power to give eternal life to all of us if we follow His gospel*]. Wherefore, he commandeth none that they shall not partake of his salvation [*salvation is available to all people*].

25 Behold, doth he cry unto any, saying: Depart from me? Behold, I say unto you, Nay; but **he saith: Come unto me all ye ends of the earth**, buy milk and honey, without money and without price. [*In other words, it makes no difference how rich or poor you are. The gospel of Jesus Christ is available to all.*]

26 Behold, **hath he commanded any that they should depart out of the synagogues, or out of the houses of worship?** Behold, I say unto you, **Nay** [*No*].

Be careful how you interpret the word "free" in the next verse. Misinterpreted, it could lead to the false beliefs associated with predestination, being saved by grace alone, etc. In the context of Nephi's teachings, it means that Christ's gospel—His Atonement and exaltation—is available to all people, regardless of status or circumstance. By the Final Judgment, everyone, whether here on earth or later in the spirit world [*see D&C 138*] will have been given an absolutely fair and just opportunity to exercise agency to accept or reject the Savior's gift of exaltation.

27 **Hath he commanded any that they should not partake of his salvation?** Behold I say unto you, **Nay**; but he hath given it **free** for all men; and he hath commanded his people that they should persuade all men to repentance [*we are to take the gospel to everyone*].

28 Behold, **hath the Lord commanded any that they should not partake of his goodness?** Behold I say unto you, **Nay**; but **all men are privileged the one like unto the other, and none are forbidden** [*God is completely fair*].

Next, Nephi defines priestcraft. There is much of priestcraft in our world today.

29 He commandeth that **there shall be no priestcrafts**; for, behold, **priestcrafts are that men preach and set themselves up for a light unto the world, that they may get gain** [*to get personal wealth*] **and praise of the world; but they seek not the welfare of Zion**.

Next, Nephi reviews things that lead to exaltation, which is the highest degree of glory in the celestial kingdom, where families are together forever and husbands and wives become gods.

30 Behold, the Lord hath forbidden this thing [*priestcraft*]; wherefore, the Lord God hath given a commandment that **all men should have charity**, which charity is **love**. And except they should have charity they were nothing. Wherefore, **if they should have charity they would not suffer the laborer in Zion to perish**.

31 But the laborer in Zion shall labor for Zion; for **if they labor for money** [*if material possessions become their main goal*] **they shall perish.**

32 And again, the Lord God hath commanded that men should **not murder**; that they should not lie; that they should **not steal**; that they should **not take the name of the Lord their God in vain** [*including making covenants with God in the name of Jesus Christ, and then not keeping them*]; that they should **not envy**; that they should **not have malice** [*hatred*]; that they should **not contend one with another**; that they should **not commit whoredoms** [*sexual immorality*]; and that they should do none of these things; for whoso doeth them shall perish [*die spiritually, and sometimes physically*].

Nephi summarizes his powerful sermon here by emphasizing again that the gospel of Christ is available to all.

33 For **none of these iniquities** [*forms of wickedness*] **come of the Lord**; for he doeth that which is good among the children of men; and he doeth nothing save it be plain unto the children of men; and **he inviteth them all to come unto him and partake of his goodness; and he denieth none that come unto him, black and white, bond and free, male and female; and he remembereth the heathen; and all are alike unto God, both Jew and Gentile** [*in other words, all people*].

2 NEPHI 27

This chapter is similar to Isaiah 29 in the Bible, only it is considerably more accurate since it comes from Nephi's copy of Isaiah taken from the brass plates of Laban.

This prophecy was given by Isaiah about 700 BC, near the end of his ministry. It deals with the last days, including the Restoration of the gospel through the Prophet Joseph Smith and many specific details about the coming forth of the Book of Mormon. It is one of those chapters of scripture that bear extra strong witness of the truth of prophecies given by the Lord's prophets.

Isaiah begins by giving a general prophecy about the out-of-control wickedness that will be among all peoples upon the earth in the last days leading up to the Second Coming of Christ.

1 But, behold, **in the last days, or in the days of the Gentiles** [*when the times of the Gentiles are being fulfilled; see Luke 21:24, meaning when the gospel is being taken to everyone except the Jews*]—yea, behold all the nations of the Gentiles and also the Jews, both those who shall come upon this land [*the land of the Book of Mormon*] and those who shall be upon other lands, yea, even **upon all the lands of the earth**, behold, **they will be drunken** [*out of control*] **with iniquity and all manner of abominations** [*they will be hooked on wickedness; wickedness will be very widespread*]—

2 And **when that day shall come they shall be visited of the Lord of Hosts** [*will receive a wake up call, so to speak, from the Lord*], **with thunder** and with **earthquake**, and with a great **noise**, and with **storm**, and with **tempest**, and with the **flame of devouring fire** [*the burning at the Second Coming; see D&C 5:19*].

Next, Isaiah prophesies that once the gospel is restored in the last days, none will be successful in stopping its progress.

3 **And all the nations that fight against Zion** [*the Lord's work and his people*], and that distress her, **shall be as a dream of a night vision**; yea, it shall be unto them [*wicked nations*], even as unto a hungry man which dreameth, and behold he eateth [*in his dream*] but he awaketh and his soul is empty [*he is still hungry*]; or like unto a thirsty man which dreameth, and behold he drinketh but he awaketh and behold he is faint [*still hungry and thirsty*], and his soul hath appetite; yea, **even so shall the multitude of all the nations be that fight against Mount Zion** [*the Lord's work; they, the wicked, will never be satisfied and will ultimately come up empty.*

Persecutors of the Saints never feel satisfied and can't seem to leave them alone].

4 For **behold, all ye that doeth iniquity** [*who commit sin and live wickedly*], **stay yourselves and wonder** [*stop and think*], for ye shall cry out, and cry; yea, **ye shall be drunken** [*out of control*] **but not with wine**, ye shall stagger but not with strong drink [*you will stagger about in wickedness because you reject the prophets; see verse 5*].

5 For behold, **the Lord hath poured out upon you the spirit of deep sleep** [*has had to withdraw His spirit; you are living in spiritual darkness; compare with Alma 12:11*]. For behold, **ye have closed your eyes**, and **ye have rejected the prophets**; and **your rulers** [*righteous leaders*], **and the seers** [*prophets*] **hath he** [*the Lord*] **covered** [*taken away*] because of your iniquity.

> Next begins an incredibly detailed prophecy of the coming forth of the Book of Mormon. This is a reminder of how completely the Lord knows the future. Remember, that Isaiah is prophesying this about 700 BC, which makes it over 2,500 years before the Book of Mormon was first published in 1830!

6 **And it shall come to pass** [*in the last days; see verse 1*] **that the Lord God shall bring forth unto you the words of a book** [*the Book of Mormon*], and they shall be the words of them which have slumbered [*people who have already passed away, such as Nephi, Mormon, Moroni, etc.*].

7 **And behold the book shall be sealed** [*referring to the sealed portion of the gold plates; see verses 10, 21; see also Ether 5:1*]; and in the book shall be a revelation from God, from the beginning of the world to the ending thereof.

8 Wherefore, because of the things which are sealed up, **the things which are sealed** [*the sealed portion of the plates*] **shall not be delivered** [*translated, etc.*] **in the day of the wickedness and abominations of the people**. Wherefore, the book [*sealed portion*] shall be kept from them.

> The fact that the sealed portion of the plates will not be translated and given to the people while "wickedness and abominations" exist makes us wonder if it might not be until the Millennium before we get the rest of the Book of Mormon. But we do not know for sure.

9 **But the book** [*the unsealed portion of the gold plates*] **shall be delivered unto a man** [*Joseph Smith*], **and he shall deliver** [*translate, etc.*] **the words of the book, which are the words of those who have**

slumbered in the dust [*Book of Mormon prophets*], **and he** [*Joseph Smith*] **shall deliver these words unto another** [*refers prophetically to the incident in which Martin Harris gave a copy of characters taken from the plates to Professor Charles Anthon; see JS—H 1:63–65*];

10 **But the words which are sealed** [*sealed portion of the plates*] **he shall not deliver** [*translate, etc.*], neither shall he deliver the book. For the book shall be sealed by the power of God, **and the revelation which was sealed** [*the sealed portion*] **shall be kept in the book** [*kept with the plates*] **until the own due time of the Lord** [*until the Lord says it is time to translate it; see verse 22*], that they [*the contents of the sealed portion*] may come forth; for behold, **they reveal all things from the foundation of the world unto the end thereof.**

People often wonder what is in the sealed portion of the Book of Mormon plates. Verse 10, above, at least gives us a hint—namely, that they contain "all things from the foundation of the world unto the end thereof." What a treasure that will be!

11 **And the day cometh that the words of the book which were sealed** [*the sealed portion, see verses 8 and 10*] **shall be read upon the house tops** [*shall be made available to everyone*]; and they shall be read by the power of Christ; and all things [*compare with D&C 101:32–34*] shall be revealed unto the children of men which ever have been among the children of men, and which ever will be even unto the end of the earth.

Having spoken some about the sealed portion of the gold plates, which Joseph Smith received from angel Moroni on the Hill Cumorah, next, Isaiah gives specific details about the coming forth of the Book of Mormon as we have it. He will begin by telling about the Three Witnesses to the Book of Mormon.

12 **Wherefore, at that day when the book** [*gold plates*] **shall be delivered** [*by Angel Moroni*] **unto the man** [*Joseph Smith*] **of whom I have spoken, the book shall be hid from the eyes of the world** [*no one will be allowed to see the gold plates*], **that the eyes of none shall behold it save** [*except*] **it be that three witnesses** [*Oliver Cowdery, David Whitmer, and Martin Harris; see D&C 17, heading and verse 1*] **shall behold** [*see*] **it, by the power of God, besides him** [*Joseph Smith*] to whom the book shall be delivered; **and they shall testify to the truth of the book and the things therein.**

We will take a moment here and read the testimony of these three witnesses. Notice how they held carefully to the guidelines given in Isaiah's prophecy, above. In fact, the Lord gave additional instructions to Martin Harris, Oliver Cowdery, and David Whitmer as to what they should say in their testimony, as follows:

D&C 17:3–6

3 And ***after that you have obtained faith, and have seen them with your eyes, you shall testify of them, by the power of God****;*

4 And this you shall do that my servant Joseph Smith, Jun., may not be destroyed, that I may bring about my righteous purposes unto the children of men in this work.

5 And ***ye shall testify that you have seen them****, even as my servant Joseph Smith, Jun., has seen them; for it is by my power that he has seen them, and it is because he had faith.*

6 ***And he has translated the book****, even that part which I have commanded him,* ***and*** *as your Lord and your God liveth* ***it is true.***

Now, let us read the Testimony of Three Witnesses, which you can find at the front of your Book of Mormon:

The Testimony of Three Witnesses

BE IT KNOWN unto all nations, kindreds, tongues, and people, unto whom this work shall come: That ***we****, through the grace of God the Father, and our Lord Jesus Christ,* ***have seen the plates*** *which contain this record, which is a record of the people of Nephi, and also of the Lamanites, their brethren, and also of the people of Jared, who came from the tower of which hath been spoken. And* ***we*** *also* ***know*** *that they have been* ***translated by the gift and power of God****, for his voice hath declared it unto us; wherefore* ***we know of a surety that the work is true****. And we also testify that we have seen the engravings which are upon the plates; and* ***they have been shown unto us by the power of God****, and not of man. And we declare with words of soberness, that an angel of God came down from heaven, and he brought and laid before our eyes, that* ***we beheld and saw the plates, and the engravings thereon; and we know that it is by the grace of God the Father, and our Lord Jesus Christ, that we beheld and bear record that these things are true****. And it is marvelous in our eyes. Nevertheless, the voice of the Lord commanded us that we should bear record of it; wherefore, to be obedient unto the commandments of God,* ***we bear testimony of these things****. And we know that if we are faithful in Christ, we shall rid our garments of the blood of all men, and be found spotless before the judgment-seat of Christ, and shall dwell with him eternally in the heavens. And the honor be to* *the Father, and to the Son, and to the Holy Ghost, which is one God. Amen.*

OLIVER COWDERY
DAVID WHITMER
MARTIN HARRIS

We will now continue with 2 Nephi 27, as of verse 13.

13 And there is **none other which shall view it** [*the gold plates*], **save it be a few** [*except for a few others, including the Eight Witnesses; see their recorded witness at the front of your Book of Mormon*] **according to the will of God**, to bear testimony of his word unto the children of men; for the Lord God hath said that the words of the faithful [*Book of Mormon prophets*] should speak as if it were from the dead.

There is one other recorded witness of the gold plates who was not called upon to bear witness to the world, as directed in verse 13, but who, nevertheless, saw the gold plates. Her name was Mary Whitmer. She is the mother of David Whitmer. Her husband, Peter Whitmer Sr., invited Joseph Smith and Oliver Cowdery to come to the family farm in Fayette, New York, and continue the work of translating the gold plates there, after persecution became too dangerous for them to remain in Harmony, Pennsylvania.

David Whitmer came with his horse and buggy to Harmony and transported Joseph and Oliver to Fayette. Emma Smith stayed behind to finish some details and soon joined Joseph at the Whitmer home in Fayette. Having extra people to feed and take care of was an extra burden for Mother Whitmer, which overwhelmed her at times, but she never complained. One evening, as she went to the barn to milk the cows, Moroni appeared to her and expressed appreciation for her kindness in hosting the Prophet and Oliver and offered to show her the plates so she would know for sure that she was helping with the work of the Lord. He did so. Mary Whitmer's son, David, reported this incident as follows:

"She was met out near the yard by the same old man (the Angel Moroni seen earlier by David, judging by her description of him) who said to her: 'You have been very faithful and diligent in your labors, but you are tired because of the increase of your toil; it is proper therefore that you should receive a witness that your faith may be strengthened.' Thereupon he showed her the plates" (Report of Elders Orson Pratt and Joseph F. Smith, pp. 772–73; spelling standardized). This quote is used in the Institute of Religion student manual for Church history, *Church History in the Fulness of Times*, pp. 57–58).

Next, Isaiah speaks of you and me and all others who will bear their testimony of the truth of the Book of Mormon when it comes forth in the last days.

14 Wherefore, **the Lord God will proceed to bring forth the words of the book; and in the mouth of as many witnesses** [*missionaries, you, me, etc.*] **as seemeth him good will he establish his word**; and wo be unto him that rejecteth the word of God!

Now Isaiah goes back to Joseph Smith as he works on translating the gold plates. As mentioned above, this is an incredibly detailed prophecy of the future.

While in the process, Joseph made a copy of some of the characters or writings on the gold plates for his friend, Martin Harris, who was serving as a scribe for the translation. Martin wanted to take the copy to Professor Charles Anthon in New York who was said to be an expert scholar in ancient languages, to see if the characters really were from an ancient language. Starting with verse 15, next, you will see that Isaiah prophesies what actually took place with Martin Harris and Professor Anthon.

15 But behold, it shall come to pass that the Lord God shall say unto him [*Joseph Smith*] to whom he shall deliver the book: **Take these words which are not sealed** [*a copy of some of the characters from the unsealed portion of the gold plates*] **and deliver them to another** [*Martin Harris*], **that he may show them unto the learned** [*Professor Charles Anthon and Dr. Mitchell; see JS—History 1:64–65*], **saying: Read this**, I pray thee. **And the learned** [*Charles Anthon*] **shall say: Bring hither the book, and I will read them** [*bring me the gold plates, and I will translate them*]**.**

Isaiah even gives details as to the motives of Mitchell and Anthon.

16 And now, **because of the glory of the world and to get gain will they** [*Anthon and Mitchell*] **say this**, and not for the glory of God.

17 **And the man** [*Martin Harris*] **shall say: I cannot bring the book, for it is sealed**.

18 **Then shall the learned say: I cannot read it.**

When Martin Harris told Professor Anthon that he was not allowed to bring the gold plates to him, Anthon said, "I cannot read a sealed book." You can read this in the Pearl of Great Price, Joseph Smith—History, chapter 1, verse 65. It is an exact fulfillment of Isaiah's prophecy!

Next, Isaiah continues with more prophetic detail. He basically says that after Martin Harris takes the copies of the characters to the two language experts, Professor Anthon and Dr. Mitchell, and

Anthon asks Martin to bring the plates to him for him to translate, and Martin say he can't, that Joseph Smith will be the one to translate the plates. Joseph Smith will be worried that he has no training to translate the plates, but Isaiah prophesies that the Lord will help Joseph to do the job.

19 Wherefore it shall come to pass, that **the Lord God will deliver again the book and the words thereof to him** [*Joseph Smith*] **that is not learned** [*who has no education for translating ancient records*]**; and the man that is not learned shall say: I am not learned**.

20 **Then shall the Lord God say unto him** [*Joseph Smith*]: **The learned shall not read them** [*Professors Anthon and Mitchell will not be allowed to translate the plates*], for they have rejected them, and **I** [*the Lord*] **am able to do mine own work**; wherefore **thou shalt read** [*you will translate*] **the words which I shall give unto thee** [*with the help of the Urim and Thummim*].

21 **Touch not the things which are sealed** [*don't even peek at the sealed portion of the gold plates*], **for I will bring them forth in mine own due time**; for I will show unto the children of men that I am able to do mine own work.

22 Wherefore, **when thou** [*Joseph Smith*] **hast read the words which I have commanded thee** [*when you have finished the translation of the portion of the Book of Mormon plates that I want you to*], **and obtained the witnesses which I have promised unto thee**, then shalt thou **seal up the book again, and hide it up unto me**, that I may preserve the words which thou hast not read [*the sealed portion*], until I shall see fit in mine own wisdom to reveal all things unto the children of men.

With respect to the instruction to "hide it up unto me" in verse 22, above, it is interesting to note that as Joseph Smith finished the translation of the plates, he and Oliver Cowdery did just that. Brigham Young relates that they took the plates back to the Hill Cumorah, where the hill opened up for them and they entered a large room filled with other plates and records. This incident is related by Brigham Young in the *Journal of Discourses*, 19:38 as follows.

"I will take the liberty to tell you of another circumstance that will be as marvelous as anything can be. This is an incident in the life of Oliver Cowdery, but he did not take the liberty of telling such things in meeting as I take. I tell these things to you, and I have a motive for doing so. I want to carry them to the ears of my brethren and sisters, and to the children also, that they may grow to an understanding of some things that seem to be entirely hidden from the human family. Oliver Cowdery went with the Prophet Joseph when he deposited these plates. Joseph did not translate all of the plates; there was a portion of them sealed, which you can learn from the Doctrine and Covenants. When Joseph got the plates, the angel instructed him to carry them back to the hill Cumorah, which he did. Oliver says that when Joseph and Oliver went there, the hill opened, and they walked into a cave, in which there was a large and spacious room. He says he did not think, at the time, whether they had the light of the sun or artificial light; but that it was just as light as day.

"They laid the plates on a table; it was a large table that stood in the room. Under this table there was a pile of plates as much as two feet high, and there were altogether in this room more plates than probably many wagon loads; they were piled up in the corners and along the walls. The first time they went there the sword of Laban hung upon the wall; but when they went again it had been taken down and laid upon the table across the gold plates; it was unsheathed, and on it was written these words: 'This sword will never be sheathed again until the kingdoms of this world become the kingdom of our God and his Christ.' I tell you this as coming not only from Oliver Cowdery, but others who were familiar with it, and who understood it just as well as we understand coming to this meeting, enjoying the day, and by and by we separate and go away, forgetting most of what is said, but remembering some things. So is it with other circumstances in life. I relate this to you, and I want you to understand it. I take this liberty of referring to those things so that they will not be forgotten and lost" (Young, *Journal of Discourses*, 19:38–39).

In verse 23, next, Isaiah's prophecy says that the Lord Himself bears testimony that He is capable of getting this work done.

23 **For behold, I am God; and I am a God of miracles**; and I will show unto the world that I am the same yesterday, today, and forever [*I use the same gospel to save people; I am totally reliable, dependable*]; and **I work not among the children of men save it be according to their faith**.

Isaiah teaches another important lesson to us at the end of verse 23, above. It is basically that we determine how much the Lord is involved in our lives by our agency as we exercise faith in Him or as we chose not to exercise faith in Him.

Next, continuing the amazing detail contained in this prophecy, Isaiah tells us one of the things the Savior will tell Joseph Smith during the First Vision in the spring of 1823, when the Father and the Son appeared to young Joseph.

24 **And again it shall come to pass that the Lord shall say unto him** [*Joseph Smith; see JS—History 1:19*] **that shall read** [*translate*] **the words** [*the gold plates*] that shall be delivered him:

Jesus quoted Isaiah, next, as He answered Joseph Smith's question as to which church to join, during the First Vision.

25 Forasmuch as this people draw near unto me with their mouth, and with their lips do honor me, but have removed their hearts far from me, and their fear towards me [*their concept of God*] is taught by the precepts of men—

26 Therefore, **I will proceed to do a marvelous** [*"astonishing"*] **work among this people, yea, a marvelous work and a wonder** [*the Restoration of the gospel through Joseph Smith*], for the wisdom [*the false wisdom*] of their wise and learned shall perish, and the understanding of their prudent shall be hid [*pushed aside by revealed truth*].

27 And **wo unto them** [*the wicked*] **that seek deep to hide their counsel** [*evil plots*] **from the Lord!** And their works are in the dark; and they say: Who seeth us, and who knoweth us? And they also say: Surely, your turning of things upside down [*twisting of truth to make it fit their own teachings*] shall be esteemed as [*will be like*] the potter's clay [*claiming they can get along without God, like the situation described in Isaiah 45:9, where the potter's clay tries to tell the potter what to do*]. **But behold, I will show unto them** [*the wicked*], **saith the Lord of Hosts, that I know all their works**. For shall the work [*the pot*] say of him [*the potter*] that made it, he made me not? Or shall the thing framed [*the building or whatever*] say of him [*the carpenter, craftsman*] that framed it [*built it*], he had no understanding [*he doesn't know me; "God doesn't know us. We can be wicked and successfully hide from God"; or, "You wicked are just as foolish as the potter's clay that claims it made itself into a pot and has no accountability to its maker."*]?

Next, Isaiah will prophesy that the land of Israel will blossom with literal forests and with truth, spiritual growth, etc., after the Restoration. This is being very dramatically fulfilled, literally, today, as millions upon millions of trees are being planted in the southern portions of the Holy Land. It appears that significant spiritual growth for the Jews is yet future.

28 But **behold, saith the Lord of Hosts: I will show unto the children of men** [*all people*] **that it is yet a very little while** [*after the Book of Mormon comes forth*] **and Lebanon** [*the Holy Land*] **shall be turned into a fruitful field; and the fruitful field shall be esteemed as a forest**.

Next, Isaiah continues his prophecy by showing us what the results of the coming forth of the Book of Mormon and the Restoration of the true Church will be.

29 **And in that day shall the deaf hear the words of the book, and the eyes of the blind shall see out of obscurity and out of darkness** [*the spiritually deaf and blind will be healed of their lack of personal spirituality as a result of the Restoration, Book of Mormon, etc.*].

30 And **the meek also shall increase** [*shall gain strength and power with God*], and **their joy shall be in the Lord**, and **the poor among men shall rejoice in the Holy One of Israel** [*the righteous will know the Savior again*].

31 For assuredly as the Lord liveth they shall see that **the terrible one** [*tyrants, wicked rulers*] **is brought to naught** [*is reduced to nothing*], **and the scorner** [*one who ridicules the work of the Lord*] **is consumed**, **and all that watch for iniquity** [*in Church leaders and members; see D&C 45:50*] **are cut off**;

Next, in verse 32, Isaiah continues with more examples of dishonest people who will eventually be cut off by the Lord.

32 And **they that make a man an offender for a word** [*via corrupt lawyers and corrupt judicial system*], **and lay a snare for him that reproveth in the gate** [*try to destroy the honest person who attempts to straighten out corrupt governments, etc.; the "gate" was an alcove in Jerusalem's wall where officials and citizens met to discuss matters*], **and turn aside the just for a thing of naught** [*destroy good people for unimportant matters*].

In a fascinating and ingenious way, Isaiah next portrays Jacob, the father of the twelve sons who eventually became the twelve tribes of Israel, as having been embarrassed over the centuries to admit that the Israelites are related to him. However, in the last days, after the Book of Mormon is published, when Israelites (including us) are strong, faithful Saints, Jacob is no longer embarrassed to claim us as his posterity. Rather, he is proud to be our ancestor.

33 Therefore, thus saith the Lord, who redeemed Abraham, concerning the house of Jacob [*Israel; God's covenant people*]: **Jacob shall not now be ashamed**, neither shall

his face now wax pale [*Father Jacob will no longer have to be embarrassed about the behavior of his posterity*].

34 But **when he seeth his children** [*his posterity being faithful to God in the last days*], **the work of my** [*the Lord's*] **hands** [*now righteous*], in the midst of him, **they** [*righteous Israel*] **shall sanctify my** [*God's*] **name**, and sanctify the Holy One of Jacob [*Christ*], and **shall fear** [*respect*] **the God of Israel** [*Christ*].

Isaiah now summarizes the results of the coming forth of the Book of Mormon and the Restoration of the true Church in one final sentence.

35 **They also that erred in spirit shall come to understanding, and they that murmured shall learn doctrine** [*by studying the truths of the gospel made available by the Book of Mormon and the Restoration of the true Church*].

2 NEPHI 28

Nephi has just helped us to better understand Isaiah's writings regarding the last days, in which we now live, and the coming forth of the Book of Mormon. Now he will explain what Isaiah said and teach us many lessons from it.

1 AND now, behold, my brethren, **I have spoken unto you, according as the Spirit hath constrained** [*instructed*] **me**; wherefore, I know that they [*the prophecies of Isaiah*] must surely come to pass [*be fulfilled*].

2 And **the things which shall be written out of the book** [*the Book of Mormon*] **shall be of great worth unto the children of men** [*all people*], and especially unto our seed [*the Lamanites*], which is a remnant of [*a part of*] the house of Israel [*the descendants of Abraham, Isaac, and Jacob*].

Nephi now explains that there will be much arguing and debating between churches in the last days and warns that such churches will claim to be the Lord's Church.

3 For **it shall come to pass in that day** [*in the last days especially*] **that the churches which are built up, and not unto the Lord** [*and are not the Lord's true Church*], **when the one shall say unto the other: Behold, I, I am the Lord's; and the others shall say: I, I am the Lord's**; and thus shall every one say that hath built up churches, and not unto the Lord—

4 **And they shall contend** [*argue and debate*] **one with another**; and their priests shall contend one with another, and they shall teach with their learning, and deny the Holy Ghost, which giveth utterance.

The phrase "deny the Holy Ghost" in verse 4, above, is not the same as denying the Holy Ghost as in becoming a son of perdition. In this context, it means to refuse to be inspired by the Holy Ghost or to live unworthily of inspiration.

5 **And they deny the power of God**, the Holy One of Israel [*Christ*]; **and they say unto the people: Hearken unto us** [*listen to us*], and hear ye our precept [*listen to our teachings*]; for behold **there is no God today, for the Lord and the Redeemer hath done his work**, and he hath given his power unto men; [*In other words, among other things, they will teach that there is no such thing as more scripture, continuing revelation, prophets and apostles, etc. The Bible is it, and there is nothing beyond that.*]

Nephi continues to describe what false priests and teachers will teach their followers in the last days. We see a lot of such teachings in many religions today, as well as in schools, university classes, and so forth.

6 Behold, hearken ye unto my precept; **if they shall say there is a miracle wrought by the hand of the Lord, believe it not**; for this day he is not a God of miracles; **he hath done his work**. [*In other words, there are no such things as miracles today. They stopped with the Bible.*]

Next, Nephi prophesies that there will be many in the last days who believe in the philosophy that sin is not that big of a deal and we shouldn't worry about it.

7 Yea [*indeed*], and **there shall be many which shall say: Eat, drink, and be merry, for tomorrow we die; and it shall be well with us**.

Next, Nephi warns against those who believe in God and believe in accountability but do not believe that the standards of the gospel are all that strict, nor that God's punishments will be all that bad. We see this all around us today, even among some members of the Church. Satan is quite successful in getting people to believe these ideas.

8 And **there shall also be many which shall say: Eat, drink, and be merry; nevertheless, fear God**—he will justify in committing a little sin; yea, lie a little, take the advantage of one because of his words [*for example, sue people in court because of something they said so you can get their money or stuff*], dig a pit for thy neighbor [*do bad things to others*]; there is no harm in this; and do all these things, for tomorrow we die; **and if it so be that we are guilty, God will beat us with a few stripes** [*punish us with a few gentle*

lashes], **and at last we shall be saved in the kingdom of God**.

9 Yea, and **there shall be many which shall teach after this manner**, false and vain [*useless*] and foolish doctrines, and shall be puffed up in their hearts [*full of pride, thinking that they can change or water down God's commandments*], and shall seek deep to hide their counsels from the Lord [*will try to get away with what they are teaching*]; and their works shall be in the dark [*as Isaiah said in 2 Nephi 27:27*].

10 And the blood of the saints [*righteous people, including prophets, who gave their lives to keep and teach the standards of the gospel*] **shall cry from the ground against them** [*shall bear witness against their false teachings, when the Book of Mormon, which was buried in the ground (the gold plates) comes forth to the world*].

11 Yea, **they have all gone out of the way** [*they have all gone astray from the true gospel of Jesus Christ*]; they have become corrupted.

Nephi now warns us against some of the things that can lead people into such foolish thinking and rebellious behaviors.

12 Because of **pride**, and because of **false teachers**, and **false doctrine**, their churches have become corrupted [*have left the true gospel*], and their churches are lifted up [*are prideful*]; because of pride they are puffed up.

13 **They rob the poor** because of their fine sanctuaries [*they spend their money on fancy churches and don't help the poor and the needy*]; they rob the poor because of their fine clothing; and **they persecute the meek and the poor in heart**, because in their **pride** they are puffed up.

14 **They wear stiff necks and high heads** [*they are full of pride*]; yea, and because of **pride**, and **wickedness**, and **abominations** [*very evil and wicked deeds*], and **whoredoms** [*sexual immorality*], they have all gone astray save it be a few, who are the humble followers of Christ; nevertheless, they are led, that in many instances they do err because they are taught by the precepts of men. [*All the more reason to stick very strictly to the words of our modern prophets.*]

15 O the wise [*in their own minds*], and the learned [*the highly educated who do not have faith in God*], and the rich, that are **puffed up in the pride of their hearts**, and all those who preach **false doctrines**, and all those who **commit whoredoms**, and **pervert** [*twist and misrepresent*] **the right way of the Lord**, wo, wo, wo be unto them, saith

the Lord God Almighty, for they shall be thrust down to hell!

Nephi is giving us one of the most powerful sermons ever on the attitudes, philosophies, and behaviors that will lead to the downfall of stable and safe society in the last days.

16 **Wo unto them** [*trouble and punishment will come to those*] **that turn aside the just** [*the righteous; this can include corrupt judicial systems*] **for a thing of naught** [*for something of no significance*] **and revile against that which is good** [*tear down that which is good*], and say that it is of no worth! For the day shall come that the Lord God will speedily visit [*punish*] the inhabitants of the earth; and in that day that they are fully ripe in iniquity they shall perish [*when they get to the point that they are completely wicked, they will be destroyed*].

After describing such awful wickedness and ignoring of God and His commandments, Nephi reminds us that it is still not too late for such people to repent. This is a wonderful reminder of the kindness and mercy of the Lord. He paid for all sins and wants us to accept His gift of the Atonement by repenting as needed. When we repent quickly when we slip up, our life is much happier!

17 But behold, **if the inhabitants of the earth shall repent** of their wickedness and abominations [*extra wicked sins*] **they shall not be destroyed**, saith the Lord of Hosts.

Next, Nephi teaches clearly that Satan and his evil followers will not have power forever.

18 But behold, **that great and abominable church** [*the kingdom of the devil; see 1 Nephi 14:10, 22:22–23*], the whore of all the earth, **must tumble to the earth**, and great must be the fall thereof. [*In other words, when the time is right, Satan's kingdom with all his evil followers will fall.*]

Next, Nephi shows that the Lord will use strong means to try to wake the wicked up so that they can still repent and return to Him. It is clear that He still loves them and wants them to come home to Him.

19 For the kingdom of the devil must shake, and **they** [*the wicked*] **which belong to it must needs be** [*have to be*] **stirred up unto repentance**, or the devil will grasp them with his everlasting chains, and they be stirred up to anger, and perish;

In verse 20, below, Nephi reminds us that one of the devil's most powerful tools is anger against righteousness.

20 For behold, **at that day shall he rage in the hearts of the**

children of men, and stir them up to anger against that which is good.

Perhaps you've noticed that Satan is very cunning. If he can't get people involved in serious wickedness, which often leads to anger against the righteous, he gently convinces them that things aren't as bad as the prophets say, so that they relax in their worldly lifestyles and become sloppy in living the gospel, while still "active in the Church" in their own minds. Nephi describes this next in verse 21.

21 And others will he pacify, and **lull them away into carnal security** [*make them very comfortable in the security of worldly things*], that they will say: All is well in Zion; yea, Zion prospereth, all is well—**and thus the devil cheateth their souls, and leadeth them away carefully down to hell.**

Apostle George Albert Smith, who later became the President of the Church, described how Satan leads people "carefully down to hell" as follows:

"Now, I want you to note that: 'And thus the devil cheateth their souls and leadeth them away carefully down to hell.' And that is the way he does it, that's exactly the way he does it. He does not grab you bodily and take you into his territory, but he whispers, 'Do this little evil,' and when he succeeds in that, another little evil and another, and, to use the expression, 'He cheateth their souls.' That's what he does. He makes you believe you are gaining something when you are losing. So it is every time we fail to observe a law of God or keep a commandment; we are being cheated, because there is no gain in this world or in the world to come but by obedience to the law of our heavenly Father. Then again, that peculiar suggestion, 'And he leadeth them carefully away down to hell' is significant, that is his method. Men and women in the world today are subject to that influence, and they are being drawn here and there, and that whispering is going on and they do not understand what the Lord desires them to do, but they continue in the territory of the evil one, subject to his power where the Spirit of the Lord will not go" (Smith, in Conference Report, Apr. 1918, p. 40).

Next, Nephi describes yet another tool of the devil; namely, he gets them to believe that there is no such thing as hell or the devil.

22 And behold, **others he flattereth away, and telleth them there is no hell**; and **he saith unto them: I am no devil, for there is none**—and **thus he whispereth in their ears, until he grasps them with his awful chains**, from whence there is no deliverance.

Next, Nephi teaches strongly that such people will absolutely have to stand before God someday and be judged for their wickedness.

23 Yea, **they are grasped with death** [*spiritual death; the death of their spirituality*], **and hell**; and death, and hell, and the devil, **and all that have been seized therewith must stand before the throne of God, and be judged according to their works**, from whence they must go into the place prepared for them, even **a lake of fire and brimstone**, which is endless torment.

Near the end of verse 23, above, you saw the phrase, "lake of fire and brimstone." Brimstone is white-hot, molten sulphur, so hot that it is in a liquid state. There is really no such thing as a "lake of fire and brimstone," but the words are designed to make the wicked realize that, unless they repent, they will end up in hell, and it is not a fun place to be.

Symbolically, Nephi now summarizes what he has taught so well in the previous verses.

24 Therefore, **wo be unto him that is at ease in Zion** [*doesn't worry much about living the gospel*]!

25 **Wo be unto him that crieth: All is well** [*the world is not as wicked as the prophets say it is; it is really quite okay*]!

26 Yea, **wo be unto him that hearkeneth** [*believes*] **unto the precepts** [*teachings and philosophies*] **of men, and denieth the power of God, and the gift of the Holy Ghost**!

27 Yea, **wo be unto him that saith: We have received, and we need no more** [*we don't need any more revelation from God*]!

28 **And in fine** [*in summary*], **wo unto all those who tremble, and are angry because of the truth of God**! For behold, he that is built upon the rock [*Christ and His gospel*] receiveth it [*the gospel*] with gladness; and he that is built upon a sandy foundation [*the devil's ways*] trembleth lest he shall fall.

Next, Nephi prophesies that there will be many in the last days who will teach that there is no such thing as continuing revelation through modern prophets.

29 **Wo be unto him that shall say: We have received the word of God, and we need no more** of the word of God, for we have enough!

Verse 30, next, is a great lesson in how we can qualify to receive continuing revelation ourselves, both through our prophets and through the Holy Ghost for our personal needs and responsibilities and for continuing personal growth toward God.

30 For behold, thus saith the Lord God: I will give unto the children of men **line upon line, precept upon precept** [*commandment upon commandment; rule upon rule; instruction upon instruction, etc.*], here a little and there a little; and **blessed are those who hearken unto** [*listen to and obey*] **my precepts, and lend an ear unto my counsel**, for they shall learn wisdom; for **unto him that receiveth I will give more**; and **from them that shall say, We have enough, from them shall be taken away even that which they have**.

Perhaps you've noticed someone whom you know who once had a strong testimony but who now does not have it anymore. The last phrase of verse 30, above, explains what has happened.

31 **Cursed** [*to be stopped in progress toward becoming like God*] **is he that putteth his trust in man, or maketh flesh his arm** [*depends on people's thinking rather than listening to God's teachings*], or shall hearken unto the precepts [*the philosophies and teachings*] of men, save [*unless*] their precepts shall be given by the power of the Holy Ghost.

32 **Wo be unto the Gentiles**, saith the Lord God of Hosts! For notwithstanding [*even though*] I shall lengthen out mine arm unto them from day to day [*even though I keep reaching out to them, inviting them to repent and come unto Me*], **they will deny me** [*they refuse*]; **nevertheless, I will be merciful unto them, saith the Lord God, if they will repent and come unto me**; for **mine arm is lengthened out all the day long** [*I will keep trying to save them*], saith the Lord God of Hosts.

2 NEPHI 29

In this chapter, Nephi tells us that there will be much opposition to the Book of Mormon because Satan will succeed in getting people to believe that the Bible is the end of revelation from God. My companions and I ran into this thinking many times during my mission.

These people often quoted from the last chapter of Revelation in the Bible, saying that verse 18 teaches that there can be no more scripture. We will take a moment here and quote Revelation 22:18, and then show what is wrong with their interpretation.

Revelation 22:18

*18 For I testify unto every man that heareth the words of the prophecy of this book, **If any man shall add unto these things, God shall add unto him the plagues that are written in this book:***

One of the problems with using Revelation 22:18 to try to prove that the Book of Mormon cannot be additional revelation from God is that the book of Revelation is not the last book of the New Testament. Bible scholars agree that the Gospel of John (think Matthew, Mark, Luke, and John) was written after John wrote Revelation.

Therefore, the whole gospel of John was written after the book of Revelation. Not only that, but Ezekiel, in the Old Testament, specifically prophesies that there will be a book of scripture that will be added to the Bible (see Ezekiel 37:16–20). This is a direct prophecy of the Book of Mormon (Ezekiel calls it "the stick of Joseph").

And so, it is clear that there will be additional scripture after the Bible. What Revelation 22:18 means is that nobody should add their own false doctrine and thinking to what is written in the book of Revelation or twist its teachings to fit their own incorrect thinking.

In fact, we find a similar warning in Deuteronomy 4:2, in the Old Testament.

Let's see how Nephi tells us that, in the last days, people will reject the Book of Mormon because they believe that the Bible is all the scripture and revelation that God is going to give us.

1 BUT behold, **there shall be many** [*this thought will continue in verse three; you will see another long dash there*]—at that day [*in the last days*] when I [*the Lord*] shall proceed to do a marvelous work among them [*when I restore the gospel among them, including bringing forth the Book of Mormon*], that I may remember [*keep*] my covenants which I have made unto the children of men, that I may set my hand again the second time to recover my people, which are of the house of Israel;

2 And also, that I may remember [*keep*] the promises which I have made unto thee, Nephi, and also unto thy father, that I would remember your seed [*posterity*]; and that the words of your seed should proceed forth out of my mouth unto your seed [*through the Book of Mormon*]; and my words shall hiss [*signal*] forth unto the ends of the earth, for a standard unto my people, which are of the house of Israel;

Next is the specific prophecy that people will oppose the Book of Mormon because they already have the Bible.

3 And because my words shall hiss forth—**many of the Gentiles shall say: A Bible! A Bible! We have got a Bible, and there cannot be any more Bible.**

Watch now as the Lord answers this reasoning for opposing additional revelation and scripture in no uncertain terms! Also, He will give a wonderful compliment to the Jews for giving us what we have in the Bible.

4 But **thus saith the Lord God: O fools, they shall have a Bible; and it shall proceed forth from the Jews**, mine ancient covenant people. And what thank they the Jews for the Bible which they receive from them? Yea, what do the Gentiles [*the non-Jews who got the Bible from the Jews*] mean [*do they give proper credit to the Jews*]? **Do they remember the travails, and the labors, and the pains of the Jews, and their diligence** [*steady, hard work*] **unto me, in bringing forth salvation** [*the teachings of the Bible*] **unto the Gentiles?**

5 **O ye Gentiles, have ye remembered the Jews**, mine ancient covenant people? **Nay**; but ye have cursed them, and have hated them, and have not sought to recover them. But behold, I will return all these things upon your own heads [*you will be held accountable*]; for **I the Lord have not forgotten my people** [*the Jews*].

Next comes one of the favorite quotes of many returned missionaries.

6 **Thou fool, that shall say: A Bible, we have got a Bible, and we need no more Bible**. Have ye obtained a Bible save it were by the Jews?

We are taught next that we are not the only ones who have received revelation and scriptures from the Lord. This reminds us that there are many records yet to come forth in the due time of the Lord.

7 **Know ye not that there are more nations than one?** Know ye not that I, the Lord your God, have created all men, and that I remember those who are upon the isles of the sea [*upon all the continents and in all nations*]; and that I rule in the heavens above and in the earth beneath; **and I bring forth my word unto the children of men, yea, even upon all the nations of the earth?**

8 **Wherefore murmur ye** [*why do you complain*], **because that ye shall receive more of my word?** Know ye not that the testimony of two nations is a witness unto you that I am God, that I remember one nation like unto another? Wherefore, I speak the same words unto one nation like unto another. And when the two nations shall run together the testimony of the two nations shall run together also.

9 And I do this that I may prove unto many that I am the same yesterday, today, and forever [*I am*

completely fair to all people]; and that I speak forth my words according to mine own pleasure. And **because that I have spoken one word ye need not suppose that I cannot speak another; for my work is not yet finished; neither shall it be until the end of man, neither from that time henceforth and forever.** [*In other words, there will be no end to continuous revelation.*]

10 Wherefore, **because that ye have a Bible ye need not suppose that it contains all my words**; neither need ye suppose that I have not caused more to be written.

11 For **I command all men, both in the east and in the west, and in the north, and in the south, and in the islands of the sea, that they shall write the words which I speak unto them**; for out of the books which shall be written I will judge the world, every man according to their works, according to that which is written.

12 For behold, **I shall speak unto the Jews and they shall write it** [*the Bible*]; **and I shall also speak unto the Nephites and they shall write it** [*the Book of Mormon*]; **and I shall also speak unto the other tribes of the house of Israel, which I have led away, and they shall write it** [*they have written scriptures too*]; **and I shall also speak unto all nations of the earth and they shall write it** [*still more written scriptures*].

13 And it shall come to pass that **the Jews shall have the words of the Nephites** [*the Book of Mormon*], **and the Nephites shall have the words of the Jews** [*the Bible*]; **and the Nephites and the Jews shall have the words of the lost tribes of Israel**; and **the lost tribes of Israel shall have the words of the Nephites and the Jews.** [*In other words, the time will come when we will have all these scriptures!*]

It is important to note in verse 14, next, that there are many lands to which the house of Israel will be gathered. In a significant sense, members today are being "gathered" to stakes of Zion wherever they live.

Hopefully, you have noticed that our modern prophets today are saying much about the gathering of Israel. No doubt, you will hear much more. It is exciting to realize that each of us is playing a role in this mighty gathering of Israel in preparation for the Second Coming of the Savior. As we help others to live the gospel and come unto Christ, we are helping to "gather Israel."

14 And it shall come to pass that **my people, which are of the**

house of Israel, shall be gathered home unto the lands of their possessions; and my word also shall be gathered in one [*all of the written scriptures will support and strengthen each other, as is the case with the Bible and the Book of Mormon*]. And **I will show unto them that fight against my word and against my people, who are of the house of Israel, that I am God, and that I covenanted with Abraham that I would remember** [*keep My promises to*] **his seed** [*posterity*] forever.

2 NEPHI 30

As Nephi finishes his message to his people (and to us) in this chapter, he reminds all of us that God is completely fair and that all people will ultimately get a completely fair chance to hear, understand, and accept or reject the gospel. In other words, everyone will have a fair chance to be part of the Lord's covenant people. No one is favored over another as the big picture unfolds.

1 AND now behold, my beloved brethren, I would speak unto you; for **I, Nephi, would not suffer** [*allow*] **that ye should suppose that ye are more righteous than the Gentiles shall be.** For behold, except ye [*unless you*] shall keep the commandments of God ye shall all likewise perish; and because of the words which have been spoken **ye need not suppose that the Gentiles are utterly destroyed**.

Next, Nephi emphasizes that choosing whether or not to become part of the Lord's covenant people is a matter of individual agency. And anyone who choses to repent, be baptized, and live the gospel becomes a member of God's covenant people—in other words, a member of the Church.

2 For behold, I say unto you that **as many of the Gentiles as will repent are the covenant people of the Lord** [*all people who are baptized and remain faithful are part of the Lord's covenant people*]; **and as many of the Jews as will not repent shall be cast off** [*will no longer be part of the Lord's covenant people*]; **for the Lord covenanteth with none save it be** [*except*] **with them that repent and believe in his Son**, who is the Holy One of Israel.

As Nephi continues, he teaches about the coming forth of the Book of Mormon and shows that when it comes, it means that the last days before the Second Coming of Christ are just beginning. The Book of Mormon will be a major tool for converting people to The Church of Jesus Christ of Latter-day Saints, and they will take the Book of Mormon to Nephi's descendants, the Lamanites. And so, Nephi's descendants will also get the chance to learn about who they are and return to Christ.

3 And now, I would prophesy somewhat more concerning the Jews and the Gentiles. For **after the book** [*the Book of Mormon*] **of which I have spoken shall come forth, and be written unto the Gentiles** [*translated and be taken out to the Gentiles by missionaries from the Church*], and sealed up again unto the Lord [*and the gold plates are returned to the Hill Cumorah for safe keeping; see* Journal of Discourses, *volume 19, page 38*], **there shall be many which shall believe the words which are written** [*many will believe the Book of Mormon and be converted to the Church*]; **and they** [*the converts*] **shall carry them** [*the words of the Book of Mormon*] **forth unto the remnant of our seed** [*the Lamanites*].

4 **And then shall the remnant of our seed know concerning us** [*the Book of Mormon peoples*], **how that we came out from Jerusalem, and that they are descendants of the Jews** [*that their ancestors, Lehi and his family, originally came from the Holy Land*].

5 **And the gospel of Jesus Christ shall be declared among them** [*the Lamanites*]; wherefore, **they shall be restored unto the knowledge of their fathers** [*ancestors*], **and also to the knowledge of Jesus Christ**, which was had among their fathers.

6 **And then shall they rejoice**; for they shall know that it is a blessing unto them from the hand of God; **and their scales of darkness** [*spiritual darkness*] **shall begin to fall from their eyes**; and many generations shall not pass away among them, save [*until*] **they shall be a pure and a delightsome people**.

You and I are witnesses of the tremendous work now taking place among the Lamanites, especially in places such as Mexico, Central America, and South America. The fulfillment of Nephi's prophecy about the Book of Mormon being taken to his descendants is underway on a grand scale!

Next, the Lord turns our attention to the future gathering of the Jews and their conversion to believe in Christ. Most Jews today still do not believe that Jesus is the Son of God, so this part of Nephi's prophecy is still going to happen in the future.

7 And it shall come to pass that **the Jews** which are scattered **also shall begin to believe in Christ; and they shall begin to gather in upon the face of the land** [*they will start to be gathered back to their original lands, after the Book of Mormon comes through Joseph Smith*]; **and as many as**

shall believe in Christ shall also become a delightsome people. [*In other words, they too will be set free from spiritual darkness and unbelief in Christ.*]

Again, a reminder that the coming forth of the Book of Mormon is a very significant point in the history of the earth. Its coming forth signals the final Restoration of the gospel before the Second Coming of the Lord. It will bring the final great gathering of Israel to the true gospel, out of all the earth, in preparation for the final prophesied scenes before the Savior comes. In order for this gathering to be accomplished, we must take the gospel to all nations. This work is certainly underway. You are watching it and will no doubt help with it if you stay active and faithful in the Church.

8 **And it shall come to pass that the Lord God shall commence his work** [*begin His work after the Book of Mormon comes forth*] **among all nations, kindreds, tongues, and people** [*in other words, throughout the whole world*], to bring about the restoration of his people upon the earth [*the gathering of Israel*].

9 And **with righteousness shall the Lord God judge** the poor, and reprove with equity for the meek of the earth. And he shall smite the earth with the rod of his mouth; and with the breath of his lips shall he slay the wicked.

Next, Nephi tells us that in the last days, as the Second Coming gets closer, there will be a more and more obvious division between those who stay loyal to the gospel of Christ and those who do not. It appears that there will be less and less "gray area." You are either with the Lord or far away from Him.

These divisions between the righteous and the wicked will become wider and wider until the actual Second Coming, at which time the wicked will be burned and thus the "division" will be complete.

10 For the time speedily cometh that the Lord God shall cause a great division among the people, and **the wicked will he destroy; and he will spare his people,** yea, **even if it so be that he must destroy the wicked by fire** [*which He will at the Second Coming*].

Next, Nephi quotes Isaiah, who uses symbolism to tell us that when the Savior comes to rule the earth for the Millennium, He will be a wonderfully righteous ruler.

11 **And righteousness shall be the girdle of his loins** [*symbolically, Christ will be dressed in righteousness*], **and faithfulness the girdle of his reins** [*symbolically, Christ will be dressed in faithfulness; reins (kidneys) symbolized the deepest feelings and desires of the heart in Isaiah's day; Nephi is quoting Isaiah's prophecy in 2 Nephi 21:5*].

The great, final division between the righteous and the wicked, spoken of above, will bring in the Millennium, as depicted in the remaining verses of this chapter. Watch how Isaiah uses animals that are usually enemies to each other to symbolize the wonderful peace that will exist during the Millennium.

12 And **then shall the wolf dwell** [*live*] **with the lamb**; and **the leopard shall lie down with the kid** [*baby goat*], and **the calf, and the young lion, and the fatling, together**; and **a little child shall lead them** [*herd them without being in danger*]. [*There will be peace during the Millennium.*]

13 And **the cow and the bear shall feed** [*graze together*]; **their young ones shall lie down together**; and the lion shall eat straw like the ox.

14 And **the sucking** [*nursing*] **child shall play on the hole of the asp** [*will play with formerly poisonous serpents*], and **the weaned child** [*toddler*] **shall put his hand on the cockatrice's** [*poisonous serpent's*] **den**.

15 **They shall not hurt nor destroy in all my holy mountain** [*the entire world will be at peace during the Millennium*]; for **the earth shall be full of the knowledge of the Lord** as the waters cover the sea [*the gospel of Christ will eventually cover the whole earth*].

16 Wherefore, **the things of all nations shall be made known**; yea, all things shall be made known unto the children of men. [*If it hasn't already happened by this time, this sounds like the time when all the records or scriptures of other nations will come forth.*]

17 There is nothing which is secret save it shall be revealed; there is no work of darkness save it shall be made manifest in the light; and there is nothing which is sealed upon the earth save it shall be loosed.

18 Wherefore, **all things which have been revealed unto the children of men shall at that day be revealed**; and **Satan shall have power over the hearts of the children of men no more, for a long time** [*for a thousand years; see D&C 29:11*]. And now, my beloved brethren, I [*Nephi*] make an end of my sayings.

2 NEPHI 31

In the next three chapters, Nephi will, in effect, say goodbye to us. Knowing that he has very little time remaining as our teacher, we will want to pay close attention to what he says by way of counsel in these last few pages.

1 AND **now I, Nephi, make an end of my prophesying unto you**, my beloved brethren. And I cannot write but a few things, which I know must surely come to pass [*will surely happen*]; neither can I write but a few of the words of my brother Jacob.

First, Nephi will teach us about what is known as "the doctrine of Christ."

2 **Wherefore** [*therefore*], **the things which I have written sufficeth me** [*will have to be enough*], **save it be** [*except for*] **a few words which I must speak concerning the doctrine of Christ**; wherefore, **I shall speak unto you plainly**, according to the plainness of my prophesying.

The word "prophesying" as used here, in context, can mean two things. First: literally prophesying of future events. Second: it can also mean "teaching."

3 For **my soul delighteth in plainness**; for after this manner doth the Lord God work among the children of men. [*In other words, the true gospel, properly taught, is very plain and simple, and that is how the Lord teaches.*] For the Lord God giveth light unto the understanding [*to our minds*]; for he speaketh unto men according to their language, unto their understanding.

First, Nephi will teach us about John the Baptist, who will baptize Jesus in just under 600 years from Nephi's time. This is a reminder that Nephi is a great prophet.

4 Wherefore, I would that ye should **remember that I have spoken unto you concerning that prophet** [*John the Baptist*] which the Lord showed unto me, **that should baptize the Lamb of God** [*Jesus*], **which should take away the sins of the world** [*who would perform the Atonement*].

Members of the Church often wonder why Christ had to be baptized, or if He actually had to be baptized, or if perhaps He did it only to serve as an example for all of us. Nephi will give us the correct answer in the next verses.

5 And now, **if the Lamb of God**, he being holy [*perfectly free from sin*], **should have need to** [*had to be*] **be baptized by water**, to fulfil all righteousness [*to be obedient to the will of the Father*], **O then, how much more need have we, being unholy, to be baptized, yea, even by water!**

Nephi is an excellent teacher. First, he gets us thinking. Then he makes sure we come up with the correct answer to his questions.

6 And now, **I** would **ask** of **you**, my beloved brethren, **wherein** [*in*

what way] **the Lamb of God** [*Christ*] **did fulfil all righteousness in being baptized by water?**

7 Know ye not that he was holy? But notwithstanding [*even though*] he being holy, he showeth [*set an example*] unto the children of men that, according to the flesh [*as a mortal being*] **he humbleth himself before the Father, and witnesseth unto the Father that he would be obedient unto him in keeping his commandments**.

> Having answered his questions, telling us that Christ did have to be baptized, in order to keep the Father's commandments, Nephi now teaches us that the Holy Ghost came upon the Savior, like He does upon us if we are worthily baptized and confirmed (see verse 12).

8 Wherefore, after he was baptized with water **the Holy Ghost descended upon him in the form of a dove**.

> Sometimes, in gospel discussions talking about the Savior's baptism, students wonder if the Holy Ghost really turns Himself into a dove on occasions, as He bears witness of Christ. The Prophet Joseph Smith answered this question as follows:
>
> "The Holy Ghost is a personage, and is in the form of a personage. It does not confine itself to the *form* of the dove, but in *sign* of the dove. The Holy Ghost cannot be transformed into a dove" (Smith, *Teachings of the Prophet Joseph Smith*, p. 275).
>
> So, we know that the Holy Ghost does not turn into a dove.
>
> Next, Nephi continues teaching us why Jesus had to be baptized, including that it shows us that there is only one way to get onto the covenant path, and that is through proper baptism.

9 And again, it showeth unto the children of men the straitness [*narrowness*] of the path, and the narrowness of the gate [*baptism*], by which they should enter, **he having set the example before them.**

10 And he said unto the children of men: **Follow thou me.** Wherefore, my beloved brethren, can we follow Jesus save we shall be willing to keep the commandments of the Father?

11 And **the Father said: Repent ye, repent ye, and be baptized in the name of my Beloved Son.**

12 And also, the voice of the Son came unto me, saying: **He that is baptized in my name, to him will the Father give the Holy Ghost, like unto me** [*Christ*]; wherefore, **follow me, and do the**

things which ye have seen me do [*in other words, follow My example*].

Now we will continue with Nephi's teachings of the doctrine of Christ.

13 Wherefore, my beloved brethren, I know that if ye shall **follow the Son**, with full purpose of heart, acting **no hypocrisy** [*honestly wanting to do the right thing*] and no deception before God, but with real intent, **repenting of your sins, witnessing unto the Father that ye are willing to take upon you the name of Christ, by baptism**—yea, by following your Lord and your Savior down into the water [*being baptized*], according to his word, behold, then shall ye **receive the Holy Ghost**; yea, **then cometh the baptism of fire and of the Holy Ghost** [*the Holy Ghost will continue to teach you and strengthen your testimony that the gospel is true*]; and then can ye speak with the tongue of angels [*you can speak with the same testimony and understanding that angels have about Christ*], and shout praises unto the Holy One of Israel [*Christ*].

14 But, behold, my beloved brethren, thus came the voice of the Son unto me, saying: **After ye have repented** of your sins, **and witnessed unto the Father that ye are willing to keep my commandments, by the baptism of water, and have received the baptism of fire and of the Holy Ghost**, and can speak with a new tongue [*you can speak as one who has a true testimony of Christ and His gospel*], yea, even with the tongue of angels, **and after this should deny me, it would have been better for you that ye had not known me.** [*This is a serious warning about the accountability of one who has gained a testimony from the Holy Ghost.*]

The imagery of being "baptized by fire" by the Holy Ghost is a reminder that the Holy Ghost works with us after we receive the Gift of the Holy Ghost, to make us clean from our sins and bad behaviors. The symbolism of burning imperfections out of us through the help of the Holy Ghost comes from what is known as the refiner's fire. A refiner is one who takes rock that has metal in it (such rocks are called "ore") and heats it until the metal and rock melt and separate.

A refiner of gold, for instance, heats ore in a crucible (a special pot that can handle high heat) until both the rock (imperfections) and the gold (symbolic of the person being refined or prepared for exaltation) melts. The gold is heavier than the rock; therefore, it settles to the bottom of the crucible, and the rock floats to the top, where it can be scraped off. As the "refiner's fire" continues, more ore is added, and the level of gold rises, and more "imperfections" are taken away by the refiner (symbolic of Christ and His Atonement). Eventually, the crucible is filled with pure gold (symbolic of a person ready for exaltation).

Next, Nephi bears testimony to us that he has heard the voice of Heavenly Father.

15 **And I heard a voice from the Father**, saying: **Yea** [*yes*], **the words of my Beloved** [*Christ*] **are true and faithful** [*are absolutely correct*]. **He that endureth to the end, the same shall be saved.**

16 And now, my beloved brethren, **I know by this that unless a man shall endure to the end, in following the example of the Son of the living God, he cannot be saved.**

One way of looking at the phrase "endure to the end" is as follows: The word "end" often means "goal" or "purpose" as used in the scriptures. Therefore, "endure to the end" could mean "endure until you have reached the goal of exaltation," or "endure until you have satisfied the purpose of your having been sent to earth," which would obviously be that you live the gospel as best you can right up until you die.

You will see, in verses 17 and 18, that Nephi reviews and repeats his major messages in the previous verses.

17 Wherefore, **do the things** which I have told you **I have seen that your Lord and your Redeemer should** [*will*] **do** [*be baptized and keep your commitments like Christ will*]; for, for this cause have [*this is why*] they been shown unto me, that ye might know the gate by which ye should enter. For **the gate by which ye should enter is repentance and baptism by water**; and **then cometh a remission of your sins by fire and by the Holy Ghost.**

18 **And then are ye in this strait** [*narrow*] **and narrow path** [*the "narrow and narrowing path"; in other words, the more righteous you become, the narrower the path you allow yourself to walk because of the "light" that the Holy Ghost is shining for you*] **which leads to eternal life** [*exaltation*]; yea, **ye have entered in by the gate**; **ye have done according to the commandments of the Father and the Son**; and **ye have received the Holy Ghost**, which witnesses of the Father and the Son, unto the fulfilling of the promise which he hath made, that if ye entered in by the way ye should receive.

Next, Nephi asks a very important question.

19 And now, my beloved brethren, **after ye have gotten into this strait and narrow path, I would ask if all is done?** Behold, I say unto you, **Nay**; for ye have not come thus far save it were by the word of Christ with unshaken faith in him, relying wholly upon the merits of him who is mighty to save.

Verse 20, next, is a strong reminder that it is all right to humbly plan on exaltation. Many members might think that planning on being exalted is a bit arrogant and smacks of pride. Not so, according to Nephi in verse 20. The word "hope" as used in the Book of Mormon is a much more positive and a much stronger word than hope as used in modern English.

20 Wherefore, ye must **press forward with a steadfastness in Christ, having a perfect brightness of hope**, and a love of God and of all men. Wherefore, if ye shall **press forward**, **feasting upon the word of Christ**, and **endure to the end**, behold, thus saith the Father: **Ye shall have eternal life** [*exaltation in the highest degree in the celestial kingdom; see D&C 131:1–4*].

Another way to say "endure to the end" in verse 20, above, might be "continue improving to the goal." If we keep honestly trying to live the gospel, and keep repenting as needed, we can plan on making it back to heaven and living with Heavenly Father and the Savior, in our own family unit, in exaltation, where families are forever.

Nephi now finishes his marvelous sermon on the doctrine of Christ. Watch how he summarizes what he has taught us over the last several verses.

21 And now, behold, my beloved brethren, **this is the way**; and there is **none other way nor name given under heaven whereby man can be saved in the kingdom of God** [*there is no other way to get to exaltation*]. And now, behold, **this is the doctrine of Christ**, and **the only and true doctrine of the Father, and of the Son, and of the Holy Ghost**, which is one God [*in other words, the three members of the Godhead work together in perfect unity for the purpose of saving us*], without end. Amen.

2 NEPHI 32

Nephi is just about finished teaching us. He can see by the power of prophecy and the Holy Ghost that many of us still do not understand what he meant in 2 Nephi 31:13 when he said, "Then can ye speak with the tongue of angels." Therefore, he will proceed to explain more as to what he meant for us to understand. He will start with what we should do after we have entered the covenant path by being baptized and receiving the gift of the Holy Ghost.

1 AND now, behold, my beloved brethren, **I suppose that ye ponder** [*are thinking*] **somewhat in your hearts concerning that which ye should do after ye have entered in by the way**. But, behold, why do ye ponder these things in your hearts [*what is it that you don't understand*]?

2 Do ye not **remember that I said unto you that after ye had received the Holy Ghost ye could speak with the tongue of angels?** And now, how could ye speak with the tongue of angels save [*unless*] it were by the Holy Ghost?

As mentioned in 2 Nephi 31:13, in one of the notes in brackets, a major part of "speaking with the tongue of angels" is that of having the same testimony and understanding of the Savior and His gospel that angels have. The logic in this is that since angels speak by the power of the Holy Ghost (verse 3, next) and since we can also teach or bear testimony by that same power, we can have the same understanding as they do about Christ. This is a very powerful and wonderful truth!

3 **Angels speak by the power of the Holy Ghost**; wherefore [*therefore*], **they speak the words of Christ**. Wherefore [*this is the reason*], I said unto you, feast upon the words of Christ; for behold, the words of Christ will tell you all things what ye should do.

4 **Wherefore, now after I have spoken these words, if ye cannot understand them it will be because ye ask not, neither do ye knock**; **wherefore** [*this is why*], **ye are not brought into the light**, but must perish in the dark. [*In other words, now it is up to us to use our moral agency to choose to ask the Father for additional inspiration from the Holy Ghost as needed, to understand Nephi's inspired words.*]

Next, Nephi repeats again to help us understand his teaching. He is very anxious that we understand what he has taught us about the doctrine of Christ in chapter 31. It appears from Nephi's emphasis that the doctrine of Christ is the gospel of Christ in its most basic form. Therefore, understanding the doctrine of Christ is necessary for any other thorough understanding of any doctrines of the plan of salvation.

5 For behold, again I say unto you that **if ye will enter in by the way** [*repentance and baptism*], **and receive the Holy Ghost, it will**

show unto you all things what ye should do.

6 Behold, **this is the doctrine of Christ**, and there will be no more doctrine given until after he shall manifest himself unto you in the flesh [*until after He comes to perform His mortal ministry*]. And when he shall manifest himself unto you in the flesh [*as a mortal being*], the things which he shall say unto you shall ye observe to do.

Nephi is a tenderhearted teacher and prophet, and he wishes he could do even more to help save every soul. But there are limits, set by individual agency. And although this has to be, it still causes pain in the hearts of righteous teachers.

7 And now **I, Nephi, cannot say more**; the Spirit stoppeth mine utterance, and **I am left to mourn because of the unbelief, and the wickedness, and the ignorance, and the stiffneckedness** [*pride and lack of humility*] **of men**; for **they will not search knowledge** [*this requires effort; it is an agency choice that many people will not make*], **nor understand great knowledge, when it is given unto them in plainness**, even as plain as word can be.

Next, Nephi emphasizes the role of sincere prayer in gaining knowledge through the Holy Ghost. He also warns us to pray even if we do not feel like praying. As people yield to Satan's temptations, they generally stop praying to God. Thus, they cut off communication with Heavenly Father, who could help them keep from being pulled down by the devil.

8 And now, my beloved brethren, I perceive that ye ponder still in your hearts; and it grieveth me [*it causes me pain and concern*] that I must speak concerning this thing. **For if ye would hearken unto the Spirit which teacheth a man to pray ye would know that ye must pray**; for **the evil spirit** [*Satan*] **teacheth not a man to pray, but teacheth him that he must not pray**.

9 But behold, I say unto you that **ye must pray always, and not faint** [*not give up*]; that ye must not perform any thing unto the Lord save in the first place ye shall pray unto the Father in the name of Christ, that he will consecrate thy performance unto thee [*He will see that it benefits you*], that thy performance may be for the welfare of thy soul.

2 NEPHI 33

This is the last chapter of Nephi's writings, and we will feel his great love for his people and for us as he carefully chooses his final words to us. In verse 1, below, he humbly claims that he is not "mighty in writing," but we would humbly disagree. He is a mighty prophet and teacher, and we will look forward to meeting him in the next life.

Next, you will see another well-known quote from the Book of Mormon dealing with the role of the Holy Ghost in teaching.

1 AND now I, Nephi, cannot write all the things which were taught among my people; neither am I mighty in writing, like unto speaking; **for when a man speaketh by the power of the Holy Ghost the power of the Holy Ghost carrieth it unto the hearts of the children of men.**

> Did you notice that the Holy Ghost "carrieth it **unto** the hearts" rather than **into** the hearts? The word "unto" implies that the Holy Ghost will carry the message right up to your heart, but you must let it in.
>
> Next, Nephi points out that many people miss out on important gospel truths, inspiration, etc., because they refuse to listen to the Holy Ghost.

2 But **behold, there are many that harden their hearts against the Holy Spirit**, that it hath no place in them; wherefore, **they cast many things away** [*they reject many things*] which are written and esteem them as things of naught [*they consider the scriptures to be of no worth*].

3 **But I, Nephi, have written** what I have written, **and I esteem** [*consider*] **it as of great worth**, and especially unto my people. For I pray continually for them by day, and mine eyes water my pillow by night, because of them; and I cry unto my God in faith, and I know that he will hear my cry [*prayer*].

4 And **I know that the Lord God will consecrate my prayers for the gain of my people** [*I know my prayers will be effective*]. **And the words which I have written in weakness will be made strong unto them** [*the Holy Ghost can make the scriptures speak clearly and strongly to us*]; for it **persuadeth them to do good**; it **maketh known unto them of their fathers** [*ancestors*]; **and it speaketh of Jesus, and persuadeth them to believe in him, and to endure to the end, which is life eternal** [*exaltation; living with God, becoming gods, and having our own families forever*].

5 And **it speaketh harshly against sin**, according to the plainness of the truth; wherefore, **no man will be angry at the words which I have written save** [*unless*] **he shall be of the spirit of the devil.**

6 **I glory in plainness**; I glory in truth; I glory in my Jesus, for he hath redeemed my soul from hell.

Above, Nephi expresses his love of "plainness." You may have noticed that Christ is the author of plainness and that Satan is the author of complexity. In fact, many false doctrines, which compete with the simple "plain and precious" truths of the gospel, become so complex that they are not understandable.

7 **I have charity for my people, and great faith in Christ that I shall meet many souls spotless at his judgment-seat.**

There is a major message that is very encouraging taught by Nephi in verse 7, above. It is that he has confidence that many of us will make it to exaltation. We should pay close attention to his choice in using the word "spotless." Many members of the Church have the mistaken idea that we have to be perfect as we get to our final judgment on Judgment Day. This is not true. Christ was the only completely perfect individual to ever live on earth. If we get confused and use the word "perfect" in place of the word "spotless," we will get very discouraged.

If we understand and follow the doctrine of Christ—in other words, live the gospel—as taught by Nephi in the previous chapter, we will qualify for the Savior's Atonement to cleanse us completely from sins. Thus, we will be spotless or, in other words, perfectly clean and pure, and we will have an enjoyable Judgment Day.

8 **I have charity for the Jew**—I say Jew, because I mean them from whence [*where*] I came [*in other words, there were people from all of the tribes of Israel living in the Jerusalem area, and because they lived in the Jerusalem area, they were called Jews*].

9 **I also have charity for the Gentiles** [*all other people besides the Jews; by this definition, most of us are Gentiles*]. But behold, **for none of these can I hope except they shall be reconciled unto Christ** [*unless they put their lives in harmony with Christ by living the gospel*], **and enter into the narrow gate** [*repentance and baptism; see 2 Nephi 31:17*], **and walk in the strait** [*"narrow"*] **path** [*the covenant path*] **which leads to life** [*eternal life; exaltation*], **and continue in the path until the end of the day of probation** [*until the time your life and testing is over*].

10 **And now, my beloved brethren, and also Jew, and all ye ends of the earth** [*in other words, everyone*], **hearken** [*listen carefully*] **unto these words and believe in Christ**; and if ye believe not in these words believe in Christ [*if you don't believe my words, at least believe in Christ*]. **And**

if ye shall believe in Christ ye will believe in these words, for they are the words of Christ, and he hath given them unto me; and **they teach all men that they should do good**.

Next, Nephi invites people to judge for themselves whether the things he has taught are the words of Christ. And he strongly bears testimony that they are, and that they will know for sure on Judgment Day that they have made a bad mistake if they reject them.

11 **And if they are not the words of Christ, judge ye—for Christ will show unto you, with power and great glory, that they are his words, at the last day** [*on Judgment Day*]; and **you and I shall stand face to face before his bar** [*where Christ sits to judge us*]; and **ye shall know that I have been commanded of him to write these things**, notwithstanding [*in spite of*] my weakness.

In verse 12, next, we feel Nephi's great Christlike love for all people as he prays for as many as possible to be saved in celestial glory.

12 **And I pray the Father in the name of Christ that many of us, if not all, may be saved in his kingdom** at that great and last day [*on Judgment Day*].

Nephi now bids us all a powerful and emotional farewell. You can feel his deep and sincere concern for our eternal welfare.

13 **And now, my beloved brethren**, all those who are of the house of Israel, and all ye ends of the earth [*in other words, everyone*], **I speak unto you as the voice of one crying from the dust** [*he is speaking to us from the ground, so to speak, where the gold plates were buried on the Hill Cumorah*]: **Farewell until that great day shall come** [*until Judgment Day comes*].

14 **And you that will not partake of the goodness of God, and respect the words of the Jews** [*the Bible*], **and also my words** [*Nephi's portion of the Book of Mormon*], **and the words which shall proceed forth out of the mouth of the Lamb of God** [*and everything Christ teaches*], behold, **I bid you an everlasting farewell** [*I say goodbye forever, because we will be separated forever after Judgment Day*], **for these words shall condemn you** [*will stop your eternal progression*] **at the last day** [*on Judgment Day*].

15 For what I seal on earth, shall be brought against you at the judgment bar; for thus hath the Lord commanded me, and I must obey. Amen.

THE BOOK OF JACOB

Nephi's parents, Lehi and Sariah, had two more sons after they fled from Jerusalem and while they were traveling in the wilderness for eight years. Jacob is the older of the two sons (see 1 Nephi 18:7). He is Nephi's younger brother and would be in the neighborhood of forty-five to fifty years old at this point. In chapter 1, Jacob will talk to us about the commandment Nephi gave him to take over the small plates of Nephi and to engrave a few of his own things on them. Nephi's death is recorded by Jacob, also in chapter 1.

In chapter 2, Jacob will give some powerful messages, including a strong warning for the men among his people to stop having more than one wife. This is called "plural marriage."

Perhaps the best-known chapter of Jacob is chapter 5, which is the allegory of the tame olive tree and the wild olive trees. We will spend considerable time on this chapter.

Jacob has seen the Savior (2 Nephi 11:3) and has been well taught in the gospel by Nephi. He is kind and gentle and it bothers him to have to speak bluntly and boldly to his people in order to wake them up to the reality that they are going into apostasy, meaning that they are going away from God's teachings and the Church (see chapter two).

We are greatly blessed to have these inspired teachings of Jacob, and we can see that Mormon selected them for us (Words of Mormon 1:3–8) as he was inspired to include the small plates of Nephi in the plates that Moroni would later bury in the stone box in the Hill Cumorah and give to Joseph Smith in 1827.

JACOB 1

In this chapter, you will meet Jacob as he introduces himself to us. He will explain some differences between the large plates of Nephi and the small plates of Nephi. He will redefine the terms "Lamanites" and "Nephites" and then give a little background to the sermon he delivered to his people in the temple.

1 FOR behold, it came to pass that **fifty and five years had passed away from the time that Lehi left Jerusalem** [*so it is now a little over 540 years before Christ's birth in Bethlehem*]; wherefore [*therefore*], Nephi gave me, Jacob, a commandment concerning the small plates [*the small plates of Nephi*], upon which these things are engraven.

For more information about the various sets of plates referred to in the Book of Mormon, see "A

Brief Explanation about the Book of Mormon" in the introductory pages to your Book of Mormon.

2 And **he gave me, Jacob, a commandment that I should write upon these plates** [*the small plates*] a few of the things which I considered to be most precious; that I should not touch, save it were lightly, concerning the history of this people which are called the people of Nephi.

You can see, from verse 2, above, that Nephi told Jacob to write mainly spiritual things on the small plates or records. This is a real advantage for us because it helps us be spiritual and live the gospel. By the way, the small plates of Nephi were the plates in the stack of gold plates from which Joseph Smith translated the first six books of the Book of Mormon. So, we have basically been reading from the small plates of Nephi up to now and will continue to do so until we finish Omni.

3 **For he said that the history of his people should be engraven upon his other plates** [*the large plates of Nephi*], and that I should preserve these plates and hand them down unto my seed [*posterity, descendants*], from generation to generation.

4 **And if there were preaching which was sacred, or revelation which was great, or prophesying, that I should engraven the heads** [*main points*] **of them upon these plates** [*the small plates*], and touch upon them as much as it were possible, for Christ's sake, and for the sake of our people.

Next, Jacob says, basically, that the small plates have many prophecies on them.

5 For because of faith and great anxiety, **it truly had been made manifest** [*shown*] **unto us concerning our people, what things should happen unto them**.

6 And **we also had many revelations,** and the spirit of **much prophecy**; **wherefore** [*and so*], **we knew of Christ** and his kingdom, which should come.

7 Wherefore we labored diligently [*we worked hard*] among our people, **that we might persuade them to come unto Christ, and partake of the goodness of God, that they might enter into his rest** [*exaltation in the celestial kingdom; see D&C 84:24*], lest by any means he should swear in his wrath [*should promise in His anger that*] they should not enter in [*to heaven*], as in the provocation in the days of temptation while the children of Israel were

in the wilderness [*like in the "provoking of God"—in other words, the forty years the children of Israel spent in the wilderness because they provoked God to anger*].

8 Wherefore, **we would to God** [*we sincerely hope*] **that we could persuade all men not to rebel against God**, to provoke him to anger, **but that all men would believe in Christ**, and view his death, and suffer his cross [*do whatever it takes to follow Him*] and bear the shame of the world [*be faithful to God in spite of opposition from others*]; wherefore, I, Jacob, take it upon me to fulfil the commandment of my brother Nephi.

Next, Jacob talks briefly about how each of their kings was named "Nephi," no matter what his actual name was.

9 **Now Nephi began to be old, and he saw that he must soon die**; wherefore, he anointed a man to be a king and a ruler over his people now, according to the reigns of the kings.

10 **The people having loved Nephi exceedingly** [*very much*], he having been a great protector for them, having wielded the sword of Laban in their defence, and having labored in all his days for their welfare—

11 **Wherefore, the people were desirous to retain in remembrance his name**. And whoso should reign in his stead were called by the people, second Nephi, third Nephi, and so forth, according to the reigns of the kings; and thus they were called by the people, let them be of whatever name they would [*no matter what their real name was, they were called "King Nephi"*].

12 And it came to pass that **Nephi died**.

Next, as stated above, Jacob redefines the terms "Lamanites" and "Nephites." It is important that we keep these new definitions in mind as we continue our Book of Mormon study.

13 Now **the people which were not Lamanites were Nephites**; nevertheless, they were called Nephites, Jacobites, Josephites, Zoramites, Lamanites, Lemuelites, and Ishmaelites.

14 But I, Jacob, shall not hereafter distinguish them by these names, but **I shall call them Lamanites that seek to destroy the people of Nephi, and those who are friendly to Nephi I shall call Nephites**, or the people of Nephi, according to the reigns of the kings.

Next, Jacob tells us about the serious problem that is growing among his people: men are beginning to take plural wives—in other words, more than one wife at a time—which is against the commandment of the Lord.

In Jacob 2:27 and 30, Jacob will explain that if the Lord wants men to have plural wives, He will command it, like He did in the early days of the Church. But the Lord had not commanded it for Jacob's people, so it was a sin and was a form of sexual immorality.

15 And now it came to pass that **the people of Nephi**, under the reign [*rule*] of the second king, **began to** grow hard in their hearts, and **indulge themselves somewhat in wicked practices** [*started to allow themselves to commit serious sins*], such as like unto David of old **desiring many wives and concubines** [*woman servants whom they also married*], and also Solomon, his son.

Next, Jacob points out that his people also started paying too much attention to getting wealthy and getting stuff. This is often called "materialism," and pride usually goes along with it.

16 Yea, and **they also began to search much gold and silver, and began to be lifted up somewhat in pride** [*they were also getting caught up in materialism and pride*].

Next, Jacob tells us that his sermon, which he will give to his people in chapters 2 and 3, was designed to make them aware of three major tools of the devil—namely, sexual immorality, materialism, and pride. Satan uses these three categories of sin to tempt all of us.

17 Wherefore **I, Jacob, gave unto them these words as I taught them** in the temple, having first obtained mine errand [*my talk*] from the Lord.

18 For **I, Jacob, and my brother Joseph had been consecrated priests and teachers of this people, by the hand of Nephi** [*Nephi ordained Jacob and Joseph to be priesthood leaders over the people*].

The terms "priests" and "teachers" as used here don't refer to the Aaronic Priesthood, rather, to responsibilities within the Melchizedek Priesthood. Joseph Fielding Smith, who became one of the Presidents of the Church, explained this as follows:

"Under these conditions **the Nephites officiated by virtue of the Melchizedek Priesthood from the days of Lehi to the days of the appearance of our Savior among them**. It is true that Nephi 'consecrated Jacob and Joseph' that they should be priests and teachers over the land of the Nephites, but the fact that plural terms *priests and teachers* were used indicates that this was not a reference to the definite office in the priesthood in either case, but it was a general assignment to teach, direct, and admonish the people. Otherwise the terms *priest and teacher* would have been given, in the singular. Additional light is thrown on this appointment showing that these two brothers of Nephi held the Melchizedek Priesthood, in the sixth chapter, second verse of 2 Nephi, where Jacob makes this explanation regarding the priesthood which he and Joseph held: 'Behold, my beloved brethren, I, Jacob, having been called of God, and ordained *after the manner of his holy order*, and having been consecrated by my brother Nephi, unto whom ye look as a king or a protector, and on whom ye depend for safety, behold ye know that I have spoken unto you exceeding many things.'

"This seems to be a confirmation of the ordinations that he and his brother Joseph received in the Melchizedek Priesthood. All through the Book of Mormon we find references to the Nephites officiating by virtue of the Higher Priesthood (Melchizedek Priesthood) after the holy order." (Smith, *Answers to Gospel Questions,* 1:124)

Next, Jacob explains that he and his brother, Joseph, took their responsibilities to teach their people very seriously. This reminds us that we should do our best in our own church callings also.

19 **And we did magnify our office unto the Lord** [*we fulfilled the responsibilities of our offices and callings*], **taking upon us the responsibility, answering the sins of the people upon our own heads** [*considering that we were responsible for our people's sins*] **if we did not teach them the word of God with all diligence** [*to the very best of our ability*]; wherefore, by laboring with our might their blood might not come upon our garments [*that we would not be held accountable for their sins*]; **otherwise their blood would come upon our garments** [*we would be held responsible for their sins*], and we would not be found spotless at the last day [*we would not be free from sin on Judgment Day*].

JACOB 2

In this chapter, Jacob will go to the temple and teach his people. He will deal with the three major topics—materialism, pride, and sexual immorality—that were mentioned in the last chapter. As he speaks about sexual immorality, meaning sexual sins, he will deal with the topic of plural marriage.

1 **THE words which Jacob, the brother of Nephi, spake unto**

the people of Nephi, after the death of Nephi:

2 Now, my beloved brethren, I, Jacob, according to the responsibility which I am under to God, to magnify mine office [*to fulfill my calling*] with soberness, and that I might rid my garments of your sins [*not be responsible for your sins*], **I come up into the temple this day that I might declare unto you the word of God**.

Preparing to deliver this particular sermon has been very hard on Jacob. He is a kind, tender man and does not like to make people feel bad or hurt their feelings. He is like our modern prophets.

3 And **ye yourselves know that I have hitherto** [*up to now*] **been diligent in the office of my calling** [*worked hard to do what I am supposed to in my calling as a leader over you*]; but I this day am weighed down with much more desire and anxiety for the welfare of your souls than I have hitherto been. [*He is worried more about them now than he has ever been.*]

4 For behold, **as yet** [*up to now*], **ye have been obedient unto the word of the Lord**, which I have given unto you.

Next, in verse 5, you will see that as a prophet, Jacob can tell or discern what is in the minds and thoughts of his people by the power of the Holy Ghost. It is his stewardship to do so. Our prophets do the same, and we see it, especially as they address us at the general conferences of the Church.

5 But behold, hearken ye unto me [*listen carefully to what I say*], and know that **by the help of the all–powerful Creator of heaven and earth I can tell you concerning your thoughts, how that ye are beginning to labor in sin,** which sin appeareth very abominable [*terribly sinful*] unto me, yea, and abominable unto God.

The phrase "labor in sin" as used in verse 5, above, as a very interesting and insightful term. Sin creates much more stress and work (labor) than righteousness does. This is true both on an individual basis as well as on a national level.

For instance, righteousness promotes peace, and thus the labors and productivity of the people go to building up of the standard of living for everyone. On the other hand, wickedness requires the formation and financing of police, armies, self-defense, locks, security systems, guards, and so forth. In summary, righteousness builds, produces, and creates prosperity, while wickedness eats up prosperity.

6 Yea, **it grieveth my soul** [*causes me a lot of worry*] **and causeth me to**

shrink with shame before the presence of my Maker [*God*], that I must testify unto you concerning the wickedness of your hearts. [*Jacob is ashamed of his people's behaviors.*]

7 And **also it grieveth me that I must use so much boldness of speech concerning you**, before [*in front of*] your wives and your children, many of whose feelings are exceedingly tender and chaste [*pure*] and delicate before God, which thing is pleasing unto God;

> It is weighing heavily upon Jacob's heart that many righteous members, including the wives of men who have started taking plural wives, have come to this meeting expecting to be cheered up and encouraged, to have their day brightened by listening to their prophet. But it is not going to happen.

8 **And it supposeth me** [*I suppose*] **that they have come up hither** [*here to this meeting at the temple*] **to hear the pleasing word of God**, yea, the word which healeth the wounded soul.

9 **Wherefore, it burdeneth** [*weighs down*] **my soul** that I should be constrained [*required*], because of the strict commandment which I have received from God, to admonish [*teach and warn*] you according to your crimes, to enlarge the wounds of those who are already wounded [*by your sins*], instead of consoling and healing their wounds; and those who have not been wounded, instead of feasting upon the pleasing word of God have daggers placed to pierce their souls and wound their delicate minds.

10 But, notwithstanding [*in spite of*] the greatness of the task, **I must do according to the strict commands of God, and tell you concerning your wickedness and abominations** [*extremely serious sins*], in the presence of the pure in heart, and the broken heart, and under the glance of the piercing eye of the Almighty God [*in other words, God is watching me to see if I will tell you what He commanded me to tell you*].

11 Wherefore [*therefore*], **I must tell you the truth according to the plainness of the word of God**. For behold, as I inquired [*asked*] of the Lord, thus came the word unto me, saying: Jacob, get thou up into the temple on the morrow [*the next day*], and declare the word which I shall give thee unto this people.

> First, Jacob teaches and warns them about materialism; in other words, making money and having things, personal wealth and possessions, as a top priority in their

lives, rather than living the gospel as their most important goal in life. This leads to pride.

12 And now behold, my brethren, **this is the word** which I declare unto you, that **many of you have begun to search for gold, and for silver, and for all manner of precious ores** [*rocks that have gold, silver, copper, etc., in them*], in the which this land, which is a land of promise unto you and to your seed, doth abound most plentifully. [*There is a lot of gold and silver, etc., available in this land.*]

13 And **the hand of providence** [*God*] **hath smiled upon you most pleasingly** [*God has blessed you a lot*], that you have obtained many riches; and because some of you have obtained more abundantly than that of your brethren [*because some of you have gotten more wealth than others*] **ye are lifted up in the pride of your hearts**, and wear stiff necks [*you won't bow your heads in humility*] and high heads [*you are prideful*] because of the costliness of your apparel [*clothing*], and persecute your brethren **because ye suppose that ye are better than they**.

14 And now, my brethren, **do ye suppose that God justifieth you** [*approves your behavior*] **in this thing?** Behold, I say unto you, **Nay.** But he condemneth you, and if ye persist in these things [*if you keep doing this*] his judgments [*punishments*] must speedily come unto you.

15 **O that he would show you that he can pierce you**, and with one glance of his eye he can smite you to the dust [*destroy you completely*]!

16 **O that he would rid you from this iniquity** [*wickedness*] and abomination. And, **O that ye would listen unto the word of his commands, and let not this pride of your hearts destroy your souls!**

Next, Jacob teaches his people a simple method of overcoming pride and materialism.

17 **Think of your brethren like unto yourselves**, and be familiar [*generous*] with all and free with your substance [*your money and things*], that they may be rich like unto you.

Some people think that wealth itself is evil. This is not the case. It is how individuals handle wealth and what goes on in their minds and hearts that counts. What Jacob says next is very important and quite well known among members of the Church today.

18 But **before ye seek for riches, seek ye for the kingdom of God**.

19 **And after ye have obtained a hope in Christ** [*after you have become strong and active in the gospel*] **ye shall obtain riches, if ye seek them**; and **ye will seek them for the intent to do good**—to clothe the naked, and to feed the hungry, and to liberate the captive, and administer relief to the sick and the afflicted. [*In other words, if you remain loyal and faithful to God, and if you gain wealth, it will not ruin you because you will keep things in proper perspective.*]

20 And **now**, my brethren, **I have spoken unto you concerning pride**; and those of you which have afflicted your neighbor, and persecuted him because ye were proud in your hearts, of the things which God hath given you, **what say ye of it** [*what have you got to say for yourselves*]?

21 **Do ye not suppose that such things are abominable** [*a big sin*] **unto him** [*God*] **who created all flesh?** And the one being [*person*] is as precious in his sight as the other. And all flesh is of the dust; and for the selfsame end [*purpose*] hath he created them, that they should keep his commandments and glorify him forever.

Jacob wishes that he could end his sermon at this point and let his people go home. It would be a great relief to him to do so. But one of the responsibilities of a leader is to deliver the word of the Lord to his people without leaving part of it out. In the next verses, Jacob expresses this and then delivers the rest of the message.

22 And **now I make an end of speaking unto you concerning this pride**. And **were it not that I must speak unto you concerning a grosser** [*bigger*] **crime, my heart would rejoice exceedingly because of you.**

23 **But the word of God burdens me** [*is weighing me down*] **because of your grosser crimes**. For behold, thus saith the Lord: This people begin to wax in iniquity [*are beginning to grow in wickedness*]; they understand not the scriptures, for they seek to excuse themselves in committing whoredoms [*sexual immorality*], because of the things which were written concerning David, and Solomon his son.

Jacob's people have obviously read in the brass plates about David and Solomon in our Old Testament and are using this as an excuse to break the commandment that the Lord gave Lehi (see Jacob 3:5) that his people should not have plural wives, which was still commonly practiced in Old Testament lands when Lehi left Jerusalem in 600 BC.

First, Jacob tells his people that they must not use David and Solomon as role models, because they both lost their souls as this practice got out of hand with them. For instance, King David, who had killed Goliath as a young man, had Bathsheba's husband killed intentionally in battle so he could marry her as a plural wife after he found out she was expecting their child. Thus, David tried to cover up adultery with murder. As a result, David lost his exaltation (see D&C 132:39). David was not a good example for Jacob's people to follow.

As for Solomon, 1 Kings 11:3, in the Old Testament, informs us that he had seven hundred wives and three hundred concubines (second-class wives), and the Bible goes on to record that Solomon began worshiping idols, which was pleasing to many of his wives who had other religions. Thus, Solomon also left God because of his abuse of plural marriage. He too was not a good example for Jacob's people to follow.

No wonder Jacob told his people the following:

24 **Behold** [*listen carefully*], **David and Solomon truly had many wives and concubines, which thing was abominable** [*a terrible sin*] before me, saith the Lord.

Next, Jacob explains to his people that one of the reasons that God led Lehi and his family out of the Jerusalem area was that the Jews had gotten so wicked that they were going to be attacked and destroyed or led away into captivity. One of their big sins was sexual immorality using the excuse of plural wives or polygamy.

25 Wherefore, **thus saith the Lord, I have led this people forth out of the land of Jerusalem**, by the power of mine arm, **that I might raise up unto me a righteous branch** [*people*] from the fruit of the loins of Joseph [*from the descendants of Joseph who was sold into Egypt*].

26 **Wherefore** [*therefore*], **I the Lord God will not suffer** [*allow*] **that this people shall do like unto them of old.**

As Jacob continues, he will give us the only reason for having plural wives in verses 27 and 30. It is simple. When the Lord commands it, it is okay. Otherwise, it is not okay.

27 Wherefore, my brethren, hear me, and hearken to the word of the Lord: **For there shall not any man among you have save it be one wife; and concubines he shall have none;**

28 For **I, the Lord God, delight in** the **chastity** [*sexual purity*] of women. **And whoredoms** [*sexual*

sins] **are an abomination** [*a very big sin*] **before me**; thus saith the Lord of Hosts.

29 Wherefore, **this people shall keep my commandments**, saith the Lord of Hosts, **or cursed be the land for their sakes**.

30 For **if I will, saith the Lord of Hosts, raise up seed unto me** [*children who are righteous*], **I will command my people** [*to practice plural marriage*]; **otherwise they shall hearken unto these things** [*the rule given in verse 27*].

A common question that comes up in classes is, "Will I be required to practice plural marriage if I attain exaltation?" The answer is "No," according to Bruce R. McConkie. He gives the answer as follows:

"Plural marriage is not essential to salvation or exaltation. Nephi and his people were denied the power to have more than one wife and yet they could gain every blessing in eternity that the Lord ever offered to any people" (McConkie, *Mormon Doctrine*, 578).

Next, the Lord tells Jacob's people why He does not want the Nephites to have plural wives.

31 **For behold, I, the Lord, have seen the sorrow, and heard the mourning of the daughters of my people in the land of Jerusalem**, yea, and in all the lands of my people, **because of the wickedness and abominations of their husbands**.

32 **And I will not suffer** [*allow*], saith the Lord of Hosts, **that the cries of the fair daughters of this people**, which I have led out of the land of Jerusalem, **shall come up unto me against the men of my people**, saith the Lord of Hosts.

Next, the Lord gives the men of Jacob's people a very strong warning not to continue having more than one wife at a time and not to commit adultery or any sexual sins. If they keep doing it, they will be destroyed!

33 For **they shall not lead away captive the daughters of my people** because of their tenderness, **save I shall visit them with a sore curse, even unto destruction**; for they shall not commit whoredoms [*sexual sins*], like unto them of old, saith the Lord of Hosts.

Next, Jacob reminds the men among his people that they already know the commandments of the Lord to them on this topic. Therefore, they are accountable for going against God's law on this matter.

34 And now behold, my brethren, **ye know that these**

**commandments were given to
our father, Lehi**; wherefore, **ye
have known them before** [*you
already knew this commandment*]; and **ye
have come unto great condem-
nation**; for ye have done these
things which ye ought not to have
done.

35 Behold, ye have done greater
iniquities than the Lamanites,
our brethren. **Ye have broken the
hearts of your tender wives, and
lost the confidence of your chil-
dren, because of your bad exam-
ples** before them; and the sob-
bings of their hearts ascend up to
God against you. And because of
the strictness of the word of God,
which cometh down against you,
many hearts died, pierced with
deep wounds.

JACOB 3

Next, Jacob gives encouragement to those of his people who have not broken these commandments of God. This is a good reminder to us that even though there may be many people who become wicked, there are usually still a number of people who remain righteous and try their best to keep God's commandments. We need to try to stay righteous always, and Jacob will give us some good advice for how to do it.

1 BUT behold, I, Jacob, would
speak unto you that are pure in
heart. **Look unto God with firm-
ness of mind**, and **pray unto him
with exceeding faith**, and he will
console you in your afflictions,
and he will plead your cause [*He
will be on your side*], and send down
justice upon those who seek your
destruction.

2 O all ye that are pure in heart,
lift up your heads [*be happy and
optimistic*] and **receive the pleas-
ing word of God** [*study and accept
the gospel*], and **feast upon his love**;
for ye may, if your minds are firm,
forever.

One of the most important messages of the gospel is the effectiveness of the Atonement of Christ. Jacob will now warn, invite, and remind the wicked among his people to repent. It is not too late.

3 But, **wo, wo, unto you that are
not pure in heart, that are filthy
this day before God**; for **except
ye repent the land is cursed for
your sakes** [*unless you repent, you will
be destroyed*]; **and the Lamanites**,
which are not filthy like unto you,
nevertheless they are cursed with
a sore cursing [*because they have gone
astray from the gospel*], **shall scourge**
[*keep bothering and attacking*] **you even
unto destruction**.

4 And the time speedily cometh, that **except ye** [*the wicked among the Nephites*] **repent they shall possess the land of your inheritance** [*they will take your land from you*]**, and the Lord God will lead away the righteous out from among you**. [*He did this by having Mosiah lead the righteous out of the land of Nephi to Zarahemla; see Omni 1:12–15.*]

5 Behold, **the Lamanites** your brethren, whom ye hate because of their filthiness and the cursing which hath come upon their skins, **are more righteous than you**; for they have not forgotten the commandment of the Lord, which was given unto our father—that they should have save it were one wife, and concubines they should have none, and there should not be whoredoms committed among them.

6 And now, **this commandment they observe to keep**; wherefore, because of this observance, in keeping this commandment, **the Lord God will not destroy them**, but will be merciful unto them; and one day they shall become a blessed people. [*We are watching the fulfilling of this prophecy today.*]

7 **Behold, their husbands love their wives, and their wives love their husbands; and their husbands and their wives love their children**; and their unbelief and their hatred towards you is because of the iniquity of their fathers [*who taught them to hate the Nephites*]; wherefore, how much better are you than they, in the sight of your great Creator?

8 O my brethren, I fear that unless ye shall repent of your sins that their skins will be whiter than yours, when ye shall be brought with them before the throne of God. [*They will be more pure and clean on Judgment Day than you.*]

The sinful practice of plural marriage to satisfy their lustful desires among the Nephites at the time of Jacob's sermon to his people was a form of severe hypocrisy. Remember, "hypocrisy" is when a person wants to commit sins but still wants to look righteous in other people's eyes. They looked down at the Lamanites, yet they were guilty of gross sin themselves. Jacob explains this next.

9 Wherefore [*therefore*], **a commandment I give unto you**, which is the word of God, **that ye revile** [*be critical*] **no more against them because of the darkness of their skins; neither shall ye revile against them because of their filthiness; but ye shall remember your own filthiness**, and remember that their filthiness

came because of their fathers [*the unrighteous traditions of their ancestors*].

Next, in verse 10, Jacob reminds the wicked among his people why they are hypocrites.

10 Wherefore, ye shall **remember your children, how that ye have grieved their hearts because of the example that ye have set before them**; and also, remember that ye may, because of your filthiness, bring your children unto destruction, and their sins be heaped upon your heads at the last day.

Just a quick word about the phrase "bring your children unto destruction" in verse 10, above. Remember that God is completely fair to all people, including children who are given bad examples, and thus grow up away from the gospel. If they do not get a fair chance in this life, such children will have a fair chance in the spirit world (see D&C 137:7–8; see also D&C 50:7, where the Lord tells us that those who are deceived by hypocrites "shall be reclaimed"). This doctrine is very comforting.

Next, Jacob gives one of the finest calls to repentance found anywhere in the scriptures.

11 **O my brethren, hearken** [*listen carefully*] **unto my words**; **arouse the faculties of your souls** [*wake up and think!*]; **shake yourselves that ye may awake from the slumber of death** [*wake yourselves up and avoid the death of your spirituality*]; and **loose yourselves** [*rescue yourselves*] **from the pains of hell** that ye may not become angels to the devil, to be cast into that lake of fire and brimstone [*lake of fiery, liquid, burning sulphur, symbolic of hell*] which is the second death [*being kept out of God's presence forever*].

12 **And now I, Jacob, spake** [*spoke*] **many more things unto the people of Nephi**, warning them against fornication [*having sex before marriage*] and lasciviousness [*all forms of sexual immorality*], and every kind of sin, telling them the awful consequences [*results, effects*] of them.

Next, Jacob mentions that he can hardly begin to tell us everything that took place among his people, on the small plates of Nephi. He reminds us that more details are kept on the large plates.

13 And **a hundredth part of the proceedings of this people**, which now began to be numerous, **cannot be written upon these plates** [*the small plates of Nephi*]; but many of their proceedings are written upon the larger plates [*the large plates of Nephi*], and their wars, and their contentions, and the reigns of their kings.

14 **These plates** [*this section of the small plates of Nephi*] **are called the plates of Jacob, and they were made by the hand of Nephi**. And I make an end of speaking these words.

JACOB 4

At the end of chapter 4, Jacob told us that the plates he was engraving or writing on were made by his brother, Nephi. Can you imagine how much work it would take to even make thin metal plates, let alone engrave on them with a thin, sharp-pointed metal tool? Engraving plates was a very painstaking task, and next, Jacob takes a moment to call our attention to this. It will be nice to meet Jacob in the next life and tell him thanks for his patient, hard work in giving us his part of the Book of Mormon.

1 NOW behold, it came to pass that I, Jacob, having ministered much unto my people in word (and I cannot write but a little of my words, **because of the difficulty of engraving our words upon plates**), and we know that the things which we write upon plates must remain [*will be permanent*];

Next, Jacob mentions that the only thing they can write on that will last is metal plates.

2 But **whatsoever things we write upon anything** [*such as animal skins or whatever*] **save** [*except*] **it be upon plates** [*metal plates*] **must** [*will*] **perish and vanish away**; but we can write a few words upon plates, which will give our children, and also our beloved brethren, a small degree of knowledge concerning us, or concerning their fathers—

3 Now in this thing we do rejoice; and **we labor diligently to engraven these words upon plates**, hoping that our beloved brethren and our children will receive them with thankful hearts, and look upon them that they may learn with joy and not with sorrow, neither with contempt, concerning their first parents [*concerning us, their ancestors*].

Next, Jacob bears testimony to his descendants down through the ages.

4 For, **for this intent have we written these things, that they may know that we knew of Christ**, and we had a hope [*an assurance*] of his glory **many hundred years before his coming**; and not only we ourselves had a hope of his glory, but also all the holy prophets which were before us.

Next, Jacob explains the purpose of the law of Moses. The law of Moses was the many rules, laws, and commandments, including animal sacrifices, that Moses gave the children of Israel as he led them out of Egyptian captivity. The law of Moses was a schooling to help the people grow and develop from the sometimes-lower ways of thinking and living they developed as slaves in Egypt to the ability to accept the Savior's higher laws and ordinances of the true gospel of salvation.

5 Behold, **they** [*the prophets before us*] **believed in Christ** and worshiped the Father in his name, **and also we worship the Father in his name**. And for this intent we keep **the law of Moses, it pointing our souls to him**; and for this cause it [*the proper use of the law of Moses*] is sanctified unto us for righteousness, even as it was accounted unto Abraham in the wilderness to be obedient unto the commands of God in offering up his son Isaac, which is a similitude of God and his Only Begotten Son. [*Abraham was symbolic of the Father, and Isaac was symbolic of the sacrificing of the Son.*]

Next, Jacob teaches us a great lesson in the value of scripture study. Watch as he teaches us why we should regularly read and study the scriptures and the words of the living prophets.

6 Wherefore [*this is why*], **we search the prophets** [*the scriptures*], and **we have many revelations and the spirit of prophecy**; and having all these witnesses **we obtain a hope, and our faith becometh unshaken** [*our testimonies become very strong*], insomuch [*so that*] that we truly can command in the name of Jesus and the very trees obey us, or the mountains, or the waves of the sea.

7 Nevertheless, the Lord God showeth us our weakness **that we may know that it is by his grace, and his great condescensions** [*willingness to work with people who are so much less capable than He*] unto the children of men, **that we have power to do these things**.

8 Behold, **great and marvelous are the works of the Lord**. How unsearchable are the depths of the mysteries of him [*it is impossible for us to comprehend God at this point; but we will someday; compare with D&C 88:49*]; and it is impossible that man should find out all his ways. And **no man knoweth of his ways save it be revealed unto him**; wherefore, brethren, despise not the revelations of God.

Next, in verse 9, Jacob reminds us how powerful God is as a way of reminding us that we should listen to and follow His counsel (verse 10).

9 For behold, **by the power of his word man came upon the face of the earth, which earth**

was created by the power of his word. Wherefore, if God being able to speak and the world was, and to speak and man was created, O then, why not able to command the earth, or the workmanship of his hands [*including us*] upon the face of it, according to his will and pleasure?

> Next is another famous quote among members of the Church. It reminds us to avoid telling the Lord how to run things, rather to listen carefully to Him so that we learn.

10 **Wherefore, brethren, seek not to counsel the Lord, but to take counsel from his hand**. For behold, ye yourselves know that he counseleth in wisdom, and in justice, and in great mercy, over all his works.

11 **Wherefore, beloved brethren, be reconciled unto him** [*become in harmony with the Father*] **through the atonement of Christ**, his Only Begotten Son, and ye may obtain a resurrection [*a celestial resurrection; see the next lines*], according to the power of the resurrection which is in Christ, and be presented as the first-fruits of Christ [*the best results of Christ's Atonement; namely, a celestial resurrection*] unto God [*the Father*], having faith, and obtained a good hope of glory in him [*Christ*] before he manifesteth himself in the flesh.

> The last phrase of verse 11, above, is very significant doctrinally. It shows us that Christ's Atonement worked even before it was actually performed. Thus, Jacob's people could be forgiven of sins even though the Savior had not yet come to earth to serve His atoning mission.

12 And now, beloved, marvel not that I tell you these things; for why not speak of the atonement of Christ, and attain to a perfect knowledge of him, as to attain to the knowledge of a resurrection and the world to come?

> As mentioned previously, the word "prophesy" has at least two meanings in the context of the scriptures. For one thing, it means to foretell the future. Another definition is "teach." Both definitions seem to apply to verse 13, next.

13 Behold, my brethren, he that prophesieth, let him prophesy to the understanding of men [*so that people can understand what you are saying*]; **for the Spirit speaketh the truth** and lieth not [*truth is simple*]. **Wherefore, it speaketh of things as they really are, and of things as they really will be**; wherefore [*this is why*], these things are manifested unto us plainly, for the salvation of our souls. But

behold, we are not witnesses alone in these things; for God also spake them unto prophets of old.

You have probably noticed that many of Jacob's teachings are rather well known among Church members. Next, we see a rather famous statement, "Don't look beyond the mark." In other words, don't miss the obvious. Watch as Jacob teaches it.

14 But behold, the Jews were a stiffnecked [*stubborn and prideful*] people; and **they despised the words of plainness** [*they loved to complicate things*], and killed the prophets, **and sought for things that they could not understand** [*this is typical of many teachers of philosophy today*]. Wherefore, because of their blindness [*because they couldn't see spiritual, simple things*], **which blindness came by looking beyond the mark**, they must needs fall; for **God hath taken away his plainness from them**, and delivered unto them [*allowed them to come up with*] many things which they cannot understand, because they desired it. And because they desired it [*because they exercised their agency so unwisely*] God hath done it, that they may stumble.

Pay close attention to what Jacob says in the next four verses. He will set the stage for Jacob, chapter five, in which the allegory or parable of the tame and wild olive trees is given. The main point leading up to chapter five is, "How can the Jews (or any people, for that matter) who reject the Savior so completely, ever come back?" Jacob will pose this question specifically in verse 17.

In verse 15, Jacob tells us that he is going to prophesy that the Jews will reject Jesus when He comes to earth for His mortal mission. This will be about 500 years in the future from when Jacob lived.

15 And **now I, Jacob, am led on by the Spirit unto prophesying**; for I perceive by the workings of the Spirit which is in me, that by the stumbling of the Jews **they will reject the stone** [*Christ*] **upon which they might build and have safe foundation**.

16 But behold, according to the scriptures, this stone [*Christ*] shall become the great, and the last, and the only sure foundation, upon which the Jews can build.

17 And now, my beloved, **how is it possible that these** [*the Jews*], **after having rejected the sure foundation, can ever build upon it** [*can ever return to Christ*], that it may become the head of their corner [*become the "chief cornerstone" of their lives; compare with Ephesians 2:20*]?

In verse 18, next, Jacob lets us know that he is quite nervous about getting his point across in chapter five. There is a message for us in this. If we get too anxious or worried about what the Lord asks us to do, we can ruin our ability to listen to the Holy Ghost and we may not get the job done right. While many of us will get nervous about teaching or speaking, we would do well to have sufficient faith to calm us down enough so we can be effective instruments in the Lord's hands.

18 Behold, my beloved brethren, **I will unfold this mystery** [*I will show you how the Jews can return to Christ*] unto you; **if I do not, by any means, get shaken from my firmness in the Spirit, and stumble because of my over anxiety for you**.

JACOB 5

In the last two verses of Jacob, chapter 4, Jacob told us that he would tell us how it is possible for the Jews to come unto Christ and build their lives upon His gospel, after having rejected Him and crucified Him. Jacob will use chapter 5 to tell us how this is possible. This parable is often referred to as "The Allegory of the Tame and Wild Olive Trees." An "allegory" is a story or parable that symbolizes things in real life. This allegory comes from the writings of Zenos (see verse 1), a prophet whose writings were on the brass plates but are not found in the Bible.

If you are willing to work a little harder to understand this chapter of Jacob's writings, it will benefit you a lot for the rest of your life because you will hear about this allegory many times as you discuss the gospel in classes and in other discussions.

Over many years of teaching seminary and institute classes, I found that the following chart was very helpful to my students in understanding this parable or allegory. You may wish to copy this chart and glue it into your own Book of Mormon. You may also want to make specific notes in your own copy of the Book of Mormon by the verses where these definitions are needed.

Key Features of the Allegory of the Tame and Wild Olive Trees

Item

1. The vineyard
2. Master of the vineyard
3. The servant
4. Tame olive tree
5. Wild olive tree
6. Branches
7. The roots of the tame olive tree
8. Fruit of the tree
9. Digging, pruning, fertilizing
10. Transplanting the various branches
11. Grafting
12. Decaying branches
13. Casting the branches into the fire

Interpretation

1. The world
2. Jesus Christ
3. The Lord's prophets
4. The house of Israel, the Lord's covenant people
5. Gentiles, or non-Israel (later in the parable, wild branches are apostate Israel)
6. Groups of people
7. The gospel covenant and promises made by God that constantly give life and sustenance to the tree
8. The lives or works of men
9. The Lord's work with his children, which seeks to persuade them to be obedient and produce good fruit
10. The scattering of groups throughout the world, or restoring them to their original position
11. The process of spiritual rebirth wherein one is joined to the covenant
12. Wickedness and apostasy
13. The judgment of God

One major message of this chapter is that the Lord keeps working with us individually and as peoples and nations. He has some successes with each of us and some failures. Nevertheless, He keeps working and doing all He can, without violating our agency, to bring us back to the Father, permanently. As we go through the Allegory the first time, we will emphasize this theme. We will give some possible interpretations. We will note that the Lord of the vineyard makes four specific visits to His vineyard (the world) as follows:

1. Verses 4–14
2. Verses 15–28
3. Verses 29–51
4. Verses 52–77

First, Jacob asks his people if they remember reading about the allegory of the tame and wild olive trees in the writings of Zenos.

1 BEHOLD, my brethren, **do ye not remember to have read the words of the prophet Zenos**, which he spake [*spoke*] unto the house of Israel [*the Lord's covenant people*], saying:

2 Hearken [*listen carefully*], O ye house of Israel, and hear the words of me, a prophet of the Lord.

3 For behold, thus saith the Lord, I will liken thee, O house of Israel, like unto a tame olive-tree [*I will compare the Lord's covenant people, Israel, to a tame olive tree*], which a man [*Jesus*] took and nourished in his vineyard [*the world*]; and it grew, and waxed old [*grew old*], and began to decay [*apostasy, meaning when people go away from God and His teachings*].

4 And it came to pass that the master of the vineyard [*Christ*] went forth, and **he saw that his olive-tree** [*His covenant people, Israel*] **began to decay** [*go into apostasy*]; and he said: **I will prune it** [*cut off the most wicked and rebellious people and cut out false doctrines, etc.*], and **dig about**

it, and **nourish it**, **that perhaps it may shoot forth young and tender branches** [*people who believe in God and are faithful to the gospel*], **and it perish not** [*so that the gospel doesn't die out completely*].

5 And it came to pass that **he pruned it, and digged about it, and nourished it according to his word** [*as He had promised to do, including when He sent us here from pre-mortality*].

> Next, Zenos tells us that the Lord's efforts to save His covenant people, Israel, worked with a few but, overall, the majority ignored His efforts.

6 And it came to pass that after many days **it began to put forth somewhat a little, young and tender branches; but behold, the main top** [*the majority of His covenant people at that time*] thereof **began to perish** [*had fallen away from Him*]. [*One possible fulfillment among many of this could be the apostasy of ancient Israel. Another could be the people of Nephi over the centuries.*]

7 And it came to pass that **the master of the vineyard saw it** [*Jesus saw the apostasy*], **and he said unto his servant: It grieveth me** [*it makes Me sad*] **that I should lose this tree** [*the covenant people of the Lord*]; wherefore, **go and pluck the branches from a wild olive-tree, and bring them hither** [*here*] unto me; and **we will pluck off those main branches** [*of apostate Israel*] which are beginning to wither away [*dry up and die*], **and we will cast them into the fire that they may be burned** [*the punishments and destructions of God sent upon the wicked*].

> In verse 8, the Lord seems to be scattering various groups of people and also gathering some of them, as He has done throughout history. Remember, this allegory is quoted to show how the Lord works to save His people.

8 And behold, saith the Lord of the vineyard [*Christ*], **I take away many of these young and tender branches** [*groups of people*], **and I will graft them whithersoever I will** [*I will scatter them wherever I want to*]; **and it mattereth not that if it so be that the root** [*covenants*] **of this tree** [*the tame olive tree; Israel*] **will perish**, I may preserve [*gather*] the fruit thereof unto myself; wherefore, I will take these young and tender branches, and **I will graft them whithersoever I will** [*scatter them throughout the world*].

9 **Take thou the branches of the wild olive-tree** [*Gentiles*], **and graft them in, in the stead thereof** [*in place of Israel*]; and these [*groups of apostate people of covenant Israel*] **which I have plucked off I will**

cast into the fire and burn them, that they may not cumber [*clutter*] the ground of my vineyard.

10 And it came to pass that **the servant of the Lord of the vineyard did according to the word of the Lord of the vineyard**, and **grafted in the branches of the wild olive tree**.

Next the Lord explains to the servant, who represents prophets, that He is doing everything He can to save His covenant people.

11 And the Lord of the vineyard caused that it should be digged about, and pruned, and nourished, **saying unto his servant: It grieveth me that I should lose this tree; wherefore, that perhaps I might preserve the roots thereof** that they perish not, that I might preserve them unto myself, **I have done this thing**.

You can see from verse 12, next, that it is the job of the Lord's prophets to watch over God's children here on earth.

12 Wherefore, go thy way; **watch the tree, and nourish it, according to my words** [*the gospel*].

Next, in verses 13 and 14, the Lord scatters some of the people of covenant Israel to some far away places on the earth.

13 And **these will I place in the nethermost** [*farthest away*] **part of my vineyard**, whithersoever I will, it mattereth not unto thee [*I know what I'm doing*]; and I do it that I may preserve unto myself the natural branches of the tree; and also, that I may lay up fruit thereof against the season [*I want to bring people home to Me forever*], unto myself; for it grieveth me that I should lose this tree and the fruit thereof.

14 And it came to pass that **the Lord of the vineyard** went his way, and **hid the natural branches of the tame olive-tree** [*the scattering of Israel*] **in the nethermost parts of the vineyard**, some in one and some in another, according to his will and pleasure.

This is the end of the first visit of the Lord to the earth, mentioned in the notes at the beginning of this chapter.

15 And it came to pass that a long time passed away, and the Lord of the vineyard said unto his servant: **Come, let us go down into the vineyard**, that we may labor in the vineyard. [*This is the second visit referred to at the beginning of the chapter. A major message here is that the Lord constantly sends His prophets and missionaries to the world to give them chance after chance to hear and accept the gospel.*]

16 And it came to pass that **the Lord of the vineyard, and also the servant, went down into the vineyard to labor** [*the Savior is much involved with His prophets in leading and helping us here*]. And it came to pass that the servant said unto his master: Behold, look here; behold the tree.

17 And it came to pass that **the Lord of the vineyard looked and beheld the tree** in the which the wild olive branches [*Gentiles*] had been grafted; and it had sprung forth and begun to bear fruit [*many of the Gentiles had accepted and lived the gospel*]. And he beheld [*saw*] that it was good; and **the fruit thereof was like unto the natural fruit** [*there is no difference between Israelite members of the Church and Gentile members of the Church, if they keep their covenants made at baptism, etc.*].

18 And **he said unto the servant: Behold, the branches of the wild tree** [*the Gentile converts to the Church*] **have taken hold of the moisture of the root thereof** [*have made and kept gospel covenants*], that the root thereof hath brought forth much strength; and because of the much strength of the root **thereof the wild branches have brought forth tame fruit** [*the Gentile converts are solid members of the Church*]. Now, **if we had not grafted in these branches, the tree thereof would have perished.** [*One possible meaning of this phrase is that the European converts strengthened the early Church.*] And now, behold, I shall lay up much fruit, which the tree thereof hath brought forth; and the fruit thereof I shall lay up against the season, unto mine own self [*I will bring many home to the Father*].

19 And it came to pass that **the Lord of the vineyard** [*Christ*] **said unto the servant** [*His prophets*]: Come, **let us go to the nethermost part of the vineyard**, and behold if [*see if*] the natural branches [*the people of Israel whom I have scattered*] of the tree have not brought forth much fruit also [*have become faithful in the gospel too*], that I may lay up of the fruit thereof against the season, unto mine own self.

20 And it came to pass that they went forth whither the master had hid the natural branches of the tree, and he said unto the servant: Behold these; and he beheld **the first** that it **had brought forth much fruit** [*had many faithful converts*]; and he beheld also that it was good. And he said unto the servant: Take of the fruit thereof, and lay it up against the season, that I may preserve it unto mine own self; for behold, said he, this

long time have I nourished it, and it hath brought forth much fruit. [*Much success, with many souls brought home to heaven.*]

> Next, the servant asks the Lord an interesting question; namely, why did He scatter these people to such a poor place, one of the worst possible spots, in the world? Watch what the Lord says to him.

21 And it came to pass that the servant said unto his master: **How comest thou hither** [*here*] **to plant this tree, or this branch of the tree? For behold, it was the poorest** [*worst*] **spot in all the land of thy vineyard**.

22 And the Lord of the vineyard said unto him: **Counsel me not**; I knew that it was a poor spot of ground; wherefore, I said unto thee, I have nourished it this long time, and thou beholdest that it hath brought forth much fruit.

> Verse 22, above, is a reminder that there are wonderful Saints who live in very poor circumstances.

23 And it came to pass that the Lord of the vineyard said unto his servant: Look hither; **behold I have planted another branch** [*another group*] of the tree also; and thou knowest that this **spot of ground was poorer than the first**. But, behold the tree. I have nourished it this long time, and **it hath brought forth much fruit** [*we have had many faithful converts here*]; therefore, gather it, and lay it up against the season, that I may preserve it unto mine own self.

24 And it came to pass that the Lord of the vineyard said again unto his servant: Look hither, and behold **another branch** also, which I have planted; behold that I have nourished it also, and it **hath brought forth fruit**.

> One important message from these verses is that the Lord has much success with many people, no matter where they are throughout the world. This is very encouraging.

> Verse 25, next, seems to fit Lehi's group after they landed in America (see verses 43–45). Some of them were faithful ("tame fruit"), at this point (the Nephites), and some became "wild fruit" at this point (the Lamanites).

25 And he said unto the servant: Look hither and behold the last. Behold, this have I **planted in a good spot of ground**; and I have nourished it this long time, and **only a part of the tree hath brought forth tame fruit, and the other part of the tree hath brought forth wild fruit** [*apostasy*]; behold, I have nourished this tree like unto the others [*they have all been*

treated fairly and had opportunities to accept the gospel].

26 And it came to pass that **the Lord of the vineyard said unto the servant**: Pluck off the branches that have not brought forth good fruit, and **cast them into the fire**.

27 **But behold, the servant said unto him: Let us** prune it, and dig about it, and **nourish it a little longer**, that perhaps it may bring forth good fruit unto thee, that thou canst lay it up against the season.

Did you notice what is happening to the servant, as mentioned in verse 27, above? He has grown and matured to the point that he does not want to destroy the wicked yet. He loves them and wants to give them some more chances to repent! There is a lesson in this for each of us. As we become closer to the Lord, we want to become more merciful and patient, like He is.

28 And it came to pass that **the Lord of the vineyard and the servant of the Lord** of the vineyard **did nourish all the fruit of the vineyard**.

Next, we have the third visit mentioned at the beginning of the chapter. There seems to be a feeling of urgency because time is running out.

29 And it came to pass that a long time had passed away, and the Lord of the vineyard said unto his servant: **Come, let us go down into the vineyard, that we may labor again in the vineyard.** For behold, **the time draweth near, and the end soon cometh**; wherefore, I must lay up fruit against the season, unto mine own self.

30 And it came to pass that **the Lord of the vineyard and the servant went down into the vineyard**; and they came to the tree [*Israel*] whose natural branches had been broken off [*scattered*], and the wild branches had been grafted in; and behold **all sorts of fruit did cumber** [*clutter*] **the tree**. [*Perhaps the universal apostasy with all kinds of churches and all kinds of false doctrines, creeds, and practices.*]

31 And it came to pass that the Lord of the vineyard did taste of the fruit [*judged the products of false churches*], every sort according to its number. And **the Lord of the vineyard said: Behold, this long time have we nourished this tree** [*from the beginning we have worked patiently with Israel*], **and I have laid up unto myself against the season much fruit** [*and we have had much success*].

32 **But** behold, **this time** [*the great apostasy after Jesus and His Apostles were gone and the true Church was no longer on earth*] **it hath brought forth much fruit, and there is none of it which is good**. And behold, there are all kinds of bad fruit [*there are all kinds of ways to be wicked*]; and it profiteth me nothing, notwithstanding all our labor; and now it grieveth me that I should lose this tree.

Next, notice that the Lord is now involving the servant more actively in making decisions about what to do.

33 And **the Lord of the vineyard said** unto the servant: **What shall we do unto the tree**, that I may preserve again good fruit thereof unto mine own self?

34 **And the servant said** unto his master: Behold, because thou didst graft in the branches of the wild olive-tree they have nourished **the roots**, that they **are alive** and they have not perished; wherefore thou beholdest that they are yet good.

35 And it came to pass that **the Lord of the vineyard said** unto his servant: **The tree profiteth me nothing, and the roots thereof profit me nothing so long as it shall bring forth evil fruit** [*I can't save people unless they are honestly striving to live righteously*].

36 Nevertheless, **I know that the roots are good**, and for mine own purpose I have preserved them; and because of their much strength they have hitherto brought forth, from the wild branches, good fruit.

37 But behold, **the wild branches have grown and have overrun the roots thereof**; and because that the wild branches have overcome the roots **thereof it hath brought forth much evil fruit**; and because that it hath brought forth so much evil fruit [*people are allowing so much wickedness into their lives that*] thou beholdest that it beginneth to perish; and **it will soon become ripened** [*so wicked*], that it may be cast into the fire, except we should do something for it to preserve it.

38 And it came to pass that **the Lord** of the vineyard **said** unto his servant: Let us go down into the nethermost parts of the vineyard, and behold if the natural branches have also brought forth evil fruit. [*Let's go see what is happening in the far away parts of the earth.*]

39 And it came to pass that **they went down into the nethermost parts of the vineyard** [*possibly*

America among the ancient Lamanites]. And it came to pass that **they beheld that the fruit** of the natural branches had become corrupt also; yea, the first and the second and also the last; and they **had all become corrupt** [*the people had all become wicked*].

40 And **the wild fruit** [*apostasy*] of the last **had overcome that part of the tree** [*the Nephites?*] **which brought forth good fruit**, even that the branch had withered away and died [*the Church had died out completely*].

41 And it came to pass that **the Lord of the vineyard wept**, and said unto the servant: What could I have done more for my vineyard?

Did you notice, in verse 41, above, that the Lord was so sad because of the wickedness of His people that He cried? He has given all of us our agency and will not violate it, but it makes Him sad, indeed, when we choose the wrong rather than the right.

42 Behold, I knew that all the fruit of the vineyard, save it were these, had become corrupted. And **now these which have once brought forth good fruit have also become corrupted** [*have gone bad*]; and now all the trees of my vineyard are good for nothing save it be to be hewn down and cast into the fire.

43 And **behold this last** [*Lehi's people, see verse 25*], whose branch hath withered away [*who have now gone into apostasy*], **I did plant in a good spot of ground** [*America*]; yea, even that **which was choice unto me above all other parts of the land** [*2 Nephi 1:5*] of my vineyard [*the whole earth*].

44 And thou beheldest that **I also cut down that** [*the Jaredites?*] **which cumbered** [*cluttered with their wickedness*] **this spot of ground, that I might plant this tree** [*Lehi?*] **in the stead thereof** [*in place of it*].

45 And thou beheldest that **a part** thereof [*the Nephites?*] **brought forth good fruit**, and a part thereof [*the Lamanites?*] **brought forth wild fruit**; and because I plucked not the branches thereof and cast them into the fire, behold, **they** [*the Lamanites?*] **have overcome the good branch** [*the Nephites?*] that it hath withered away.

46 And now, behold, notwithstanding [*in spite of*] all the care which we have taken of my vineyard [*the earth*], **the trees thereof have become corrupted, that they bring forth no good fruit**; and these I had hoped to preserve, to have laid up fruit thereof

against the season, unto mine own self. But, behold, **they have become like unto the wild olive-tree** [*the wicked*], and they are of no worth but to be hewn down and cast into the fire; and it grieveth me that I should lose them.

You can see from verse 47, next, that the Lord does everything He can to save us without violating our agency.

47 But **what could I have done more in my vineyard?** Have I slackened mine hand, that I have not nourished it [*have I not tried hard enough*]? Nay, I have nourished it, and I have digged about it, and I have pruned it, and I have dunged [*fertilized*] it; and I have stretched forth mine hand almost all the day long, and the end draweth nigh. And it grieveth me that I should hew down all the trees of my vineyard, and cast them into the fire that they should be burned. **Who is it that has corrupted my vineyard?**

The question at the end of verse 47 is an important one. The answer is in verse 48.

48 And it came to pass that the servant said unto his master: **Is it not the loftiness** [*pride*] of thy vineyard—**have not the branches thereof overcome the roots** [*people are shallow in living the gospel, are not keeping their covenants*] which are good? And because **the branches have overcome the roots** thereof, behold they grew faster than the strength of the roots, **taking strength unto themselves** [*perhaps meaning not following the Brethren*]. Behold, **I say, is not this the cause that the trees of thy vineyard have become corrupted?**

49 And it came to pass that **the Lord of the vineyard said** unto the servant: Let us go to and hew [*cut*] down the trees of the vineyard and cast [*throw*] them into the fire, that they shall not cumber [*clutter*] the ground of my vineyard, for I have done all. What could I have done more for my vineyard?

50 But, behold, **the servant said** unto the Lord of the vineyard: Spare it a little longer.

51 **And the Lord said**: Yea, I will spare it a little longer, for it grieveth me that I should lose the trees of my vineyard.

Beginning with verse 52, we see the gathering of Israel in the last days.

52 Wherefore, **let us take of the branches of these which I have planted in the nethermost parts of my vineyard**, and let us **graft them into the tree from whence they came** [*let's gather Israel from all*

the world and bring them back into the true Church and onto the covenant path]; and let us pluck from the tree those branches whose fruit is most bitter, and graft in the natural branches of the tree in the stead thereof.

As stated in verse 52, above, converts do not suddenly become "lifelong members." It takes time and effort to change old habits and break away from inappropriate traditions. But with patience and continued help from the Holy Ghost, it happens over time.

53 And **this will I do that the tree may not perish**, that, perhaps, I may preserve unto myself the roots [*the covenants made in the true Church*] thereof for mine own purpose.

54 And, behold, **the roots of the natural branches of the tree which I planted whithersoever I would are yet alive**; wherefore, that I may preserve them also for mine own purpose, I will take of the branches of this tree, and I will graft them in unto them. Yea, **I will graft in unto them the branches of their mother tree** [*the Restoration of the gospel*], that I may preserve the roots [*the original covenants, doctrines, etc.*] also unto mine own self, that when they shall be sufficiently strong perhaps they may bring forth good fruit unto me, and I may yet have glory in the fruit of my vineyard.

In the next verses, we see the beginnings of the last days gathering of Israel in all the world.

55 And it came to pass that **they took from the natural tree which had become wild, and grafted in unto the natural trees, which also had become wild**.

56 And **they also took of the natural trees which had become wild, and grafted into their mother tree**.

Verse 57, next, reminds us that people don't become perfect suddenly. Rather, they come into the Church and still have some false notions and ideas that have to gradually be taken away and replaced with the true teachings and doctrines of the gospel.

57 And the Lord of the vineyard said unto the servant: **Pluck not the wild branches from the trees, save it be those which are most bitter** [*this is how the Lord works with each of us too*]; and in them ye shall graft according to that which I have said.

58 And **we will nourish again the trees of the vineyard**, and we will trim up the branches thereof; and we will pluck from the trees those branches which are ripened

[*in wickedness*], that must perish, and cast them into the fire.

59 And this I do that, perhaps, the roots thereof may take strength because of their goodness; and because of the change of the branches, **that the good may overcome the evil**.

60 And because that I have preserved the natural branches and the roots thereof, and that I have grafted in the natural branches again into their mother tree, and have preserved the roots of their mother tree, that, **perhaps, the trees of my vineyard** [*all peoples of the earth*] **may bring forth again good frui**t and **that I may have joy again** in the fruit of my vineyard, and, perhaps, **that I may rejoice exceedingly** that I have preserved the roots and the branches of the first fruit—

> Verse 61 seems to refer to the final gathering of Israel in the last days. The Lord calls many servants to help Him. We are in that number. Note that He is working closely with us.

61 Wherefore, go to, and **call servants, that we may labor diligently with our might** in the vineyard, **that we may prepare the way**, that I may bring forth again the natural fruit [*covenant people*], which natural fruit [*personal righteousness*] is good and the most precious above all other fruit [*all other lifestyles*].

62 Wherefore, let us go to and labor with our might **this last time** [*the day you and I live in, often called "the dispensation of the fulness of times"*], for behold **the end** [*of the world*] **draweth nigh** [*is getting near*], and **this is for the last time that I shall prune my vineyard** [*the last time before the Second Coming of Christ*].

> In verse 63, next, you will see that the Gentiles, meaning, in this case, all people who are not Jews, will get the gospel first in the last days. Most of us are in this group. The Jews will be last to get the gospel preached to them as a people, in the last days.
>
> During and just after the time of Christ's mission on earth, the Jews were the first to get the gospel preached to them, and the Gentiles were last.
>
> In the scriptures we often read to the effect that the first will be last and the last will be first, meaning that the Jews were first to get the gospel back in the time of Christ and they will be the last to get it now. Whereas the Gentiles were last to get it back then but will be the first to get it now, beginning with the Restoration of the gospel through Joseph Smith.

63 Graft in the branches; **begin at the last** [*the Gentiles*] **that they may**

be first, and that the first [*the Jews*] **may be last**, and dig about the trees, both old and young, the first and the last; and the last and the first, that all may be nourished once again for the last time [*before the Second Coming*].

64 Wherefore, dig about them [*loosen the soil around them*], and prune them, and dung [*fertilize*] them once more, **for the last time, for the end draweth nigh** [*the end of the world before the Second Coming is getting near*]. **And if it be so that these last grafts shall grow, and bring forth the natural fruit** [*if we get converts as we gather scattered Israel and many remain faithful*], then shall ye prepare the way for them, that they may grow.

> You've seen this next message several times in the allegory. It teaches that we must be patient with new converts, as well as lifelong members, and be very careful not to criticize them right out of the Church. This is how the Holy Ghost works with each of us.

65 **And as they begin to grow** ye shall **clear away** the branches which bring forth **bitter fruit** [*such as bad habits, false ideas about the gospel, etc.*], **according to the strength of the good** and the size thereof; and **ye shall not clear away the bad thereof all at once**, lest the roots thereof should be too strong for the graft [*for fear that the change in their lives as new members of the Church will be too hard for them to adjust to*], and the graft thereof shall perish [*and they become inactive or leave the Church*], and I lose the trees of my vineyard.

66 For it grieveth me that I should lose the trees of my vineyard; wherefore [*that is why*] **ye shall clear away the bad according as the good shall grow** [*as their testimonies grow*], that the root and the top may be equal in strength, **until the good shall overcome the bad,** and the bad be hewn down and cast into the fire, that they cumber not the ground of my vineyard; and **thus will I sweep away the bad out of my vineyard**.

> Looking at the last phrase of verse 66, above, you can see that another part of the meaning of these verses is that, as good people throughout the world are gathered as converts to the gospel and baptized into the Church, there will be more and more destruction among the wicked, leading to the complete destruction of the wicked at the time of the Second Coming.

67 And **the branches of the natural tree will I graft in again into the natural tree** [*through the

Restoration of the true Church and the preaching of the gospel to all the world];

68 And **the branches of the natural tree will I graft into the natural branches of the tree** [*the gathering of Israel*]; and thus will I bring them together again, that they shall bring forth the natural fruit, **and they shall be one** [*faithful Saints throughout the world will be united in the gospel*].

69 And **the bad shall be cast away**, yea, even out of all the land of my vineyard; for behold, **only this once will I prune my vineyard.** [*In other words, this is the last time the gospel will go forth to all the world, and then the Second Coming will come.*]

70 And it came to pass that the Lord of the vineyard sent his servant; and **the servant went and did as the Lord had commanded him, and brought other servants; and they were few** [*there will be relatively few members of the Church, compared to the population of the world, in the last days to carry the gospel to all the world*].

71 And the Lord of the vineyard said unto them: Go to, and labor in the vineyard, with your might. For behold, **this is the last time** that I shall nourish my vineyard [*this is the last time I will preach the gospel to all the world before I come again*]; for **the end is nigh at hand** [*the Second Coming is close*], and the season speedily cometh; **and if ye labor with your might with me ye shall have joy in the fruit** [*missionaries and members have great joy as they help spread the gospel*] which I shall lay up unto myself against the time which will soon come.

72 And it came to pass that **the servants did go and labor with their mights; and the Lord of the vineyard labored also with them**; and they did obey the commandments of the Lord of the vineyard in all things.

73 And there **began to be the natural fruit again in the vineyard** [*the Church began to grow*]; **and the natural branches began to grow and thrive exceedingly** [*a description of the amazing growth of the Church in the last days*]; and the wild branches [*the wicked; also false doctrines and wicked behaviors among converts and members of the Church*] began to be plucked off and to be cast away; and they did keep the root and the top thereof equal, according to the strength thereof.

Perhaps you are aware that, throughout the history of the world, each time the gospel has been restored, it has finally died out because of apostasy (falling away from the true Church) and it had to be restored again later.

But this time, in our day, it will not die out again, but will keep growing until the Savior comes, and then, during the Millennium, it will grow to fill the whole earth.

Verses 74 and 75, next, show us that this time, the Church will continue to grow and Israel will continue to be gathered successfully, as taught us by our prophets today. You and I are constantly being invited by our living prophet and other Church leaders to help gather Israel today.

74 **And thus they labored, with all diligence** [*faithfulness and steadiness*], **according to the commandments of the Lord** of the vineyard, even **until the bad had been cast away** out of the vineyard, **and the Lord had preserved unto himself** that the trees had become again **the natural fruit** [*faithful members of the Church who remain on the covenant path*]; and they became like unto one body; and the fruits were equal; and **the Lord of the vineyard had preserved unto himself the natural fruit** [*faithful members of the Church in the last days*], which was most precious unto him from the beginning.

Notice that, among other things, verse 75, next, emphasizes that we will have much joy with the Lord as we help gather Israel to Him.

75 And it came to pass that when **the Lord of the vineyard saw that his fruit was good, and that his vineyard was no more corrupt**, he called up his servants, and said unto them: Behold, for this last time have we nourished my vineyard; and thou beholdest that I have done according to my will; and I have preserved the natural fruit, that it is good, even like as it was in the beginning. And **blessed art thou** [*faithful members in the last days*]; for **because ye have been diligent in laboring with me** in my vineyard, and **have kept my commandments**, and have brought unto me again the natural fruit, that my vineyard is no more corrupted, and the bad is cast away, behold **ye shall have joy with me** because of the fruit of my vineyard.

Verse 76 refers to the Millennium, which is the 1,000 years of peace on earth after the Second Coming, followed by the "little season" at the end of the Millennium, when Satan and his evil followers are let loose for the final battle between his forces and the forces of good, depicted by verse 77.

76 For behold, for a long time will I lay up of the fruit of my vineyard unto mine own self against the

season, which speedily cometh; and for the last time have I nourished my vineyard, and pruned it [*cut out the bad and shaped the good, as in pruning fruit trees*], and dug about it [*cultivated it to help it grow*], and dunged it [*fertilized it*]; wherefore **I will lay up unto mine own self of the fruit, for a long time** [*the Millennium*], according to that which I have spoken.

77 **And when the time cometh that evil fruit shall again come into my vineyard** [*the little season at the end of the thousand years*], then will I cause the good and the bad to be gathered; and the good will I preserve unto myself, and the bad will I cast away into its own place [*Final Judgment*]. **And then cometh the season and the end; and my vineyard will I cause to be burned with fire** [*a quick review of what was said in the previous verses*].

JACOB 6

Jacob will now explain some of the basic teachings of the allegory of the tame and wild olive trees that we read in chapter 5. It is very helpful to us to have a prophet explain things to us.

In verse 1, Jacob bears his testimony to us that the prophecies in the allegory of Zenos will certainly come true. And we can easily see that we are living in the time when verses 50 to 76 of chapter 5 are being fulfilled, as the gospel goes to all the world.

1 AND now, behold, my brethren, as I said unto you that I would prophesy, behold, this is my prophecy—that the things which this prophet **Zenos spake, concerning the house of Israel, in the which he likened** [*compared*] **them unto a tame olive-tree** [*a domestic olive tree that produces good fruit*], **must surely come to pass** [*will certainly be fulfilled*].

2 And **the day that he** [*the Lord*] **shall set his hand again the second time** [*the Restoration through the Prophet Joseph Smith*] **to recover his people, is** the day, yea, even **the last time, that the servants of the Lord shall go forth in his power** [*the final missionary work to gather the righteous before the Second Coming*], to nourish and prune his vineyard; and **after that the end soon cometh**.

3 And how blessed are they [*missionaries and faithful members*] **who have labored diligently in his vineyard** [*throughout the earth*]; and how cursed are they who shall be cast out into their own place [*the wicked; see D&C 88:114*]! And **the world shall be burned with fire** [*at the Second Coming*].

4 And **how merciful is our God** unto us, **for he remembereth** [*keeps His promises to*] **the house of Israel**, both roots and branches [*no matter where they have been scattered throughout the world*]; **and he stretches forth his hands unto them all the day long** [*constantly invites them to repent and return to Him*]; and they are a stiffnecked [*prideful*] and a gainsaying [*always rebelling and denying God*] people; **but as many as will not harden their hearts shall be saved in the kingdom of God** [*a simple fact*].

5 Wherefore, my beloved brethren, I beseech [*beg*] of you in words of soberness that ye would **repent, and come with full purpose of heart** [*with all of your heart*], and **cleave unto** [*hold tightly to*] **God** as he cleaveth unto you. And **while his arm of mercy is extended towards you in the light of the day** [*while you have a chance to respond*], harden not your hearts [*don't rebel and reject Him*].

6 **Yea, today** [*do it right now*], if ye will hear his voice, harden not your hearts; for why will ye die [*spiritually*]?

Jacob gives a stern warning in verses 7–10, next.

7 For behold, **after ye have been nourished by the good word of God all the day long, will ye bring forth evil fruit** [*will you keep sinning and rebelling*], **that ye must be hewn down and cast into the fire** [*do you want to be destroyed*]?

8 Behold, **will ye reject these words?** Will ye reject the words of the prophets; and will ye reject all the words which have been spoken concerning Christ, after so many have spoken concerning him; **and deny the good word of Christ, and the power of God, and the gift of the Holy Ghost**, and quench the Holy Spirit, and make a mock of the great plan of redemption, which hath been laid for you?

9 **Know ye not that if ye will do these things**, that the power of the redemption and the resurrection, which is in Christ, will bring you to stand with shame and awful guilt before the bar [*the judgment bar*] of God?

10 **And according to the power of justice** [*the law of justice*], for justice cannot be denied [*cannot be robbed; see Alma 42:25*], **ye must go away** into that lake of fire and brimstone [*white hot fire and molten sulphur*], whose flames are unquenchable [*can't be put out*], and whose smoke ascendeth up forever and ever, which lake of fire and

brimstone is endless torment [*is symbolic of endless suffering*].

You can feel Jacob's deep love for his people in verse 11, next.

11 **O then, my beloved brethren, repent ye, and enter in at the strait** [*narrow*] **gate** [*repentance and baptism*], **and continue in the way** [*on the path*] **which is narrow, until ye shall obtain eternal life** [*exaltation*].

12 **O be wise; what can I say more?**

13 Finally, **I bid you farewell, until I shall meet you before the pleasing bar of God** [*Judgment Day will be pleasant for the righteous*], which bar striketh the wicked with awful dread and fear. Amen.

JACOB 7

In this chapter, we will meet an antichrist. An antichrist is a person who teaches that there will be no Christ and who does everything he or she can do to teach against Christ and His gospel.

The antichrist we meet here is named Sherem. He is the first of three antichrists we will meet in the Book of Mormon. The other two are Nehor (Alma 1) and Korihor (Alma 30). Sherem is typical of many who oppose the Church today. You will see that he is well-educated as far as the world is concerned and thinks he is better than other people. He is full of pride and is cocky. By studying what happens when he meets Jacob, we can learn several things to watch out for in such enemies of righteousness.

1 AND now it came to pass after some years had passed away, **there came a man among the people of Nephi, whose name was Sherem.**

Remember that the prophets from clear back at the beginning have taught the people that Jesus would come to earth and carry out His Atonement for all of us. Now, here comes Sherem among Jacob's people and tells them it is not true.

2 And it came to pass that **he began to preach among the people, and to declare unto them** [*tell them*] **that there should be no Christ**. And he preached **many things which were flattering** unto the people [*things they wanted to hear*]; and this he did that he might overthrow the doctrine of Christ. [*He did this intentionally in an attempt to stop people from believing in Christ.*]

3 And **he labored diligently** [*he worked hard at this*] that he might lead away the hearts of the people, insomuch that **he did lead away many hearts** [*he was quite successful*];

and he knowing that I, Jacob, had faith in Christ who should come, **he sought much opportunity that he might come unto me.**

You may have noticed that many apostates today and others who are angry at the Church seek opportunities to debate the leaders of the Church in public. Satan's methodology does not seem to change.

4 And **he was learned, that he had a perfect knowledge of the language of the people** [*he was very well educated and very skilled in public speaking*]; **wherefore, he could use much flattery** [*telling people what they wanted to hear*], **and much power of speech, according to the power of the devil**. [*The devil can inspire people and help them be skillful in leading people astray.*]

Next, we see that Sherem was not very wise in choosing Jacob as his next victim, because Jacob had seen angels and had seen Jesus (2 Nephi 11:3).

5 And **he had hope to shake me from the faith** [*he hoped to get me to not believe in Christ*], **notwithstanding the** [*even though I had had*] **many revelations and the many things which I had seen concerning these things**; for **I truly had seen angels**, and they had ministered unto me. And **also, I had heard the voice of the Lord** speaking unto me in very word, from time to time; **wherefore** [*and that's why*], **I could not be shaken**.

Perhaps you can picture Sherem swaggering up to Jacob and addressing him with a touch of sarcasm in his voice. He even calls him "Brother." Note the skill with which he attacks Jacob and the gospel with phrases designed to make people doubt the truth of the gospel.

6 And it came to pass that he came unto me, and on this wise did he speak unto me, saying: **Brother Jacob, I have sought much opportunity that I might speak unto you**; for I have heard and also know that thou goest about much, preaching **that which ye call the gospel, or the doctrine of Christ**.

7 And **ye have led away much of this people** that **they pervert the right way of God** [*they twist around the true teachings of God*], **and keep not the law of Moses which is the right way**; and convert the law of Moses into the **worship of a being** [*Christ*] **which ye say shall come many hundred years hence** [*in the future*]. And now behold, I, Sherem, declare unto you that this is blasphemy [*a terribly wrong and evil thing to teach*]; for **no man knoweth of such things; for he cannot tell of things to come**. [*No one can know*

the future. This statement will come back to cause trouble for Sherem in verse 9; also, among other things, he is denying the existence of true prophets.] **And after this manner did Sherem contend against me** [*this is how Sherem argued against me*].

8 But behold, **the Lord God poured in his Spirit into my soul**, insomuch that [*so that*] I did confound [*stop, confuse*] him in all his words.

9 And I said unto him: Deniest thou the Christ who shall come? And he said: If there should be a Christ, I would not deny him; but **I know that there is no Christ, neither has been, nor ever will be.**

Sherem is already in trouble. In verse 7, above, he claimed that no one can know the future. In verse 9, he contradicts himself. He says, in effect, that he knows the future and that there never will be a Christ.

10 **And I said unto him: Believest thou the scriptures** [*Old Testament*]? **And he said, Yea.**

Jacob's approach to Sherem in verse 11, next, is rather gentle. It is a reminder to us to be gentle, if possible, with people who do not believe like we do. He is trying to give him an "out" for what he has previously claimed. This is a kind approach because, if taken advantage of by Sherem, his ego is not so much at stake. Rather, he simply needs to be taught the truth. However, sadly, he will not take advantage of this opportunity to salvage his ego.

Verse 11 is also a powerful reminder to us that the Old Testament, in its original, pure form, clearly taught about Christ.

11 And I said unto him: **Then ye do not understand them** [*the scriptures*]; **for they truly testify of Christ**. Behold, I say unto you that **none of the prophets have written, nor prophesied, save** [*except*] **they have spoken concerning this Christ**.

Next, Jacob will bear pure, simple testimony to Sherem. This is a reminder to us of the power of this approach to teaching and spreading the gospel.

12 And this is not all—**it has been made manifest unto me, for I have heard and seen**; and **it also has been made manifest unto me by the power of the Holy Ghost; wherefore, I know** if there should be no atonement made all mankind must be lost.

Next, we hear the sarcasm in Sherem's voice as he rejects Jacob's humble testimony and demands a sign.

13 And it came to pass that he said unto me: **Show me a sign** by this power of the Holy Ghost, in the which ye know so much.

Jacob is a kind man and doesn't want Sherem to get in trouble with God by demanding a sign of some kind to prove that Christ will come. But he knows that Sherem has agency to ask for a sign if he wants to.

14 **And I said** unto him: **What am I that I should tempt God to show unto thee a sign in the thing which thou knowest to be true?** [*Jacob knows by the power of the Spirit that Sherem actually knows the truth.*] **Yet thou wilt deny it, because thou art of the devil** [*you are like the devil, who is also a liar*]. Nevertheless, not my will be done; but **if God shall smite thee** [*if God strikes you down . . . ; this is not the kind of sign Sherem had in mind*], **let that be a sign unto thee** that he has power, both in heaven and in earth; and also, **that Christ shall come**. And thy will, O Lord, be done, and not mine.

15 And it came to pass that when I, Jacob, had spoken these words, **the power of the Lord came upon him, insomuch that he fell to the earth**. And it came to pass that he was nourished for the space of many days [*the people kept him alive by feeding him for several days*].

The fact that Sherem did not die immediately is a reminder of the kindness of the Lord to even the worst of sinners. Despite Sherem's sarcastic attitude and damaging false teachings, he is an individual of infinite worth. The Lord shows tender mercy in giving him some time to think it over before he dies. It will work, according to verses 17–19.

16 And it came to pass that **he said unto the people: Gather together on the morrow** [*tomorrow*], for I shall die; wherefore, **I desire to speak unto the people before I shall die**.

17 And it came to pass that on the morrow the multitude were gathered together; and **he spake plainly unto them and denied the things which he had taught them** [*told them he had been lying*]**, and confessed the Christ** [*told them he knew that Christ would come*]**, and the power of the Holy Ghost, and the ministering of angels.**

18 And **he spake plainly unto them, that he had been deceived** [*fooled*] **by the power of the devil**. And he spake of hell, and of eternity, and of eternal punishment. [*Sherem has a very good gospel doctrinal vocabulary, probably indicating that he*

knew the gospel well before he apostatized and started being an antichrist.]

19 And he said: **I fear lest I have committed the unpardonable sin** [*the sin against the Holy Ghost, which cannot be forgiven*], for I have lied unto God; for I denied the Christ, and said that I believed the scriptures; and they truly testify of him. And because I have thus lied unto God I greatly fear lest my case shall be awful; but I confess unto God.

Many students of the scriptures wonder whether Sherem would qualify to be a son of perdition (meaning he would be banished to live with the devil after Judgment Day), which is what happens if you commit the unpardonable sin. While Final Judgment is up to the Savior (John 5:22), we can note that one who becomes a son of perdition would think and act completely like the devil (see D&C 76:31–35) and would not be sorry for what he did like Sherem was.

20 And it came to pass that **when he had said these words** he could say no more, and **he gave up the ghost** [*he died*].

21 And when **the multitude** had witnessed that he spake these things as he was about to give up the ghost, they **were astonished exceedingly** [*because people are usually totally honest when they know they are dying*]; insomuch that the power of God came down upon them, and they were overcome that they fell to the earth. [*Many were reconverted or had their testimonies strengthened.*]

22 **Now, this thing was pleasing unto me, Jacob, for I had requested it** [*the reconversion of those who had followed Sherem*] of my Father who was in heaven; for he had heard my cry and answered my prayer.

23 And it came to pass that **peace and the love of God was restored again among the people**; and they searched the scriptures [*key to avoiding personal apostasy*], and hearkened [*listened*] no more to the words of this wicked man.

Next, Jacob will be sad about the fact that they were unsuccessful in bringing the Lamanites of his day back into the Church.

24 And it came to pass that many means were devised to reclaim and restore the Lamanites to the knowledge of the truth; **but it all was vain** [*their efforts did no good*], for they delighted in wars and bloodshed, and they had an eternal hatred against us, their brethren. And they sought by the power of their arms [*weapons*] to destroy us continually.

Some people are very much opposed to having our government build up stockpiles of weapons for our defense as a nation. Here, the Book of Mormon applies to us in our day by advising us on this matter.

25 Wherefore [*this is why*], **the people of Nephi did fortify against them with their arms, and with all their might** [*they built up stockpiles of weapons*], trusting in the God and rock of their salvation; wherefore, they became as yet, conquerors of their enemies.

We can feel the greatness of Jacob as a serious and tender man of God, as he says goodbye to us in verses 26 and 27.

26 And it came to pass that I, Jacob, began to be old; and the record of this people being kept on the other plates of Nephi [*the large plates*], wherefore, I conclude this record [*Jacob's portion of the small plates of Nephi*], declaring that **I have written according to the best of my knowledge**, by saying that the time passed away with us, and also our lives passed away like as it were unto us a dream, we being a lonesome and a solemn people, wanderers, cast out from Jerusalem, born in tribulation, in a wilderness, and hated of our brethren, which caused wars and contentions; wherefore, we did mourn out our days.

Next, Jacob will turn over the responsibility for keeping the plates and engraving upon them to his son, Enos.

27 **And I, Jacob, saw that I must soon go down to my grave** [*I saw that I would soon die*]; **wherefore, I said unto my son Enos: Take these plates**. And I told him the things which my brother Nephi had commanded me, **and he promised obedience unto the commands. And I make an end of my writing upon these plates** [*the small plates*], which writing has been small; **and to the reader I bid farewell**, hoping that many of my brethren may read my words. Brethren, **adieu**.

"Adieu," which means "goodbye" in French, may sound a bit strange in the Book of Mormon. Some critics of the Book of Mormon point out this use of a French word and use it against Joseph Smith. What they don't realize is that "adieu" was commonly used in Joseph Smith's day to bid farewell. In fact, American English is loaded with words adapted over time from several different European languages.

THE BOOK OF ENOS

ENOS 1

Enos is the son of Jacob. In this brief but powerful chapter, we will be taught much about many things, including how to have our faith strengthened for a specific occasion and how to know if our sins have been forgiven.

First, we will be reminded that the teachings of righteous parents often come to bless their children long after the teachings were given.

1 BEHOLD, it came to pass that **I, Enos, knowing my father that he was a just** [*strict with himself in living the gospel*] **man**—for **he taught me in his language, and also in the nurture and admonition of the Lord** [*he taught me how to live the gospel*]—and blessed be the name of my God for it—

> Next, Enos tells us that he wanted to be forgiven of his sins. We can see that he was taught the gospel well in his home as he grew up, so he knew that he should pray for forgiveness as needed.

2 And **I will tell you of the wrestle** [*struggle involving strong effort*] **which I had before God, before I received a remission of my sins** [*a reminder that receiving forgiveness of our sins requires real effort on our part*].

3 Behold, I went to hunt beasts in the forests; and **the words which I had often heard my father speak concerning eternal life, and the joy of the saints, sunk deep into my heart**.

> It appears that Enos was quite concerned about his standing with God, whether or not God approved of how he was living his life. Thus, his thoughts of an adventurous day hunting turned into a deep yearning to be forgiven of sins and be clean before his Maker. Enos teaches us in verse 4 that these things often require much effort and patience. In fact, you will see that he prayed all day long and into the night.

4 And my soul hungered [*to be pure and clean*]; and I kneeled down before my Maker [*God, my Creator*], and **I cried unto him in mighty prayer** and supplication [*pleading*] for mine own soul; and **all the day long** did I cry unto him; yea, and **when the night came I did still raise my voice high that it reached the heavens**.

There are no doubt many ways to pray as long as Enos did, when one is praying for help with very important and serious matters. For example, a person could be saying the words of the prayer out loud or silently, or a combination of both.

Another way might be how I did it many years ago when I was praying to know whether or not I should marry a girl I had been dating. I really needed to know and wanted to know, so I rode a horse up into the mountains above our home, tethered the horse to some oak brush, and spent the next four hours praying for an answer. I opened my prayer as usual, but didn't close it yet. Instead, I asked Heavenly Father to direct my thoughts as I considered whether or not she and I were right for each other. Then, I did a lot of thinking.

Finally, after about four hours, the distinct thought came strongly into my mind to break up with her. It was very clear. So, I closed my prayer in the name of Jesus Christ, and rode the horse back down off the mountain and broke up with her that evening.

There are obviously many other ways to pray "all the day long" and into the night, including praying for help, and then spending quite a bit of time reading the scriptures to increase our ability to hear the promptings of the Holy Ghost.

5 And **there came a voice unto me, saying: Enos, thy sins are forgiven thee**, and thou shalt be blessed.

6 And I, Enos, knew that God could not lie; wherefore, **my guilt was swept away**.

The phrase "swept away" in verse 6, above, is a wonderful reminder of the power of the Atonement of Jesus Christ to cleanse and heal. One can feel the power of his or her sins being "swept away"!

The speed and completeness of this cleansing apparently startled Enos a bit and caused him to marvel.

This is one way we can know if our sins have been forgiven. The Holy Ghost can give us a feeling of peace and calm. When this happens, it is important not to second-guess or analyze the feeling too much, which can lead to doubting the feeling, but rather, accept it with a prayer of gratitude and then move ahead in life, trying even harder and more consistently to stay firmly on the covenant path by being stricter with ourselves in living the gospel.

Next, Enos wonders how such a feeling of forgiveness can come so swiftly and completely.

7 And I said: **Lord, how is it done?**

8 And he said unto me: **Because of thy faith in Christ**, whom thou hast never before heard nor seen. And many years pass away before he shall manifest himself in the flesh; wherefore, go to [*move ahead in your life*], thy faith hath made thee whole.

In the next verses, we are taught an interesting pattern. First, we must be concerned with our own standing with God. When this is in proper condition, through daily repentance and working to stay on the covenant path, the Spirit enables us to be concerned about our immediate family. With that in place, our attention then goes to others, including our enemies. In other words, when we are at peace with God, we are then enabled by the Spirit to truly love others, including our enemies. We will see this clearly taught as we continue with Enos.

9 Now, it came to pass that **when I had heard these words** [*when I knew that I had been forgiven of my sins and was acceptable before God*] **I began to feel a desire for the welfare of my brethren, the Nephites**; wherefore, I did pour out my whole soul unto God for them [*I prayed hard for them*].

10 And while I was thus struggling in the spirit, behold, **the voice of the Lord came into my mind again**, saying: **I will visit** [*bless*] **thy brethren according to their diligence in keeping my commandments.** [*In other words, they have agency too, and I must not violate the rules of honoring agency as I deal with them.*] **I have given unto them this land, and it is a holy land; and I curse it not save it be for the cause of iniquity** [*I will not punish them unless they turn wicked*]; wherefore, I will visit thy brethren according as I have said; and their transgressions will I bring down with sorrow upon their own heads.

11 And after I, Enos, had heard these words, my faith began to be unshaken in the Lord; and **I prayed unto him with many long strugglings for my brethren, the Lamanites** [*who were the enemies of the Nephites at this point in time*].

12 And it came to pass that **after I had prayed and labored with all diligence**, the Lord said unto me: **I will grant unto thee according to thy desires, because of thy faith**.

13 And now behold, **this was the desire which I desired of him**—that if it should so be, that my people, the Nephites, should fall into transgression, and by any means be destroyed, and the Lamanites should not be destroyed, **that the Lord God**

would preserve a record of my people, the Nephites; even if it so be by the power of his holy arm, that it might be brought forth at some future day unto the Lamanites, that, perhaps, they might be brought unto salvation—

Enos's desire has been granted by the coming forth of the Book of Mormon to the Lamanites in this dispensation.

14 For at the present our strugglings were vain [*not doing any good*] in restoring them to the true faith. And they swore in their wrath [*anger*] that, **if it were possible, they would destroy our records** and us, and also all the traditions of our fathers.

Referring back to the bolded phrase in verse 14, perhaps you've noticed that it is often the case with wicked dictators and their evil-minded followers that they destroy or attempt to destroy written history—in fact, any history of the people over whom they wield unrighteous dominion. This has been repeated over and over again throughout history. It is Satan's way to destroy good ties with past generations.

15 Wherefore, I knowing that the Lord God was able to preserve our records, I cried [*prayed*] unto him continually, for **he had said unto me: Whatsoever thing ye shall ask in faith, believing that ye shall receive in the name of Christ, ye shall receive it** [*compare with D&C 46:30 and 50:30*].

16 And I had faith, and **I did cry unto God that he would preserve the records**; and he covenanted with me that he would bring them forth unto the Lamanites in his own due time [*when the time was right according to His wisdom and knowledge*].

17 **And I, Enos, knew it would be according to the covenant which he had made; wherefore my soul did rest** [*I had peace about this matter of our records being preserved*].

18 And the Lord said unto me: Thy fathers [*ancestors*] have also required of me this thing; and **it shall be done unto them according to their faith**; for their faith was like unto thine.

19 And now it came to pass that **I, Enos, went about among the people of Nephi**, prophesying of things to come, and testifying of the things which I had heard and seen.

As Enos finishes teaching us, he points out what happens to people individually as well as as a society when they reject the gospel. This has repeated many, many times throughout history and is happening in many places today. One key indicator of this happening is that the further from God people stray, the more bizarre their dress and behavior becomes. We see this in verse 20, next.

20 And I bear record that **the people of Nephi did seek diligently to restore the Lamanites unto the true faith in God. But our labors were vain** [*didn't do any good*]; their hatred was fixed, and they were led by **their evil nature** that they became **wild, and ferocious**, and a **blood-thirsty** people, **full of idolatry** [*worshipping idols and other things besides God*] and **filthiness**; **feeding upon beasts of prey** [*animals that hunt other animals for food*]; dwelling in tents, and wandering about in the wilderness **with a short skin girdle about their loins** and their **heads shaven**; and their skill was in the bow, and in the cimeter, and the ax. And **many of them did eat nothing save it was raw meat**; and they were continually seeking to destroy us.

21 And it came to pass that **the people of Nephi did till the land** [*used farming to raise food*], and **raise all manner of grain**, and of **fruit,** and **flocks of** herds, and flocks of all manner of **cattle** of every kind, and **goats**, and **wild goats**, and also **many horses**.

22 And **there were exceedingly many prophets among us**. And the people were a stiffnecked people, hard to understand [*the people were not humble, so they couldn't understand the gospel very well*].

Next, Enos reminds us how important it is that our prophets speak plainly to us about dangers to our well-being; otherwise, many people won't listen to them.

23 And **there was nothing save it was** [*except it was*] **exceeding** [*extreme*] **harshness**, preaching and prophesying of wars, and contentions, and destructions, **and continually reminding them of death, and the duration of eternity, and the judgments** [*punishments*] **and the power of God**, and all these things—stirring them up continually **to keep them in the fear of the Lord**. I say there was **nothing short of these things**, and exceedingly great plainness of speech, **would keep them from going down speedily to destruction**. And after this manner do I write concerning them [*this is how I have to describe them*].

24 And **I saw wars between the Nephites and Lamanites in the course of my days** [*during my life*].

As Enos now prepares to say goodbye to us, we can calculate that Lehi and Sariah's family and descendants have now been in America for about 170 years.

25 And it came to pass that I began to be old, and **an hundred and seventy and nine years had passed away from the time that our father Lehi left Jerusalem**.

Remember, Enos is Jacob's son, which makes Lehi and Sariah his grandparents and makes Nephi his uncle.

26 And **I saw that I must soon go down to my grave** [*I will die soon*], having been wrought [*worked*] upon by the power of God that I must preach and prophesy unto this people, and declare the word according to the truth which is in Christ. And I have declared it in all my days, **and have rejoiced in it above that of the world** [*I have loved the gospel more than anything else in the world*].

Remember that when we first met Enos, he was very concerned about being forgiven of his sins and about being okay with God. Verse 27, next, tells us that he achieved those goals wonderfully well during the rest of his life, and now, he knows by the power of the Holy Ghost that he will indeed live with Christ and Heavenly Father after he dies.

We can have the same peace at the end of our lives if we have tried sincerely and with real effort to live the gospel. This includes using the Atonement of Christ by sincerely repenting a lot as needed throughout our lives.

27 And **I soon go to the place of my rest, which is with my Redeemer**; for I know that in him I shall rest. And **I rejoice in the day when my mortal shall put on immortality** [*I am looking forward to the day when I am resurrected*], and shall stand before him; **then shall I see his face with pleasure**, and he will say unto me: Come unto me, ye blessed, there is a place prepared for you in the mansions of my Father. Amen.

THE BOOK OF JAROM

JAROM 1

Jarom is the son of Enos, which means he is the grandson of Jacob and the great grandson of Lehi and Sariah. He will review and remind us of many of the teachings of his father and grandfather. He will not write very much but will show us that the efforts of many prophets preaching the gospel clearly and strongly are paying off.

1 NOW behold, **I, Jarom, write a few words according to the commandment of my father, Enos**, that our genealogy may be kept.

2 And as **these plates are small** [*the small plates of Nephi*], **and as these things are written for the intent of the benefit of our brethren the Lamanites**, wherefore, **it must needs be** [*it is necessary*] **that I write a little**; but I shall not write the things of my prophesying, nor of my revelations. For what could I write more than my fathers [*ancestors*] have written? For have not they revealed the plan of salvation? I say unto you, Yea; and this sufficeth me [*this is sufficient for me*].

It is clear from what Jarom writes that it is requiring every effort on the part of him and the righteous leaders of his people to stop the wave of apostasy among them.

3 Behold, **it is expedient** [*necessary*] **that much should be done among this people**, because of the hardness of their hearts [*insensitivity to righteousness*], and the deafness of their ears [*they don't listen to or pay attention to the gospel and spiritual things*], and the blindness of their minds [*they close their minds to the teachings of God*], and the stiffness of their necks [*they are full of pride and are not humble*]; **nevertheless, God is exceedingly merciful unto them, and has not as yet swept them off from the face of the land.**

According to the next verses, it seems that their society is much like ours today. The righteous are becoming more and more righteous, and those who are sloppy about the gospel are getting further and further into the ways of the world. And the preaching and teachings of their prophets and church leaders seem to be working since many are becoming increasingly spiritually sensitive, according to verses 4 and 5.

4 And there are **many among us** who **have many revelations**, for **they are not all stiffnecked.** And **as many as are not stiff-necked and have faith, have communion with the Holy Spirit** [*receive much inspiration from the Holy Ghost*], which maketh manifest unto the children of men [*people*], according to their faith.

5 And now, behold, two hundred years had passed away [*since Lehi left Jerusalem*], and the people of Nephi had waxed [*grown*] strong in the land. **They observed to keep the law of Moses and the sabbath day holy** unto the Lord. **And they profaned not; neither did they Blaspheme** [*they did not swear or speak crudely about sacred things*]. And **the laws of the land were exceedingly strict.** [*Good laws help preserve good people.*]

Next, Jarom shows us how the Lamanites had become different than the Nephites.

6 And they were scattered upon much of the face of the land, and the Lamanites also. And they were exceedingly more numerous than were they of the Nephites; and **they** [*the Lamanites*] **loved murder and would drink the blood of beasts** [*a direct violation of Old Testament law; see Genesis 9:4*].

7 And it came to pass that **they came many times against us, the Nephites, to battle. But our kings and our leaders were mighty men in the faith of the Lord**; and they taught the people the ways of the Lord; wherefore [*this is why*], we withstood [*defended ourselves against*] the Lamanites and swept them away out of our lands, and began to fortify [*strengthen the defenses of*] our cities, or whatsoever place of our inheritance.

Next, we are taught and reminded that prosperity as a society is an inevitable result of personal righteousness among its citizens.

8 And **we multiplied exceedingly** [*our population increased rapidly*], and spread upon the face of the land, **and became exceedingly rich** in gold, and in silver, and in precious things, and in fine workmanship of wood, in buildings, and in machinery, and also in iron and copper, and brass and steel, making all manner of [*all kinds of*] tools of every kind to till the ground, and weapons of war—yea, the sharp pointed arrow, and the quiver, and the dart, and the javelin, **and all preparations for war**.

Again, we have a guideline in these two verses, 8 and 9, that it is wise to be prepared for war, even in times of peace.

9 **And thus being prepared to meet the Lamanites, they did not prosper** [*succeed*] **against us**. But the word of the Lord was verified [*was proven to be true*], which he spake [*spoke*] unto our fathers [*ancestors*], saying that: **Inasmuch as ye will keep my commandments ye shall prosper in the land**.

10 And it came to pass that the prophets of the Lord did threaten the people of Nephi, according to the word of God, **that if they did not keep the commandments, but should fall into transgression** [*committing sins*], **they should be** [*would be*] **destroyed** from off the face of the land.

11 **Wherefore, the prophets, and the priests, and the teachers, did labor diligently, exhorting with all long-suffering** [*patience*] **the people to diligence; teaching the law of Moses, and the intent for which it was given; persuading them to look forward unto the Messiah** [*Christ*], **and believe in him** to come **as though he already was** [*as if He had already come and performed His earthly ministry and the Atonement*]. And after this manner did they teach them.

Did you notice the very important teaching Jarom gave us in verse 11, above? It is that the Atonement of Christ worked for people before He carried it out on earth. In other words, people who lived before Christ could repent and be forgiven of their sins, even though Jesus had not come to earth yet. This is one of the proofs that the Atonement is infinite in its reach. It even worked for us in our premortal existence, according to a talk by Elder Jeffrey R. Holland, given in the October 1995 general conference. It was called "This Do in Remembrance of Me," and it can be found in the November 1995 *Ensign*, page 68.

12 And it came to pass that **by so doing they kept them from being destroyed upon the face of the land** [*this is similar to what our prophets are doing for us today*]; **for they did prick their hearts** [*get their attention*] **with the word** [*the gospel*], **continually stirring them up unto repentance**.

13 And it came to pass that two hundred and thirty and eight years had passed away—after the manner of wars, and contentions, and dissensions, for the space of much of the time.

14 And **I, Jarom, do not write more, for the plates are small**. But behold, my brethren, ye can go to the other plates of Nephi [*the

large plates of Nephi]; for behold, upon them the records of our wars are engraven, according to the writings of the kings, or those which they caused to be written.

15 And **I deliver these plates into the hands of my son Omni**, that they may be kept according to the commandments of my fathers.

THE BOOK OF OMNI

OMNI 1

Omni is the great-great-grandson of Lehi and Sariah. The book of Omni covers many years and record keepers, as you will quickly find out as you begin to read it. In it we will be given important background about King Mosiah I and about King Benjamin. You will need this background information in order to understand the setting of the Book of Mosiah, which you will be reading soon.

1 BEHOLD, it came to pass that **I, Omni, being commanded by my father, Jarom, that I should write somewhat upon these plates** [*the small plates of Nephi*], to preserve our genealogy—

2 Wherefore, **in my days**, I would that ye should know that **I fought much** with the sword to preserve my people, the Nephites, from falling into the hands of their enemies, the Lamanites. **But behold, I of myself am a wicked man** [*this is a sad confession*], and I have not kept the statutes [*laws*] and the commandments of the Lord as I ought to have done.

3 And it came to pass that **two hundred and seventy and six years had passed away** [*since Lehi and his family left Jerusalem*], and we had many seasons of peace; and we had many seasons of serious war and bloodshed. Yea, and in fine [*in summary*], two hundred and eighty and two years had passed away, and I had kept these plates [*the small plates*] according to the commandments of my fathers; and **I conferred them upon my son Amaron**. And I make an end.

4 And **now I, Amaron, write** the things whatsoever I write, which are few, in the book of my father.

5 Behold, it came to pass that three hundred and twenty years had passed away, and **the more wicked part of the Nephites were destroyed**.

6 For **the Lord would not suffer** [*allow*], after he had led them out of the land of Jerusalem and kept and preserved them from falling into the hands of their enemies, yea, he would not suffer **that the words should not be verified**, which he spake unto our fathers, saying that: **Inasmuch as ye will not keep my commandments**

ye shall not prosper in the land [*things will not go well for you*].

7 Wherefore, **the Lord did visit them in great judgment** [*great punishments*]; **nevertheless, he did spare the righteous** that they should not perish, but did deliver them out of the hands of their enemies.

8 And it came to pass that **I did deliver the plates unto my brother Chemish**.

9 Now **I, Chemish, write** what few things I write, in the same book with my brother; for behold, I saw the last which he wrote, that he wrote it with his own hand; and **he wrote it in the day that he delivered them unto me.** And after this manner we keep [*this is how we kept*] the records, for it is according to the commandments of our fathers. And I make an end.

10 Behold, I, **Abinadom**, am the son of Chemish. Behold, it came to pass that I **saw much war and contention** between my people, the Nephites, and the Lamanites; and I, with my own sword, have taken the lives of many of the Lamanites in the defence of my brethren.

Next, Abinadom makes a rather sad commentary about the status of continuing revelation among his people as they become increasingly wicked.

11 And behold, the record of this people is engraven upon plates which is had by the kings, according to the generations; and **I know of no revelation save** [*except*] **that which has been written, neither prophecy**; wherefore, that which is sufficient is written. And I make an end.

Amaleki will give us very valuable background about King Mosiah I and also about King Benjamin.

First, he tells us that the Nephites got so wicked that the righteous people among them had to flee away and find a new place to live. Mosiah was their leader as they did so.

12 Behold, **I am Amaleki,** the son of Abinadom. Behold, **I will speak unto you somewhat concerning Mosiah**, who was made king over the land of Zarahemla; for behold, **he being warned of the Lord that he should flee out of the land of Nephi**, and **as many as would hearken unto the voice of the Lord should also depart out of the land with him**, into the wilderness—

There is symbolism for us in the fleeing into the wilderness. Sometimes, we must flee others or circumstances in which we find ourselves compromising the standards of the gospel. When we do so, we often find ourselves alone and out of our comfort zone, in a wilderness as it were. But, if we faithfully continue through the wilderness, we ultimately end up in a land of promise where the desired blessings and security are given us by God.

13 And it came to pass that **he did according as the Lord had commanded him**. And they departed out of the land into the wilderness, as many as would hearken unto the voice of the Lord; and **they were led by many preachings and prophesyings**. And they were admonished [*taught, warned, and encouraged*] continually by the word of God; and they were led by the power of his arm, through the wilderness **until they came down into the land which is called the land of Zarahemla**.

Next, we are introduced to the Mulekites, called the people of Zarahemla in the Book of Mormon, that Mosiah and his people discovered as they fled from the wicked in their own land. Mulek was one of the sons of wicked King Zedekiah, who was the wicked king in Jerusalem when Lehi and his family fled into the wilderness (see notes after 1 Nephi 1:3 in this book). According to the biblical account, all of the sons of Zedekiah were killed when he was taken captive and blinded. But, from the Book of Mormon account, we know that Mulek somehow escaped and, along with others, made his way to the New World. They are not referred to in the Book of Mormon as Mulekites but are commonly called by that name in gospel conversations.

14 **And they** [*Mosiah and his people*] **discovered a people, who were called the people of Zarahemla** [*Mulekites*]. Now, **there was great rejoicing among the people of Zarahemla**; and also Zarahemla [*the leader of the Mulekites, who was a descendant of Mulek*] did rejoice exceedingly, because the Lord had sent the people of Mosiah with the plates of brass which contained the record of the Jews.

15 Behold, it came to pass that **Mosiah discovered that the people of Zarahemla** [*Mulekites*] **came out from Jerusalem** at the time that Zedekiah, king of Judah, was carried away captive into Babylon.

16 And they [*the Mulekites*] journeyed in the wilderness, and were **brought by the hand of the Lord across the great waters** [*the ocean*], **into the land where Mosiah discovered them**; and they had dwelt there from that time forth.

In verse 17, next, we are reminded of the absolute necessity of having scriptures and written records. Otherwise, people can forget God and their language can get corrupted or changed and messed up.

17 And at the time that Mosiah discovered them, they had become exceedingly [*very*] numerous. Nevertheless, they had had many wars and serious contentions, and had fallen by the sword [*had been killed in battle*] from time to time; and **their language had become corrupted**; and **they had brought no records** [*scriptures or other written records*] **with them**; and **they denied the being of their Creator**; **and Mosiah, nor the people of Mosiah, could understand them** [*could not understand their language, even though their people had originally come from Jerusalem like Lehi and his family had, probably a little over 300 years ago*].

Next, we see that Mosiah was a wise man, and he had his people teach their language to the Mulekites, the people of Zarahemla, so that they could all understand each other.

18 But it came to pass that **Mosiah caused that they should be taught in his language**. And it came to pass that after they were taught in the language of Mosiah, **Zarahemla** [*the leader of the Mulekites*] **gave a genealogy of his fathers** [*ancestors*], according to his memory; and they are written, but not in these plates [*the small plates*].

19 And it came to pass **that the people of Zarahemla, and of Mosiah, did unite together**; and **Mosiah was appointed to be their king.**

Next, Amaleki, who is the keeper of the records and is telling us all this (see verse 12), tells us about a large stone that the people of Zarahemla (the Mulekites) had. It had a brief history of the Jaradites engraved on it. The Jaredites (you will read about them in the Book of Ether in the Book of Mormon) had come to America shortly after the Tower of Babel, mentioned in Genesis, chapter 11, in the Bible. This huge tower was built a few hundred years—some histories say about 700 years—after the Flood. The wicked people who built it figured they could build it high enough to get to heaven. Because the wicked inhabitants of the land would not listen to their prophets and repent, the Lord changed their language so they couldn't understand each other, and the work on the tower stopped.

Mosiah was able to translate the engravings on the stone by the gift and power of God and found that they included an account of a Jaredite named Coriantumr, who had lived with the Mulekites for about nine months, after his people were all destroyed. Verses 20–22 summarize what I have just told you.

20 And it came to pass **in the days of Mosiah, there was a large stone** [*containing some history of the Jaredites*] **brought unto him with engravings on it**; and **he did interpret the engravings by the gift and power of God**.

21 And **they gave an account of one Coriantumr** [*the last Jaredite except for Ether*], **and the slain of his people** [*the Jaredites; see the book of Ether*]. And Coriantumr was discovered by the people of Zarahemla [*the Mulekites*]; and he dwelt with them for the space of nine moons [*nine months*].

22 **It also spake a few words concerning his fathers** [*ancestors*]. And **his first parents** [*the first of his people, the Jaredites*] **came out from the tower** [*the Tower of Babel; see Genesis 11*], **at the time the Lord confounded** [*confused, changed*] **the language of the people**; and the severity of the Lord fell upon them according to his judgments, which are just; and their bones [*Jaredite bones*] lay scattered in the land northward [*north of Zarahemla*].

Amaleki now switches topics and tells us about King Benjamin. King Mosiah I was King Benjamin's father. Next, Amaleki will give us some background concerning King Benjamin, whose famous talk we will study in the book of Mosiah.

23 Behold, **I, Amaleki, was born in the days of Mosiah**; and I have lived to see his death; **and Benjamin, his son, reigneth** [*now rules as king*] **in his stead** [*in his place*].

24 And behold, **I have seen, in the days of king Benjamin, a serious war and much bloodshed between the Nephites and the Lamanites**. But behold, the Nephites did obtain much advantage over them; yea, insomuch that **king Benjamin did drive them out of the land of Zarahemla**.

25 And it came to pass that **I began to be old; and, having no seed** [*children*], **and knowing king Benjamin to be a just** [*righteous*] **man** before the Lord, wherefore, **I shall deliver up these plates unto him**, exhorting [*urging*] all men to come unto God, the Holy One of Israel, and **believe in prophesying, and in revelations, and in the ministering of angels, and in the gift of speaking with tongues, and in the gift of interpreting languages, and in all things which are good; for there is nothing which is good**

save it comes from the Lord; and that which is evil cometh from the devil.

Amaleki bears strong testimony to us as he begins to draw his brief writings to a close.

26 And **now, my beloved brethren, I would that ye should come unto Christ**, who is the Holy One of Israel, and partake of his salvation, and the power of his redemption [*His power to redeem us from the effects of sin and death*]. Yea, come unto him, and **offer your whole souls as an offering unto him**, [*since Christ offered His "whole soul" for you*] and **continue in fasting** and **praying**, and **endure to the end**; and as the Lord liveth ye will be saved.

What Amaleki tells us next is very helpful when we get to Mosiah 7:1–9. We will use **bold**, as usual, to point these things out (and to demonstrate that you can carefully highlight or underline certain words in your scriptures as a way of making sentences or writing sentences).

27 And now I would speak somewhat concerning **a certain number** who **went** up into the wilderness **to return to the land of Nephi** [*from which Mosiah and his righteous followers had fled*]; for there was a large number who were desirous to possess the land of their inheritance [*their original homeland*].

28 Wherefore, **they went up into the wilderness**. And their leader being a strong and mighty man, and a stiffnecked [*proud*] man, wherefore he caused a **contention** among them; and they were **all slain** [*killed*], **save** [*except*] **fifty**, in the wilderness, and **they returned again to the land of Zarahemla.**

29 And it came to pass that **they also took others** to a considerable number [*a fairly large group*], **and took their journey again into the wilderness**.

30 And **I, Amaleki, had a brother, who also went with them; and I have not since known concerning them**. And I am about to lie down in my grave; and these plates are full. And I make an end of my speaking.

In Mosiah 7:1–9, we will pick up the history of Amaleki's brother and those he went with to the land of Nephi, after seventy-nine years have passed.

THE WORDS OF MORMON

WORDS OF MORMON 1

By referring to the chronology information at the end of the chapter heading for The Words of Mormon, in your Book of Mormon, you will see that Mormon is writing this about 385 years after Christ's birth. The Words of Mormon are a transition from the small plates of Nephi (1 and 2 Nephi, Jacob, Enos, Jarom, and Omni) to the book of Mosiah.

Mormon was a great prophet and military general among the Nephites near the end of their civilization, when most of them had turned wicked. The record of his life and service is written in the book of Mormon within the Book of Mormon, starting after Forth Nephi. He was the prophet who had all the historical records or plates of the Nephites and made a shortened version of the history of the Nephites, which his son, Moroni, gave to Joseph Smith. Joseph Smith translated the portion of the stack of gold plates that was not sealed, and we have the translation now as the Book of Mormon.

As we read Words of Mormon, Mormon will explain that after he had abridged (condensed, summarized) the large plates of Nephi, leading down through history from the time Lehi left Jerusalem until the reign of King Benjamin (in the first part of Mosiah), he found the small plates of Nephi as he searched through all the records he had. This small set of plates brought special feelings to his soul, so he included them (under inspiration) in the stack of plates that Joseph Smith would be given by Moroni on the Hill Cumorah in the fall of 1827.

By the time Mormon is writing this, almost all of his people have been killed and he is getting the records or plates ready to hand over to his son, Moroni. It will not be long before Mormon, himself, will be killed by the Lamanites.

1 AND **now I, Mormon, being about to deliver up** [*give*] **the record which I have been making into the hands of my son Moroni**, behold I have witnessed almost all the destruction of my people, the Nephites.

2 And **it is many hundred years after the coming of Christ** that I deliver these records into the hands of my son; and it supposeth me [*I suppose*] that he will witness [*see*] the entire destruction of my people. **But may God grant that he may survive them, that he may write somewhat concerning them, and somewhat**

concerning Christ, that perhaps some day it may profit [*help*] them.

3 And **now, I speak somewhat concerning that which I have written**; for **after I had made an abridgment** [*a summary*] **from the plates of Nephi, down to the reign of this king Benjamin**, of whom Amaleki spake, **I searched among the records** which had been delivered into my hands, **and I found these plates** [*the small plates of Nephi*], which contained this small account of the prophets, from Jacob [*including Lehi and Nephi*] down to the reign of this king Benjamin, and also many of the words of Nephi.

In verse 4, next, Mormon bears his testimony to us that he knows that the things on the small plates of Nephi are true.

4 And **the things which are upon these plates pleasing me**, because of the prophecies of the coming of Christ; and my fathers knowing that many of them have been fulfilled; yea, and **I also know that as many things as have been prophesied concerning us down to this day have been fulfilled, and as many as go beyond this day must surely come to pass** [*will surely be fulfilled*]—

5 Wherefore [*therefore*], **I chose these things** [*the small plates*], **to finish my record upon them**, which remainder of my record [*the rest of the Book of Mormon from Mosiah to Mormon*] I shall take from the plates of Nephi [*the large plates of Nephi*]; and I cannot write the hundredth part [*the tiniest bit*] of the things of my people.

6 But behold, **I shall take these plates** [*the small plates*], **which contain these prophesyings and revelations, and put them with the remainder of my record**, for they are choice unto me; and I know they will be choice unto my brethren.

Mormon is a great teacher, and next he teaches us that there are times when we are impressed by the Spirit to do something, even though we don't understand why at the time.

7 And I do this for a wise purpose; for **thus it whispereth me, according to the workings of the Spirit of the Lord which is in me. And now, I do not know all things**; **but the Lord knoweth all things** which are to come; wherefore, he worketh in me [*inspires me*] to do according to his will.

Mormon shows his great love and Christlike character next by praying for the wicked people around him, including his enemies.

8 And **my prayer to God is** concerning my brethren, **that they may once again come to the knowledge of God, yea, the redemption of Christ; that they may once again be a delightsome people**.

9 And **now I, Mormon, proceed to finish out my record**, which I take from the plates of Nephi; and I make it according to the knowledge and the understanding which God has given me.

Now, Mormon finishes telling us about the transition in the record to the reign of King Benjamin.

10 Wherefore, it came to pass that **after Amaleki had delivered up** [*had given*] **these plates** [*the small plates*] **into the hands of king Benjamin**, he took them and put them with the other plates [*the large plates and other records*], which contained records which had been handed down by the kings, from generation to generation until the days of king Benjamin.

11 **And they were handed down from king Benjamin, from generation to generation until they have fallen into my hands.** [*We understand from* Journal of Discourses, *volume 19, page 38, that there were the equivalent of several wagon loads of records.*] And I, Mormon, pray to God that they may be preserved from this time henceforth. And **I know that they will be preserved; for there are great things written upon them**, out of which my people and their brethren shall be judged at the great and last day [*Judgment Day*], according to the word of God which is written.

Mormon will now give us some background information about King Benjamin, son of Mosiah I, to get us ready to read the Book of Mosiah.

12 And now, **concerning this king Benjamin—he had somewhat of contentions** [*fighting, arguing, etc.*] **among his own people.**

It in interesting to see, in verse 13, next, that they still had the sword of Laban, which Nephi took from Laban when he got the brass plates. As you will see, King Benjamin will use it in battle.

In fact, when Joseph Smith and Oliver Cowdery took the gold plates back to the Hill Cumorah, after the translation was complete, the hill opened up and they entered a room with many Nephite records. Among other things, they saw the sword of Laban. So, we know that it still exists. You can read about this in *Journal of Discourses*, Volume 19, page 38.

13 And it came to pass **also** that **the armies of the Lamanites came** down out of the land of Nephi, **to battle against his people**. But behold, **king Benjamin gathered together his armies, and he did stand against them; and he did fight with the strength of his own arm** [*he personally fought against the Lamanites, along with his soldiers*], **with the sword of Laban** [*which Nephi took from Laban*].

14 And **in the strength of the Lord** they did contend [*fight*] against their enemies, until they had slain many thousands of the Lamanites. And it came to pass that they did contend against the Lamanites until they had driven them out of all the lands of their inheritance.

Next, Mormon mentions some of the other serious troubles that King Benjamin had to deal with among his people.

15 And it came to pass that after **there had been false Christs**, and their mouths had been shut, and they punished according to their crimes;

16 And after there had been **false prophets**, and **false preachers and teachers** among the people, and all these having been punished according to their crimes; **and after there having been much contention and many dissensions away unto the Lamanites** [*there had been much apostasy, and many wicked Nephites joined the Lamanites*], **behold, it came to pass that king Benjamin, with the assistance of the holy prophets who were among his people—**

17 For behold, **king Benjamin was a holy man, and he did reign over his people in righteousness; and there were many holy men in the land, and they did speak the word of God with power and with authority**; and they did use much sharpness because of the stiffneckedness [*rebellion and pride and wickedness*] of the people—

18 Wherefore, **with the help of these, king Benjamin**, by laboring with all the might of his body and the faculty of his whole soul, and also the prophets, **did once more establish peace in the land**.

SOURCES

Anderson, Richard Lloyd. *Investigating the Book of Mormon Witnesses.* Salt Lake City: Shadow Mountain, 1989.

Authorized King James Version of the Bible. Salt Lake City, Utah: The Church of Jesus Christ of Latter-day Saints, 1979.

Book of Mormon Student Manual, Religion 121 and 122. Salt Lake City: The Church of Jesus Christ of Latter-day Saints, 1989.

Church History in the Fulness of Times, Religion 341–43. Salt Lake City: The Church of Jesus Christ of Latter-day Saints, 1980.

Collier, John. *The Indians of the Americas.* New York: W. W. Norton & Company, 1947.

Dibble, Johnathan A. "Delivered by the Power of God: The American Revolution and Nephi's Prophecy." *Ensign,* Oct. 1987.

Doctrine and Covenants Student Manual, Religion 324 and 325. Salt Lake City: The Church of Jesus Christ of Latter-day Saints, 1981.

Holland, Jeffrey R. "'This Do in Remembrance of Me.'" *Ensign,* Nov. 1995.

Jacobs, Wilbur R. *The Frontier in American History.* Tuscon, Arizona: University of Arizona Press, 1986.

Jacobs, Wilbur R. "The Indian and the Frontier in American History—A Need for Revision." *Western Historical Quarterly.* Jan. 1973.

Journal of Discourses. 26 vols. London: Latter-day Saints' Book Depot, 1854–86.

Kimball, Spencer W. "Our Paths Have Met Again." *Ensign,* Dec. 1975.

Kimball, Spencer W. "The Blessings and Responsibilities of Womanhood." *Ensign,* Mar. 1976.

Kimball, Spencer W. *The Miracle of Forgiveness.* Salt Lake City: Bookcraft, 1969.

Latourette, Kenneth Scott. *A History of the Expansion of Christianity, The Great Century.* Vol. 4. New York: Harper and Brothers, 1941.

Library of Aboriginal American Literature. Edited by Daniel Garrison Brinton. 8 vols. Philadelphia: William F. Fell & Co., 1890.

Ludlow, Daniel H. *A Companion to Your Study of The Book of Mormon.* Salt Lake City: Deseret Book, 1976.

Martin Luther edition of the German Bible, which Joseph Smith said was the most correct of any then available.

Maxwell, Neal A. "On Being a Light." Address delivered at the Salt Lake Institute of Religion, Jan. 2, 1974.

Maxwell, Neal A. "'According to the Desire of [Our] Hearts.'" *Ensign*, Nov. 1996.

McConkie, Bruce R. *Millennial Messiah.* Salt Lake City: Deseret Book, 1983.

McConkie, Bruce R. *Mormon Doctrine.* 2nd ed. Salt Lake City: Bookcraft, 1966.

Moldenke, Harold and Alma Moldenke. *Plants of the Bible.* Mineola, New York: Dover Publications, Incorporated, 1986.

Nibley, Hugh. *Since Cumorah: The Book of Mormon in the Modern World.* Salt Lake City: Deseret Book, 1970.

Old Testament Student Manual, 1 Kings through Malachi, Religion 302. Salt Lake City: The Church of Jesus Christ of Latter-day Saints, 1981.

Petersen, Mark E. *The Great Prologue.* Salt Lake City: Deseret Book, 1976.

Reynolds, George and Janne M. Sjodahl. *Commentary on the Book of Mormon.* 7 vols. Salt Lake City: Deseret Press, 1976.

Richards, LeGrand. "Prophets and Prophecy." In Conference Report, Oct. 1975; or *Ensign*, Nov. 1975.

Richards, LeGrand. *Israel! Do You Know?* 4th ed. Salt Lake City: Shadow Mountain, 1990.

Smith, George Albert. In Conference Report, Apr. 1918.

Smith, Joseph. *History of The Church of Jesus Christ of Latter-day Saints.* Edited by B. H. Roberts. 2d ed. rev., 7 vols., Salt Lake City: The Church of Jesus Christ of Latter-day Saints, 1932–51.

Smith, Joseph. *Messenger and Advocate*, Apr. 1835.

Smith, Joseph. *Teachings of the Prophet Joseph Smith.* Selected and arranged by Joseph Fielding Smith. Salt Lake City: Deseret Book, 1976.

Smith, Joseph F., Anthon H. Lund, and John Henry Smith. First Presidency Statement. *Improvement Era*, Aug. 1916.

Smith, Joseph F., John R. Winder, and Anthon H. Lund. First Presidency Message. *Messages of the First Presidency of The Church of Jesus Christ of Latter-day Saints.* 6 vols. Compiled by James R. Clark. Salt Lake City: Bookcraft, 1965.

Smith, Joseph Fielding. *Answers to Gospel Questions.* Compiled by Joseph Fielding Smith. 5 vols. Salt Lake City: Deseret Book, 1957–66.

Smith, Joseph Fielding. *Church History and Modern Revelation.* 4 vols. Salt Lake City: Deseret Book, 1947.

Smith, Joseph Fielding. *Doctrines of Salvation.* Compiled by Bruce R. McConkie. 3 vols. Salt Lake City: Bookcraft, 1954–56.

Smith, Lucy Mack. *History of Joseph Smith by His Mother.* Salt Lake City: Stevens & Wallis, Inc., 1945.

Talmage, James E. *Articles of Faith.* Salt Lake City: Deseret Book, 1981.

"The Family: A Proclamation to the World." First Presidency and Council of the Twelve Apostles. *Family Guide Book.* Salt Lake City: Church of Jesus Christ of Latter-day Saints, 1995.

Wasserman, Jacob. *Columbus: Don Quixote of the Seas.* Translated by Eric Sutton. Boston: Little, Brown, and Co., 1930.

Young, Brigham. *Discourses of Brigham Young.* Compiled by John A. Widtsoe. Salt Lake City: Deseret Book, 1954.

NOTES

NOTES

NOTES

NOTES

NOTES

NOTES

NOTES

NOTES

NOTES

NOTES

NOTES

NOTES

NOTES

NOTES

NOTES

ABOUT THE AUTHOR

David J. Ridges taught for the Church Educational System for thirty-five years and has taught for several years at BYU Campus Education Week. He taught adult religion classes and Know Your Religion classes for BYU Continuing Education for many years. He has also served as a curriculum writer for Sunday School, seminary, and institute of religion manuals.

He has served in many callings in the Church, including Gospel Doctrine teacher, bishop, stake president, and patriarch. He and Sister Ridges served a full-time eighteen-month mission, training senior CES missionaries and helping coordinate their assignments throughout the world.

Brother Ridges and his wife, Janette, are the parents of six children and make their home in Springville, Utah.

Scan to visit

www.davidjridges.com